Guided Comprehension for English Learners

Maureen McLaughlin

INTERNATIONAL
Reading Association

800 BARKSDALE ROAD, PO BOX 8139
NEWARK, DE 19714-8139, USA
www.reading.org

Executive Editor, Publications Shannon Fortner
Managing Editor Christina M. Terranova
Editorial Associate Wendy Logan
Design and Composition Manager Anette Schuetz
Design and Composition Associate Lisa Kochel

Project Editor Matthew W. Baker

Art Cover Design: Alissa Jones; Cover and Interior Photography (pp. 1, 89, 225): Maureen McLaughlin, Sun Nannan, Leslie Fisher

The publisher would appreciate notification where errors occur so that they may be corrected in subsequent printings and/or editions.

Library of Congress Cataloging-in-Publication Data
McLaughlin, Maureen.
Guided comprehension for English learners / Maureen McLaughlin.
p. cm.
Includes bibliographical references and index.
ISBN 978-0-87207-884-0
1. English language--Study and teaching--Foreign speakers. 2. Reading comprehension--Study and teaching. I. International Reading Association. II. Title.
PE1128.A2M423 2012
428.0071--dc23

2012007668

Suggested APA Reference
McLaughlin, M. (2012). *Guided Comprehension for English learners*. Newark, DE: International Reading Association.

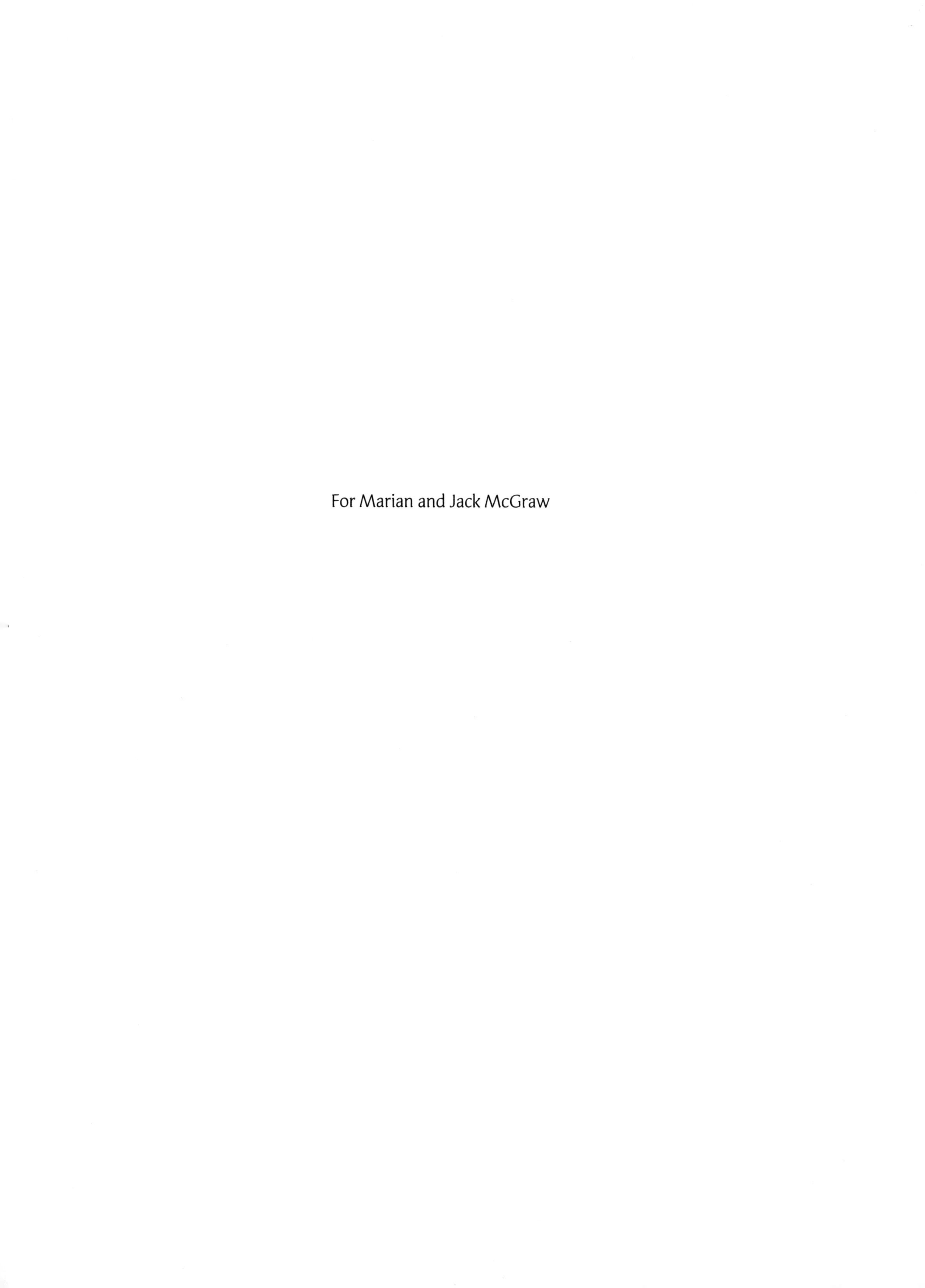

For Marian and Jack McGraw

CONTENTS

ABOUT THE AUTHOR

Maureen McLaughlin is a professor of reading education at East Stroudsburg University of Pennsylvania in East Stroudsburg, Pennsylvania, USA. She earned her doctorate at Boston University in reading and language development. Prior to her tenure at East Stroudsburg University, Maureen spent 15 years as a classroom teacher, reading specialist, and department chair in a public school system.

Maureen was a member of the Board of Directors of the International Reading Association from 2005–2008, and she will serve as IRA President in 2013–2014. She was the recipient of IRA's Jerry Johns Outstanding Teacher Educator in Reading Award in 2010. The author of numerous publications about the teaching of reading, reading comprehension, content area literacies, and the Common Core State Standards, Maureen recently published the second editions of *Guided Comprehension in the Primary Grades* and *Guided Comprehension in Grades 3–8*. She also wrote *Content Area Reading: Teaching and Learning in an Age of Multiple Literacies* (Allyn & Bacon, 2010). A frequent speaker at international, national, and state conferences, Maureen is a consultant to schools and universities throughout the world.

PREFACE

The Guided Comprehension Model was developed more than a decade ago to help reading educators teach students how to comprehend text. In this volume, I introduce the Guided Comprehension Model for English Learners and explain how we can use it to teach English learners, our fastest growing student population, to understand what they read.

The Guided Comprehension Model is based on the idea that reading is a social constructivist process. Underpinned by current research and beliefs about best practice, the Model provides a detailed, research-based, classroom-tested process for teaching reading from a comprehension-based perspective. When we use the Model to teach English learners, we teach these students to become active, strategic readers by providing explicit strategy instruction, numerous opportunities for engagement, and a variety of texts and instructional settings.

My goal in writing this volume has been to integrate what we know about teaching English learners with what we know about teaching students how to comprehend. This publication has afforded me opportunities to create a new stage for the Guided Comprehension Model (i.e., the Engaging Prereading Sequence for English Learners), integrate the latest research base for teaching English learners, include 12 Guided Comprehension lessons for English learners, share ideas for differentiating instruction, present theme resources, and include examples of student work. Writing this volume has also afforded me an opportunity to revise the appendixes to accommodate English learners. Evidence of this can be found in the strategy applications and new teaching examples in Appendix A, culturally relevant booklists and revised forms for organizing and managing centers and routines (Appendix B), updated sources of leveled texts (Appendix D), and ideas for making home–school connections (Appendix E).

Although this book is filled with innovations, I have simultaneously continued to focus on our ultimate goal: helping students to become good readers—readers who actively engage with text and naturally use a variety of skills and a repertoire of strategies to facilitate the construction of meaning.

We know from a variety of research studies that comprehension strategies and the skills that support them can be taught. We also know that Guided Comprehension, a context in which students learn comprehension skills and strategies in a variety of settings, has emerged as a highly successful teaching framework. The Guided Comprehension Model fosters students' transactions with text by integrating explicit and guided instruction of comprehension strategies, multiple levels and types of text, and varied opportunities for strategy application.

This new volume is divided into two parts. Part One features a detailed description of the Guided Comprehension Model for English Learners, including its research base, multiple stages, assessment connections, and use of leveled texts. Twelve theme-based Guided Comprehension lessons for English learners are presented in Part Two. The lessons, which focus on three themes, also include connections to the Common Core State Standards, student examples, assessment possibilities, ideas for differentiating instruction, and teacher commentaries. Resources that support the Guided Comprehension Model for English Learners are featured in the appendixes.

The seven chapters in Part One focus on using the Guided Comprehension Model and the research that supports it to teach English learners:

- Chapter 1 delineates the evidence base for teaching English learners.
- Chapter 2 details the Guided Comprehension Model for English Learners. The 10 research-based tenets that support the Model's emergence from research and current beliefs about best practice are delineated. Guided Comprehension connections are made to each tenet.
- Chapter 3 describes the four stages of the Model and how they function when teaching English learners. This discussion includes the presentation of the comprehension strategies and related teaching ideas.
- Chapter 4 focuses on comprehension centers for English learners. A wide variety of ideas for creating centers and related activities are described, and modifications for English learners are detailed.
- Chapter 5 explains comprehension routines, including Literature Circles, Reciprocal Teaching, and Cross-Age Reading Experiences. The components of each routine are delineated, and modifications for English learners are presented.
- Chapter 6 discusses the multiple roles of assessment in Guided Comprehension, makes connections to the Common Core State Standards, and describes a variety of practical measures.
- Chapter 7 discusses the various roles of leveled text in Guided Comprehension. Factors that influence student accessibility and text type and structure are also presented.

Chapters 1–7 are also linked to practical, reproducible resources in the appendixes, which have been adapted for or created to be used with English learners.

In Part Two, which includes Chapters 8–10, 12 lessons focused on three Guided Comprehension themes are introduced:

1. Animals of the Past...Animals of the Present
2. Favorite Authors: Eve Bunting, Doreen Cronin, Gary Soto, and Gary Paulsen
3. Biographies: The Stories of Our Lives

Each theme includes the following elements:

- Theme description
- Theme-based plan for Guided Comprehension for English Learners
- Four Guided Comprehension lessons for English learners
- Connections to the Common Core State Standards
- Planning forms
- Teacher commentaries and Think-Alouds
- Samples of student work
- Ideas for differentiating instruction

- Theme-based resources including related texts, websites, performance extensions across the curriculum, and culminating activities

The appendixes are filled with resources for teaching English learners. New samples of student work are featured in Appendix A, which provides strategy descriptions, graphic organizers, and reproducible blacklines. Resources for organizing and managing comprehension centers and routines are presented in Appendix B. Assessment materials and leveled text resources are the focus of Appendixes C and D. Home–school connections are featured in Appendix E, and Guided Comprehension planning and scheduling forms are presented in Appendix F.

Guided Comprehension for English Learners is designed to be a teacher-friendly, comprehensive resource. It contains everything you need to teach Guided Comprehension to English learners. Whether you are a classroom teacher, staff developer, reading specialist, literacy coach, ESL teacher, or teacher educator, this is a book that will remain on your desk and emerge dog-eared and well used over the years.

Acknowledgments

As always, there are many people to thank for making this book possible. I express my appreciation to family, colleagues, and friends for their insight, understanding, and support. I am also particularly grateful to the following people:

- Alexandria Gibb
- Mary Ellen Rock
- Ethel Fritz
- Stephanie Romano
- Rhonda Sutton
- Rebecca Norman
- Nancy and Rachel Sun
- Jessica Armour
- Ashley Heller
- Leslie Fisher
- Francesca McCutchan
- Stroudsburg School District, Stroudsburg, Pennsylvania
- Shannon Fortner, IRA Executive Editor of Publications, for her extraordinary knowledge of the publication process
- Matt Baker, Project Manager, for his insight, patience, and unparalleled editorial expertise

Finally, I thank you for joining me as we continue our search for greater understanding of reading comprehension. I hope you find *Guided Comprehension for English Learners* to be a valuable teaching resource, one that you and your colleagues will use to further our common goal of helping students understand what they read.

—*MM*

PART ONE

Guided Comprehension: A Teaching Model for English Learners

Part One provides a detailed description of the Guided Comprehension Model for English Learners, including its research base, multiple stages, assessment connections, and use of leveled text.

Theoretical Underpinnings: Chapter 1 presents the research base for teaching English learners. Focuses include creating classroom communities, being a culturally responsive educator, and setting high standards for English learners. In Chapter 2, the 10 research-based tenets that support the Guided Comprehension Model for English Learners' emergence from research and current beliefs about best practice are presented. Guided Comprehension connections are made to each tenet.

The Guided Comprehension Model for English Learners: In Chapter 3, the four stages of the Model are explained. This discussion includes the presentation of the comprehension strategies and related teaching ideas.

Comprehension Centers for English Learners: Comprehension centers are the focus of Chapter 4. A wide variety of ideas for creating centers and related activities are described. How to organize and manage comprehension centers is a special emphasis of this chapter.

Comprehension Routines: Literature Circles, Reciprocal Teaching, and Cross-Age Reading Experiences are explained in Chapter 5. The components of each routine are detailed and ideas for classroom implementation are presented.

Assessments: In Chapter 6, the multiple roles of assessment in Guided Comprehension are discussed and connections are made to the Common Core State Standards and World-Class Instructional Design and Assessment (WIDA) English Language Proficiency Standards. A variety of practical assessments are also described. Guided Comprehension connections are provided for each assessment. Then the Guided Comprehension Profile, an organizational framework for documenting student progress, is introduced.

Leveled Texts: The various roles of leveled text in Guided Comprehension are presented in Chapter 7. Factors that influence student accessibility and text type and structure are discussed. This is followed by descriptions of elements essential for choosing books for student success. Finally, methods of leveling and organizing classroom texts are delineated.

CHAPTER 1

English Learners and Reading Comprehension: What Teachers Need to Know

As literacy professionals, we have a special interest in teaching English learners—students who speak one or more languages and are learning English (Opitz & Harding-DeKam, 2007). Learning English as an additional language is a critical task because in today's classrooms, teachers and students use language for a variety of purposes, including creating meaning, establishing social relationships, organizing learning, and re-creating culture and language (Iddings, Risko, & Rampulla, 2009). Further,

> Language is what enables students to communicate, language is what makes collaboration possible, and using language is a way of transmitting and negotiating knowledge. But language is precisely the barrier that English learners face when they sit in the classroom. (Pilgreen, 2006, p. 41)

Our goal is to teach the English learners in our classes to become active, engaged readers. To help our students do this, we need to understand all we can about how to teach them (Fitzgerald & Graves, 2004; Young & Hadaway, 2006).

Researchers report that the most important feature of English learners is their diversity (Peregoy & Boyle, 2005; Short & Echevarria, 2004). English learners have diverse backgrounds, languages, and educational experiences—all of which we, as teachers, need to accommodate. Researchers agree that modifications should be made when we are teaching English learners (August, Goldenberg, Saunders, & Dressler, 2010; Goldenberg, 2010). As a result, the Guided Comprehension Model for English Learners has been modified from the original Model in several ways. These modifications are detailed in Chapter 3.

This chapter examines what various researchers suggest literacy professionals need to know when teaching English learners. The categories that follow have been culled from the work of a variety of researchers (Au, 2009; Au & Raphael, 2010; August et al., 2010; Avalos, Plasencia, Chavez, & Rascón, 2007; Barone, 2010; Brock, Youngs, Oikonomidoy, & Lapp, 2009; de Jong, 2010; Goldenberg, 2010; Helman, 2009; Iddings et al., 2009; Manyak, 2007; Manyak & Bauer, 2008; McIntyre, 2010; McLaughlin, 2010a; Mohr, 2004; Mohr & Mohr, 2007; Ogle & Correa-Kovtun, 2010; Peregoy & Boyle, 2005; Short & Echevarria, 2004; Villegas & Lucas, 2007; Watts-Taffe & Truscott, 2000; Yoon, 2007). The ideas range from being culturally and linguistically responsive educators, to explicitly teaching English learners the components of literacy, to continuing to engage in ongoing professional development.

Be Culturally Responsive

Gay (2000, 2002) defines culturally responsive teaching as using students' cultural knowledge, background knowledge, and learning styles to make learning more effective. Culturally responsive educators teach to and through the strengths of these students.

Villegas and Lucas (2002) concur, noting that culturally responsive teachers (a) are socioculturally conscious, (b) have affirming views of students' diverse backgrounds, (c) see themselves as capable of initiating change to make schools more equitable, (d) understand the constructivist nature of reading and are capable of teaching students how to construct personal meaning, (e) know about the lives of their students, and (f) teach lessons that build on students' background knowledge while challenging them to think beyond the familiar. Culturally responsive teachers also create connections between home and school, as well as between learning and the realities of life. They employ a variety of instructional techniques and accommodate students' learning styles while integrating multicultural literature and materials into their teaching. They also value students' cultural heritages and teach their students to do the same (Gay, 2000, 2002; Yoon, 2007).

Maintain High Expectations for English Learners

When teaching English learners, we need to view their previous experiences as strengths and maintain high expectations for their performance. As Helman (2009) notes, "When students' knowledge and background experiences, as well as their abilities, languages, and family heritage, are seen as strengths, students are empowered to be successful at school" (p. 9).

de Jong (2010) further suggests that we build on students' native language resources, use bilingual approaches to teaching, implement a curriculum that reflects students' cultural experiences, and use culturally and linguistically responsive teaching practices. Supports we use when teaching English learners—such as welcoming the students' first languages and cultures into our classrooms, ensuring the prominence of vocabulary study, incorporating visuals, employing modified graphic organizers, using a variety of grouping options, using leveled texts, and integrating culturally relevant materials—contribute to student achievement.

Create Classroom Communities and Engage English Learners

Au and Raphael (2010) suggest that we create a community of learners in our classroom. In such a community, students learn from each other, as well as from the teacher. In turn, the teacher also "shows an openness to learning from the students" (p. 209).

Creating a community of learners in which all participants are encouraged to value each other fosters student engagement and motivation. As Barone (2010) notes, student engagement is vital for English learners to avoid being lost in the background during instruction.

English learners need to be motivated to participate in class, engage in discussions, and work independently (Barone, 2010; Mohr & Mohr, 2007). It is critical that they (and all students) be active participants in learning, not passive observers (Barone, 2010; Mohr & Mohr, 2007; Yoon, 2007). Creating a culturally responsive community of learners is one way to foster English learners' active engagement in learning. Yoon (2007) suggests that teachers can also facilitate English learners' participation by showing interest in their cultures, encouraging them to share information about their cultures, demonstrating how to appreciate a variety of cultures, and encouraging mainstream students to welcome and support their learning. In fact, in Yoon's (2007) study, the English learners' increased participation appeared to result from their mainstream peers' welcoming attitudes toward them.

Explicitly Teach English Learners the Components of Literacy

The National Literacy Panel (August & Shanahan, 2007) found that English learners learning to read in English benefit from the explicit teaching of the components of literacy (e.g., phonemic awareness, phonics, vocabulary, comprehension, and writing), just as English speakers learning to read in English do. Goldenberg (2010) notes that "ELs appear to be capable of learning at levels comparable to those of English speakers, if they are provided with good, structured, explicit teaching" (p. 27). Brock et al. (2009) concur, reporting that meaningful, explicit instruction is essential for English learners. Manyak (2007) provides a rationale for this thinking:

> Given that ELs regularly face texts with more unfamiliar content and vocabulary than native speakers, ELs must be particularly strategic in activating background knowledge, inferring meanings of words, and monitoring their comprehension. Thus, the need for high-quality instruction in comprehension strategies is especially acute for ELs. (pp. 197–198)

Avalos et al. (2007) further suggest that explicit instruction for English learners should extend to Guided Reading. They recommend that instead of prompting, English learners should be coached with explicit demonstrations integrating the cueing systems during Guided Reading. The authors suggest that teachers begin by modeling the strategy and using a Think-Aloud (Davey, 1983). Next, the student uses the strategy, demonstrating it for the teacher. Then the student uses a Think-Aloud to verbalize what he or she was thinking while using the strategy. The use of Think-Alouds helps students to internalize the process.

Build on Programs and Procedures Effective for Monolingual English Speakers

Many researchers suggest that when we teach English learners, we should begin with programs and procedures that have proven successful for monolingual English speakers and modify them as necessary. August et al. (2010) note,

> The reason that common instructional procedures would be effective with ELs is probably due to the fact that students are very similar in perceptual skills, memory, capacity, ability to learn, etc., no matter what their language background, so the roles of modeling, explanation, and practice in instruction probably do not differ from one group to another. (p. 285)

Researchers make a variety of suggestions in terms of the types of modifications teachers may wish to make when teaching English learners (Au, 2009; August et al., 2010; Barone, 2010; Brock et al., 2009; Iddings et al., 2009; McLaughlin, 2010a, 2010b; Mohr, 2004; Mohr & Mohr, 2007). They recommend that teachers do the following:

- Emphasize student motivation and engagement
- Employ a structured literacy lesson format with appropriate supports
- Teach students to generate and respond to questions
- Teach patterns for narrative and informational texts
- Read aloud texts that present content, useful language patterns, or vocabulary in context to help foster oral language development
- Interact with text to make content more comprehensible
- Encourage students to engage in written responses to provide time for thought and reflection
- Provide numerous daily opportunities for students to engage in discussion
- Integrate visual aids to support and extend understanding, including picture books as supports for English learners of all ages
- Teach integrated, engaging, and enriching lessons that deepen understandings

Emphasize Student Motivation and Engagement

One way we can do this is to ensure that we connect learning to students' lives. For example, when reading informational text, such as *Tracking Trash: Flotsam, Jetsam, and the Science of Ocean Motion* (Burns, 2007), we can invite students to visit a variety of websites about the topic. When reading narrative text, such as *Just a Dream* (Van Allsburg, 2011), students can use realia bags that contain props representing characters and objects in the book to retell the story.

We can ensure that we have culturally relevant titles available at appropriate reading levels, especially when students engage in self-selection of texts. We can also draw from students' diversity as a classroom resource. For example, when reading about world cultures, we can invite students who have come from various cultures to share information about them. This can also be supported by the use of technology.

Employ a Structured Literacy Lesson Format With Appropriate Supports

Guided Comprehension lessons are based on a structured literacy lesson format that has built-in supports for English learners. Examples of these include the Engaging Prereading Sequence, small-group instructional settings, the use of visuals, and culturally relevant text. To further modify the Model, we can use additional modeling and Think-Alouds (Davey, 1983). (For examples of modeling, see the lessons in Chapters 8, 9, and 10. For a detailed example of a Think-Aloud, see Appendix A, page 248.)

We can also integrate students' native languages in our classrooms whenever possible. Examples of this include encouraging English learners to discuss readings with each other in their native language and to engage in Cross-Age Reading Experiences with partners who share the same language.

Teach Students to Generate and Respond to Questions

After teaching students how to generate and respond to questions using Ciardiello's four levels of questioning (see Chapter 3), we can rephrase questions to encourage students to respond. We can also value and elaborate on students' responses.

To encourage students to respond to questions, we can increase wait time to afford students time to think through responses and possibly engage in code-switching (thinking or speaking in one language and switching to another). We can also encourage alternative ways of responding, such as choral responses and Think–Pair–Shares (McTighe & Lyman, 1988), rather than calling on individual students to respond.

Teach Patterns for Narrative and Informational Texts

The narrative or story text pattern focuses on characters, setting, problem, attempts to resolve the problem, and resolution. It is, essentially, all the elements we use when writing or retelling a story. Informational text is different because it has multiple patterns. These include comparison/contrast, cause and effect, description, sequence, and problem/solution. When teaching these patterns, we can use paragraph frames based on each pattern, and scaffold students' learning by beginning with completed frames in a given pattern and gradually releasing control of the writing to the students. We can do this by gradually decreasing the amount of information we include on the frame and encouraging students to provide it.

Read Aloud Texts That Present Content, Useful Language Patterns, or Vocabulary in Context

We can extend students' oral language and fluency development through techniques such as choral reading, echo reading, and Readers Theatre. We can also enhance vocabulary by repeating read-alouds, ensuring multiple exposures to words, and actively engaging students (Morrow & Brittain, 2003).

Interact With Text

To interact with text, we can reread texts or the alternative bilingual versions to help students learn vocabulary and text features. We can also incorporate graphic organizers, numbering or highlighting the sections of each. Encouraging students to represent their thinking in multiple ways (such as dramatization, music, and photography) also helps to make text comprehensible.

Encourage Students to Engage in Written Responses

We can provide opportunities for students to engage in short written responses by engaging them in Tickets Out (see Appendix C, page 343); journal entries; and strategy applications, such as Bookmark Technique (see Appendix A, page 246), Concept of Definition Maps (see Appendix A, page 242), and Questions Into Paragraphs (see Appendix A, page 251).

Provide Numerous Daily Opportunities to Engage in Discussion

From a constructivist perspective, discussion affords students opportunities to refine their understanding. Students should engage in discussion multiple times during a literacy lesson. These include *before reading* to determine and activate prior knowledge, *during reading* to make connections and refine understanding, and *after reading* to extend or elaborate on ideas.

Integrate Visual Aids to Support and Extend Understanding

To accommodate students' needs in this area, we can include pictures and websites in our teaching. We can also encourage students to respond through sketching and encourage students to write stories based on wordless picture books, such as David Wiesner's *Flotsam* (2006) or Alexandra Day's *Carl Goes to Daycare* (1993).

Teach Integrated, Engaging, and Enriching Lessons

Guided Comprehension lessons are designed to deepen students' understanding. Chapters 8, 9, and 10 feature lessons that integrate numerous supports for English learners.

Integrate Leveled Texts

A wide range of accessible text at a variety of levels should be available to English learners. The array of text accommodates students' interests, and access to leveled texts accommodates their reading abilities. The access to leveled texts allows students to choose text at their independent levels when they are not with the teacher and read text at their instructional levels when they are (see Chapter 7). Ogle and Correa-Kovtun (2010) remind us that students should read materials at their instructional and independent levels every day to improve as readers.

Manyak and Bauer (2008) suggest that we should "not underestimate ELs' ability to read sophisticated texts and engage in higher-level comprehension" (p. 433). They further note that English learners' comprehension often improves when they read culturally relevant text.

Use a Variety of Grouping Options

Teachers should use multiple ways of organizing instruction to extend and build on English learners' skills (McIntyre, 2010). Instructional settings often include pairs, trios, small groups organized for a variety of purposes, and large groups.

Au (2009) notes that teachers of English learners find small-group lessons effective. McIntyre (2010) concurs and suggests that English learners should have opportunities to work with others who speak their language, as well as native English speakers. English learners may work in pairs, trios, or small groups with other English learners or with a mix of English learners and native English speakers. These settings may be teacher structured or student selected. The structure depends on the purpose. For example, a teacher may preteach strategies to English learners in a small group, or English learners and native English speakers may choose the group in which they will participate for creative activities.

It is important to note that English learners often feel more comfortable responding in pair, trio, and small-group settings. They do not seem to feel the pressure to respond immediately that they sometimes experience when working in large groups.

Teach Vocabulary

Researchers agree that vocabulary is a key element in English learners' comprehension (Blachowicz, Fisher, Ogle, & Watts-Taffe, 2006; Manyak & Bauer, 2008; McLaughlin, 2010b; NICHD, 2000; Townsend, 2009). Graves (2006) extends this thinking, noting that vocabulary knowledge not only promotes understanding but also enables ownership of language.

When teaching vocabulary, Bedore, Peña, and Boerger (2010) recommend that teachers engage in instruction that is multifaceted and focused on expanding students' understanding. Goldenberg (2010) suggests that English learners are more likely to understand words when they are explicitly taught. He also contends that English learners understand a greater number of words when the words are embedded in meaningful contexts.

Bauman and Graves (2010) suggest that "the comprehensiveness of instruction coupled with use of the native language, in support text and cognates, are powerful tools for increasing the vocabulary of ELL students" (p. 533). The authors also examined the nature of academic vocabulary, a common focus for English learners, concluding,

> Researchers, writers, and theorists tend to define academic vocabulary in one of two ways: (1) as *domain-specific academic vocabulary*, or the content-specific words used in disciplines like biology, geometry, civics, and geography; or (2) as *general academic vocabulary*, or the broad, all-purpose terms that appear across content areas but that may vary in meaning because of the discipline itself. (p. 6)

Use Formative Assessments

Many of the assessments included in Guided Comprehension are formative in nature. Formative assessment is ongoing, classroom-based, and informal. It occurs every day. McTighe and O'Connor (2005) distinguish between formative and summative assessments by viewing formative assessment as a means of improving learning and summative assessment as a way to provide reliable information about what has been achieved.

Shepard (2005) notes that formative assessment is a collaborative process in which how to improve learning is negotiated between teacher and student. Weber (1999) proposes that the results of formative assessments suggest future steps for teaching and learning. Such steps might result from observations that allow us to determine how well a student contributed to a class discussion, or informal writing that documents whether a student is able to apply a particular skill or strategy. Formative assessment not only demonstrates how students learn and what students know but also helps teachers to identify what remains unclear.

We can monitor all students' progress through formative assessments, but it is especially valuable in the case of English learners. We usually provide these students with additional supports. Observing their progress through formative assessments provides us with ongoing insights into their thinking and abilities. This information helps us to understand whether the supports we provided were effective or should be changed.

Engage in Ongoing Professional Development

Researchers tell us that appropriate professional development can help prepare us to teach English learners and to continue to learn new ways to meet their literacy needs (Brock et al., 2009; Short & Echevarria, 2004). Such professional development is available in numerous formats. Examples include joining professional organizations, reading professional journals, participating in book clubs and study groups, taking graduate courses, participating in webinars, taking in-district courses, participating in and presenting at literacy conferences, and earning a state endorsement for teaching English learners.

Li and Protacio (2010) elaborate on the need for continued professional development by noting that it should encourage collaboration among classroom teachers and ESL specialists. Mohr (2004) concurs, noting that the classroom teacher and the ESL instructor should collaborate to provide excellent instruction. Developing positive relationships with these teachers and discussing how we can best help our English learners to succeed is often an invaluable experience. For example, we can discuss supports such as preteaching, visuals, and a variety of response modes. We can organize meetings with the ESL teacher(s) and the content area teachers to develop lists of general academic vocabulary that will work across the curriculum. We can also discuss integrating students' native languages into our classes as a scaffold and understand how much scaffolding particular students may need. Other members of such a support team may include, but not be limited to, literacy coaches, upper-grade students, and community volunteers who speak students' first languages. When we partner with those who speak students' native languages, we can use the languages to help English learners access our curriculums. Villegas and Lucas (2007) suggest that materials in the students' native languages, such as informational articles, text adaptations, leveled text, or textbooks, help them build background knowledge.

Final Thoughts

In summary, Helman (2009) notes, "Educational factors that influence the literacy learning of English learners involve in-class instruction, the types and quality of lessons, involvement of the students and their communities, teacher knowledge, and students' opportunities to use language in cognitively challenging activities" (p. 13). Allison and Harklau (2010) concur, noting,

> ELs are no different from their peers, in that they fare best in classrooms in which they are part of the conversation; where their unique backgrounds, strengths, and learning characteristics are valued and respected; and where they receive affective support. (p. 140)

This chapter discussed what we need to know when teaching English learners. Chapter 2 will explore the research-based tenets that support Guided Comprehension and make connections between the research and the Guided Comprehension Model for English Learners.

CHAPTER 2

Reading Comprehension for English Learners

As literacy professionals in the 21st century, we find ourselves teaching increasingly high numbers of culturally and linguistically diverse students (Hadaway & Young, 2006). In fact, English learners are the fastest growing educational population (Young & Hadaway, 2006). Goldenberg (2010) notes that "EL students in the United States come from over 400 different language backgrounds; however, by far the largest proportion—80%—is Spanish speakers" (p. 17).

This book has been designed as a resource to help literacy professionals teach English learners how to actively construct personal meaning while reading. To accomplish this, a number of adaptations have been made to the original Guided Comprehension Model and the processes that support it. These changes are delineated in Chapter 3. This chapter details Guided Comprehension's natural emergence from current research. To illustrate this relationship, 10 research-based comprehension tenets are presented. Each is followed by a brief discussion of the tenet's connection to the Guided Comprehension Model for English Learners.

Tenets of Reading Comprehension

Studies have shown that multiple factors affect successful reading comprehension. The following research-based tenets describe the current most influential elements (McLaughlin & Allen, 2009):

- Comprehension is a social constructivist process.
- Comprehension strategies and skills can be taught.
- Differentiated reading instruction accommodates students' needs, including those of English learners and struggling readers.
- Influential reading teachers affect students' learning.
- Good readers are strategic and take active roles in the reading process.
- Reading should occur in meaningful contexts.
- Students benefit from transacting daily with a variety of texts at multiple levels.
- Vocabulary development and instruction affect reading comprehension.
- Engagement is a key factor in the comprehension process.
- Formative assessment informs comprehension instruction.

Although the tenets have strong research underpinnings, they are also designed to inform instruction. In the sections that follow, each tenet is discussed and connections are made between theory and practice. Each tenet's relation to the Guided Comprehension Model for English Learners is also described.

Comprehension Is a Social Constructivist Process

Constructivists believe that learners make sense of their world by connecting what they know and have experienced with what they are learning. They construct meaning through these connections when educators pose relevant problems, structure learning around primary concepts, seek and value students' ideas, and assess students' learning in context.

According to Short and Burke (1996), constructivism frees students of fact-driven curricula and encourages them to focus on larger ideas, allows students to reach unique conclusions and reformulate ideas, encourages students to see the world as a complex place with multiple perspectives, and emphasizes that students are responsible for their own learning and should attempt to connect the information they learn to the world around them through inquiry.

Cambourne (2002) notes that constructivism has three core theoretical assumptions:

1. What is learned cannot be separated from the context in which it is learned.
2. The purposes or goals that the learner brings to the learning situation are central to what is learned.
3. Knowledge and meaning are socially constructed through the processes of negotiation, evaluation, and transformation.

Constructivists believe that students construct knowledge by linking what is new to what is already known. In reading, this concept is reflected in schema-based learning development, which purports that learning takes place when new information is integrated with what is already known. The more experience learners have with a particular topic, the easier it is for them to make connections between what they know and what they are learning (Anderson, 1994; Anderson & Pearson, 1984). From a constructivist perspective, comprehension is viewed as

> the construction of meaning of a written or spoken communication through a reciprocal, holistic interchange of ideas between the interpreter and the message in a particular communicative context. Note: The presumption here is that meaning resides in the intentional problem-solving, thinking processes of the interpreter during such an interchange, that the content of meaning is influenced by that person's prior knowledge and experience, and that the message so constructed by the receiver may or may not be congruent with the message sent. (Harris & Hodges, 1995, p. 39)

Vygotsky's principles enhance the constructivist perspective by addressing the social context of learning (Dixon-Krauss, 1996). According to Vygotsky, students should be taught within their zones of proximal development (Forman & Cazden, 1994; Vygotsky, 1978). Instruction within the zone should incorporate both scaffolding and social mediation. As Dixon-Krauss (1996) notes when explaining this Vygotskian principle, "It is through social dialogue with adults and/or more capable peers that language concepts are learned" (p. 155). Such social interaction encourages students to think and share their ideas.

Constructivism is manifested in classrooms that are characterized by student-generated ideas, self-selection, creativity, interaction, critical thinking, and personal construction of meaning (McLaughlin & Allen, 2002b). In such contexts, authentic literacy tasks assimilate real-world experiences, provide a purpose for learning, and encourage students to take ownership of learning (Hiebert, 1994; Newmann & Wehlage, 1993).

Cambourne (2002) suggests that instructional principles emerge from constructivist theory. These principles include the following:

- Creating a classroom culture that encourages deep engagement with effective reading
- Using strategies that are a blend of explicitness, systematicity, mindfulness, and contextualization
- Creating continuous opportunities to develop intellectual unrest
- Encouraging students to develop their conscious awareness of how text functions and how we create meaning
- Designing and using tasks that will support the authentic use of the processes and understandings implicit in reading behavior

Guided Comprehension Connection

The Guided Comprehension Model is based on the view of comprehension as a social constructivist process. This is demonstrated in the Model in numerous ways, including the ultimate goal of students' transaction with text and the value placed on learning in a variety of social settings. In the constructivist process, the role of background knowledge is particularly vital for English learners. When teaching English learners, our goals concerning background knowledge are twofold: We need to ensure that our students have background knowledge about a variety of topics, and that they are able to activate it. This is supported in multiple ways in the Guided Comprehension Model for English Learners, including the preteaching of skills and strategies and the use of accessible text.

Comprehension Strategies and Skills Can Be Taught

Durkin's research in the late 1970s reported that little if any comprehension instruction occurred in classrooms (Durkin, 1978). Instead, comprehension questions, often at the literal level, were assigned and then corrected; comprehension was assessed but not taught. Studies have demonstrated that explicit instruction of comprehension strategies improves students' comprehension of new texts and topics (Hiebert, Pearson, Taylor, Richardson, & Paris, 1998).

We know that research supports the teaching of reading comprehension strategies in the primary grades (Duffy, 2001; Duke & Pearson, 2002; Hilden & Pressley, 2002; McLaughlin, 2003b). In fact, Duke and Pearson (2002) suggest incorporating "both explicit instruction in specific comprehension strategies and a great deal of time and opportunity for actual reading, writing, and discussion of text" (p. 206). Guided Comprehension strategies include the following:

- *Previewing*: Activating background knowledge, predicting, and setting a purpose
- *Self-questioning*: Generating questions to guide reading
- *Making connections*: Relating reading to self, text, and others

- *Visualizing*: Creating mental images while reading
- *Knowing how words work*: Understanding words through strategic vocabulary development, including the use of the graphophonic, syntactic, and semantic cue systems to figure out unknown words
- *Monitoring*: Asking "Does this make sense?" and clarifying by adapting strategic processes to accommodate the response
- *Summarizing*: Synthesizing important ideas
- *Evaluating*: Making judgments about the text

Pressley (2001) states that comprehension instruction should begin in the early grades with the teaching of comprehension skills, such as sequencing and questioning, and that instruction in a few strategies, such as predicting and summarizing, should occur as early as kindergarten. Linking skills and strategies can facilitate comprehension. Comprehension strategies are generally more complex than skills and often require the orchestration of several skills. Effective instruction links comprehension skills to strategies to promote strategic reading. For example, the comprehension skills of sequencing, making judgments, noting details, making generalizations, and using text structure can be linked to summarizing, which is a comprehension strategy (Lipson, 2001). These and other skills, including generating questions, making inferences, distinguishing between important and less important ideas, and drawing conclusions, facilitate students' use of one or more comprehension strategies. For example, students' ability to generate questions permeates all the Guided Comprehension strategies. (See Chapter 3, particularly Figure 2 on page 34, for more detailed information about questioning.)

Fielding and Pearson (1994) recommend a framework for comprehension instruction that encourages the gradual release of responsibility from teacher to student. This four-step approach includes teacher modeling, guided practice, independent practice, and application of the strategies in authentic reading situations. This framework is supported by Vygotsky's (1978) work on instruction within the zone of proximal development and by scaffolding, the gradual relinquishing of support as the students become more competent in using the strategies.

After explaining and modeling strategies, teachers scaffold instruction to provide the support necessary as students attempt new tasks. During this process, teachers gradually release responsibility for learning to the students, who, after practicing the strategies in a variety of settings, apply them independently.

Guided Comprehension Connection

This tenet is a core underpinning of Guided Comprehension because the Model is designed to promote comprehension as a strategy-based thinking process. It incorporates the explicit teaching of comprehension strategies and the skills that enable their use. The Model also provides multiple opportunities for practice and transfer of learning. Learning reading comprehension skills and strategies also supports national standards for English learners, including TESOL's PreK–12 English Language Proficiency Standards (2006) and the World-Class Instructional Design and Assessment (WIDA) English Language Proficiency Standards (2007).

Differentiated Reading Instruction Accommodates Students' Needs, Including Those of English Learners and Struggling Readers

Duke and Pearson's (2002) work reminds us that learners need different kinds and amounts of reading comprehension instruction. As teachers, we understand this. We know that we have students of differing capabilities in our classes, and we strive to help them to comprehend to the best of their abilities.

Differentiated instruction enables us to accommodate the diversity of students' needs (Gibson & Hasbrouck, 2008; Tyner & Green, 2005). To develop environments that promote differentiated instruction, Gibson and Hasbrouck (2008) suggest that we do the following:

- Embrace collaborative teaching and learning
- Use whole-class and small-group explicit strategy instruction
- Establish consistent routines and procedures
- Scaffold student learning
- Increase student engagement
- Teach students how to learn, as well as what to learn
- Change the way teaching occurs

We can differentiate a number of instructional components to support students as they gain competence and confidence in learning. These include *content*, the information being taught; *process*, the way in which the information is taught; and *product*, how the students demonstrate their learning (Tomlinson, 1999).

When we differentiate instruction we create multiple pathways to learning. This supports our goal of helping students to perform to their maximum potentials.

Differentiated instruction is embedded in the Guided Comprehension Model. Flexible paired and small-group instruction, multiple levels of text, and differentiated tasks are three examples of how we can accommodate individual students' needs when teaching Guided Comprehension. Examples of specific ideas for differentiating instruction for English learners, including using visual cues and providing culturally relevant texts, are presented in the theme-based lessons in Part Two of this book.

Influential Reading Teachers Affect Students' Learning

Influential reading teachers are valued participants in the learning process. As the National Commission on Teaching and America's Future (1996) has reported, the single most important strategy for achieving U.S. education goals is to recruit, prepare, and support excellent teachers for every school.

The teacher's knowledge makes a difference in student success (IRA, 2000). A knowledgeable teacher is aware of what is working well and what each student needs to be successful, and he or she knows the importance of every student having successful literacy experiences.

The teacher's role in the reading process is to create experiences and environments that introduce, nurture, or extend students' literacy abilities to engage with text. This requires that teachers engage in explicit instruction, modeling, scaffolding, facilitating, and participating (Au & Raphael, 1998).

Both reading researchers and professional organizations have delineated the characteristics of excellent reading teachers (Fountas & Pinnell, 1996; IRA, 2000; Ruddell, 1995). The following characterization of such reading teachers integrates these ideas.

Influential reading teachers believe that all children can learn. They base their teaching on the needs of the individual student, including English learners. They know that motivation and multiple kinds of text are essential elements of teaching and learning. They understand that reading is a social constructivist process that functions best in authentic situations. They teach in print-rich, concept-rich environments.

Such teachers have in-depth knowledge of various aspects of literacy, including reading, writing, and discussion. They teach for a variety of purposes, using diverse methods, materials, and grouping patterns to focus on individual needs, interests, and learning styles. They also know the strategies good readers use, and they can teach students how to use them.

Influential reading teachers view their teaching as multifaceted, and they view themselves as participants in the learning process. They integrate their knowledge of the learning cycle, learning styles, and multiple intelligences into their teaching.

These teachers understand the natural relation between assessment and instruction, and they use formative assessments in multiple ways for a variety of purposes. They use instructional strategies that provide authentic feedback to monitor the effectiveness of teaching and student performance. They know that assessment informs both teaching and learning.

Guided Comprehension Connection

Teachers who engage in Guided Comprehension are knowledgeable not only about the concept but also about their students and their linguistic and cultural backgrounds. Their goal is for all students, including English learners, to be active participants in literacy. Influential teachers know that students need accessible text, and they know how to use the Guided Comprehension Model to integrate text to accommodate each reader's interests and needs. These educators are active participants in the reading process. They know how to use a variety of materials in a variety of ways within a variety of settings. Guided Comprehension provides a context for such teaching.

Good Readers Are Strategic and Take Active Roles in the Reading Process

Numerous reading researchers have reported that much of what we know about comprehension is based on studies of good readers (Askew & Fountas, 1998; Duke & Pearson, 2002; Pearson, 2001; Pressley, 2000). They describe good readers as active participants in the reading process who have clear goals and constantly monitor the relation between the goals they have set and the text they are reading. Good readers use comprehension strategies to facilitate the construction of meaning. In Guided Comprehension, these strategies include previewing, self-questioning, making connections, visualizing, knowing how words work, monitoring, summarizing, and evaluating. Researchers believe that using a repertoire of such strategies helps students become metacognitive readers (Duke & Pearson, 2002; Palincsar & Brown, 1984; Roehler & Duffy, 1984).

Good readers read from aesthetic or efferent stances and have an awareness of the author's style and purpose (Rosenblatt, 1978, 2002). They read both narrative and expository texts and have ideas about how to figure out unfamiliar words. They use their knowledge of text structure to efficiently and strategically process text. This knowledge develops from experiences with different genres and is correlated with age or time in school (Goldman & Rakestraw, 2000).

These readers spontaneously generate questions at different points in the reading process for a variety of reasons. They know that they use questioning in their everyday lives and that it increases their comprehension. Good readers are problem solvers who have the ability to discover new information for themselves.

Good readers read widely. This provides exposure to various genres and text formats, affords opportunities for strategy use, increases understanding of how words work, provides bases for discussion and meaning negotiation, and accommodates students' interests.

Good readers construct and revise meaning as they read. They monitor their comprehension and know when they are constructing meaning and when they are not. When comprehension breaks down because of lack of background information, difficulty of words, or unfamiliar text structure, good readers know a variety of fix-up strategies to use. These strategies include rereading, changing the pace of reading, using context clues, cross-checking cueing systems, and asking for help. Most important, good readers are able to select the appropriate strategies and to consistently focus on making sense of text and gaining new understandings.

Guided Comprehension Connection

Helping all students, including English learners, to become active, strategic readers is the ultimate goal of Guided Comprehension, and students fully participate in the process. Students' roles are extensive and include engaging in comprehension as a thinking process and transacting with various levels of text in multiple settings. Students then incorporate the strategies they learn into their existing repertoire and use them as needed.

Reading Should Occur in Meaningful Contexts

Duke (2001) has delineated an expanded understanding of context for present-day learners. She suggests that context should be viewed as curriculum, activity, classroom environment, teachers and teaching, text, and society. One of the interesting aspects of this expanded notion of context is the number of influences that impact student learning. As Cambourne (2002) reminds us, "What is learned cannot be separated from the context in which it is learned" (p. 26).

Lipson and Wixson (2009) suggest that the instructional context encompasses settings, practices, and resources. The instructional settings include teacher beliefs and literate environment, classroom interaction, classroom organization, and grouping. Instructional goals, methods, activities, and assessment practices are part of instructional practice. Commercial programs, trade materials, and technology are viewed as instructional resources.

More specific, literacy-based descriptions of context include ideas offered by Gambrell (1996), Hiebert (1994), and Pearson (2001). They suggest that the classroom context is characterized by multiple factors including classroom organization and authentic opportunities to read, write, and discuss. They further note that the instruction of skills and strategies, integration of concept-driven vocabulary, use of multiple genres, and knowledge of various text structures are other contextual components.

When teaching English learners, it is essential that we create culturally responsive classrooms. Research suggests that teachers can begin this process by valuing students' cultures, explicitly teaching English learners in small-group settings, integrating multicultural literature, and holding high expectations for all students (Gay, 2000; Villegas & Lucas, 2002; Yoon, 2007).

Guided Comprehension is a context for teaching and learning comprehension strategies. It incorporates a variety of settings, practices, and resources. Students, including English learners, have numerous opportunities to read, write, and discuss using multiple genres and levels of authentic text.

Students Benefit From Transacting Daily With a Variety of Texts at Multiple Levels

Students need to engage daily with multiple levels of texts. When such levels of text are being used, teachers scaffold learning experiences and students receive varying levels of support, depending on the purpose and context of the reading. When text is challenging, students have full teacher support. For example, teachers can share the text through read-aloud. When the text is just right for instruction, students have support as needed, with the teacher prompting or responding as necessary. Finally, when the text is just right for independent reading, little or no support is needed. (For a more detailed discussion of leveled text, see Chapter 7.)

Transacting with a wide variety of genres enhances students' understanding. Experience reading multiple genres provides students with knowledge of numerous text structures and improves their text-driven processing (Goldman & Rakestraw, 2000). Gambrell (2001) notes that transacting with a wide variety of genres—including biography, historical fiction, legends, poetry, and brochures—increases students' reading performance.

In Guided Comprehension, students have opportunities to engage with a variety of texts at independent, instructional, and challenging levels on a daily basis. This includes accessible narrative and informational texts for English learners. Villegas and Lucas (2007) suggest that materials in the students' native languages, such as informational articles, text adaptations, leveled text, or textbooks, should also be available to help English learners build background knowledge.

Vocabulary Development and Instruction Affect Reading Comprehension

Vocabulary development and instruction have strong ties to reading comprehension. As the National Reading Panel (NICHD, 2000) notes, "Reading comprehension is a complex, cognitive process that cannot be understood without a clear description of the role that vocabulary development and vocabulary instruction play in the understanding of what has been read" (p. 13). Snow, Burns, and Griffin (1998) support this view, observing, "Learning new concepts and words that encode them is essential to comprehension development" (p. 217).

Harris and Hodges (1995) describe students' ever-growing knowledge of words and their meanings as *vocabulary development*. They note that vocabulary development also refers to the teaching–learning processes that lead to such growth. Vocabulary development is also influenced by the amount and variety of text students read (Baumann & Kame'enui, 1991; Beck & McKeown, 1991; Snow et al., 1998). Teacher read-alouds, which offer students access to a variety of levels of text, contribute to this process (Hiebert et al., 1998).

Blachowicz, Fisher, Ogle, and Watts-Taffe (2006) suggest that effective vocabulary instruction is characterized by the following:

- An environment that fosters word consciousness—"the awareness of and interest in learning and using new words and becoming more skillful and precise in word usage" (Graves & Watts-Taffe, 2002, p. 144)
- Students who actively participate in the process
- Instruction that integrates vocabulary with the curriculum and word learning throughout the day and across subject areas
- Instruction that provides both definitional and contextual information
- Teachers who provide multiple exposures to words
- Teachers who provide numerous, ongoing opportunities to use the words

Goldenberg (2011) further notes that "for English speakers and English learners alike, word learning is enhanced when the words are taught explicitly, embedded in meaningful contexts, and students are provided with ample repetition and use" (p. 696).

Baumann and Kame'enui (1991) suggest that explicit instruction of vocabulary and learning from context should be balanced. The instruction should be meaningful to students, include words from students' reading, and focus on a variety of strategies for determining the meanings of unfamiliar words (Blachowicz & Lee, 1991). Another important aspect of such teaching is making connections between the vocabulary and students' background knowledge.

In Guided Comprehension, all students are immersed in words. They engage daily with texts at multiple levels in a variety of settings, and they learn words through both explicit instruction and use of context clues. Students also learn vocabulary strategies in scaffolded settings that provide numerous opportunities for practice and application, paired and small-group reading, and teacher read-alouds. These techniques are known to be beneficial for English learners as well as native English speakers.

Engagement Is a Key Factor in the Comprehension Process

The engagement perspective integrates cognitive, motivational, and social aspects of reading (Baker, Afflerbach, & Reinking, 1996; Baker & Wigfield, 1999; Guthrie & Alvermann, 1999). Engaged learners achieve because they want to understand, they possess intrinsic motivations for interacting with text, they use cognitive skills to understand, and they share knowledge by talking with teachers and peers (Guthrie & Wigfield, 1997). Engaged readers are motivated by the material offered, use many strategies to comprehend the text they are reading, and are able to construct new knowledge after making connections with the text (Casey, 2008).

Engaged readers transact with print and construct understandings based on connections between background knowledge and new information. Tierney (1990) describes the process of the mind's eye and suggests readers become part of the story within their minds. Teachers can nurture and extend this by encouraging students to read for authentic purposes and respond in meaningful ways, always focusing on comprehension, personal connections, and reader response. Baker and Wigfield (1999) note that "engaged readers are motivated to read for different purposes, utilize knowledge gained from previous experience to generate new understandings, and participate in meaningful social interactions around reading" (p. 453).

Pitcher and Fang (2007) suggest, "Motivation to read is a complex construct that influences readers' choices of reading material, their willingness to engage in reading, and thus their ultimate competence in reading, especially related to academic reading tasks" (p. 379). There are seven instructional practices that increase student motivation in reading and reading comprehension: (1) setting content goals, (2) allowing students to choose what they read, (3) picking a topic of interest, (4) allowing social interactions, (5) caring about what students do, (6) using some extrinsic rewards, and (7) reading for mastery goals (Guthrie et al., 2006). Edmunds and Bauserman (2006) recommend that teachers can increase their students' motivation to read by allowing students to select their own books, by paying attention to the characteristics of the books offered, by acknowledging students' personal interests and their access to the books, and by allowing active involvement of others during the reading process.

Motivation is described in terms of competence and efficacy beliefs, goals for reading, and social purposes of reading (Baker & Wigfield, 1999). Motivated readers believe they can be successful and are willing to take on the challenge of difficult reading material. They also exhibit intrinsic reasons for reading, such as gaining new knowledge about a topic or enjoying the reading experience. Motivated readers enjoy the social aspects of sharing with others new meanings gained from their reading.

Gambrell (1996) suggests that "classroom cultures that foster reading motivation are characterized by a teacher who is a reading model, a book-rich classroom environment, opportunities for choice, familiarity with books, and literacy-related incentives that reflect the value of reading" (p. 20). Gambrell, Palmer, Codling, and Mazzoni (1996) note that highly motivated readers read for a wide variety of reasons including curiosity, involvement, social interchange, and emotional satisfaction.

Guided Comprehension Connection

The Guided Comprehension Model is based on all students' active engagement. It integrates the cognitive, motivational, and social aspects of reading. Students use strategies to think through text. Students are motivated because their interests and opportunities for success are embedded in the Model. This includes related texts, which may focus on students' cultures and be written in students' native languages. Guided Comprehension is social because students negotiate meaning and interact with teachers and peers on a daily basis.

Formative Assessment Informs Comprehension Instruction

Formative assessment captures students' performance as they engage in the process of learning. It is continuous, provides an ongoing record of student growth, and has the ability to afford insights into students' understandings at any given point in the learning experience. Formative assessment is dynamic. It reflects constructivist theory and is viewed not as an add-on but rather as a natural component of teaching and learning.

Formative assessments, which are informal in nature, can be used in a variety of instructional settings. These include scaffolded learning experiences in which students have varying degrees of teacher support. Assessing in this context captures the students' emerging abilities and provides insights that may not be gleaned from independent settings (Minick, 1987).

Guided Comprehension Connection

Formative assessment permeates the Guided Comprehension Model, occurring for multiple purposes in a variety of settings every day. Formative assessment is a natural part of learning that provides insights into students' thinking as they engage in all stages of the Model. The results of such assessments inform future teaching and learning.

As delineated in this chapter, the Guided Comprehension Model for English Learners has a sound theoretical framework. It is dynamic in nature, accommodates students' individual needs, employs a variety of texts and settings, and incorporates active, formative assessments in multiple settings.

Chapter 3 details the Guided Comprehension Model for English Learners. The Model includes a variety of modifications for English learners that focus on context, instruction, text, and assessment.

CHAPTER 3

The Guided Comprehension Model for English Learners

Guided Comprehension is a context in which students learn comprehension skills and strategies in a variety of settings using multiple levels and types of text. Although the original Guided Comprehension Model supported teaching English learners in a variety of ways—explicit instruction, leveled texts, guided small-group instruction, a variety of instructional settings, multiple modes of representing thinking—the Guided Comprehension Model for English Learners includes additional modifications to further accommodate these students. These changes include the addition of a new stage, the Engaging Prereading Sequence, which occurs prior to whole-group instruction, and a number of modifications in teacher-guided small-group instruction, centers, and routines.

This chapter explores the Guided Comprehension Model for English Learners. To begin, the categories of modifications made to accommodate English learners are delineated. These include context, instruction, text, and assessment. Next, the Model itself is explored. Stage One, the Engaging Prereading Sequence, which was created specifically for English learners, is detailed. Then the remaining stages of the Model are described. These include teacher-directed whole-group instruction, teacher-guided small-group instruction, student-facilitated comprehension centers and routines, and teacher-facilitated whole-group reflection and goal setting. Descriptions of the Guided Comprehension strategies and related skills are embedded in Stage Two.

Categories of Modifications Embedded in the Guided Comprehension Model for English Learners

Although the components of the original Guided Comprehension Model support English learners, a variety of modifications are evident in the Guided Comprehension Model for English Learners. Categories that have emerged from these modifications include context, instruction, text, and assessment.

Context

The Guided Comprehension Model for English Learners is situated in culturally responsive classroom communities. In these settings, students' cultures are valued by teachers and peers. Culturally relevant materials such as books and informational articles are readily available. Teachers view students' diversity as a resource for the classroom community. (For more detailed information about culturally responsive contexts, see Chapter 1.)

Instruction

The Guided Comprehension Model for English Learners begins with the Engaging Prereading Sequence. This stage was added at the beginning of the Model to provide English learners with opportunities to enrich and extend their background knowledge and understanding early in Guided Comprehension lessons. The Engaging Prereading Sequence, which occurs in a conversational setting, provides small-group opportunities for English learners to learn about reading comprehension strategies before the strategies are taught in a whole-group setting.

In addition to creating a new stage of the Model, numerous instructional supports for English learners have been integrated into the teaching of Guided Comprehension. Examples of these include the following:

- Creating culturally responsive classrooms
- Enriching and building English learners' background knowledge
- Ensuring that culturally relevant texts at multiple levels are available to the students
- Holding high standards for English learners and engaging them in higher order thinking and inquiry-based learning
- Encouraging English learners to be active participants in literacy
- Paying particular attention to providing wait time during discussion
- Extending the use of visual supports, particularly picture books and modified graphic organizers
- Encouraging the use of alternative modes of representing students' thinking
- Integrating students' native languages through teachers, peers, and Cross-Age Reading Experience partners
- Focusing on techniques such as choral reading and Think–Pair–Share (McTighe & Lyman, 1988) as alternatives to individual students responding orally during whole-group instruction
- Providing time for students to write responses to clarify their thinking.

Text

In Guided Comprehension, students have opportunities to engage with a variety of texts at independent and instructional levels on a daily basis. This includes accessible narrative and informational texts for English learners. Villegas and Lucas (2007) suggest that a range of culturally diverse texts in a variety of genres be available, as well as materials in the students' native languages, such as informational articles, text adaptations, leveled text, or textbooks, to help English learners build background knowledge. (See Appendix B for a list of multicultural books and a list of popular trade books available in English and other languages.)

Texts are available in a variety of formats. For example, English learners can listen to and read along with text on CDs to improve fluency and increase comprehension. They can also use wordless picture books to improve their understanding of story structure by writing the stories they see in the illustrations. Creating their own texts in response to reading or as a way of representing their thinking when engaging in inquiry-based learning is another possibility for English learners.

Assessment

Assessment permeates the Guided Comprehension Model for English Learners. In this Model, assessment has been influenced by both the Common Core State Standards (Common Core State Standards Initiative, 2010c) and the World-Class Instructional Design and Assessment (WIDA) English Language Proficiency Standards (WIDA, 2007). Formative assessment, which supports students' achievement of these standards, pervades the Guided Comprehension Models. The value of this type of informal assessment is well affirmed by the growing national interest in it.

At this point, a vast majority of states in the United States have formally adopted the Common Core State Standards, a state-led effort coordinated by the National Governors Association Center for Best Practices and the Council of Chief State School Officers. The standards were created to provide a consistent framework to prepare students for college and for work.

The Common Core State Standards embed multiple characteristics. These include that the standards

- Are aligned with college and work expectations;
- Are clear, understandable and consistent;
- Include rigorous content and application of knowledge through high-order skills;
- Build upon strengths and lessons of current state standards;
- Are informed by other top performing countries, so that all students are prepared to succeed in our global economy and society; and
- Are evidence-based. (Common Core State Standards Initiative, 2010a)

Unfortunately, at this point in time there are no Common Core State Standards for English learners.

The WIDA English Language Proficiency Standards (2007) have also influenced the Guided Comprehension Model for English Learners. The WIDA Standards, which have currently been adopted by 28 states, are in the process of being revised. It is expected that the new version of the WIDA Standards will be published in 2012. Among several revisions, the new WIDA Standards will be aligned with the Common Core State Standards.

In addition to the recent developments in standards, formative assessment, which should occur every day in every reading classroom, is the object of current interest by policymakers in the United States. Formative assessment is ongoing and classroom-based. Its results are used to inform future teaching. Examples of formative assessment include informal writing, student-constructed responses, problem solving, discussion, and strategy use. Formative assessment is employed in all the Guided Comprehension lessons presented in Part Two.

Shepard (2005) notes that formative assessment is a collaborative process in which how to improve learning is negotiated between teacher and student. Weber (1999) proposes that formative assessments suggest future steps for teaching and learning. These steps might result from observations that allow us to assess how well a student contributed to a class discussion, or informal writing that documents whether a student is able to apply a particular skill or strategy. Formative assessment not only helps to reinforce how students learn and what students know, but also helps to identify what may remain unclear, thus giving direction to future teaching.

How the Guided Comprehension Model for English Learners Works

The Guided Comprehension Model for English Learners is a framework designed to help teachers and students think through reading as a strategy-based process. The Model is based on existing research, knowledge of best practice, and personal experience. It integrates the following:

- Activation of (and/or providing of) background knowledge
- Motivation
- Explicit instruction of comprehension strategies
- Leveled independent, instructional, and challenging texts
- Formative assessment
- Scaffolded instruction (varying levels of teacher support, with gradual release of responsibility to students)
- Various genres and text types, including culturally relevant text
- Reading, writing, and discussion
- Strategy instruction and application in a variety of settings
- Independent practice and transfer of learning in multiple settings
- Reflection and goal setting

Structurally, the Model begins with Stage One, the Engaging Prereading Sequence, which is followed by three additional stages. These components progress in the following order:

Stage One: Engaging Prereading Sequence: Small-group conversational teaching focused on motivation, background knowledge, and explicit instruction

Stage Two: Teacher-directed whole-group instruction

Stage Three: Teacher-guided small-group instruction and student-facilitated comprehension centers and routines (independent practice)

Stage Four: Teacher-facilitated whole-group reflection and goal setting

The Guided Comprehension Model for English Learners is active for both teachers and students. To begin, teachers are culturally responsive. They engage in explicit instruction and select texts and strategies based on students' needs. They help students activate background knowledge and provide background knowledge if students don't have it. They assess students informally on a regular basis and motivate students to fully engage in reading, writing, and discussion. Students' active roles in Guided Comprehension include activating background knowledge, thinking through the reading

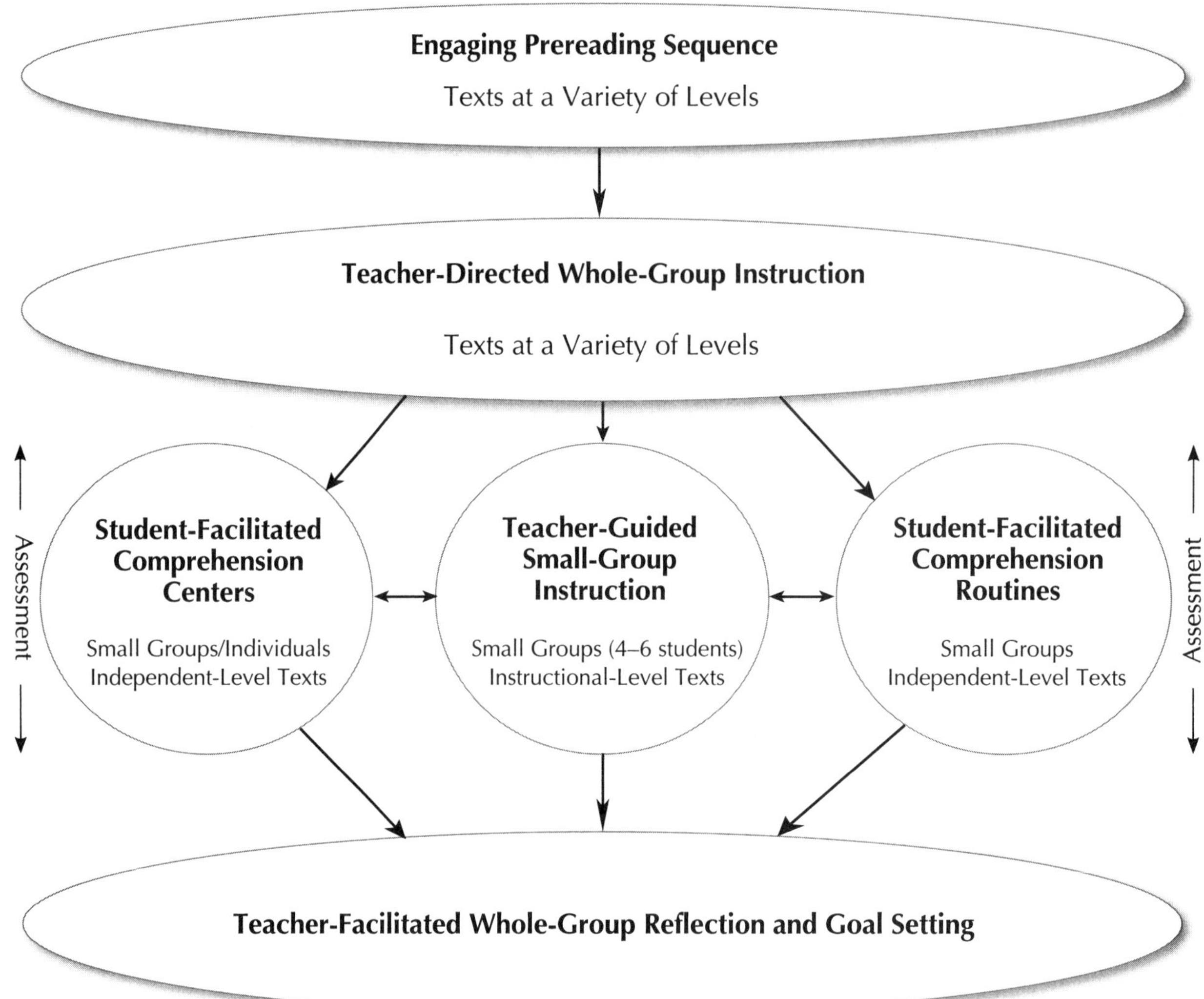

process, using skills and strategies, transacting with text at multiple levels in varied settings, and responding in a variety of ways. They also fully participate in reading, writing, and discussion.

The Guided Comprehension Model for English Learners includes opportunities for whole-group, small-group, paired, and individual literacy experiences. Students transact daily with texts at a variety of levels. Teachers engage in explicit small-group and whole-group instruction, explicitly teach comprehension skills and strategies, and work daily with Guided Comprehension small groups. Teachers also observe and assess students as they engage in guided and independent comprehension activities.

The Model progresses from the Engaging Prereading Sequence to explicit whole-group teaching, guided instruction, and independent application and transfer (see Figure 1). All components of the Model are necessary to ensure that students can independently apply comprehension strategies in multiple settings. Formative assessment permeates every aspect of the Model, facilitating the gathering of information about student progress, which continually informs teaching and learning.

Figure 1. Overview of the Guided Comprehension Model for English Learners

STAGE ONE

Engaging Prereading Sequence—Small-group conversational teaching focused on motivation, student engagement, background knowledge, and explicit instruction.

Motivate the students to engage in learning.
Activate and/or provide background knowledge.
Teach essential vocabulary.
Engage in the explicit instruction of reading comprehension strategies: explain, demonstrate, guide, practice, and reflect.
Encourage discussion.

STAGE TWO

Teacher-Directed Whole-Group Instruction—Teaching comprehension strategies using independent, instructional, or challenging text.

Explain the current strategy and discuss how it relates to the class goal.
Demonstrate the strategy using a Think-Aloud, a read-aloud, and a visual—smartboard, chart, overhead slide, or PowerPoint—and appropriate supports.
Guide student practice by continuing to read aloud additional sections of text and encouraging pairs of students to apply the strategy with support. Monitor students' applications.
Practice by asking students to apply the strategy to another section of text you have read, providing minimal support. Applications can occur in pairs or individually.
Reflect by inviting students to think about how they can use this strategy on their own.

STAGE THREE

Students apply the comprehension strategies in teacher-guided small groups and student-facilitated comprehension centers and routines. In these settings, students work with varying levels of support and use appropriate instructional- and independent-level texts.

Teacher-Guided Small-Group Instruction—Applying comprehension strategies with teacher guidance using instructional-level texts and dynamic grouping (four or five students).

Review previously taught strategies and focus on the current strategy.
Guide the students to apply the current strategy as well as previously taught strategies as they whisper read sections of the instructional-level (just right) text. Prompt the students to construct and share personal meanings. Scaffold as necessary, gradually releasing support as students become more proficient. Encourage discussion and repeat this process with other sections of text.
Practice by inviting students to work in pairs or individually to apply strategies. Encourage discussion.
Retell and Reflect by inviting students to engage in a retelling of the text they have read, and share ways in which the current strategy and the other strategies they know helped them to understand the text. Talk about ways in which students can apply the current strategy in comprehension centers and routines.

Student-Facilitated Comprehension Centers and Routines—Applying comprehension strategies individually, in pairs, or in small groups using independent-level (easy) texts.

Comprehension Centers are independent activities that provide opportunities to practice strategy application and extend understandings. (Examples: fluency center, theme center)
Comprehension Routines are procedures that foster habits of thinking and promote the comprehension of text. (Examples: Literature Circles, Cross-Age Reading Experiences)

STAGE FOUR

Teacher-Facilitated Whole-Group Reflection and Goal Setting—Reflecting on performance, sharing experiences, and setting new goals.

Share performances from Stage Three.
Reflect on students' ability to use the strategy.
Set new goals or extend existing ones.

ASSESSMENT OPTIONS

Use authentic, formative measures in all stages.

Note. Adapted for English learners from *Guided Comprehension: A Teaching Model for Grades 3–8* by M. McLaughlin & M.B. Allen, 2002, Newark, DE: International Reading Association, p. 5.

The Guided Comprehension Model for English Learners is adapted from the original Guided Comprehension Model, which was developed for grades 3–8 more than a decade ago (McLaughlin & Allen, 2002a). The Model for English Learners differs from the original Model in a number of ways:

- The new Model opens with the Engaging Prereading Sequence, a conversational gathering that involves teachers motivating English learners, activating and/or providing background knowledge, and engaging these students in explicit small-group strategy instruction.
- Teacher-guided small-group instruction has been expanded to include retellings and opportunities for English learners to whisper read with partners.
- The comprehension centers have been adapted in several ways, including additional language-based activities, culturally relevant texts, and opportunities for students to work with native English speakers, as well as those who speak the English learners' native languages.
- The comprehension routines—Literature Circles, Reciprocal Teaching, and Cross-Age Reading Experiences— have been adapted in various ways, including partner reading opportunities for English learners.
- The integration of multiple ways of representing student thinking—such as sketching, dramatizing, and singing—has been increased throughout the strategy applications.
- A variety of appropriate supports, such as the use of picture books and modifications to graphic organizers, are incorporated throughout teaching and learning.

Stage One: Engaging Prereading Sequence

In the Engaging Prereading Sequence, teachers meet with small groups of English learners in the context of an informal conversation. During this stage, the teacher has four priorities: (1) to motivate students to engage in learning, (2) to activate and/or provide background knowledge, (3) to teach essential vocabulary, and (4) to engage in the explicit instruction of reading comprehension strategies: explain, demonstrate, discuss and clarify, guide, practice, and reflect. Discussion permeates this process. (For details about the steps of explicit instruction and the use of Think-Alouds in the process, see the detailed description in Stage Two.)

This initial stage of the Model is designed to provide English learners with background knowledge about the theme and knowledge of the strategies before they are taught in the whole-class setting. When English learners engage in whole-group instruction after participating in the Engaging Prereading Sequence, they already have some background knowledge about the strategies and how they work. This new stage of the Model enables the English learners to experience success when they first learn about the strategies and, as a result, be motivated to learn more about the strategies in Stage Two. In the Engaging Prereading Sequence, the text is often culturally relevant and students are encouraged to discuss their responses with peers in English or their native languages. Introducing the text is an important component of this segment, as it is throughout the Guided Comprehension Model for English Learners. Marie Clay (1991) created an excellent format for introducing text. Her work is based on introducing stories, but the format is easily adapted for use in introducing informational text. For suggestions about how to implement Clay's process, see Appendix A, page 232.

While teachers and English learners are engaged in the Engaging Prereading Sequence, the remaining students can participate in a number of comprehension-based endeavors. These include Patterned Partner Reading (see Appendix A), informal writing, and comprehension-based centers (see Chapter 4).

Stage Two: Teacher-Directed Whole-Group Instruction

In Stage Two of Guided Comprehension, the teacher engages in explicit instruction by using a five-step process: explain, demonstrate, guide, practice, and reflect. The class is organized as a whole group during the explain and demonstrate steps, but students typically work in small groups or with partners in the guide step and on their own in the practice step, as teachers gradually release responsibility to the students. Stage Two concludes with whole-class reflection. During this stage, the level of text may be easy, just right, or challenging because the teacher is reading aloud.

Organizing for Stage Two

In Stage Two of the Model, whole-group instruction provides students with a positive sense of belonging to a culturally responsive community of learners. The sense of community is fostered by student–teacher and student–peer interactions, print-rich environments, opportunities to engage with authentic texts from a variety of genres, students who are active learners, and teachers who are knowledgeable about their students and current best practice.

Because the instruction in Stage Two of Guided Comprehension is teacher directed and allows us to fully support student learning, we can choose to teach from texts that range in level from easy to challenging. For example, we may choose to read a humorous text that is interesting to the students and works well when teaching strategies but is a bit lower in level.

Engaging in Explicit Instruction

In working with a wide variety of literacy professionals, I have heard many say that reading educators often describe teaching comprehension strategies as "going over" the strategies with students, "telling" the students about the strategies, or just sharing blacklines. Effectively teaching comprehension strategies requires more than "going over" these ideas; it requires explicit instruction—explaining, demonstrating, guiding, practicing, and reflecting.

When engaging in explicit instruction, we use authentic text and formative assessment, which is a natural part of the process. As previously noted, there are a variety of comprehension strategies incorporated into the Model. They include previewing (activating prior knowledge, setting purposes for reading, and predicting), self-questioning, making connections, visualizing, knowing how words work, monitoring, summarizing, and evaluating. Which strategies are taught will depend on the students' stages of language and literacy development.

It is important to remember that English learners will have already had explicit strategy instruction in the Engaging Prereading Sequence prior to engaging in whole-group instruction. So, when Stage Two begins, these students will already have some background knowledge about and experience in applying the strategies.

Formative assessments, which are informal in nature, provide information that helps us understand students' abilities. Examples of such assessments, which occur every day, include observation, student strategy applications, fluency checks, sketching, and informal writing.

Steps in Explicit Instruction

Regardless of the skill or strategy being taught, the explicit instruction process remains the same. It includes the following steps:

1. *Explain the skill or strategy*: Describe how the skill or strategy works and how it contributes to text comprehension. Describe a related strategy application (see Appendix A) and explain how it works.
2. *Demonstrate the skill or strategy*: Begin by introducing the text. (For details about how to do this effectively, see Marie Clay's Storybook Introductions in Appendix A.) Make connections to students' background knowledge. Next, introduce a skill or strategy, using a read-aloud, a Think-Aloud, and a smartboard, overhead projector, chalkboard, whiteboard, or poster paper. Using a Think-Aloud allows us to share our reasoning process with our students and to provide a model for students to think through their strategy use. As we think aloud, we orally explain precisely what is triggering our thoughts and how it is affecting our understanding. (For a detailed description of Think-Alouds, see Appendix A, page 248.) This can lead to the development of personal connections, questions for clarification, and refined predictions. Duffy (2001) notes the importance of wording the Think-Aloud. The following example of modeling predicting has been developed according to his suggestions:

   > Let me show you how I would make a prediction about this book. When I read the title *The Very Hungry Caterpillar*, I know from having seen a caterpillar that it is a small insect. I also know that caterpillars turn into butterflies. The secret of making predictions is to think about what you already know from your own experience with the topic of the book, in this case, caterpillars and butterflies.

   When using the Think-Aloud to demonstrate strategies, we need to explain our thinking so students have a clear idea of the cognitively active process readers experience as they transact with text.
3. *Guide the students to apply the strategy*: Read aloud the next section of the text and guide the students to apply the strategy just taught, prompting and offering assistance as necessary. When the students are comfortable with the strategy, continue scaffolding instruction by having the students work in pairs or small groups.
4. *Practice the skill or strategy*: Students begin to practice the skill or strategy independently in small groups, trios, or pairs as we gradually relinquish control of the process.
5. *Reflect on strategy use*: Invite the students to reflect on how using the strategy helped them to understand the text. Discuss the ideas shared.

When engaging in explicit instruction, always focus on the following:

- Explaining the skill or strategy and how it works
- Demonstrating using a Think-Aloud

- Guiding students to practice, prompting and offering assistance as necessary
- Providing settings for group, paired, and independent practice
- Affording opportunities to reflect on strategy use

This stage also provides multiple opportunities to integrate formative assessments. These often include teacher observation, strategy applications, discussion, informal writing, and sketching.

Throughout this framework, students' learning is scaffolded—responsibility is gradually released to the students. When students learn how the strategy works, they have our total support. When they engage in guided practice, they have our support as necessary. When they apply the strategy independently, our support is diminished and the students are in control.

Comprehension Strategies: Focus on Teaching

During Stage Two of the Model, a number of strategy applications can be used to clarify and reinforce students' understanding and application of the comprehension skills and strategies. Our goal is for students to develop a repertoire of strategies they can use independently. This section provides a definition of each comprehension strategy and a list of related applications. These lists are not exhaustive, but they do include examples that can be used successfully when teaching English learners. Appendix A contains a step-by-step process for explicit instruction of each strategy application, as well as links to various comprehension strategies, types of text, and stages of reading.

Previewing is a way of introducing the text. It includes activating background knowledge, setting purposes for reading, and predicting. The following teaching ideas support this strategy:

- Semantic Map
- Semantic Question Map
- Story Impressions
- Storybook Introductions

Self-questioning involves generating questions to guide thinking while reading. Teaching ideas that support this strategy include the following:

- Paired Questioning
- Question–Answer Relationships (QAR)
- Thick and Thin Questions

Making connections occurs when students think about the text in relation to connections they can make to self, to texts, and to others. Teaching ideas that support this strategy include the following:

- Connection Stems
- Double-Entry Journal
- Draw and Write Connections

Visualizing is creating mental images while reading. Teaching ideas that support this strategy include the following:

- Draw and Write Visualizations
- Graphic Organizers/Visual Organizers
- Guided Imagery

Knowing how words work is understanding words through strategic vocabulary development, including the use of the graphophonic, syntactic, and semantic cueing systems to figure out unknown words. The graphophonic cueing system involves creating grapheme (written letter)–phoneme (sound) matches. The syntactic cueing system deals with the structure of the language. The semantic cueing system focuses on meaning. Readers use all three cueing systems, along with other knowledge of words, to effectively engage with text. Ideas that support this comprehension strategy include the following:

- Concept of Definition Map
- Context Clues
- Semantic Feature Analysis
- Vocabulary Bookmark

Monitoring involves asking, "Does this make sense?" and clarifying by adapting strategic processes to accommodate the response. Monitoring is knowing if meaning is being constructed and what to do if it is not. The following teaching ideas support this strategy:

- Bookmark Technique
- Patterned Partner Reading
- Say Something
- Think-Alouds

Summarizing involves extracting essential information from text. In informational text, this involves the main idea and supporting details and/or details derived from text patterns. In narrative text, this involves the story elements: characters, setting, problem, attempts to resolve the problem, and resolution. Teaching ideas that support this strategy include the following:

- Lyric Retelling/Lyric Summary
- Paired Summarizing
- Questions Into Paragraphs (QuIP)
- Retelling
- Story Map

Evaluating means making judgments about text and supporting one's thinking. The following teaching ideas support this strategy:

- Evaluative Questioning
- Journal Responses

- Persuasive Writing
- Venn Diagram

Skills That Underpin the Comprehension Strategies

As noted earlier, comprehension strategies are more complex than skills and may require the orchestration of several comprehension skills. Students often begin by learning comprehension skills and then progress to learning strategies. The following list of skills is not exhaustive, but it offers a good sampling of the kinds of skills that underpin comprehension strategies:

- Decoding
- Generating Questions
- Recognizing Text Structures
- Sequencing
- Distinguishing Important From Less Important Ideas

These skills are essential components of the reading process, and they need to be taught. For example, the ability to generate questions is a skill that underpins every comprehension strategy (see Figure 2). For this reason, we should ensure that the students understand how to create questions by engaging in explicit instruction.

When teaching students about questioning, we can explain what questions are, discuss their purposes, and delineate their multiple levels. We can explain that there are many reasons for generating questions, including information seeking, connected understanding, historical speculation, imagination, and research. Busching and Slesinger (1995) note that the best way to help students develop meaningful questions is to encourage them to engage extensively in reading, writing, speaking, listening, and viewing.

Ciardiello (1998, 2007) suggests that students generate questions at four levels: memory, convergent thinking, divergent thinking, and evaluative thinking. He also provides the following signal words and cognitive operations for each category:

Memory Questions

Signal words: *who, what, where, when?*

Cognitive operations: naming, defining, identifying, designating

Convergent Thinking Questions

Signal words: *why, how, in what ways?*

Cognitive operations: explaining, stating relationships, comparing and contrasting

Divergent Thinking Questions

Signal words: *imagine, suppose, predict, if/then*

Cognitive operations: predicting, hypothesizing, inferring, reconstructing

Figure 2. Generating Questions: A Skill That Supports Comprehension Strategies

Comprehension Strategy	Narrative Text (*The Three Little Javelinas* by Susan Lowell)	Informational Text (*Wolves* by Seymour Simon)
Previewing	What is the story about? What might happen in this story?	What do I already know about wolves?
Self-Questioning	Why is one of the javelinas a girl?	How are wolf packs like families?
Making Connections	What connections can I make between this story and the original little pigs story?	What connections can I make between the text description of wolves and the text illustrations and the video we saw about wolves? To the article we read in *National Geographic World*?
Visualizing	Is my mental picture of where the javelinas live still good? Why should I change it?	What do arctic wolves look like? How do they compare/contrast with red wolves?
Knowing How Words Work	Do the words *adobe bricks* make sense in the sentence? Are they like the bricks in my house?	What clues in the text can I use to figure out the word *adaptable*?
Monitoring	Does what I'm reading make sense? If not, what can I do to clarify?	Does what I'm reading make sense? If not, what can I do to clarify?
Summarizing	What has happened so far?	What is the most important information in the book?
Evaluating	Thinking about all the little pigs stories that I know, how would I rank the javelinas' story? What can I say to justify my response?	Do I think wolves will become extinct? How can I justify my thinking?

Note. Adapted for English learners from *Guided Comprehension in the Primary Grades* (2nd ed.) by M. McLaughlin, 2010, Newark, DE: International Reading Association, p. 22.

Evaluative Thinking Questions

Signal words: *defend, judge, justify/what do you think?*

Cognitive operations: valuing, judging, defending, justifying

The teacher explains each question type and then models, first with life experiences and then with authentic text. Students engage in guided practice in a variety of settings and finally engage in independent application and transfer.

Displaying Ciardiello's question types and signal words in the classroom is beneficial for all students, including English learners. It enables them to see the information as they generate their own questions and to try to comprehend queries posed by others. Adding examples of each type of question—and a possible response—to the display provides further support for students. We can display this information on a bulletin board or a poster. We also can create a "question wall" that is similar in structure to word walls. Regardless of which format is used, the information displayed provides valuable support for student learning.

Stage Three: Teacher-Guided Small-Group Instruction and Student-Facilitated Comprehension Centers and Routines

Stage Three of the Guided Comprehension Model focuses on three instructional settings: teacher-guided small groups, student-facilitated comprehension centers, and student-facilitated comprehension routines.

Organizing for Stage Three

In Stage Three of Guided Comprehension, students have opportunities to apply comprehension skills and strategies in a variety of settings with varying levels of support. Texts in this stage vary from the instructional-level texts used in the teacher-guided small groups to the independent-level texts used when students work independently in comprehension centers and routines.

Because students can work in three different settings in this stage, having an organizational plan is essential. One way to manage this time is to use a chart that illustrates the settings in which students should be at given times (see Figure 3). (Other organizational plans can be found in Appendix B.)

Teacher-Guided Small-Group Instruction

Although Stage Three is characterized by three different instructional settings, only one is teacher-guided. In this small-group setting, students of similar abilities apply their knowledge of strategies to leveled texts to become active, engaged readers. Students are dynamically grouped and progress at individual rates, changing groups as they become prepared to transact with increasingly challenging levels of text.

When organizing for teacher-guided small-group instruction, we need to consider the following factors:

- All students in the group need to have similar instructional levels; this means that all the students in this Guided Comprehension setting should be able to read the same texts with some teacher support.
- The texts we select for use in this setting should reflect students' instructional levels as well as their interests.
- While in this small-group setting, we also need to monitor students who are working independently in the comprehension centers and routines.

Once the small groups are formed and the appropriate text is matched to students' abilities and interests, the teacher meets with one or more guided small groups every day. During this time with the students, we typically use the Guided Comprehension small-group lesson format: Review, Guide,

Figure 3. Organizing for Stage Three

Centers	Session 1	Session 2
ABC		
Drama		
Making Words		
Reader Response		
Writing		

Routines	Session 1	Session 2
Literature Circles		
Reciprocal Teaching		
Cross-Age Reading Experiences		

Teacher-Guided Small Groups		

Practice, Retell and Reflect. In the descriptions that follow, supports for English learners have been integrated into each step.

- *Review* previously taught strategies, placing particular emphasis on the current strategy. Engage students in an ongoing discussion of the strategies and how they use them. Stress connections to students' background knowledge. Encourage English learners to make connections to what they learned in the Engaging Prereading Sequence and Stage Two. Introduce the text using detailed steps, such as those proposed by Marie Clay (1991) (see Appendix A). Emphasize discussion. If possible, choose a strategy application that includes sketching or another alternative mode of representing thinking.
- *Guide* the students to apply the reading strategies during the reading of the instructional level text or—if the text is very short—the text in its entirety. Make a decision about whether you will read the text to the students, invite them to whisper read, or encourage them to read silently, based on the their English language development. (Reading the text to the students—or with them—enables the teacher to provide a strong, fluent reading model as a support for English learners. Inviting the students to whisper read the text enables the teacher to complete informal fluency checks.) Use visual aids. Prompt the students to construct personal meanings. Continue to emphasize discussion. Incorporate word study as needed. (See Appendix A for examples of teaching ideas to use for word study.) Scaffold as necessary, gradually releasing support as students become more proficient. Encourage discussion and repeat this process with other sections of text. Find an occasional opportunity to complete a fluency check or running record with individual students. To conduct a fluency check, pull your chair next to a student's and ask him or her to whisper read a short selection. For more information about running records, see Chapter 6.
- *Practice* by encouraging the students to work in pairs to apply the skills and strategies as they read the text silently or in whisper tones, or discuss strategy application as the teacher reads aloud. Invite the students to continue to engage in discussion of the text.
- *Retell and reflect* by inviting students to engage in rereading and responding to text in a variety of ways. Encourage students to take active roles in a prompted retelling of the text. Encourage them to share ways in which the skills or strategies helped them to understand the text. Extend learning by incorporating word study and discussion. Talk about ways in which the students can apply the skills or strategies in the comprehension centers and routines. Introduce the students to activities in the reader response center that relate to their Guided Reading text and explain that they will go to that center when their small-group reading ends. (As needed, you may also wish to note that students can read along with a CD of their Guided Reading text at the fluency center or engage in Patterned Partner Reading to practice their fluency and refine their understanding.)

Review the strategies. In this step, begin each guided group by reminding students about skills and strategies that have been taught previously. It is helpful to have these posted on a chart in the classroom or listed on a bookmark or other quick reference for the students. Keene and Zimmermann (1997) suggest creating "Thinking Records" using the following steps:

- Use chart paper to create a separate record for each strategy.

- Record strategy definitions.
- Include examples generated by students.
- Add questions and insights about the use of the strategy.
- Display the Thinking Records in the classroom.
- Add information about the strategies as they are learned and used.

Invite the English learners to discuss the strategies, making connections to what they learned in the Engaging Prereading Sequence and in whole-group instruction.

This review is designed to remind students that even though they need to learn the strategies, the ultimate goal is to use them in concert, developing a repertoire of strategies to use as needed to construct personal meaning. After this quick review, the group revisits the strategy application featured in that day's whole-group setting. Whenever possible, offer students an alternative mode of representing their thinking, such as adding a sketching component to the strategy application.

Encourage the students to activate background knowledge, make connections, and engage in discussion throughout the steps of this stage. Introduce the text using a detailed format and appropriate supports.

Guide students. Decide how sections of the text will be read. Depending on the stage of the English learners' language development, either invite the students to read silently or with partners in whisper tones, or, as an alternative, you can read the text aloud. Encouraging one of the students to read in whisper tones allows you to check on fluency and observe strategy use. Encourage discussion throughout this step. To facilitate this, for example, you may revisit predictions, verbalize connections, or share visualizations. You may ask, "What does this remind you of?" "Have you ever had an experience like this?" "How is this character like...?" You can also revisit students' original predictions and ask students why their thinking has changed or remained the same. After this, the students read another predetermined section of the text and stop for more guided discussion.

Practice. When students are actively engaging with the text and constructing meaning, they practice using their comprehension strategies. For example, they may make connections as they (or you) read another segment or finish reading the text. Then they may discuss their connections with the members of the small group.

Retell and reflect. The final component of teacher-guided small-group instruction includes students participating in a guided retelling of the text and reflecting on the text and strategy use through discussion. Students may make personal responses and share new information or offer insights at this point. Teachers may choose to incorporate word study and guide students to make broader connections to other texts and extend their understandings. These may be documented through writing, drawing, dramatization, or oral response. If time permits, students can reread the text to enhance understanding and practice fluency. The rereading also provides an opportunity to do a running record with one of the students. This is a good time to observe student responses and connections; this information will inform dynamic grouping, future student–text matches, and instructional planning. During discussion, it is important to invite students to reflect on their reading and to review the strategies they used to make sense of the text. This will remind students to transfer what they have learned in whole-group instruction and in their Guided Comprehension small groups to their reading of other texts in other settings. The Guided Comprehension Model for English Learners provides students with two settings for such independent practice: comprehension centers and comprehension routines.

Student-Facilitated Comprehension Centers and Routines

Comprehension centers provide purposeful, authentic settings for students to integrate and apply their comprehension strategies. Students may work in small groups, with partners, or on their own when they are engaged in the centers. Theme-based center activities for all students—including English learners—promote the integration of reading, writing, and discussion. Ideas for organizing and managing centers, as well as descriptions of a variety of centers in which English learners can engage, are presented in Chapter 4.

Students also practice and transfer what they have learned in comprehension routines. Comprehension routines are those habits of thinking and organizing that facilitate reading and response in authentic contexts. These are independent settings: This implies that students are knowledgeable about the strategies and routines, that they are provided with texts at their independent levels, and that they have ample time for practicing and transferring these processes. Routines used in the Guided Comprehension Model for English Learners are described in detail in Chapter 5.

Stage Four: Teacher-Facilitated Whole-Group Reflection and Goal Setting

In this stage of the Model, the students and teacher gather to reflect on what they have learned. This stage follows a three-step process: share, reflect, and set new goals.

Organizing for Stage Four

In this setting, we encourage students to think about what they have accomplished in the first and second stages of the Model. We want them to actualize their learning and be accountable for it. Bringing the class together also provides opportunities for closure and celebration of new knowledge.

The cyclical process of setting goals, engaging in learning experiences, reflecting on performance, and setting new goals helps students to perceive themselves as empowered, successful learners. It encourages students to think critically, observe progress, and take ownership of their learning.

It is these active roles that students are taking, not reflection itself, that is new to the educational process. In 1933, Dewey suggested that teachers become reflective practitioners to gain better understandings of teaching and learning. In 1987, Schön noted that reflection offers teachers insights into various dimensions of teaching and learning that can lead to better understanding. In the 1990s, when reflection became a valued component of evolving assessment practices, students were encouraged to engage actively in the process (Darling-Hammond, Ancess, & Falk, 1995; Hoyt & Ames, 1997; McLaughlin, 1995).

Self-reflection focuses on what students have learned and how they feel about their learning (Cooper & Kiger, 2001). It includes both self-assessment, which addresses process and product, and self-evaluation, which makes judgments about performance. Questions raised for self-assessment purposes include "What is confusing me?" and "How did I contribute to the discussion?" Questions that foster self-evaluation include "What did I do well?" and "Did I achieve my goal?"

Self-reflection offers insights into students' thinking. It not only illustrates that they are thinking but also details *how* they are thinking. According to Hoyt and Ames (1997), "Self-reflection offers students an opportunity to be actively involved in internal conversations while offering teachers an insider's view of the learning and the student's perception of self as learner" (p. 19). This focus on internal conversations parallels Tierney and Pearson's (1994) idea that "literacy learning is an ongoing conversation with oneself.... If we view learning as dynamic in character, as that evolving dialogue with oneself, then even major shifts become little more than the natural, almost inevitable, consequence of human reflection" (p. 514).

Reflection and Goal Setting in Guided Comprehension

Goal setting is a natural outgrowth of reflection. As Hansen (1998) notes, "Learning proceeds from the known to the new" (p. 45). What students have learned to a given point influences what they learn next; this is the foundation of goal setting. Students reflect on what they have learned and set future personal goals for continuous improvement. When students actively engage in creating both personal and class goals, they appear to be more motivated and take more responsibility for their learning (Clemmons, Laase, Cooper, Areglado, & Dill, 1993; Hill & Ruptic, 1994).

Because explicit instruction of reflection and goal setting is necessary, we apply the steps used in Stages One and Two. This is especially important for English learners because students may not have strong background experiences in reflection; in fact, many may not even be familiar with the concept.

- *Explain* what reflection is and how it works.
- *Demonstrate* how to reflect.
- *Guide* students to apply reflection to something they have learned. Reflection forms can be used to facilitate this process (see Appendix C).
- *Practice* by providing students with multiple opportunities for application.

After engaging in reflection, students create new personal goals. The following are examples of new goals that were shared in student–teacher conferences at various grade levels:

- My goal is to read a book with my friend.
- My new goal is to write a story from a wordless picture book.
- My new goal is to ask more kinds of questions when we talk about what we read.
- My new goal is to talk more in Literature Circle. I want to make more connections.

When students become comfortable with reflection and goal setting, they engage in transfer of their learning. In Guided Comprehension, students have opportunities to reflect on their performance as members of a whole group, small group, or pair, as well as individually. (See Appendix C for reproducible blacklines for Reflection and Goal Setting [page 342] and Student Self-Reflection and Goal Setting in Guided Comprehension [page 341].)

Because reflection and goal setting are essential components of Guided Comprehension, it is important to maintain student interest in them. The following are additional teaching ideas to foster students' engagement in these processes.

Vary the components. When planning reflection and goal setting, we make selections from the following four categories:

1. *Type of goal*: individual or whole group, short term or long term
2. *Reflection setting*: whole group, small group, paired, or individual
3. *Reflection mode*: speaking, writing, illustrating, or dramatizing
4. *Sharing setting*: whole group, small group, paired, or individual

Choices can vary according to lesson content, student learning styles, or student interest. For example, students can create new personal goals by working in pairs to reflect on their learning, create sketches to illustrate their thinking, and then share them with a small group.

There are several formats for engaging students in written reflection, two of which are Guided Comprehension Journals and Tickets Out.

Guided Comprehension Journals: Students can use Guided Comprehension Journals during all stages of the Model. For example, they can use the journals to record notes for Literature Circles, jot down questions that arise during the stages of Guided Comprehension, and engage in reflection. In Stage Four, students can use the journals to record their reflections and set new goals.

Tickets Out: This is a favorite teaching idea because it fosters reflection, helps monitor students' learning, and takes very little time. It is called Tickets Out because students hand their tickets to the teacher as they exit the classroom at the end of the period or the end of the day. To participate in this activity, students use a half sheet of paper. On the first side, they write the most important thing they learned that day. On the other side, they write one question they have about something they learned that day. Whether students put their names on their tickets is the teacher's choice.

To complete this activity, students need only about five minutes. As the students leave the room, collect the tickets with side one facing up. After students have left the room, read side one of their tickets first. This is the side on which they record the most important thing they learned that day. During this part of Tickets Out, put aside any tickets that need clarification. Remember to discuss them at the start of the next day's class.

Next, turn over the entire pile of tickets and read the questions students have about their learning. Some days, more than one student will raise the same question, and other days, not every student will have a question. During this part of Tickets Out, put aside questions that you deem valuable. Respond to these questions, which usually number between four and six, at the start of the next day's class. This helps students understand that we value their thinking and also enhances the continuity from class to class.

Tickets Out is not a time-consuming process, but it does provide valuable information. For example, it offers insight into what students value about their learning and also gives us an opportunity to monitor and clarify any misconceptions they may have. (A reproducible graphic organizer for Tickets Out can be found in Appendix C, page 343.)

Provide prompts. Providing prompts can assist students when reflecting and creating new goals in a variety of settings. Prompts help to focus students' thinking on various dimensions of learning.

Questions to Guide Reflection

- What was your goal today? Do you think you reached it?
- What did you learn today?
- What strategies did you find most helpful?
- What confused you today? How did you figure it out?
- How did your group do? What contributions did you make to your group? What contributions did others make?
- What questions do you have about what you learned today?
- How do you think you will use what you learned today?

Reflection Stems

- I was really good at...
- The best thing I learned today was...
- I found out that...
- I contributed...to our literature discussion.
- I read...and found out that...
- When I was confused today, I...

Questions to Guide Goal Setting

- What do you still need to work on?
- Where will you start next time?
- What do you hope to accomplish?
- What is your new goal?

Goal-Setting Stems

- I need to work more on...
- Tomorrow, I am going to...
- My goal for tomorrow is to...

Students can think about one or more of these prompts and then share their responses. Sharing can take place with a partner or in a small group. I often use Think–Pair–Share (McTighe & Lyman, 1988) as a framework for this. Students *think* about their learning, *pair* with a partner to discuss ideas, and then *share* their thoughts with the class. Students also can write their reflections in their Guided Comprehension Journals and then use Think–Pair–Share. This technique can be adapted for goal setting. First, students *think* about their performance and new goal(s), and then they write it. Next, they *pair* with a partner to discuss their new goal(s). Finally, they *share* their goal(s) with the whole class. Sharing with the whole class is beneficial because it shows that everyone values reflection and goal setting and provides good models for the other students.

The Guided Comprehension Model for English Learners provides a variety of settings for student learning. These include student-facilitated comprehension centers and routines, settings in which the students engage in independent practice. These components of Stage Three are examined in detail in Chapters 4 and 5.

CHAPTER 4

Creating, Organizing, and Managing Comprehension Centers

Comprehension centers provide purposeful, authentic opportunities for students to independently apply their comprehension strategies. Students may work in small groups, with partners, or on their own in this setting. Comprehension centers promote the integration of reading, writing, and discussion while offering a variety of ways for students to integrate and practice their comprehension strategies.

Student-facilitated Guided Comprehension centers for English learners are described in detail in this chapter. (It should be noted that the suggested activities will benefit a variety of students.) The chapter begins by explaining the nature of the comprehension centers and delineating their purposes. Next, issues related to center organization and management, including scheduling and student accountability, are explored. Finally, descriptions of a variety of comprehension-based centers for English learners and sample activities are presented.

Creating Guided Comprehension Centers

The time students spend in comprehension centers should be meaningful. This means that we need to be aware of students' abilities to work independently, create engaging activities, and provide motivational, accessible text. It is important to take time to teach students about the purpose of each center and how it functions. Using the five steps of explicit instruction—explain, demonstrate, guide, practice, and reflect—facilitates this process.

Center activities for English learners should accommodate a variety of learning levels, be open-ended, and be able to be completed independently, without teacher assistance. The activities should be purposeful, address a variety of interests and intelligences, and help students to think critically and creatively. The activities also should be engaging, foster discussion, extend learning, and promote decision making and student ownership of learning.

Guided Comprehension centers feature a number of supports for English learners. These include offering students opportunities to work in pairs and trios, as well as on their own. The centers also provide multiple ways in which students may represent their thinking, such as writing, sketching, dramatizing, taking photos, and singing. Texts in the centers are leveled so students can read text at their independent levels. Students can also listen to and read along with text on CDs to practice fluency. In addition, there are a variety of culturally relevant titles available in students' native languages, as well as in English. As noted earlier, teachers will explain and demonstrate each of the centers and, whenever possible, integrate visual supports, interaction with text, and hands-on learning into center activities.

The centers are usually located around the perimeter of the classroom and away from the area used by teachers and students participating in Guided Reading. The centers vary in appearance from tabletop trifold displays to file folders, pizza boxes, and gift bags. It is important to remember that the content of the center is more significant than its physical appearance.

A variety of centers can be used when implementing the Guided Comprehension Model for English Learners. Some centers are specific to reading skills, such as the ABC center and vocabulary center; others, such as the theme center, are more focused on content; still others, such as the fluency center, are process based. In addition, some centers, such as the sentence center and the writing center, are language based. Centers may be permanent throughout the year, but the topics addressed may change with themes. For example, in the poetry center, the resources could change from poems about families to poems about rain forests depending on the current theme.

During center time, students can work independently on their own or in pairs, trios, or small groups. They can make words, apply strategies while reading theme-related texts, write stories, complete form poems, work through projects, or engage in other theme-related activities. The teacher should provide a structure for these projects but make sure that the activity is open-ended to allow for students to apply thinking and personal interpretations.

The Guided Comprehension center activities for English learners are designed to promote students' language development, as well as their use of comprehension skills and strategies. (A graphic organizer to facilitate planning literacy centers can be found in Appendix B, page 292.) Suggested centers, accompanying open-ended projects, and other extensions for learning are described in this chapter; additional center activities are embedded in the theme-based lessons in Part Two.

It is important to remember to explicitly teach all students how to use each center. Demonstrating how to use the centers is especially important for English learners. When the students begin to use the centers independently, they should feel very comfortable—as if they are engaging in a well-known routine.

In addition, a number of modifications have been made for English learners when they engage in the comprehension centers. These include the following:

- Ensuring that books written in the students' native languages are among the texts available in the centers
- Making culturally relevant texts available in the centers
- Integrating multiple modes of representing thinking in student responses (sketching, singing, dramatizing)
- Inviting students to work with other English learners of the same culture when reading texts in their native languages
- Encouraging English learners to partner with native English speakers when working in centers such as fluency, question and answer, vocabulary, and other centers focused on fluency and language development

Art Center

Students use materials at the art center to visually represent their understandings of published text, to create illustrations for the texts they are writing, or to design projects they are constructing. A variety of materials and examples of specific art techniques should be available at the center. The following materials are suggested:

- All kinds of paper—colored, lined, construction, large, textured, adhesive notes
- A variety of writing and illustrating utensils—washable markers, crayons, paints, colored pencils, pencils, water colors, texture paints
- Scraps of fabric, scraps of wallpaper, contact paper, cotton balls, and macaroni (and other items to provide texture for illustrations)
- Glue sticks, white glue, tape
- Scissors—straight and patterned—and hole punchers
- Stamps—alphabet, textures, symbols, designs
- Printmaking supplies
- Wire, yarn, sticks with rounded edges, ribbon, rubber bands
- Magazines, catalogs

The center should include samples and directions for a variety of art techniques, such as drawing, collaging, painting, printmaking, and puppetry.

Fluency Center

To enrich activities at this center, teachers may encourage English learners—depending on their language development—to work with partners who are fluent, native English speakers or students who are English speakers and are also fluent in the English learners' native language. Texts in native languages provide support and help English learners to learn content.

Books on Tape or CD: Students listen to and read along with texts at their independent (easy) levels to practice their oral reading fluency. They can do this with a more fluent partner or on their own. Older students or community volunteers can put books on tape or CD so students can use them at this center. Students with expertise in the English learners' native languages can also record dual-language books to be placed at this center.

Poems: Students work with partners to read aloud engaging poems to practice their oral reading fluency. Poems may range from short, simple rhymes to humorous story poems, such as those authored by Shel Silverstein and Jack Prelutsky.

Choral Reading and Echo Reading: Students read books with repeated phrases at their independent levels to improve their oral reading fluency. Pairs or trios of students can choral read the text (read it together orally) or they can take turns being the lead voice as they engage in echo reading (one student reads a line or two, the other[s] repeat it).

Readers Theatre: Teachers provide Readers Theatre scripts based on a variety of interests at multiple levels. Students use their voices to dramatize stories. They use texts that are already in Readers Theatre format. Then they rehearse the dramatization using their voices and facial expressions as their only props. Students use Readers Theatre scripts during the performance. Scripts are available from a wide variety of sources, including publishers and websites. Examples of websites include the following:

- Reader's Theater Editions: www.aaronshep.com/rt/RTE.html
- Reader's Theater Scripts and Plays: www.teachingheart.net/readerstheater.htm
- ReadingLady.com: www.readinglady.com/index.php?name=Downloads&req=viewdownload &cid=7
- PBS Zoom by Kids, for Kids!: pbskids.org/zoom/activities/playhouse

Repeated Readings: Teachers provide passages at multiple levels that accommodate a variety of interests. These passages are selected from books and articles that have a variety of text supports, including illustrations. Students work in pairs to practice their oral reading fluency while reading passages at their independent or easy level. In the pair, one student takes on the role of the *teacher*, the other assumes the role of the *student*. The role of the *student* is to read a passage; the role of the *teacher* is to follow along in the text and listen as the *student* reads. So, both students are getting practice with the passage. The passage is read four times. Students switch roles after each reading (Samuels, 2002).

Making Books Center

Students can retell key events from stories, gather data and create reports on content area topics, or write creative pieces that can be published. These may be self-created or follow a familiar structure, such as alphabet books. The following is a list of book types and suggestions for using them.

- *Dual-Language Books*: Students, typically an English learner and a native English speaker, partner to create either a page for a dual-language book that the class is writing or an entire book that they will author. These books often relate to social studies, math, and science and have titles such as *The Dual-Language Book of...States, Countries, Insects, Weather, Clouds, Math*, and so on. The dual-language books are often written and illustrated electronically. For example, the dual-language book *What Is a Vertebrate? ¿Qúe es un Vertebrado?* was completed in PowerPoint.
- *Class Alphabet Books*: Students can create individual pages to contribute to a class alphabet book. The class alphabet books might be based on the students in the class or on a theme, such as rainforests, oceans, or weather. Titles of student books might include *Our Class Community ABC Book*, *The ABC Book of Seasons*, or *The ABC Book of Students' Hobbies*. These can be completed electronically. Older students can create alphabet books with a partner or on their own. (See Appendix B, page 288, for a list of published alphabet books that serve as great models for this activity.)
- Other types of books:

  Accordion: retelling, content area facts, creative stories with illustrations

  Origami: word books, retelling, facts, short stories, story elements

Flip/flap: word work (parts of speech, antonyms, synonyms, rhymes, prefixes/suffixes, story elements, riddles)

Slotted: journals, reading response, word books, alphabet books

Dos à dos: dialogue or buddy journal, research and report, compare/contrast

Stair-step: riddle books, sequence story events, timelines (See Appendix B, pages 299–301, for directions for making these types of books.)

Making Words Center

Students use a variety of activities to construct words. (For related blackline masters, see Appendix B, pages 309–310.)

Making Words (Cunningham, 2008): In the original version of Making Words, students manipulate the letters of a mystery word to create other words. They begin with short words and progress to longer ones. They may create the words based on clues or just list as many words as possible. Then they guess the mystery word. When creating the words, students may manipulate plastic letters, arrange magnetic letters on a cookie sheet, or use letter tiles. We can modify this activity to offer support for English learners by providing them with the completed word at the start of the activity. This is the mystery word that students typically guess at the end of the original version of Making Words. When English learners begin with the completed word, they can work with a partner or on their own to manipulate the letters to create two-, three-, and four-letter words. For example, if the students were reading Seymour Simon's *The Heart: Our Circulatory System* (2006), *heart* might be the word English learners will use to create two-, three-, and four-letter words. The word would be shared and students would make as many words as they could using the letters in that word (only once, unless a letter was repeated in the word provided). Following are some of the words they might create:

- Two-letter words: *at, he*
- Three-letter words: *tea, tar, eat, ate, art, rat*
- Four-letter words: *rate, heat, hear, tear*

Making and Writing Words (Rasinski, 1999a): In this adaptation of Making Words, students write the words they create from the letters in a mystery word. For English learners, we would again provide the completed word (the mystery word in the Making Words activity explained previously), and students would create the two-, three-, and four-letter words and then write them. Making and Writing Words provides students with opportunities to practice their handwriting and spelling.

Making and Writing Words Using Letter Patterns (Rasinski, 1999b): In this adaptation of Making and Writing Words, students use rimes (word families) and other patterns as well as individual letters to create words. Then students transfer their knowledge to create new words. Finally, they cut up the organizer to create word cards, which they use to practice the words in sentences and sorts.

Poetry Center

Teachers keep a large supply of poetry books and poetry cards at this center. They also provide blacklines for form poems and copies of lots of poems that students can read, act out, or illustrate. The following are activities students can complete at the poetry center.

Form Poems: Students create their own poems using structured formats, such as acrostics, bio-poems, cinquains, and diamantes. Blacklines of poem formats (see Appendix B, pages 312–316) for students to use and examples of completed poems are available at this center.

Poetry Frames: Students create their own versions of published poems. The teacher can create frames in which students can write their own words, keeping the structure but changing the content of the original poem. (See Appendix B, page 305, for a poetry frame for "If I Were in Charge of the World.")

Poetry Theater: In small groups, students plan and practice acting out a poem. These dramatizations include minimal theatrics and props and maximum expression through voice and actions.

Project Center

Students work on specific extensions or projects related to the theme or current events. These may include multiple modes of response such as reading, writing, illustrating, and dramatizing. Various reference materials, from newspapers to magazines to books to bookmarked sites on the Internet, should be readily available.

Author Biographies: Students self-select a favorite author and research his or her life through bookmarked websites. Then they write the biography (which includes a photo of the author) on the computer, print it, and hang it in the class's authors' corner, where other students can read it.

Bookmarks: Students create bookmarks about the book they read. They may choose what to include on the bookmark, or the teacher can provide guidelines. For example, information for narrative texts may include title, author, main character(s), the student's thoughts about the book, and illustrations of characters or events. For informational texts, students can include the title, author, key ideas learned, their reactions, and illustrations.

Book Mobile: Students create mobiles about books they have read. Students may create the mobile on their own to format the information. Information may include the title, author, setting, characters, problem, resolution, and illustration. Students may also use the mobile format to share information about the author, focus on a single narrative element (e.g., character mobiles), or review a book. Because the mobiles will be suspended from the ceiling, students can record information on both sides of the paper.

Newspaper/Newsletter: Students write newspaper articles related to a topic of study and publish them in a classroom newspaper format. Examples include articles about culturally relevant topics, articles on theme-based subjects such as coral reefs or pollution when studying oceans, book reviews, and collections of comic strip summaries/retellings presented as the comics section of the newspaper.

Press Conference (McLaughlin, 2010a): This inquiry-based activity promotes oral communication. Students choose a topic to investigate. Then they peruse newspapers, magazines, or the Internet to find at least two sources of information about the topic. After reading the articles, focusing on essential points, raising questions, and reflecting on personal insights, the student presents an informal summary of his or her research to a group of classmates or the entire class. Members of the audience then raise questions that can lead to "I Wonder" Statements that students can record in their investigative journals (see the Press Conference Summary blackline in Appendix B, page 317). Students can use Questions Into Paragraphs (QuIP) to organize the information for their Press Conference (see Appendix A, pages 251 and 278).

Questions Into Paragraphs (QuIP) (E.M. McLaughlin, 1987): Students generate questions related to the topic and use two or more sources to find answers to each question. The information is recorded on a QuIP Research Grid (see Appendix A, pages 251 and 278) and then used to write a summary paragraph or to organize research for a Press Conference.

Choose Your Own Project: Students make selections from a list of ideas to extend their thinking about what they have read (see Appendix B, page 296).

Question and Answer Center

Teachers place narrative and informational text, including theme-related books and articles, at this center. Bookmarked websites are also used. Ciardiello's (1998, 2007) levels of questioning are provided (see Chapter 3, pages 33–34). Pairs of students use Ciardiello's questioning levels and signal words to generate and respond to questions. The students can write the questions and responses in their Guided Comprehension Journals and then discuss them. Writing the questions and responses provides practice in writing the language. Students can also use the written questions and answers to review different levels of questioning.

Sentence Center

Teachers provide texts that include visual supports, examples of completed narrative and informational sentence strips, a list of suggested academic vocabulary terms, a picture dictionary, access to the class word wall, and blank strips for student use.

Story Sentence Strips: Sentence strips related to the theme being studied are kept at this center. Pairs of students can use these for numerous activities, including retelling stories and reviewing narrative text structure. Students can also create their own sentence strips.

Informational Sentence Strips: When working with informational text, pairs of students can create sentence strips that include appropriate academic vocabulary. Students can also either use teacher-provided sentence strips or create their own to recreate various text structures, including comparison–contrast and cause–effect.

Storytelling Center

Students can engage in storytelling, in which they focus on the narrative elements (characters, setting, problem, attempts to resolve the problem, and resolution) with a partner or small group. It is a good idea to provide a tape recorder at this center so students can listen to themselves tell stories.

Puppets: Students use bag and spoon puppets to retell stories the class has previously read or original stories the students have written. Puppets and copies of the related stories are kept at the center.

Realia Bags: Pairs of students tell stories based on miniature props found in bags provided at this center. The bags are labeled with story themes, such as "A Trip to the Mall" and "Snow Day," and the props represent the narrative elements—characters, setting, problem, events (attempts to resolve the problem), and solution. The Story Map blackline can be used as a guide to facilitate storytelling because it is also based on the narrative elements (see Appendix A, page 283).

Wordless Picture Books: Students tell the story of a wordless picture book, such as Alexandra Day's *Carl's Summer Vacation* (2008), *Carl's Sleepy Afternoon* (2005), *Carl Goes to Daycare* (1993), *You're a Good Dog, Carl* (2007), and *Carl's Masquerade* (1992), or David Wiesner's *Tuesday* (1991), *June 29, 1999* (1995), *Sector 7* (1999), *The Three Pigs* (2001), and *Flotsam* (2006). Students may work in pairs and/or tape record their storytelling.

Teaching Center

In this center, students work with partners and take turns being the teacher. A variety of activities can be used in this center.

Transparency Talk (Page, 2001): In this center, a student assumes the role of the teacher. He or she places transparencies containing sentences, messages, or stories the classroom teacher has prepared on the overhead projector. The "teacher" then uses these for a variety of activities including finding words he or she can read, finding all the words that begin or end with a particular sound or pattern, or reading along with a partner. (Place the projector on the floor and use a white piece of paper for a screen.)

Read the Room: The "teacher" uses a pointer and the "student" and "teacher" take turns reading room labels, a bulletin board, or a morning message as the "teacher" points to it. Then the partners switch roles.

Theme Center

Teachers provide a variety of texts at multiple levels at this center. They ensure that texts are available in multiple languages and that culturally relevant titles are represented. They also select appropriate strategy applications for students to use while reading. For example, a teacher may include Concept of Definition Maps, Connection Stems, and Bookmark Technique. (Details about these teaching ideas and the related blacklines can be found in Appendix A.) Students may also select the mode of reading in which they will engage. This often includes using the following patterns from Patterned Partner Reading:

- *Read–Pause–Make a Connection*: Partners read, stop to think, and make text–self connections.
- *Read–Pause–Retell*: Partners read, stop to think, and retell what they have read to that point.
- *Read–Pause–Sketch*: Partners read, stop to think, and then sketch an idea related to what they have read.

(To learn more about Patterned Partner Reading, see Appendix A, page 246.)

Vocabulary Center

This center may include an illustrated word wall or other display designed to facilitate multiple exposures to words. For example, cognates or roots, prefixes, and suffixes may be featured. The words may also be theme-related. Sentences may be displayed so students can use context clues to determine words' meanings.

Illustrated Vocabulary Cards: These support English learners' reading and writing while offering alternative modes of representing thinking. The format also can be changed into an Illustrated Vocabulary Notebook in which terms can be organized alphabetically or thematically.

Illustrated Word Walls: These include visuals to support English learners' learning. Pairs of students can use the words to create sentences or entries in conversational journals. When creating conversational journals, students write what each would say if they were speaking.

Word Posters: Pairs of students select a word to be the focus of the poster. Then they create a satellite arm where they add the word's meaning and, if appropriate, an illustration. Each Word Poster has four satellites, so three other pairs of students can add information about the word. The poster is then displayed for class members to reference and discuss.

Word Sorts: Students sort vocabulary words into categories provided by the teacher (closed sort) or into self-selected categories (open sort). These might include parts of speech, word roots, and specific theme subtopics. This may be completed in a hands-on fashion using word cards; then students can record their ideas on a word-sort sheet. This activity also may be completed in writing on a web or other organized structure.

Word Storm: A visual display—such as a picture from a book, a piece of art, or a poster—provides the impetus for word brainstorming. Students look at the visual and brainstorm and record words that come to mind. Then they use some or all of the words to create a sentence or paragraph about the visual.

Writing Center

This center is a place for free and structured writing. Students may write informally or use the writing process. Teachers may also structure the writing using one or more of the following ideas.

Informational Writing: Students write restaurant menus and checks; use the Internet to create brochures about theme-related topics; write newspaper articles; and develop book, movie, and music reviews.

Journals: Students write about self-selected topics or respond to teacher-provided prompts.

Patterned Writing: Students use a patterned text as a writing model. This includes repeated pattern stories, such as Laura Numeroff's (1985) *If You Give a Mouse a Cookie* (which is also available in Spanish) and form poems (see Appendix B for form poem blacklines). The pattern provides scaffolds for English learners to express their ideas.

Story Bag: Pairs of students remove items from a bag of story-related props the teacher has prepared. They write a story based on the props.

Story Collages: Instead of writing a story and then illustrating it, pairs of students create textured illustrations first and then develop stories based on them. Because the illustrations are textured (pine cones, aluminum foil, felt, sand), students can use their tactile modalities (Brown, 1993).

Story Trifold: Pairs of students write a story using a graphic that folds into three labeled parts: beginning, middle, and end (see Appendix B, page 323).

Organizing and Managing Comprehension Centers

Students can move from center to center in a variety of ways depending on the structure of the literacy schedule, the English learners' language development, and the students' level of independence. In many of the center activities, English learners work with native English speakers, who not only serve as productive partners but also as good oral reading fluency models. The following methods are used frequently.

Menu Board: One way to organize center time is to use a menu board that provides a visual organizational overview of Stage Three (see Figure 3, page 36). The students who will meet for teacher-guided small-group instruction (Guided Reading) are listed on the menu board. Center choices are also provided, and students put their names under the center name where they will work. The number of students who may work at a given center or at a given activity within a center is designated at that center and on the menu board. For example, three is the designated number of students for the making words center as posted at the activity site and on the menu board. Students continue working at their assigned centers until they complete the work they have scheduled for that day. For example, students may choose to complete a story trifold at the writing center or use a partner-reading pattern to read a book at the theme center. Using this organizational chart ensures that choice is being accommodated on multiple levels: Students can choose what goals they are trying to achieve that day, which centers to visit, how long to stay, and how to manage their time.

Required and Optional Centers: We can also provide students with a framework for required and optional centers (see Appendix B, page 322). Sometimes we may choose to assign students to the centers where they will begin, but they may choose to move later as openings at other centers occur.

Rotating Schedule: Some teachers prefer to move the students using a rotating schedule. Within this setup, students move among three or four activities, changing approximately every 20 minutes. This rotational format provides maximum control by the teacher but limits students' opportunities for choice and for learning to manage their own time.

Student Accountability

Students need to be accountable for the time they spend at the centers. Using a record-keeping system helps to keep track of which centers each student visits during the week. We can use a whole-group chart to monitor who visits which centers each week, or we can place charts at individual centers for students to record their visits. Students may also keep track of their work in their Guided Comprehension Journals (see cover sheet in Appendix B, page 304).

Student self-assessment can also contribute to our understanding of how students used their center time. Providing self-assessment forms that indicate which centers students visited, what they did, and how they think they progressed toward their goal on a particular day facilitates this process (see Appendix B, page 295).

Students can keep their center work and reflections in a two-pocket folder, where the teacher can review them weekly or biweekly. Students also can share their work with the teacher in individual conferences. Including a checklist, rubric, or other evaluative tool at each center facilitates this process (see Appendix B). At the end of Stage Four, selected works will be transferred to the students' Guided Comprehension Profiles.

Regardless of what the comprehension centers include or how they are managed, they are places for independent exploration by students. The centers should accommodate a variety of abilities, be open-ended, have clear directions, be motivational, and provide activities that are familiar to students so they can use them independently.

Ford and Opitz (2002) suggest the following guidelines for using centers to facilitate this process:

- Operate with minimal transition time and management concerns.
- Encourage equitable use of centers and activities among learners.
- Include a simple built-in accountability system.
- Allow for efficient use of teacher preparation time.
- Build the centers around classroom routines.

In the next chapter, student-facilitated comprehension routines—another setting in which students independently apply reading skills and strategies—are described in detail. The comprehension routines discussed include adapted versions of Literature Circles, Reciprocal Teaching, and Cross-Age Reading Experiences.

CHAPTER 5

Organizing and Managing Comprehension Routines

Comprehension routines are habits of thinking and organizing that facilitate reading and response in authentic contexts. These routines provide another context in which students can practice their reading comprehension strategies independently. Their purpose is to help students gain a deeper understanding of the text and to equip students with a set of strategies they can use with other texts on their own. These are independent settings, which implies that students are able to work without teacher assistance, are knowledgeable about comprehension skills and strategies, know how to use the routines, have access to texts at their independent levels, and have ample time for practicing and transferring these processes. Au and Raphael (2010) note that "using consistent routines is essential to providing English learners with an orderly, productive environment for learning" (p. 211).

Over time, routines become courses of action that are so ingrained that they can be used successfully on a regular basis. Routines that are effective for promoting comprehension in both small-group and paired settings for English learners include Literature Circles, Reciprocal Teaching, and Cross-Age Reading Experiences.

Before students can use these comprehension routines independently, they need to understand the purpose of the routines, why they are engaging with them, and how the routines function. These needs can be accommodated by using the five-step explicit instruction process—explain, demonstrate, guide, practice, and reflect—to teach the routines. This process of gradual release ensures that students' learning is scaffolded. The teacher can begin by offering total support, and, as learning progresses, he or she gradually releases control of the routines to the students. Teachers may also choose to use additional supports, such as visuals, use of native language, and Patterned Partner Reading, with English learners to ensure that they are confident when engaging in the routines.

Literature Circles, Reciprocal Teaching, and Cross-Age Reading Experiences are delineated in this chapter. These routines, along with Directed Reading–Thinking Activity and Directed Listening–Thinking Activity, are presented in a step-by-step teaching process of gradual release in Appendix A.

It is important to note that a number of modifications have been made for English learners when they engage in the comprehension routines. These include the following:

- Making culturally relevant texts available
- Integrating multiple modes of representing thinking in student responses (sketching, singing, dramatizing)

- Encouraging English learners to choose to partner with native English speakers when working in Literature Circles
- Encouraging English learners to choose to partner with native language speakers or English language speakers when working in Cross-Age Reading Experiences

Literature Circles: What We Know

Literature Circles enable students to use discussion and interaction to refine their understanding and better comprehend what they are reading. Meeting independently in small groups provides opportunities for students to become more engaged in conversation and make connections to their own experiences (Brabham & Villaume, 2000; Ketch, 2005). In Literature Circles, groups of students share their insights, questions, and interpretations of the same or theme-related texts. The goal of Literature Circles is to provide students with a setting in which to converse about texts in meaningful, personal, and thoughtful ways (Brabham & Villaume, 2000). In Guided Comprehension, this means that students are integrating their background knowledge and comprehension skills and strategies as they construct personal meaning. English learners benefit from engaging in Literature Circles in a variety of ways (Carpinelli, 2006; Casey, 2008; Day & Ainley, 2008; Day & Kroon, 2010). These include the following:

- Forming circles based on student-selected texts
- Reading in a nonthreatening atmosphere
- Engaging in both social and academic language development in small groups
- Working collaboratively, sharing ideas, refining thinking, and creating new perspectives
- Nurturing peer relationships
- Using both English and native languages
- Hearing a wide range of cultural perspectives, languages, and points of view
- Asking questions and making connections to help comprehend text
- Learning and using the Literature Circle roles
- Expanding understanding through various extension projects

Implementing Literature Circles

To facilitate students' use of Literature Circles, we need to explicitly teach the concept and actively demonstrate how to engage with text (Stien & Beed, 2004). Brabham and Villaume (2000) caution against a cookie-cutter version of how to implement Literature Circles and instead recommend designing and using them in ways that emerge from our students' needs and challenges. These circles may not all have the same format, but they all encourage the implementation of grand conversations about texts.

Literature Circles are a time of exploration and construction of personal meaning for the students. This routine is not a list of literal questions to be answered after reading. Students' personal interpretations drive the discussion. The focus is on students' inquiries, connections, and interpretations. During explicit instruction, we should make a point of modeling how to converse in meaningful ways during the demonstration step. Using Think-Alouds facilitates this process.

Daniels (2002) suggests guiding principles for using Literature Circles:

- Students self-select the books they will read.
- Temporary groups are formed based on book choice.
- Each group reads something different.
- Groups meet on a regular basis according to predetermined schedules.
- Students use drawings or writings to guide their conversations.
- Students determine the topics for discussions and lead the conversations.
- The teacher acts as a facilitator, not an instructor or leader.
- Assessment can be completed through teacher observation or student self-reflection.
- Students are actively involved in reading and discussing books.
- After reading the books, the students share their ideas with their classmates, choose new books to read, and begin the cycle anew.

When implementing Literature Circles, we can invite English learners to work with partners until they become comfortable with the routine. It is also important that all students engage in an activity in which they can get to know each other before meeting to discuss the book. This encourages students to build positive relationships with group members (Clarke & Holwadel, 2007; Daniels & Steineke, 2004). Also, self-selection, text and appropriate supports, and multiple ways of representing student thinking are key factors. Each of these is detailed in the following sections.

Self-selection. Clarke and Holwadel (2007) note the importance of having students choose the texts they will read, but students also make other choices in Literature Circles. They select the group they will join, the schedule they will follow, and the direction of the conversation. We can set the parameters for students to make these choices by providing a variety of texts (including culturally relevant titles) at multiple levels for student selection, setting minimum daily or weekly reading requirements, and prompting ideas for conversations. However, the ultimate responsibility for each group rests with the students.

Text with appropriate supports. The titles from which the students choose should be high-quality authentic literature or informational texts that relate to their experiences. The texts should help students make personal connections and prompt critical reflection (Brabham & Villaume, 2000). The books should include interesting stories with well-developed characters, rich language, and culturally relevant themes that are engaging and meaningful and generate interest from students (Noe & Johnson, 1999; Samway & Wang, 1996). The informational texts should be of interest to the students and focus on topics about which they have background knowledge.

A variety of text supports should be available to English learners when they are in Literature Circles. These include pictures, graphic organizers, partnering with a native English speaker, and using native languages as well as English.

While reading, students can jot ideas in their Guided Comprehension Journals to share during discussion. Providing prompts to help students focus their thoughts is beneficial. Examples of prompts include the following:

- I want to ask my group about...
- I think it is funny (sad, surprising, scary) that...
- I think it is interesting that...
- I think it is confusing that...
- The illustrations in this text...
- A vocabulary word I think our group should talk about is...
- This book reminds me of...

Using Bookmark Technique (McLaughlin & Allen, 2009) is a viable alternative for documenting students' ideas (see Appendix A, page 246). In this strategy application, students record their thoughts on four different bookmarks. The first contains their ideas about what they found most interesting; the second features a vocabulary word they think the group needs to discuss; the third provides information about something that was confusing; and the fourth contains ideas about illustrations, maps, or other graphics featured in the text (see Appendix A, pages 261–262, for Bookmark blacklines). The students record the page number and their thoughts on the bookmarks and place them at appropriate points in the text. Then the students use the four completed bookmarks to support their contributions to the group discussion.

Response and multiple ways to represent student thinking. After reading, students gather in their small group to share understandings from the text and make personal connections. This sharing, in the form of a conversation, helps the students to broaden their interpretations and gain new perspectives from the other members of the group.

Noe and Johnson (1999) suggest that after Literature Circle discussions have concluded, we should expand students' opportunities to respond to text by encouraging them to participate in extension activities. These activities provide students with another mode for exploring meaning, expressing their ideas about the text, making connections, and using a variety of response formats. English learners should be encouraged to represent their thinking in a variety of ways, including sketching, dramatizing, singing, and working with peers to create projects. Examples of extension projects that incorporate multiple ways of representing thinking include the following.

Book Poster: Students create an illustrated poster about the book. They include the title and author, draw or collage ideas based on the text, and include comments about what they thought of the book.

Lyric Retelling/Lyric Summary: The students in the Literature Circle meet when the reading is finished and extend their learning by engaging in a Lyric Retelling/Summary. Students begin by brainstorming individual lists of narrative elements or facts from informational text. Next, the students choose a well-known song that everyone in the group knows. Then the students use their brainstormed lists to write a retelling or summary based on the text. Finally, the group sings the Lyric Retelling/Summary for the class.

Quilt Square: Students design a quilt square to represent the book and add it to the class book quilt. They include the book's title and author and create an illustration to represent the book. They use the yarn provided to connect their square to the existing quilt. Competed class book quilts may feature theme-related texts, be genre-specific (such as favorite poetry books, biographies, or mysteries), or focus on the work of a favorite author.

Transmediations: Students change the format of the text they have read. For example, they may read a novel and change it into a story poem, read an informational text and change it into a definition poem, or read a novel or an informational text and change it into a picture book or illustrated alphabet book.

What We Thought of Our Book: Students orally present information about their book. They use drawings, make connections, and retell the story or summarize the information they read. They conclude by explaining why they would or would not suggest that other students read the book.

(For more ideas about extending students' thinking after reading, see Appendix B and the Theme Resources sections of Chapters 8–10.)

Organizing and Managing Literature Circles

There are several ways to structure and manage Literature Circles. There is no right way, but rather choices must be made to accommodate the needs and challenges of not only each grade level but also of each student in the class. Any of the existing plans for Literature Circles may be used to create successful formats. Once a meaningful plan has been selected, we make decisions about text choice, forming groups, and structuring the conversations.

Text selection. Texts for Literature Circles can be picture books, chapter books, and poetry books, but students may also read high-quality informational text (McLaughlin, 2010a; Stien & Beed, 2004). Text choices should relate to students' experiences, help them make personal connections, relate to themes, be culturally relevant, contain rich language, and prompt critical reflection (Brabham & Villaume, 2000; Noe & Johnson, 1999; Samway & Wang, 1996). These books should also be engaging, meaningful, interesting, and accessible for students. Including theme-based leveled texts ensures that students will be able to engage in the circles independently, without teacher assistance. Although students in Literature Circles usually read the same text, they can also read similar texts about the same theme or a variety of theme-related genres on multiple levels. The texts that are selected will need to accommodate a wide range of student interests and abilities.

There are multiple options for selecting texts for Literature Circles. One way is to choose books that relate to a theme, topic, genre, or author. When using this method, the teacher should choose several texts on varying levels, and the students should make reading choices based on interest and ability. Another way to select text is to create collections of text sets related to a theme or topic. Texts within each set are related but can vary in level of difficulty. Students select the theme or topic and then choose the reading material from within that set. A third way to choose reading material is to allow students to self-select and then form groups based on text similarities.

Introducing text. After selecting the texts to be used in Literature Circles, we match the books with readers. Although there are various methods for doing this, book passes and book talks are especially effective. English learners may choose to engage in text selection with a partner.

Book passes: Several books are passed among students. Each student peruses a book for a few minutes, noting the title, reading the book cover, and leafing through the pages. If the students find a book appealing, they jot the title in their Guided Comprehension Journal and pass the book to the next person. After previewing several titles, students make choices. Groups are then formed on the basis of the book selections.

Book talks: This is a short oral overview of the book, focusing on the genre, the main characters, and the plot. After the book talks, students make choices and groups are formed.

We may need to guide some students in making appropriate text choices. If text sets are used, we can introduce the theme of the set and the kinds of texts that are in it. If selections are used from an anthology, we can introduce them through book talks.

Grand conversations: Schedules, talk, and roles. Once the Literature Circles are formed, students meet and develop a schedule to determine how much they will read and to create meeting deadlines. At first, the teacher can provide the schedule as a way to model how to set these goals. Once reading goals are set, students read the text on their own or with a partner. At the designated group meeting time, the students gather to discuss the texts. Notes or sketches from their reading that have been recorded in their Guided Comprehension Journals or their Literature Circle Bookmarks inform this discussion. Prior to this point, we model how to respond to text and how to use these responses to get the group conversations started.

The time spent in Literature Circles varies by length of text, but usually 20 minutes is sufficient. We can use a minilesson to demonstrate a particular literary element—such as plot, theme, or characterization—on which the students may focus their discussion. It is important, though, that we allow each group's conversation to evolve on its own.

Gilles (1998) has identified four types of talk that often occur during Literature Circles: talk about the book, talk about the reading process, talk about connections, and talk about group process and social issues. Teachers can encourage all types of talk with demonstrations and gentle prompts during the Literature Circle conversations.

Some teachers prefer to use assigned roles and responsibilities as a way to guide the conversations. Daniels (2002) has found that the following roles, which students rotate, provide a wide level of conversation within the Literature Circle:

- The *discussion director* takes on the leadership of the group and guides the discussion. Responsibilities include choosing topics for discussion, generating questions, convening the meeting, and facilitating contributions from all members.
- The *literary luminary/passage master* helps students revisit the text. Responsibilities include selecting memorable or important sections of the text and reading them aloud expressively.
- The *connector* guides the students to make connections with the text. Responsibilities include sharing text–self, text–text, and text–world connections and encouraging others to do the same.

- The *illustrator/artful artist* creates a drawing or other symbolic response to text. Responsibilities include making the visual response and using it to encourage others to contribute to the conversation.

Teachers can also provide "role cards" with short explanations of the roles and related illustrations for English learners. This helps keep these students focused on the roles as they engage in discussion.

The advantage of using these roles is that they represent response in a variety of learning modes, including linguistic, dramatic, and visual. The disadvantage is that this structure may stifle responses. I have found that starting with clearly defined roles and then relaxing or relinquishing them as the students gain competence in Literature Circles is effective. Daniels (2002) concurs, noting that role-free discussions are the ultimate goal.

Assessment in Literature Circles

There are several ways to assess students' comprehension, contributions, and cooperation within Literature Circles. Options include self-reflection, observation, discussion, and response sheets or journal entries.

- Students may self-reflect on their contributions to the circle and the group's ability to function. Providing forms for students to record their self-reflections facilitates this process (see Appendix B, pages 307–308).
- Although the students meet independently, we can observe their conversations and make anecdotal notes or keep a checklist of the content and depth of discussions (see Appendix C, page 337). We can note who is contributing to the discussion and if full participation is lacking. We can use this data to teach the students additional ways to include all group members. We also can observe the scope of the discussion. If the students are focused on basic recall of story events, we can choose to do a minilesson on making meaningful connections with texts.
- Students' response sheets, Guided Comprehension Journals, or Literature Circle Bookmarks (see Appendix B, page 306) provide another opportunity for assessment. In this format, students take notes about the text, document understandings, and make personal connections to bring to the discussion. These written or drawn artifacts provide a window into the students' thinking about the text.

The most important thing to remember about assessment in Literature Circles is to use the assessment results. These should contribute to decisions about future instruction.

Reciprocal Teaching: What We Know

Reciprocal Teaching involves scaffolded instruction and discussion of text based on four comprehension strategies: predicting, questioning, clarifying, and summarizing. The students as well as the teacher take on the role of "teacher" in leading the discussion about the text (Palincsar & Brown, 1984). Reciprocal Teaching has three purposes:

1. To help students participate in a group effort to bring meaning to a text
2. To teach students that the reading process requires continual use of the four strategies (predicting, questioning, clarifying, summarizing) for effective comprehension
3. To provide students with the opportunity to monitor their own learning and thinking

Fashola, Slavin, Calderón, and Durán (1997) note that when English learners engage in Reciprocal Teaching, their reading comprehension increases.

Duke and Pearson (2002) describe a Reciprocal Teaching session in the following way:

> A typical Reciprocal Teaching session begins with a review of the main points from the previous session's reading, or if the reading is new, predictions about the text based on the title and perhaps other information. Following this, all students read the first paragraph of the text silently. A student assigned to act as teacher then (a) asks a question about the paragraph, (b) summarizes the paragraph, (c) asks for clarification if needed, and (d) predicts what might be in the next paragraph. During the process, the teacher prompts the student/teacher as needed, and at the end provides feedback about the student/teacher's work. (p. 225)

Implementing Reciprocal Teaching

In Guided Comprehension, students learn Reciprocal Teaching through explicit instruction before using it as an independent comprehension routine. The following steps will facilitate this process:

- Explain the procedure and the four strategies, noting their definitions, why they are important, and how they help us comprehend.
- Model thinking related to use of the four strategies by using an authentic text and Think-Alouds.
- Guide the students, in a whole-class setting, to think about their reading by providing responses for each of the strategies using verbal prompts, such as those suggested by Mowery (1995):

  Predicting
  I think...
  I bet...
  I wonder...
  I imagine...
  I suppose...

  Questioning
  Who? Where? When? What? How? Why?

  Clarifying
  I did not understand the part where...
  I need to know more about...
  This changes what I thought about...

  Summarizing
  This paragraph is about...
  The important ideas in what I read are...

- Practice by organizing the students in groups of four, and provide each group with a text to read and use as the basis of their Reciprocal Teaching.
- Assign one of the four strategies and suggested prompts to each group member.
- Invite students to engage in Reciprocal Teaching using the process modeled.
- Reflect by providing time for discussion and self-assessment forms (see Appendix B) to facilitate students' thinking about how strategy use affected their comprehension and what their future goals will be.

This process provides students with opportunities to share their thinking in a reciprocal fashion. While students are participating in their groups, we can monitor their activity and scaffold the dialogue when appropriate. Once the students are skilled at using Reciprocal Teaching, they can use it as an independent comprehension routine.

Studies by Palincsar and Brown (1984) demonstrate that students with a wide variety of abilities can use Reciprocal Teaching successfully. Although originally designed to help students who could decode well but had weak comprehension skills, all students benefit from this type of instruction because it allows them to read and understand more challenging texts (Palincsar & Brown, 1984).

Text Selection

In Reciprocal Teaching, the level of text is determined by students' abilities and the instructional setting in which this routine is being used. For example, when students are learning how to use Reciprocal Teaching in a whole-class setting or if students are using Reciprocal Teaching independently to practice using multiple comprehension strategies, texts should be at students' easy or independent reading levels.

Assessing Reciprocal Teaching

Teachers can assess students in Reciprocal Teaching groups by observing their ability to successfully use the strategies (see Appendix C, page 338). Students may self-reflect on contributions (see Appendix B, page 321) or may keep notes of the ideas they contributed. This information will help teachers create whole-class or small-group minilessons on using the strategies.

Cross-Age Reading Experiences: What We Know

Cross-Age Reading Experiences generally involve a novice working on a specific task with a more knowledgeable person for a particular period of time. This type of learning is especially applicable in education, where practitioners frequently model and scaffold learning for less-experienced learners. Forman and Cazden (1994) note that such educational practices reflect Vygotsky's thinking about adult–child relationships and offer an alternative to traditional adult–child interactions. In educational contexts, there are a variety of people who may play the role of the more knowledgeable other in cross-age relationships with our students. These people include community volunteers, upper-grade students, and classroom aides.

In Guided Comprehension, Cross-Age Reading Experiences are routines that involve exploration, strategy application, and the construction of personal meaning. The resulting learning experiences are meaningful and memorable for all involved. English learners benefit from Cross-Age Reading Experiences in multiple ways. These include the following:

- Reading narrative and informational text in a relaxed setting
- Developing collaborative partnerships
- Choosing texts
- Practicing reading comprehension strategies
- Using native languages and English
- Extending thinking about texts in a variety of ways

Implementing Cross-Age Reading Experiences

When planning Cross-Age Reading Experiences, there are a number of factors to consider. To begin, the cross-age partners must be identified. Students from upper grades, community members, and classroom aides are among those who may volunteer for this position. Obviously it is ideal to have some cross-age partners who speak the English learners' native languages. As Iddings, Risko, and Rampulla (2009) note, English learners should have a range of opportunities for linguistic experimentations involving their first and second languages to increase their comprehension of texts.

Once the partners are selected, a few informal training sessions should be held. These meetings may focus on modeling read-alouds, reviewing comprehension strategies, demonstrating upcoming teaching ideas, and discussing the role of the partner in the cross-age experience. It is important that the partners understand that this routine is part of the Guided Comprehension Model and that it is a time for students to practice and transfer comprehension strategies. It is also helpful to introduce a range of texts, including culturally relevant books, to the partners.

Scheduling is another important consideration. The partners will need to be available during the same time periods. Community volunteers and classroom aides should be able to work with students on a consistent basis. Upper-grade students may be available only once a week for a limited amount of time, but they still provide important models for students. Examples of Cross-Age Reading Experiences situated within theme-based Guided Comprehension lessons can be found in Chapters 8–10.

English learners can also use easier texts, including picture books, to help develop their fluency and word recognition. When they are comfortable with their fluent reading of such texts, they may in turn develop Cross-Age Reading Experiences with students in lower grades. These situations are wonderfully rewarding for both the English learners and the younger learners.

Text Selection

Both narrative and informational text can be used in Cross-Age Reading Experiences. The text will vary by type and genre according to the theme of study. Culturally relevant titles should also be included. The reading materials should be at students' easy or independent levels so they can read them without teacher assistance.

Assessment in Cross-Age Reading Experiences

Self-assessments similar to those that emerge from Literature Circles and Reciprocal Teaching also can be used for Cross-Age Reading Experiences (see Appendix B, page 298, and Appendix C, page 336).

Stage Three of Guided Comprehension provides English learners with a variety of meaningful settings in which to practice comprehension skills and strategies. In teacher-guided small-group instruction, students' reading has teacher support as needed. In student-facilitated comprehension centers and routines, students engage in independent applications. Student assessment and leveled texts are integral components of all three of these settings.

In the next chapter, the roles of assessment in Guided Comprehension are discussed. Connections to standards and a variety of practical assessment measures are also presented.

CHAPTER 6

Assessment in Guided Comprehension

Assessment is a natural component of teaching and learning. It helps us gain insights into students' abilities, needs, experiences, and interests. We use assessment results to inform our teaching and to help students to achieve their maximum potentials.

When we are teaching, we use assessments for a variety of purposes. For example, before teaching we use diagnostic assessments to determine what students know, to learn about their interests, and to identify approximate reading levels. While we are teaching, we use formative assessments to document student progress and check for understanding. After we have taught, we use summative assessments to determine what students have learned and to gain insights into how successful our teaching has been.

When assessing English learners, we need to be particularly aware of students' language development. Our goal is to ensure that language issues do not interfere with the content of the assessments. As a result, we often modify assessments for English learners. Understanding English learners' backgrounds and working with ESL teachers can help us gain a greater understanding of students' language capabilities. The ESL teachers can also assist in administering informal assessments in students' first languages.

This chapter focuses on practical approaches to assessing English learners. To begin, the dynamic nature of assessment and its multiple roles in Guided Comprehension are discussed. Next, the chapter delineates how to prepare to assess English learners and steps we might follow when assessing these students. Then a variety of modifications we can make for English learners are explored. This is followed by a discussion of practical measures and everyday formative assessments. Next, connections are made to the Common Core State Standards (Common Core State Standards Initiative, 2010c) and World-Class Instructional Design and Assessment (WIDA) English Language Proficiency Standards (WIDA, 2007). Finally, Guided Comprehension Profiles—tools to organize and manage student progress—are explained. Throughout the chapter, connections are made to Appendix C, which contains a variety of reproducible assessments and assessment forms.

The Multiple Roles of Assessment in Guided Comprehension

Assessment in Guided Comprehension is dynamic in nature. It occurs in an ongoing manner, offers insights into students' thinking, chronicles student development, and is a natural component of teaching and learning (McLaughlin, 2002a, 2002b). This aligns with constructivist thinking about purposeful assessments (Tierney, 1998) and supports Vygotsky's belief that assessment should extend to scaffolded experiences to capture students' emerging abilities (Minick, 1987).

Assessment in Guided Comprehension has several purposes, including the following:

- To provide an approximate range of reading levels for students
- To offer insights into student attitudes and interests
- To facilitate student–text matches
- To inform grouping for teacher-guided instruction
- To check for student understanding
- To provide insights into students' thinking
- To offer insights into students' language development
- To document students' performance
- To provide information for evaluative purposes

Assessment permeates every stage of the Guided Comprehension Model for English Learners and occurs in a variety of forms and settings. For example, we use diagnostic assessments to determine approximate student reading levels and analyze students' use of skills and strategies to decode and comprehend. These assessments provide valuable information for grouping students for small-group instruction in Stage Three and for guiding our decisions about which texts to use and which strategies to teach. We employ formative measures to monitor student learning as we are teaching and guiding. These assessments allow us to check for student understanding in a continuous, ongoing manner and to adjust our teaching to better meet the needs of our students. We use summative assessments to examine what students have learned over time and to help us make instructional decisions for future lessons.

Preparing to Assess English Learners

As we think about how we will assess English learners, we should consider what we might do to prepare to assess them. For example, we may want to focus on the following:

- Ensuring that English learners are given consideration within the district's curriculum, instruction, and assessment.
- Working as a team with the ESL teacher(s) and other teachers across the curriculum.
- Striving to understand students' unique backgrounds.
- Teaching English learners how to generate and respond to questions.
- Assessing for specific purposes.
- Explaining assessment as a natural part of teaching and learning.
- Nurturing an atmosphere of trust.
- Preparing supports as needed, based on the English learners' language development.
- Planning to actively engage students in the assessments.

Assessing English Learners

As we engage in assessing English learners, we should consider using several supports. These include the following:

- Explicitly teaching students how to complete the assessment.
- Scaffolding students' use of assessments—in small groups, with partners, and on their own. (Depending on students' language development, consider assessing English learners with partners or in a small group.)
- Providing students with examples of what we will learn from the assessments.
- Using the students' native languages as an assessment resource. This may extend to allowing English learners to use their first language to complete literacy tasks.
- Using authentic, culturally meaningful text to accommodate students' interests and backgrounds.
- Providing alternative ways for students to represent their thinking (such as orally and by using graphic organizers).
- Explaining the assessment results to the students. Share with their parents, as appropriate.
- Using the assessment results to inform future instruction and modify it, as necessary.

Modifying Assessments for English Learners

Depending on the English learners' language development, there are a variety of ways in which we may choose to further modify assessments. These include the following:

- Provide paired or small-group settings in which English learners might be assessed.
- Engage ESL teachers to assist with assessments that may involve the students' first languages.
- Invite assistants to record students' responses (such as classroom aides or Cross-Age Reading Experience partners).
- Offer students alternative modes of response.
- Use visuals and other supports.
- Begin each section of the assessment with an example response.

Practical Assessment Measures

When preparing to teach Guided Comprehension, we assess for a variety of purposes. We gather information to learn about students' reading backgrounds and interests, to determine approximate range of reading levels, and to gain insights into students' knowledge of strategies and their ability to apply them. Results of these assessments inform several aspects of our planning, including lesson content, student–text matches, and grouping students for guided instructional settings.

A number of practical, effective assessments are presented in this section. A description of each measure, an explanation of its functions, and details of its connection to Guided Comprehension are featured.

Assessments to Learn About Students' Backgrounds and Interests

Some assessments provide insights into students' pasts that enable us to better understand their present attitudes toward and performance in reading. Examples of these measures include attitude surveys, interest inventories, literacy histories, motivation profiles, and peer interviews. (Reproducible copies of these measures are included in Appendix C. Note that these forms are written in English. ESL teachers can translate the forms into students' native languages and assist in obtaining English learners' responses.)

Attitude surveys. Attitude surveys are designed to illuminate students' feelings about reading and writing and the resulting impact on motivation and effort. The most common formats are question and response, sentence completion, and selected response. Information we can obtain from attitude surveys includes how students feel about various aspects of reading and writing, how they would define reading and writing, and how they would describe successful readers and writers. Information gleaned from these surveys also provides insights into factors that may have contributed to students' current attitudes toward literacy. (Reproducible reading and writing attitude surveys can be found in Appendix C, pages 326 and 327.)

The completed attitude surveys provide information about students' perceptions of literacy processes. They also offer information about students' reading preferences that we can use when making student–text matches and selecting texts for Stages Two and Three.

Interest inventories. Interest inventories are informal surveys designed to provide information about students' personal interests. They usually include topics such as students' reading preferences, hobbies, and special interests. The most common formats for interest inventories are question and response or incomplete sentences. These surveys are relatively easy to complete, and they provide information about numerous topics including the following: genre and author preferences, what students are currently reading, and whether students choose to read beyond required assignments. (Examples of interest inventories can be found in Appendix C, pages 330 and 331.)

Completed interest inventories provide information about students' backgrounds. We can use that knowledge to make decisions related to motivating students and making student–text matches.

Literacy histories. Literacy histories chronicle students' literacy development from earliest memory to present day (McLaughlin & Vogt, 1996). They facilitate students' ability to make connections between their past literacy experiences and their current beliefs.

To create their personal literacy histories, students engage in questioning and reflection. Sources they use to construct their histories range from family memories to early-grade writing samples to copies of favorite books. Students can choose the mode of presentation; they have submitted everything from timelines to scrapbooks filled with family photos. To model this assessment, we as teachers share our own literacy histories and provide students with prompts to guide the process. (Reproducible copies of the literacy history prompts are included in Appendix C, page 332.)

Literacy histories help us learn about the present by examining the past. They provide students' personal insights into their literacy development and contribute to our understanding of students' current attitudes toward literacy.

Motivation to Read Profile. The Motivation to Read Profile (Gambrell, Palmer, Codling, & Mazzoni, 1996) consists of two instruments: the Reading Survey and the Conversational Interview. The cued response survey, which requires 15–20 minutes for group administration, assesses the self-concept of a reader and value of reading. The interview, which features open-ended free response questions and requires 15–20 minutes for individual administration, assesses the nature of motivation, such as favorite authors and interesting books. The Conversational Interview (included in Appendix C, pages 333–335) has three emphases: narrative text, informational text, and general reading.

Guided Comprehension Connection

Knowledge of what motivates students to read both narrative and informational text enhances our understanding of our students and informs meaningful text selection.

Peer Interview. The Peer Interview (McLaughlin, 2010a) is comprised of eight questions that focus on family, education, and special interests. It is designed to be used by classmates to help them get to know each other. To model completing this assessment, we can interview a student and ask the student to interview us. (A reproducible Peer Interview is included in Appendix C, page 339.)

Guided Comprehension Connection

Guided Comprehension fosters multiple opportunities for students to work with each other every day. The Peer Interview helps students to get to know each other and to become more comfortable working with each other. It also contributes to students' understanding of their peers' backgrounds.

Attitude surveys, interest inventories, literacy histories, motivation profiles, and peer interviews provide background information that informs our understanding of individual students and their literacy needs. These measures contribute vital information as we seek to provide optimum literacy experiences for our students. These assessments are easy to administer, require little time, and provide insights that may not be discerned from other literacy assessments.

Assessments to Learn About Students' Reading Levels and Strategy Use

Some measures provide information about how students use cueing systems, and others pair miscue analysis with comprehension assessments. Examples of these measures include oral reading assessment with miscue analysis, running records, and published leveled passages kits such as the Comprehensive Reading Inventory (which includes reading passages in Spanish), Qualitative Reading Inventory–5, Developmental Reading Assessment 2: Grades K–3, and Fountas and Pinnell Benchmark Assessment System: Grades K–2 and 3–8.

Miscue analysis. Miscue analysis (Goodman, 1997) helps us to assess students' use of the graphophonic, syntactic, and semantic cueing systems. Miscues indicate how a student's oral reading varies from the written text. In miscue analysis, students read aloud, and we record their attempts, self-corrections, and miscues. Recording the students' attempts and analyzing the miscues provides us with valuable information for our teaching.

To analyze miscues, Goodman, Watson, and Burke (1987) suggest we use the following four questions:

1. Does the miscue change the meaning?
2. Does the miscue sound like language?
3. Do the miscue and the text word look and sound alike?
4. Was an attempt made to self-correct the miscue?

To facilitate the use of the miscue analysis, we select some "anchor books"—both fiction and nonfiction at varying levels—and invite students to do an informal oral reading, which we tape record. At this point, we code and analyze all their attempts, self-corrections, and miscues. We also ask the students to do a brief retelling of this text. These two pieces of information provide approximate student reading levels and insights into their strategy use and comprehension. There are some defined accuracy percentages that may influence the determination of a reader's range of levels: below 90%, frustration; 90–95%, instructional; 96–100%, independent. When assessing students' levels, we also need to consider factors such as background knowledge about the content, interest in the text, and supports within the text.

Miscue analysis provides approximate reading levels, helps us to make matches between readers and texts, and informs instruction.

Running records. Running records were developed by Marie Clay (1993) as a way to observe, record, and analyze what a child does in the process of reading. The teacher assumes the role of a neutral observer for the purpose of taking a record of the child's independent reading behavior. Running records provide qualitative and quantitative information about what a reader knows and what needs to be learned next. In addition, running records help the teacher to make informed decisions concerning instructional needs, approximate reading levels, grouping for Guided Reading, and making student–text matches. (To learn how to use running records, see *Running Records: A Self-Tutoring Guide* [2000] by Johnston and *Assessment and Instruction of Reading and Writing Difficulties: An Interactive Approach* [2009] by Lipson and Wixson.)

Running records are used to assess students for placement and advancement purposes in teacher-guided small groups and to inform the teacher's understanding of students' reading.

Comprehensive Reading Inventory: Measuring Reading Development in Regular and Special Education Classrooms. The Comprehensive Reading Inventory: Measuring Reading Development in Regular and Special Education Classrooms (Cooter, Flynt, & Cooter, 2006) is the only literacy assessment on the market that addresses phonemic awareness, phonics, fluency, vocabulary, and comprehension. It is designed for use in regular and special education classrooms and has special sections devoted to assessing students whose first language is Spanish. Reading passages in Spanish are included in this assessment.

This assessment, which offers the advantage of reading passages in Spanish, provides information necessary to place students in teacher-guided small groups and to create student–text matches in Guided Comprehension.

Qualitative Reading Inventory–5. The Qualitative Reading Inventory–5 (Leslie & Caldwell, 2010) is a comprehensive assessment that ranges from preprimer to high school. It includes narrative and informational leveled passages, questions to assess prior knowledge, and word lists. To assess comprehension, students can retell passages or respond to implicit and explicit questions. The leveled passages and word lists enable the teacher to estimate students' reading levels, match students with appropriate texts, and verify suspected reading difficulties. Because there are so many components to this measure, we need to make choices when using it. For example, we may choose to do the miscue analysis and then use either the retelling checklist or the comprehension questions that accompany each leveled passage to determine students' instructional levels. The leveled passages also can be used to assess silent reading comprehension.

Guided Comprehension Connection

This assessment provides information necessary to place students in teacher-guided small groups and to create student–text matches.

Developmental Reading Assessment 2: Grades K–3. The Developmental Reading Assessment 2: Grades K–3 assessment kit (Beaver & Carter, 2009) includes a variety of fiction and nonfiction texts at primary grade levels. Detailed record-keeping forms help the teacher document student levels, reading behaviors, and comprehension over time.

This assessment provides information necessary to determine student placement in teacher-guided small groups and to create student–text matches.

Fountas and Pinnell Benchmark Assessment System: Grades K–2 and 3–8. The Fountas and Pinnell Benchmark Assessment System: Grades K–2 and 3–8 assessment kits (Fountas & Pinnell, 2008a, 2008b) provide graded word lists, fiction and nonfiction leveled readers, and detailed forms for analyzing and recording students' comprehension, writing, and fluency over time.

Fountas and Pinnell (2011) also have an assessment system for Spanish-speaking students: *Sistema de evaluación de la lectura.* The assessments in this kit are not translations of the passages in the Benchmark Assessment Systems but rather new materials developed by bilingual literacy experts under the supervision of Fountas and Pinnell. These comprehensive materials, which are designed to be used one on one, help determine students' reading levels and assist in creating student–text matches.

Guided Comprehension Connection

These assessments help us to determine approximate reading levels for students in teacher-guided small groups. This, in turn, helps us to make student–text matches and plan appropriate instruction.

Formative Assessments to Learn About Students' Everyday Progress

Formative assessments are the object of current national interest in the United States. We use formative assessments in everyday teaching and learning. These are informal measures that offer insights into students' understanding and inform our teaching. In fact, because the feedback occurs immediately, teachers can adjust their teaching while they are engaged in it. Formative assessments also provide an ongoing record of student growth and can be used to document students' progress in meeting educational standards. Three examples of formative assessments are informal student writing, strategy applications, and teacher observation.

Informal student writing. Informal student writing is a flexible assessment. It can be used for numerous purposes, including monitoring students' understanding, applying strategies, summarizing and synthesizing information, documenting student thinking, recording personal responses, and as a mode of reflection and goal setting. We observe and analyze student writing for multiple purposes, including content, focus, organization, language structure, use of vocabulary, and knowledge of sight words and spelling patterns.

Specific examples of informal writing activities that can be used as formative assessments include Language Experience, Dialogue Journals, Investigative Journals, Response Journals, and Tickets Out.

Language Experience: The Language Experience Approach (LEA) promotes reading and writing through the use of student experiences and oral language. Typically the student has an experience and dictates a story about it to the teacher or Cross-Age Reading Experience partner. Then the story becomes the text and literacy activities are constructed around it. LEA has had a high success rate because the text, which is based on students' interests, is student-generated and incorporates vocabulary that students are comfortable using. Even the level of text complexity is determined by the students. LEA has been used successfully with students in all grades, as well as with English learners.

Dialogue Journals: When engaging in Dialogue Journals, students write an entry and a student partner replies. Teachers and students can also create Dialogue Journals together. The Dialogue Journal is very personal and can address a range of topics.

Investigative Journals: When students learn about informational topics that interest them (such as tsunamis, outer space, and biographies of famous inventors), they may raise questions about the topic in their Investigative Journals. The students then use the questions as the focuses of applications, such as Questions Into Paragraphs (QuIP; E.M. McLaughlin, 1987) or Press Conference (McLaughlin, 2010a). (See Appendix A, page 251, for more detailed information about QuIP, and Chapter 4, pages 49–50, for Press Conference.)

Response Journals: In this type of journal, students record short, informal written responses to teacher prompts, text prompts, or student-generated prompts. For example, if a student had read *Murphy Meets the Treadmill* (Ziefert, 2001), he or she might have responded by writing about connections to dogs, the treadmill, or both.

Tickets Out: Students complete Tickets Out at the end of class. The tickets, which are either backlines (see Appendix C) or index cards, are two sided. On side one, students write the most important thing they learned in class. On side two, students write one question they have about what they learned in class. Tickets Out has multiple purposes. It requires students to reflect on what they have learned and raise questions about what was taught. The teacher collects the tickets as students leave the classroom. Next, the teacher reads all the "side ones" first, pulling out any ideas that need to be commented on or discussed further. Then the teacher reads all the "side twos." This time, he or she pulls out questions that are representative of students' concerns. There are typically four to six of these questions. The next day, the teacher begins class by discussing the information gleaned from Tickets Out. This helps the students to understand that the teacher values their ideas and cares about their learning. It also provides a smooth transition into the next day's class.

Informal writing is a mode of expression that informs all stages of the Guided Comprehension Model for English Learners. It is a formative assessment that documents students' thinking and provides evidence of learning.

Strategy applications. Strategy applications are formative assessments that offer insights into students' understanding. For example, Concept of Definition Maps document what students know about a particular term, and retellings demonstrate what students know about using narrative text structure to summarize. Appendix A features an extensive listing of strategy applications that can be used as formative assessments.

Strategy applications are the mainstay of Guided Comprehension. Some applications—such as the Concept of Definition Map (Schwartz & Raphael, 1985), Semantic Question Map (McLaughlin, 2010a, 2010b), Questions Into Paragraphs (E.M. McLaughlin, 1987), and Venn Diagram—include graphic organizers. Detailed descriptions of applications, examples, the steps involved in explicit instruction, and reproducible copies of the graphic organizers can be found in Appendix A.

Teacher observation. Observation is one of the most flexible formative assessments because it can offer information about virtually any aspect of literacy in which students engage. For example, we can observe English learners as they read, write, and discuss. We can also monitor their ability to stay on task when working independently and use observation to assess their fluency, record ideas about their engagement, or comment on their roles during cooperative learning activities.

Before we begin observing, we need to establish a purpose and determine how we will record the information gleaned from this measure. For example, if we are observing a student who is doing an oral retelling, we can use a checklist that includes information such as the characters, setting, problem, attempts to resolve the problem, resolution, and a section for us to record additional comments. In contrast, if we are observing a student's contribution to a cooperative activity, our checklist might include items such as the student's preparation for the group's work, engagement with peers, and contributions to the group. (Reproducible observation guides for comprehension routines can be found in Appendix C, pages 336–338.)

Observation is an informal technique that can be used in all stages of the Guided Comprehension Model for English Learners to gain insights into students' performance and inform our planning of future learning experiences.

What we want to know about our students determines which assessments we use. Therefore, our goal is not to use all these measures to assess each reader but rather to make choices and use the measures that provide the information we need.

The assessments described in this section are practical, can be used for multiple purposes, and offer valuable insights into students' backgrounds and abilities. In addition to these measures, informal assessment opportunities, including strategy applications, are embedded in all stages of the Guided Comprehension Model for English Learners. These formative measures are situated in a variety of instructional settings and provide occasions for students to demonstrate what they know through multiple modes of response, including reading, writing, discussion, sketching, drama, and singing.

Connections to the Common Core State Standards and WIDA English Language Proficiency Standards

We are living in a high-stakes testing environment that has put pressure on students to do well and on teachers to ensure that students demonstrate proficiency. Although the pressure is great, we should resist the temptation to teach to the test and instead focus on providing excellent reading instruction. This, coupled with the knowledge that the single most important influence in student learning is the teacher (Gambrell, Malloy, & Mazzoni, 2007), will produce the desired results. Guided Comprehension offers a sound, research-based foundation for meaningful reading instruction. It focuses on student understanding, explicit strategy instruction, and multiple types and levels of text. It also emphasizes knowledge of text structure and encourages question generation at multiple levels. In addition, Guided Comprehension promotes student writing. When we view reading and writing as inextricable processes, students become more aware of how they think and more adept at sharing their thoughts.

Although the Common Core State Standards (Common Core State Standards Initiative, 2010c) are currently receiving a great deal of attention in the United States, they do not include specific standards or modifications for English learners. The Application of Common Core State Standards for English Language Learners (Common Core State Standards Initiative, 2010b), however, suggests that in order for English learners to meet high academic standards, they should have access to the following:

- Qualified teachers
- Literacy-rich school environments
- Instruction that develops foundational skills
- Meaningful, quality coursework
- Opportunities for classroom discourse and interaction
- Ongoing assessment and feedback to guide learning
- Speakers of English to serve as models and provide support

The World-Class Instructional Design and Assessment (WIDA) Consortium supports academic language development and academic achievement for linguistically diverse students through high academic standards in grades K–12. More than half of the states in the United States have adopted WIDA's English Language Proficiency (ELP) Standards (WIDA, 2007).

The WIDA Consortium has issued a report titled *Alignment Study Between the Common Core State Standards in English Language Arts and Mathematics and the WIDA English Language Proficiency*

Standards, 2007 Edition, PreKindergarten Through Grade 12 (WIDA, 2011). Key findings of the analysis include the following:

- There are strong links between the WIDA Standards and the Common Core State Standards across the majority of grade-level clusters.
- Speaking and Listening domains are strongly linked for all grades.
- The language domains of Reading, Writing, and the language of Mathematics link for the majority of grades.
- The WIDA ELP Standards go beyond current requirements in federal guidance by not only matching but also broadly covering and meeting the cognitive demands of the Common Core State Standards.

(More detailed information about WIDA's ELP Standards is available at www.wida.us/standards/elp.aspx.)

As noted in the WIDA ELP Standards (2007),

> The WIDA ELP Standards served as the prototype for Teachers of English to Speakers of Other Languages (TESOL's) 2006 *Prek-12 English Language Proficiency Standards*, so that is another helpful source to draw upon for classroom assessment, curriculum and instruction. (p. 68)

While WIDA has been striving to align its standards with the Common Core State Standards, the Teachers of English to Speakers of Other Languages (TESOL) have found the Common Core State Standards to be lacking in terms of accommodating English learners. Leaders of that association note the following:

> Information and explanation on implementing the Common Core Standards with English language learners should be incorporated and interwoven throughout the standards so that all teachers understand their implications for this population. This would include discussion on issues such as background knowledge and native-language literacy, time necessary for development and mastery of skills, and under-schooling in native language, and how these would impact English language learners in their progress toward attaining specific standards. (TESOL, 2010, p. 2)

Guided Comprehension Profiles

We use Guided Comprehension Profiles to organize and manage student assessments. These profiles are strategy-based collections of assessments and indicators of student progress. Maintaining the profiles is an active process for both the students and teacher. As our students transact with texts and people in multiple settings in a variety of modes, we collect information to document their progress. Although Guided Comprehension offers numerous opportunities for assessment, there are some measures such as student writing, oral reading fluency, and comprehension that we systematically include. We use the results of these assessments to document student progress, refine guided instruction groups, and inform future instruction.

We store the students' assessments and work samples in pocket folders, and we use a Profile Summary Sheet to organize assessment information. This offers an at-a-glance overview of student progress and facilitates reporting student progress. (A reproducible copy of this organizer is included in Appendix C, page 329.)

In the Guided Comprehension Model for English Learners, assessment is viewed as a natural part of instruction, a dynamic process in which both students and teacher actively participate. In the next chapter, using assessments to create student–text matches is discussed. Reader and text factors that influence our selection of leveled texts are also explained.

CHAPTER 7

Leveled Text: An Essential Resource for Reading Comprehension

If we want English learners to achieve at their maximum potentials, we need to use leveled, accessible, engaging text that is culturally relevant. Providing students with text they *can* read and *want* to read promotes achievement. This implies that students should have access to a rich and varied collection of leveled texts in addition to core programs and classroom libraries.

Leveled texts lead to successful reading and to students who are motivated to read. This type of text is a critical component of reading comprehension instruction. If the text is accessible, students can read it. If the text is leveled, students can read it at their instructional level during teacher-guided small groups or at their independent level when they engage in independent practice. For example, when students are participating in Guided Reading, they can read instructional-level texts with some assistance from the teacher. When students are engaged in independent practice, such as comprehension centers or routines, they can read independent-level texts with no assistance from the teacher. If the text is of interest, students will choose to read it.

The focus of this chapter is the role of text selection in reading comprehension instruction. Student reading levels, student interests, and text selection are the first considerations discussed. Next, the reader and text factors that influence accessibility are shared. Then the rationale for using leveled texts, suggestions for making decisions about the ease or difficulty of text, and ideas for organizing texts are presented.

Student Reading Levels, Student Interests, and Text Selection

When considering which texts to use during Guided Comprehension, it is important to begin by determining the reading levels and interests of our students. There are a number of informal reading assessments that we can use to help determine students' approximate reading abilities. We also use informal measures to learn about students' interests. Details about these assessments and measures can be found in Chapter 6.

Student Reading Levels

When trying to determine reading levels for English learners, we must again focus on ensuring that these students' language abilities do not interfere with their reading of the text. Other critical concerns about the text include that it is accessible, of interest to the reader, and culturally relevant. (A list of culturally relevant titles can be found in Appendix B.) It is also important to remember that some English learners may benefit from reading text in their native language. A number of authors of popular books written in English have published the same titles in Spanish and other languages. Doreen Cronin, Gary Paulsen, Dav Pilkey, and Seymour Simon are just a few of the authors who have published titles in more than one language. (A list of these authors and their publications can be found in Appendix B.)

General guidelines for determining students' reading levels relate to word accuracy, comprehension, and fluency. For *word accuracy*, the text is considered easy if students can read it with 95–100% accuracy, provided the fluency and comprehension are appropriate. The instructional level is reached when students can read most of the text but there are some challenges with words or content. This is usually between 90% and 94% accuracy. Students who read a text below 90% accuracy often struggle with fluency and comprehension because they must use so much of their cognitive focus to figure out unknown words. This is considered a frustration level. At this level, key words are often misunderstood and comprehension is compromised.

In addition to word accuracy, *comprehension* must also be assessed. This often involves determining students' background knowledge as well as their ability to retell or summarize what was read, effectively discuss the text, or predict what will happen next. If a student is unable to successfully complete such tasks, the text may be too difficult.

Fluency, the third factor, is directly related to comprehension. In fact, Rasinski (2010) notes that fluency is the ability to read accurately and expressively at a natural rate with good phrasing and good comprehension. Fluency checks, which can easily be completed during Guided Reading, contribute to our understanding when creating appropriate student–text matches. We can complete fluency checks by asking individual students to whisper read during teacher-guided small groups.

When we assess students' word accuracy, comprehension, and fluency, we gain insights into their reading abilities. Although the results of these informal measures are approximations, they do provide a starting point for making appropriate student–text matches for guided and independent practice.

Student Interests

Student interests are essential considerations when making student–text matches. We can easily learn about students' interests by engaging them in informal conversations or inviting them to complete interest inventories (see Chapter 6 and Appendix C, pages 330 and 331, for examples). When students are reading texts that interest them, they are more motivated to read and generally have more background knowledge about the topic of the text. This makes reading the text easier and more enjoyable for students.

Text Selection

Once we have determined students' reading levels and interests, we can begin considering texts that will contribute to students' reading success. A common way to do this is to use leveled texts, reading materials that begin at a certain level and become progressively difficult (Brabham & Villaume, 2002). The criteria for leveling text may be standards set by well-respected literacy professionals,

Figure 4. Text Levels and the Guided Comprehension Model

Text Level	Teacher Support	Guided Comprehension
Independent	No teacher support needed. (Just right when students are reading on their own and practicing strategy application.)	Stage Three: Independent Centers and Routines
Instructional	Some teacher support needed. (Just right when guiding small groups.)	Stage One: Engaging Prereading Sequence Stage Three: Teacher-Guided Small Groups
Challenging	Full teacher support needed. (Just right when doing teacher read-alouds in whole group.)	Stage Two: Teacher-Directed Whole Groups

Note. Adapted from *Guided Comprehension in the Primary Grades* (2nd ed.) by M. McLaughlin, 2010, Newark, DE: International Reading Association, p. 67.

such as Marie Clay or Irene Fountas and Gay Su Pinnell, or they may involve the use of readability formulas, such as the Fry Readability Graph (1977), which consider length of text, length of sentences, and complexity of vocabulary. Another approach is to level text by considering a variety of text or reader factors. Whichever method is used, leveled text is an essential resource when we create student–text matches.

Students can usually engage with multiple levels of text depending on the setting in which they are reading. For example, when students read on their own, they can read independent-level or "easy" text. At this level, students have familiarity with the genre and content, can read all or most of the words, and can comprehend with no help. When students are reading with the support of a teacher, they can read instructional-level or "just right" text. At this level, students have some familiarity with the content and genre, know most of the words, and can comprehend with some teacher support. Students can also experience independent, instructional, and challenging texts when the teacher reads to them in teacher-directed whole-group instruction or during daily read-alouds. This means that even though students should not read challenging or frustration-level texts on their own, they can experience such texts when we share them through read-alouds or books on CD. Figure 4 illustrates how leveled texts are generally situated in the Guided Comprehension Model for English Learners. It is important to remember that these text levels are approximations and that factors beyond the text influence student accessibility.

Factors That Influence Accessibility

There are several factors that influence the accessibility of a text; some reside in the reader, others are determined by the text. Reader factors include interest and motivation, background knowledge, and sociocultural identities (Dzaldov & Peterson, 2005; Pitcher & Fang, 2007). Text factors include text type and structure, text length, content, vocabulary, language, and literary features (Brabham & Villaume, 2002; Dzaldov & Peterson, 2005; Hadaway & Young, 2010; Rog & Burton, 2001). Considering these factors helps us to make good text selections for reading instruction as well as independent practice.

Reader Factors

Reader factors such as interest and motivation, background knowledge, and sociocultural identities influence text selection. Dzaldov and Peterson (2005) suggest that these factors are as important as text features when making text choices for students. Similarly, Pitcher and Fang (2007) report that knowing students' interests, instructional backgrounds, experiential backgrounds, and sociocultural identities is as important or more important than text features and levels when making good matches between readers and texts.

Interest and motivation. Students who read materials on topics of interest tend to read more, can read more difficult materials, and are more motivated to read (Wigfield & Guthrie, 1997). Reading motivation is influenced by several factors, including content goals, student book choice, social structures for learning, teacher involvement, and rewards (Guthrie et al., 2006). When students are interested, they will work harder at constructing meaning. In addition, student self-efficacy, a student's belief about his or her ability to be successful, is a crucial factor in reading motivation that is connected to interest in reading and amount of time spent reading (Bogner, Raphael, & Pressley, 2002). Student motivation is influenced by students' previous experience with texts. Students who have spent years reading textbook chapters and answering the questions at the end can have negative feelings when asked to read for information. This is also true for students who have had stories so segmented for vocabulary study or detail recall that the major themes and meaning have been lost. Students who have had positive, successful experiences with texts have greater motivation to read and therefore tend to read more, often trying longer or more challenging texts.

Background knowledge. Readers' background knowledge of text content, language, and text type influences accessibility. When students have a great deal of experience with a specific topic or type of text, they have a network of ideas in their minds that allows them to make connections with the new information. This often helps them to make predictions and inferences while reading. They also have knowledge of specific vocabulary and language patterns that helps them to read with meaning at a good pace. This is true for both narrative and informational texts and is influenced by the amount of time spent reading each type.

Sociocultural identities. Social and cultural identities influence students' interests as well as their ability to read and understand texts. When characters and contexts are familiar, students can make connections to the content or story line, and that makes the text easier to read. Dzaldov and Peterson (2005) report that students who are not familiar with certain versions of fairy tales struggle to read and understand these texts, even if the texts are at a lower level than versions more familiar to the students.

Teachers who consider students' social and cultural backgrounds when planning instruction create culturally responsive learning environments in which students feel engaged and successful. Holmes, Powell, Holmes, and Witt (2007) recommend having classroom libraries that represent a variety of culturally relevant texts, which will help English learners to make connections and help all students build awareness of and greater sensitivity toward one another.

Text Factors

When considering students' abilities and interests, it is important to match those with the supports and challenges present in the text. Text features to consider when deciding on appropriateness of a book for English learners include text type and structure, text length, language and literary features, complexity of the content, and uniqueness of the vocabulary (Brabham & Villaume, 2002; Dzaldov & Peterson, 2005; Rog & Burton, 2001). Hadaway and Young (2010) further suggest that the levels of language, content familiarity, vocabulary, textual support, and cultural fit should be considered when selecting texts for English learners.

Text type and structure. Texts are organized in different ways depending on their purpose. Narrative text tells a story and usually includes the basic story elements: characters, setting, problem, attempts to resolve the problem, and resolution. This format is very familiar to students because they have heard and read many stories. This knowledge of the text structure helps students anticipate what might happen next in the story and, consequently, the story is often easier for students to read. On the other hand, informational texts provide facts about a topic. There are five main informational text structures: description, sequence, cause and effect, compare and contrast, and problem and solution (McLaughlin, 2010a). These are often less familiar to students and, consequently, may be more challenging to read. Additionally, the syntax and vocabulary in these texts may be more difficult for students.

Goldman and Rakestraw (2000) have drawn the following three conclusions from existing research on students' knowledge of text structure:

1. Readers use their knowledge of structure in processing text.
2. Knowledge of structural forms of text develops with experience with different genres, and is correlated with age/time in school.
3. Making readers more aware of genre and text structure improves learning.

Text length. As students become more competent readers, they are able to read longer texts. These stories are more complex and may have many characters and multiple story lines. Longer informational texts often include several subtopics and many more facts. Although a long text is not always a more difficult text, length is one factor to consider when thinking about the appropriateness of text for a particular reader. We also need to consider the setting in which the student will be reading. For example, in Guided Reading, which usually lasts only 20 minutes, shorter texts usually work better.

Text content. Text content is a critical factor in text selection because readers must be able to make connections between what they know and what they are reading. This requires that students either have background knowledge about the topic or gain some knowledge about it before they begin reading. For stories, this may include knowledge of how narrative texts work, such as character and plot development, or conflict and resolution. Additionally, much of the story may be told with dialogue between and among characters, making inferential thinking important to understand the plot. In informational texts, content includes the topic and how it is presented. As such texts get more challenging, the information is presented in more detail, with many more complex and abstract concepts. Also, the number of content-specific words generally increases. We must consider the content and how it is presented in the text when trying to determine text level and student accessibility. The size of print, the number or availability of pictures or other visual cues, the range of punctuation, the layout and organization of print, and the number of words per page are also influential factors in this category.

Vocabulary, language structure, and supports. To understand and make meaning from a text, students need to be able to understand most of the words they read. If they come to a word they do not know, they need to be reading with enough understanding to infer the meaning of the unknown word. When there are too many unknown words, students lose the meaning of the text and focus more of their working memory on decoding. As texts become more challenging, the vocabulary usually becomes more complex. For example, there are differences in the types of words students encounter in narrative and informational text. In a narrative text, there may be several difficult words, but they often represent other concepts that the students already understand (Hiebert, 2006). That is not usually true with informational text. Many of the difficult words in informational texts are content-specific words that are critical to understanding. This is also true for English learners. Vocabulary is critical to their success in school (Carlo, August, & Snow, 2005). This is particularly true of academic vocabulary, which is comprised of words that have precise meanings essential to understanding content area text. This often poses greater challenges for English learners than the vocabulary found in stories (Graves, 2006).

Supports, including visuals such as illustrations, photographs, charts, and maps, can help English learners make connections to text. It is important to know whether students have had experience in successfully using such supports.

Considering all these text factors is essential when we choose texts and create student–text matches. Figure 5 features a list of reader factors and text factors as well as prompts we can use to determine the appropriateness of text when making these matches.

Choosing Texts to Promote Student Success

Before making student–text matches, we need to assess our students, be aware of their interests, and ensure that we have a wide range of engaging texts at a variety of levels available for student use. We also need to consider how to organize the texts so students can easily access books at the appropriate levels.

Figure 5. Factors to Consider When Matching Students and Text

Reader Factors	Questions to Consider
Interest and Motivation	• Is the topic of interest to students? • Will students find the text engaging?
Background Knowledge	• Is the story or topic familiar? • What previous experiences with reading and reading instruction have students had? • How much experience have students had with this genre or type of text? • Do students know the vocabulary necessary to construct meaning from this text?
Sociocultural Identities	• Is the text culturally connected to students? • Is the language simple and direct? • Is the vocabulary familiar to students? • Are there illustrations to help students understand the text?

Text Factors	Questions to Consider
Length of Text	• Do students have the stamina to read this text? • Will students be able to maintain interest in this text?
Text Type and Structure	• Are students familiar with this type of text? • How much experience have students had reading this type of text? • Do students understand the structure of this text? Can they use the structure to help set a purpose or understand what they read?
Page Layout	• Do students know how to use pictures and other visual cues to help them read and understand? • Is the text considerate toward the students? Is it appropriate for their developmental and achievement levels?
Text Content	• How much background knowledge do students have about this topic? • How much experience do they have with this content? • How familiar are the students with the language patterns and vocabulary used in this text? • Are students familiar with the format in which the content is presented?
Vocabulary and Literary Features	• Are there many difficult words in this text? • Do students have the background knowledge to infer the meanings of many of the words? • Do students have enough knowledge of language to make inferences and understand the subtle messages in the text? • Do students understand the use of literary devices and how authors use them to tell the story?

Note. Reprinted from *Guided Comprehension in the Primary Grades* (2nd ed.) by M. McLaughlin, 2010, Newark, DE: International Reading Association, p. 71.

Student Information

Before planning meaningful Guided Comprehension instruction, we need to determine each student's independent and instructional level and gather information about his or her interests and background. We use this information for three purposes: to form teacher-guided small groups, to provide appropriate text for students to read when working in the comprehension-based centers and routines, and to inform text selection for teacher-directed whole-group instruction. Miscue analysis (Goodman, 1997), which we can use to assess students' oral reading and comprehension, is a viable source of this information. There are also several commercially prepared assessment tools that allow teachers to assess students' reading levels, fluency, and comprehension. (For further discussion of a variety of these assessments, see Chapter 6.)

Hunt (1996) suggests that students also contribute to determining text accessibility. He recommends that students engage in self-evaluation during independent reading by responding to questions such as the following:

- Did you have a good reading class today?
- Were you able to concentrate as you read independently?
- Did the ideas in the book hold your attention?
- Were you bothered by others or outside noises?
- Could you keep the ideas in the book straight in your mind?
- Did you get mixed up in any place? Were you able to fix it?
- Were there words you did not know? How did you figure them out?
- Were you hoping the book would end, or were you hoping it would go on and on?

Although these questions require only yes or no responses, they do provide insights into students' perceptions of their performance. Other ways to gather similar information include holding individual student–teacher conferences and using informal measures such as quick writes and Tickets Out (see Appendix C, page 343).

We also need to gather data about student experiences and interests. As noted earlier, this can be accomplished through interviews, observations, or interest inventories. (See Chapter 6 for a more complete discussion of diagnostic measures.)

Text Information

Once we have the appropriate information about our students, we need to consider what texts we will use. We use the following steps to facilitate this process:

1. *Identify the texts available in the classroom*: These may include but not be limited to core programs, anthologies, trade books, textbooks, magazines, newspapers, online text, poetry books, and picture books.
2. *Organize the texts to facilitate Guided Comprehension*: We use the following questions to accomplish this:
   - Does this text add to existing content area study or knowledge?

- Can this text be used in a genre study?
- Does this text exemplify a particular style, structure, language pattern, or literary device?
- Can this text be used to teach a comprehension strategy?
- Are there multiple copies of the text available?
- Does this text match a particular student's interests?
- Is this a good example of a text structure?
- Is this text part of a series?
- Is it written by a favorite author?

These questions can be used with both narrative and informational texts. This includes individual stories in literature anthologies, as well as individual articles within magazines.

3. *Acquire additional materials to ensure ample accessible texts for all readers*: It is important to have some sets of books to use during teacher-guided small groups, but it is also necessary to have a wide array of texts varying in type, genre, length, content, and level. All students should have a multitude of accessible books within the classroom, including picture books, informational texts, poetry books, and magazines. We keep in mind the following ideas when adding to classroom collections:

- Content areas—informational and narrative texts to supplement studies in math, science, and social studies
- Student interests—a variety of texts (narrative, informational, poetry) about diverse topics to match students' interests
- Read-aloud—texts that offer examples of a variety of text structures and engaging story lines to be used to demonstrate comprehension processes and fluency
- Anchor books—texts used in whole-group and small-group instruction to demonstrate a specific strategy or routine
- Sets of books—four to six copies of the same title to be used in Guided Comprehension teacher-guided small groups; these should be based on students' levels and interests, as well as the strategies that can be taught using them
- Text sets—series books, favorite author, genre, topic; several books that have a common characteristic

Once we have accumulated the texts, we need to organize them to accommodate all stages of the Guided Comprehension Model.

Methods for Leveling Texts

All text levels are approximations, and there is no specific rule for determining them. Text ease or difficulty is determined by both text and reader factors. Each text will need to be evaluated with specific readers in mind. Leveling systems, teacher judgment, paralleling books, and using leveled lists developed by others facilitate this process.

Leveling Systems

Several systems exist that will help determine the approximate level of a text. These take into consideration factors such as format, language structure, and content (Weaver, 2000). The following are examples of these formulas: the Fry Readability Index (Fry, 1977), Lexile Framework for Reading Book Database (www.lexile.com), and Scholastic's Teacher Book Wizard (www.scholastic.com/bookwizard). The Fry Readability Index takes into consideration sentence length and number of syllables for three random 100-word selections within a text. These two numbers are plotted on a graph and an approximate reading level is provided for each selection. The Lexile Framework for Reading Book Database has thousands of books leveled using the Lexile leveling system. This system takes into consideration word frequency and sentence length. The higher the Lexile score, the more difficult the text is related to those two features. Scholastic's Teacher Book Wizard allows teachers to enter a book title and find an approximate level based on the leveling system. In addition, you can enter a book title and find other books that have similar levels. Leveling systems provide helpful information about the ease or difficulty of a text and also help to find books that may be similar in level. For examples of books from these websites and other website resources for leveled texts, see Appendix D.

Teacher Judgment

Although these leveling systems provide a starting point, teacher judgment may be the method used most frequently in leveling texts for English learners. When we engage in leveling, it is important to identify reader factors, such as familiarity with content or genre, as well as motivation to read, when trying to match a text with a reader.

We often use the following processes for leveling texts:

- Separate books into narrative, informational, and poetry.
- For each type of book, divide the books into harder and easier.
- Take each pile of books and sort by hardest to easiest (repeat this process as necessary).
- Label or color-code levels for student access.

Although these methods do not provide exact text levels, they do allow us to organize our books by type and by degree of difficulty. This information is very helpful when teaching students to select texts, or for us to guide students in that selection process.

Paralleling Books

Another way to level texts is to match classroom books with published leveled texts that have similar text features, such as length, font size, number of illustrations, and genre. This process, called paralleling books, provides a format for informally identifying approximate levels of existing classroom materials. Appendix D has lists of model books that represent approximate levels.

Published Lists and Websites for Leveled Books

Many publishers provide lists of leveled titles that we can use in creating student–text matches and in all stages of Guided Comprehension. We can use these lists as resources for identifying anchor books as well as for assessment purposes. Many of these sets of leveled books, which include narrative and informational texts, are available for purchase. Examples of companies that publish leveled books in English or Spanish for English learners include Benchmark, Heinemann, Houghton Mifflin Harcourt, and Pearson. More detailed information about these products can be found in Appendix D.

Classroom Text Organization

Once we have leveled our classroom collections, our goal is to organize the texts efficiently to promote their optimum use. This includes texts for use in whole-group and small-group teaching, as well as texts for students to use during comprehension centers and routines. To facilitate accessing texts for our teaching, Harvey and Goudvis (2000) suggest accumulating a master list of titles and organizing them according to what they have to offer as teaching models. Approaches to such organization include listing books by strategy to be modeled, by book title, by genre and level, and by topic and level.

To provide accessible texts for student-facilitated comprehension centers and routines, we use the following methods of organization:

- *Class book baskets*: Creating book baskets by author, series, content, or approximate reading level is one method. With our help, students can then make selections from a whole collection of books in the basket.
- *Individual book baskets*: We can also help students to create individual book baskets in which they keep an ongoing collection of books they want to read. This eliminates any "down time" when students need to select a text for independent reading.
- *Individual student booklists*: Students keep these lists in the back of their Guided Comprehension Journals. Titles can be added to the list in an ongoing manner to accommodate student progress. This often happens when students share ideas from their reading in Stage Four of the Guided Comprehension Model for English Learners or when we share book talks of new and favorite books.

To further facilitate text organization, Szymusiak and Sibberson (2001) recommend that books in classroom collections be placed face out so that readers can easily see the covers and preview the texts, and that sections for fiction, nonfiction, and poetry be marked clearly.

The two most important factors in matching students with appropriate texts are students' reading levels and interests. We can determine students' range of approximate reading levels by using informal assessments. Additionally, we can learn much about students' interests through simple inventories. This information helps us to create meaningful matches between students and texts.

PART TWO

Theme-Based Guided Comprehension Lessons for English Learners

Focus: Situating Guided Comprehension in a variety of themes.

Theme Overviews: The planning graphic that appears at the start of each theme is based on Wiggins and McTighe's (2008) belief that we should begin the planning process by identifying the desired results. In this case, the desired results are expressed as the theme's goals and resulting connections to the Common Core State Standards. The next step is determining acceptable evidences; these are listed as assessments on the graphic. The final step is planning learning experiences and instruction. These are represented by the texts, comprehension strategies, teaching ideas, and instructional settings such as comprehension centers and routines. Website resources complete the plan.

Themes: Four Guided Comprehension lessons are provided for each theme. The lessons were written and taught by classroom teachers whose students include English learners. You will notice a change in voice as each teacher speaks about his or her classroom teaching experience. The Guided Comprehension Lesson Overviews are plans these teachers wrote for their lessons. The lessons focus on a variety of comprehension skills and strategies and multiple types and levels of theme-related texts. The lessons also include multiple modes of representation and critical and creative thinking. Theme-based resources including related texts and websites, suggestions for performance extensions across the curriculum, and a culminating activity follow each set of lessons. The chart at right presents an overview of the themes, including the comprehension strategies and teaching ideas that are embedded in each lesson.

Theme Topics, Strategies, and Strategy Applications

Chapter 8: Animals of the Past...Animals of the Present
Previewing: Semantic Question Map
Summarizing: Lyric Summary/Lyric Retelling
Knowing How Words Work: Concept of Definition Map
Monitoring: Say Something

Chapter 9: Favorite Authors: Eve Bunting, Doreen Cronin, Gary Paulsen, and Gary Soto
Visualizing: Draw and Write Visualizations
Making Connections: Connection Stems
Summarizing: Draw and Write Retellings
Evaluating: Evaluative Questions

Chapter 10: Biographies: The Stories of Our Lives
Monitoring: Patterned Partner Reading
Self-Questioning: Thick and Thin Questions
Making Connections: Double-Entry Journal
Summarizing: Questions Into Paragraphs (QuIP)

CHAPTER 8

Animals of the Past...Animals of the Present

Whether we are thinking about extinct dinosaurs that roamed the earth millions of years ago or creatures that exist today, animals fascinate us. Although dinosaurs ceased to exist 65 million years ago, we are still learning about them today. Every time dinosaur fossils are unearthed, it is a time of discovery. This often leads to revelations about new kinds of dinosaurs, which captures the interest and imaginations of children and adults alike. We are equally fascinated by animals that exist today. It seems to be the nature of the animal—its appearance, its habitat, and its behavior—that keeps us engaged. In this Guided Comprehension theme, we meet all different kinds of animals from dinosaurs to polar bears, wolves, bats, and sea turtles.

The animals theme was of particular interest to English learners in the classes in which these lessons were taught. The teachers held high expectations for the students throughout the lessons, and their hopes were fulfilled. The teachers created culturally responsive classrooms in which diversity was appreciated by all. They valued all students' cultural heritages and used that information to support teaching and learning in an educational community. They also used the Guided Comprehension Model for English Learners, a structured lesson format, and appropriate supports, including visuals and adapted graphic organizers, to teach.

In conversations held during the Engaging Prereading Sequence, it was clear that these English learners had background knowledge about a variety of animals and that they were comfortable discussing the topic in this small-group setting. The teachers were particularly attentive to motivating students, activating background knowledge, and sharing engaging read-alouds. During the Engaging Prereading Sequence, students actively participated as the teachers engaged them with interesting, accessible text; provided meaningful visual supports; invited students to respond in multiple modes (speaking, writing, sketching, dramatizing, and singing); provided sufficient wait time when questions were raised; taught essential vocabulary in context; and explicitly taught reading comprehension strategies.

When the English learners moved on to whole-group instruction, they were comfortable, well prepared, and eager to participate. In this setting, opportunities to work with partners and multiple modes of response were prevalent throughout explicit instruction. The comprehension strategy focus was the same one they learned to use during the Engaging Prereading Sequence, so they were already familiar with it. In addition, these lessons occasionally focused on the teaching of reading skills. A prime example of this focused on teaching students how to generate and respond to questions at multiple levels (see Chapter 3, page 22). Text supports and wait time were provided, and students were actively engaged. In teacher-guided small-group instruction, students often had the opportunity to read text with a partner or on their own. They engaged in discussion and practiced using comprehension skills and strategies. Students were also able to represent their thinking in multiple ways.

In Guided Comprehension centers and routines, English learners partnered with native language speakers or native English speakers, depending on the nature of the activity. For example, when reading theme-related texts in their native language to support their understanding in the theme center, they worked with native language speakers. Conversely, when engaging in activities at the fluency center, the students would typically work with native English speakers. In addition, culturally relevant texts, including titles published in native languages, were available in the centers. In these settings, multiple opportunities were provided for students to interact with text to make content more comprehensible.

The sample Theme-Based Plan for Guided Comprehension: Animals of the Past...Animals of the Present (see Figure 6) offers an overview of the thinking and resources that support the theme. It makes connections to the Common Core State Standards (CCSS; Common Core State Standards Initiative, 2010c) and presents a sampling of assessments, texts, technology resources, comprehension strategies, teaching ideas, comprehension centers, and comprehension routines. The plan begins by delineating examples of student goals and related Common Core College and Career Readiness Anchor Standards for Reading, Writing, Speaking and Listening, and Language. The student goals for this theme include the following:

- Use appropriate comprehension skills and strategies
- Interpret and respond to text in a variety of ways
- Write a variety of types of text
- Communicate effectively

The CCSS for English Language Arts (Common Core State Standards Initiative, 2010c) delineate grade-level expectations in reading, writing, speaking, and listening. Their purpose is to prepare all students to be college and career ready. This includes English learners.

The CCSS (Common Core State Standards Initiative, 2010c, p. 7) suggest that students who are college and career ready

- Demonstrate independence
- Build strong content knowledge
- Respond to the varying demands of audience, task, purpose, and discipline
- Comprehend as well as critique
- Value evidence
- Use technology and digital media strategically and capably
- Understand other perspectives and cultures

In this theme, the lessons are aligned with the Common Core College and Career Readiness Anchor Standards for Reading, Writing, Speaking and Listening, and Language. The key features of these standards include the following (Common Core State Standards Initiative, 2010c, p. 8):

Figure 6. Theme-Based Plan for Guided Comprehension: Animals of the Past...Animals of the Present

Goals and Common Core College and Career Readiness Anchor Standards for Reading, Writing, Speaking and Listening, and Language

Students will

- Use appropriate comprehension skills and strategies
- Interpret and respond to text
- Write a variety of types of text
- Communicate effectively

For related College and Career Readiness Standards and Common Core State Standards, see pages 94–97.

Assessment

The following measures can be used for a variety of purposes, including diagnostic, formative, and summative assessment:

Concept of Definition Map
Lyric Summary
Observation
Retelling
Running Records
Say Something
Semantic Question Map
Student Writing

Text

1. *The Encyclopedia of Awesome Dinosaurs* (Benton, 2000) and *The Ultimate Dino-pedia: The Most Complete Dinosaur Reference Ever* (Lessem, 2010)
2. *The Ultimate Book of Dinosaurs: Everything You Always Wanted to Know About Dinosaurs—But Were Too Terrified to Ask* (Dowswell, Malam, Mason, & Parker, 2002)
3. *Do Penguins Get Frostbite? Questions and Answers About Polar Animals* (Berger & Berger, 2000)
4. *Bats* (Gibbons, 2000)

Technology Resources

Dinorama
magma.nationalgeographic.com/ngexplorer/0203/adventures/
Zoom Dinosaurs
www.enchantedlearning.com/subjects/dinosaurs/toc.shtml
Animal Planet: Dolphins Explored
animal.discovery.com/features/dolphins/facts/facts.html

Comprehension Strategies

1. Previewing
2. Summarizing
3. Knowing How Words Work
4. Monitoring

Teaching Ideas

1. Semantic Question Map
2. Lyric Summary/Lyric Retelling
3. Concept of Definition Map
4. Say Something

Comprehension Centers

Students will apply the comprehension strategies and related teaching ideas in the following comprehension centers:

Art Center
Fluency Center
Making Books Center
Poetry Center
Project Center
Question and Answer Center
Theme Center
Vocabulary Center
Writing Center

Comprehension Routines

Students will apply the comprehension strategies and related teaching ideas in the following comprehension routines:

Literature Circles
Reciprocal Teaching
Cross-Age Reading Experiences

- Reading: Text complexity and the growth of comprehension
- Writing: Text types, responding to reading, and research
- Speaking and Listening: Flexible communication and collaboration
- Language: Conventions, effective use, and vocabulary

The Common Core State Standards addressed in this theme follow. These standards are directly related to the College and Career Readiness Anchor Standards for Reading, Writing, Speaking and Listening, and Language. (For a complete listing of the Common Core State Standards for English Language Arts, see www.corestandards.org/assets/CCSSI_ELA%20Standards.pdf.)

College and Career Readiness Standards for Reading

The categories of the College and Career Readiness Anchor Standards for Reading featured in these lessons include the following:

- Key Ideas and Details
- Craft and Structure
- Integration of Knowledge and Ideas
- Range of Reading and Level of Text Complexity

Key Ideas and Details

Examples of CCSS for Reading that support the anchor standards in this category include the following:

- Ask and answer questions to demonstrate understanding of a text, referring explicitly to the text as the basis for the answers
- Refer to details and examples in a text when explaining what the text says explicitly and when drawing inferences from the text
- Determine two or more main ideas of a text and explain how they are supported by key details; summarize the text
- Cite the textual evidence that most strongly supports an analysis of what the text says explicitly as well as inferences drawn from the text

Craft and Structure

Examples of CCSS for Reading that support the anchor standards in this category include the following:

- Read with sufficient accuracy and fluency to support comprehension
- Determine the meaning of general academic and domain-specific words or phrases in a text relevant to a topic or subject area
- Compare and contrast the overall structure (e.g., chronology, comparison, cause/effect, problem/solution) of events, ideas, concepts, or information in two or more texts

Integration of Knowledge and Ideas

Examples of CCSS for Reading that support the anchor standards in this category include the following:

- Draw on information from multiple print or digital sources, demonstrating the ability to locate an answer to a question quickly or to solve a problem efficiently
- Integrate information from several texts on the same topic in order to write or speak about the subject knowledgeably
- Evaluate the advantages and disadvantages of using different mediums (e.g., print or digital text, video, multimedia) to present a particular topic or idea

Range of Reading and Level of Text Complexity

Examples of CCSS for Reading that support the anchor standards in this category include the following:

- By the end of the year, read and comprehend informational texts at the high end of the grade-level text complexity band independently and proficiently

College and Career Readiness Standards for Writing

The categories of the College and Career Readiness Anchor Standards for Writing featured in these lessons include the following:

- Text Types and Purposes
- Production and Distribution of Writing
- Research to Build and Present Knowledge
- Range of Writing

Text Types and Purposes

Examples of CCSS for Writing that support the anchor standards in this category include the following:

- Write opinion pieces on topics or texts, supporting a point of view with reasons and information
- Write informative/explanatory texts to examine a topic and convey ideas and information clearly
- Write narratives to develop real or imagined experiences or events using effective technique, descriptive details, and clear event sequences

Production and Distribution of Writing

Examples of CCSS for Writing that support the anchor standards in this category include the following:

- Produce clear and coherent writing in which the development and organization are appropriate to task, purpose, and audience
- With guidance and support from peers and adults, develop and strengthen writing as needed by planning, revising, editing, rewriting, or trying a new approach
- With some guidance and support from adults, use technology, including the Internet, to produce and publish writing as well as to interact and collaborate with others
- Use technology, including the Internet, to produce and publish writing and present the relationships between information and ideas efficiently as well as to interact and collaborate with others

Research to Build and Present Knowledge

Examples of CCSS for Writing that support the anchor standards in this category include the following:

- Conduct short as well as more sustained research projects based on focused questions, demonstrating understanding of the subject under investigation

Range of Writing

Examples of CCSS for Writing that support the anchor standards in this category include the following:

- Write routinely over extended time frames (time for research, reflection, and revision) and shorter time frames (a single sitting or a day or two) for a range of discipline-specific tasks, purposes, and audiences

College and Career Readiness Anchor Standards for Speaking and Listening

The categories of the College and Career Readiness Anchor Standards for Speaking and Listening featured in these lessons include the following:

- Comprehension and Collaboration
- Presentation of Knowledge and Ideas

Comprehension and Collaboration

Examples of CCSS for Speaking and Listening that support the anchor standards in this category include the following:

- Engage effectively in a range of collaborative discussions (one-on-one, group, and teacher-led) with diverse partners on grade-appropriate topics and texts, building on others' ideas and expressing their own clearly

Presentation of Knowledge and Ideas

Examples of CCSS for Speaking and Listening that support the anchor standards in this category include the following:

- Report on a topic or text or present an opinion, sequencing ideas logically and using appropriate facts and relevant, descriptive details to support main ideas or themes; speak clearly at an understandable pace
- Include multimedia components (e.g., graphics, sound) and visual displays in presentations when appropriate to enhance the development of main ideas or themes
- Integrate multimedia and visual displays into presentations to clarify information, strengthen claims and evidence, and add interest

College and Career Readiness Anchor Standards for Language

The categories of the College and Career Readiness Anchor Standards for Language featured in these lessons include the following:

- Conventions of Standard English
- Knowledge of Language
- Vocabulary Acquisition and Use

Conventions of Standard English

Examples of CCSS for Language that support the anchor standards in this category include the following:

- Demonstrate command of the conventions of standard English grammar and usage when writing or speaking

Knowledge of Language

Examples of CCSS for Language that support the anchor standards in this category include the following:

- Use knowledge of language and its conventions when writing, speaking, reading, or listening

Vocabulary Acquisition and Use

Examples of CCSS for Language that support the anchor standards in this category include the following:

- Determine or clarify the meaning of unknown and multiple-meaning words and phrases based on grade-level reading and content, choosing flexibly from a range of strategies

Examples of assessments used in the theme-based Guided Comprehension lessons include observation, running records and retellings, skill and strategy applications, and other formative assessments. The Guided Comprehension lessons, which were designed and taught by classroom teachers, are based on the following strategies and corresponding teaching ideas:

- Previewing: Semantic Question Map
- Summarizing: Lyric Summary/Lyric Retelling
- Knowing How Words Work: Concept of Definition Map
- Monitoring: Say Something

The texts used in teacher-directed whole-group instruction include *The Encyclopedia of Awesome Dinosaurs* (Benton, 2000), *The Ultimate Dino-pedia: The Most Complete Dinosaur Reference Ever* (Lessem, 2010), *The Ultimate Book of Dinosaurs: Everything You Always Wanted to Know About Dinosaurs—But Were Too Terrified to Ask* (Dowswell, Malam, Mason, & Parker, 2002), *Do Penguins Get Frostbite? Questions and Answers About Polar Animals* (Berger & Berger, 2000), and *Bats* (Gibbons, 2000).

Numerous additional theme-related resources—including texts, websites, performance extensions across the curriculum, and a culminating activity—are presented in the Theme Resources at the end of the chapter.

In this theme, students' independent strategy applications occur in the comprehension centers and comprehension routines. The centers include art, fluency, making books, poetry, project, question and answer, theme, vocabulary, and writing. The routines include Literature Circles, Reciprocal Teaching, and Cross-Age Reading Experiences. Sample websites complete the overview.

The four Guided Comprehension lessons that follow are presented through first-person teacher commentaries. Examples of student work are featured throughout the lessons.

Guided Comprehension Lessons

Animals of the Past...Animals of the Present
Guided Comprehension Strategy: Previewing
Teaching Idea: Semantic Question Map

STAGE ONE: Engaging Prereading Sequence for English Learners

We began our Engaging Prereading Sequence by meeting in a sitting area I had created for our conversations. I had previously met with the students in this small group to explain what the Engaging Prereading Sequence was and what we would be doing when we met. I had told them that we would be having a conversation that would help them to take an active role in our reading when the class met in whole group. I had explained that we would be talking about some topics they already knew about and some that may be new to them. I told them that we would be talking about background knowledge and how to activate it. I also noted that we would be using the ideas we discussed later in whole group.

When we began our conversation, I reminded the students our topic today would be dinosaurs. I shared photos and other information about dinosaurs. I also read short segments about dinosaurs from DinoDatabase at www.dinodatabase.com/dinothry.asp and from paleobiology .si.edu/dinosaurs, a site maintained by the Smithsonian Institution National Museum of Natural History. I noticed the students' faces were beaming as we talked about the prehistoric animals. I could tell that they were highly motivated and that they had background knowledge about dinosaurs. As our discussion of dinosaurs progressed, I invited the students to sketch a dinosaur, write a fact about it, and then tell a partner about it. (Alejandro's sketch of and facts about a T-rex appear in Figure 7.) This activity was very successful, and the descriptions further affirmed the students' background knowledge of the animals.

After that, I asked the students if they knew where any of the dinosaurs had lived. After taking a few moments to think, most of the students thought the answer was *everywhere*. I brought up the United States Geological Survey website (pubs.usgs.gov/gip/dinosaurs/where.html) and showed the students that they were all exactly right. A lot of fossils—remains of ancient animals and plants—have been found recently in China and the United States, but when dinosaurs came into existence nearly 230 million years ago, they were everywhere. I also explained that when the dinosaurs first came into existence, all of the world's land masses were joined together in one C-shaped land named Pangaea. The students were fascinated by this information. Samuel, a student from Senegal, said, "So, the land of Senegal and the land of the United States were once joined together?" I explained that was correct, because all the land masses were joined together millions of years ago. Next, we took a few moments to study graphics on the website that showed how the land masses separated over time. Then we looked at a globe. We located all of our families' homelands and noted that not only had they all been homes to dinosaurs but they also had all been joined together long ago.

Next, I focused on the word *prehistoric*, because I knew it appeared in the book we would be reading in our whole-group setting. I began by showing *prehistoric* in a paragraph about dinosaurs. I wanted to discuss it in context. The sentence said, "Dinosaurs were prehistoric animals." I asked the students to think about the word and talk to a partner about what the word might mean. Then the

Guided Comprehension: Animals of the Past...Animals of the Present
Previewing: Semantic Question Map

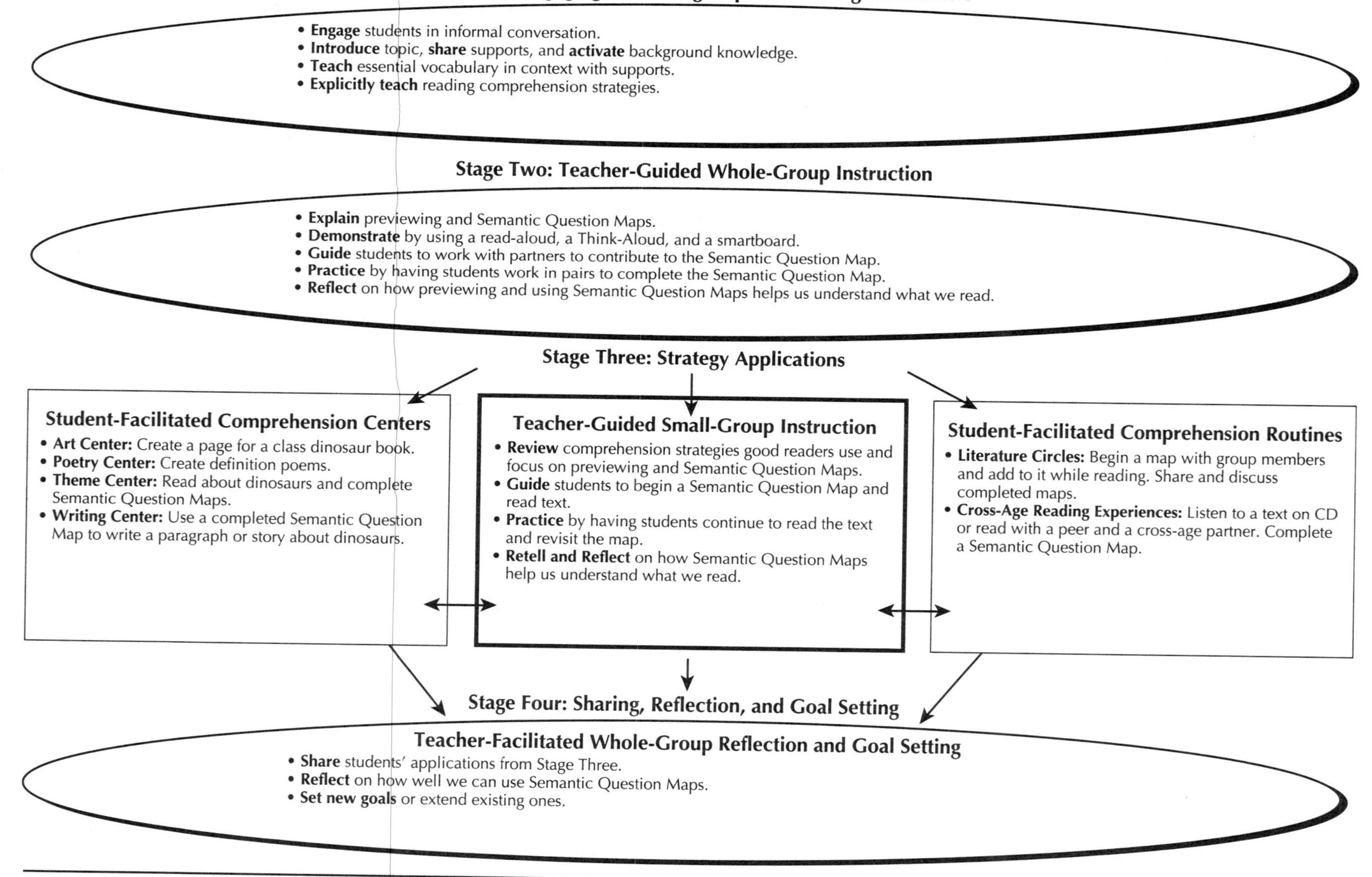

Figure 7. Alejandro's Sketch of and Facts About a T-Rex

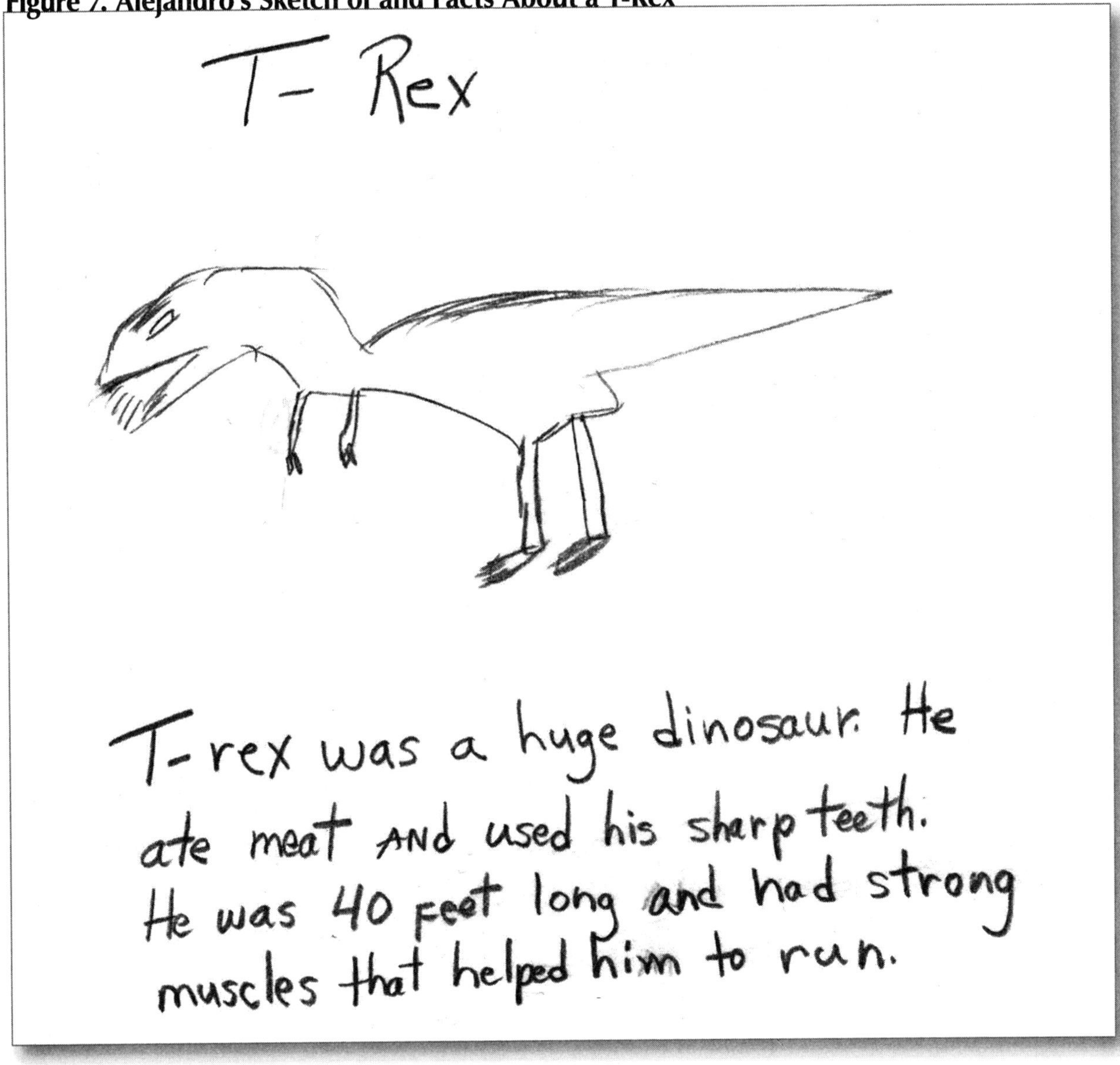

students shared their thinking. Basically, they thought it meant dinosaurs were from long ago. I told them that was true, but we could probably learn more about that word.

I made connections to cultures—mine and the students'—and talked about family histories. Then I moved on to discussing histories of countries. After that, I asked the students to talk to their partners about what they thought a *history* was. I was careful to provide sufficient time for students to think before they began sharing. Then I listened carefully as the students talked. I was pleased to note that several ideas focused on a similar meaning. Stephano said, "A history is like a story. My family history is the story of me and my family." Other students extended similar ideas to their countries and their cultures. I concluded the discussion by asking volunteers to share their thoughts. Everyone participated. Next, I explained the meaning of *pre*. Our class had been studying prefixes, and *pre* already appeared on our "Prefix, Root, and Suffix Wall." I said,

> You will remember that *pre* means "before." Our Engaging Prereading Sequence happens *before* we meet for teaching in whole group. If you have a 3- or 4-year-old brother or sister, he or she may go to *preschool*. That means that because they are so young, they go to another school *before* they go to kindergarten. You may also hear on television that some news has happened in the *predawn* hours. That means it happened during the night—*before* dawn, before the sun came up. So, when we hear the word *prehistoric*, what do you think that means?

After providing a few moments for students to think, I invited them to share their ideas with a partner. Shortly thereafter, I began inviting students to share their ideas with the small group. Ideas the students shared included, "Before there was history" and "Before people wrote a story about what was going on." I concluded this section of the discussion by noting that dinosaurs were prehistoric animals. Maria commented, "They were here a really long time ago—before there was a history." Everyone agreed, and several of the students asked exactly how long ago the dinosaurs were on Earth. We did a quick Internet search to answer that question, and I noted that we would learn more about that in whole group.

Next, I turned our conversation back to the types of dinosaurs and what we might want to know about them. I followed this by engaging in explicit instruction about the Semantic Question Map.

Explain: I began by adapting Marie Clay's Book Introduction (see Appendix A, page 232) to information from websites. I chose to use text from websites because the English learners in my class seemed to find it highly motivational. I shared the title of each site and used visual aids as I guided students through a few selected links. I also reminded the students about the meaning of *prehistoric*, which appeared in the text, and that dinosaur names have special meanings. I pointed out that *saurus* means "lizard" and that *brachio-*, *stego-*, and *tyranna-* each had a different meaning: *Brachiosaurus* means "arm lizard," *stegosaurus* means "plated lizard," and *tyrannosaurus* means "tyrant lizard." We stopped to look at pictures of these dinosaurs, talked about why the dinosaurs may have been given those names, and posted the names and pictures on our dinosaur wall.

Then I explained previewing and used a Think-Aloud to demonstrate how the Semantic Question Map works. I shared the graphic organizer for the Semantic Question Map and pointed to a completed Semantic Map on the smartboard. I said, "The Semantic Question Map is like the Semantic Map we use because it has a focus word and we need to think about ideas to complete it. It is different from the Semantic Map because the Semantic Question Map has four questions that we need to answer." Then I noted that we would have only two questions on our Semantic Question Map and that they would be numbered.

Demonstrate: Next, I shared the Semantic Question Map about dinosaurs with the students. I thought aloud and said, "Question one is asking about different kinds of dinosaurs. I know *Tyrannosaurus rex* is a type of dinosaur, so I will write that on our map." Following that, I invited students to add some dinosaurs to our list. They suggested *triceratops* and *stegosaurus*. We discussed the additional dinosaurs.

Guide: Then I thought aloud about question two. I said, "Question two is asking what dinosaurs ate. I think the answer was included in the short segment I just read. Let's take a moment to think about that." Then Maria said, "I remember! Dinosaurs ate plants." Alberto said, "They ate meat, too." Everyone agreed.

Practice: When we had completed the two questions on our map, I prompted the students and we quickly summarized everything we had discussed about the prehistoric creatures we call

Figure 8. Semantic Question Map: Dinosaurs

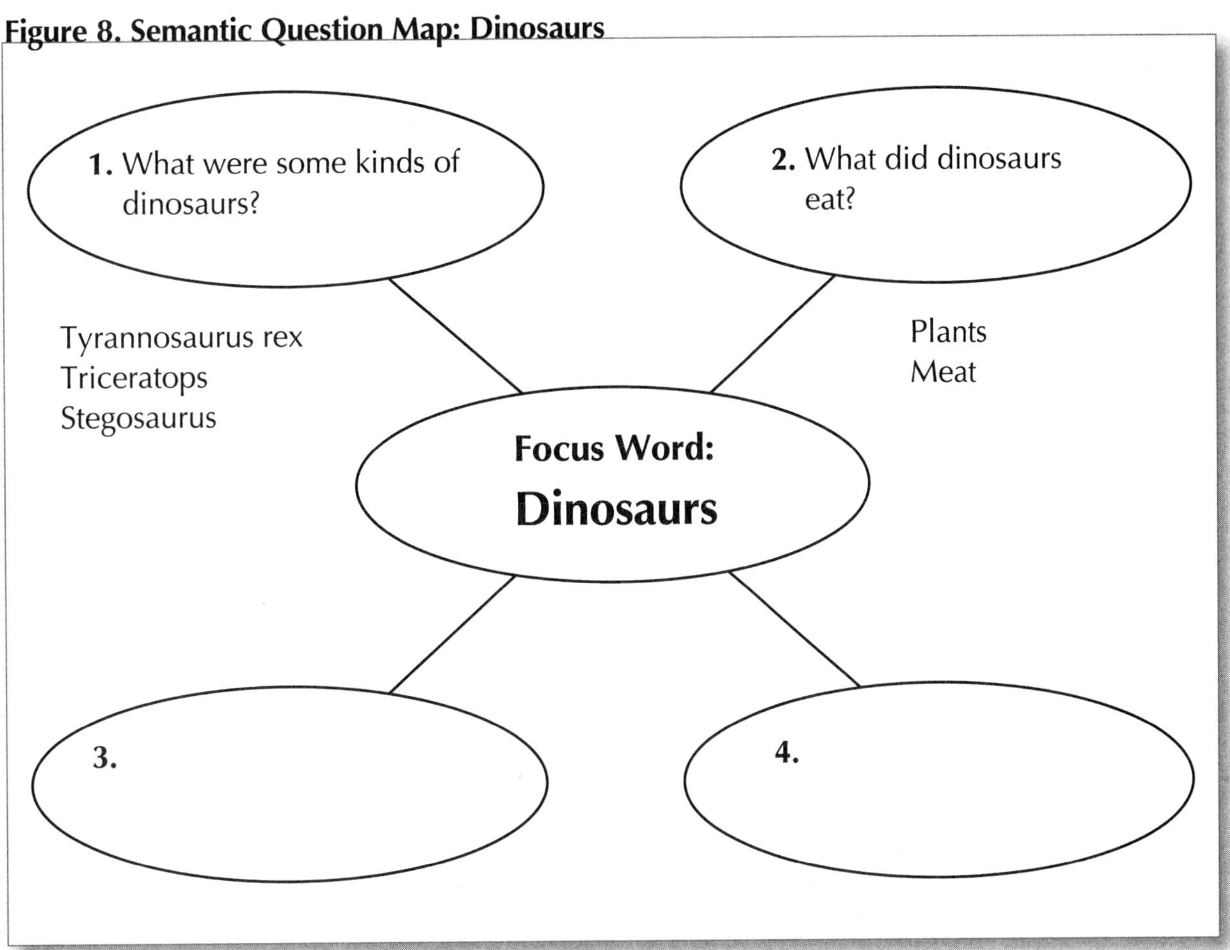

dinosaurs. (Figure 8 features the Semantic Question Map, including the English learners' questions "What were some types of dinosaurs?" and "What did dinosaurs eat?") The English learners were highly motivated, their background knowledge was activated, they had learned additional information about dinosaurs, and they knew what a Semantic Question Map was and how it worked. Then we moved into Stage Two, the whole-group setting.

STAGE TWO: Teacher-Directed Whole-Group Instruction

Texts: *The Encyclopedia of Awesome Dinosaurs* (Benton, 2000); *The Ultimate Dino-pedia: The Most Complete Dinosaur Reference Ever* (Lessem, 2010)

Explain: I began by explaining previewing. Next, I focused on previewing and how using Semantic Question Maps can help us to organize and learn information about focus words.

Demonstrate: I demonstrated by using a read-aloud, a Think-Aloud, and showing a Semantic Question Map on the smartboard. I introduced the texts by reading the titles and explaining that they were books that provided a lot of information about dinosaurs. I showed the covers of the books, explained how they were structured, and shared several chapter topics. Then the students and I discussed the types of information we would find in the books. After that, I approached the Semantic Question Map (see Appendix A, page 280). There was a centered oval for the focus word and webbed question categories, including *How did it look? How long and tall was it? How much did it weigh? How did it move?* and *What did it eat?* I said, "I will write *brachiosaurus* inside the oval because that is the focus word for this Semantic Question Map." Then I said, "Now I need to think about what I already know about brachiosauruses." I read question one, *How did it look?* and I said, "I think that brachiosauruses had long necks, so I will write *long neck* underneath this category." Then I thought aloud about what I knew about each of the remaining questions and wrote the following underneath each one: *tall, heavy, very slowly,* and *plants.* I explained to the students that I would read information about the brachiosaurus from the text and revisit the Semantic Question Map to verify or revise the ideas I had written on the map and to include additional information we might learn from the text. Then I read aloud the segment of text. When I finished, I returned to the Semantic Question Map and noted that the information I had included on the map was correct. Then I reviewed each question to see if I had new information to add. I was careful to refer to the questions by number so the students could locate them easily. The students worked with partners to contribute suggestions based on the reading.

Guide: I guided pairs of students to think about the questions on our Semantic Question Map as they listened to me read aloud more information about brachiosauruses from the texts. These segments of text provided more detailed information, so when I asked the pairs of students what they would like to add to our Semantic Question Map, they offered suggestions such as the following: "75 feet long," "50 to 70 tons," "legs like tree trunks," and "hardly able to move." The students wrote their ideas on our map under the appropriate categories.

Practice: Students practiced by listing additional details to add to our Semantic Question Map as I read aloud another section of text. When I finished, they added "teeth had shaped edges" to our map and noted the information we had written on our map was supported by the ideas in the texts. Then we used our map to create an oral summary. Our completed Semantic Question Map about brachiosauruses appears in Figure 9.

Reflect: We reflected on what we had learned about brachiosauruses and how the Semantic Question Map helped us to organize our thinking. We decided that we would leave our map on display and add new information to the categories as we learned more about this kind of dinosaur. The students asked if we could create Semantic Question Maps for other kinds of dinosaurs, and I noted we would be doing that in Stage Three. We also talked about how the organization of the map helped us to remember the information. Finally, we discussed how we would use Semantic Question Maps in other settings.

STAGE THREE: Teacher-Guided Small-Group Instruction

Text: *Dinosaur Bones* (Barner, 2001) (Texts varied according to students' abilities.)

Review: I began by reviewing the comprehension strategies good readers use and focused on previewing and Semantic Question Maps. I introduced *Dinosaur Bones* and explained that this text was a picture book that contained both a poem and facts about dinosaurs. I shared the cover, showed the format of the book through a picture walk, and read the poem aloud. Then I briefly discussed the book with the students and asked which dinosaur they would like to use as the focus of our map. They chose *Tyrannosaurus rex,* and I wrote that in the center oval of the poster board Semantic Question Map I had prepared before our lesson. It contained the same questions we had addressed during Stage Two.

Figure 9. Semantic Question Map: Brachiosaurus

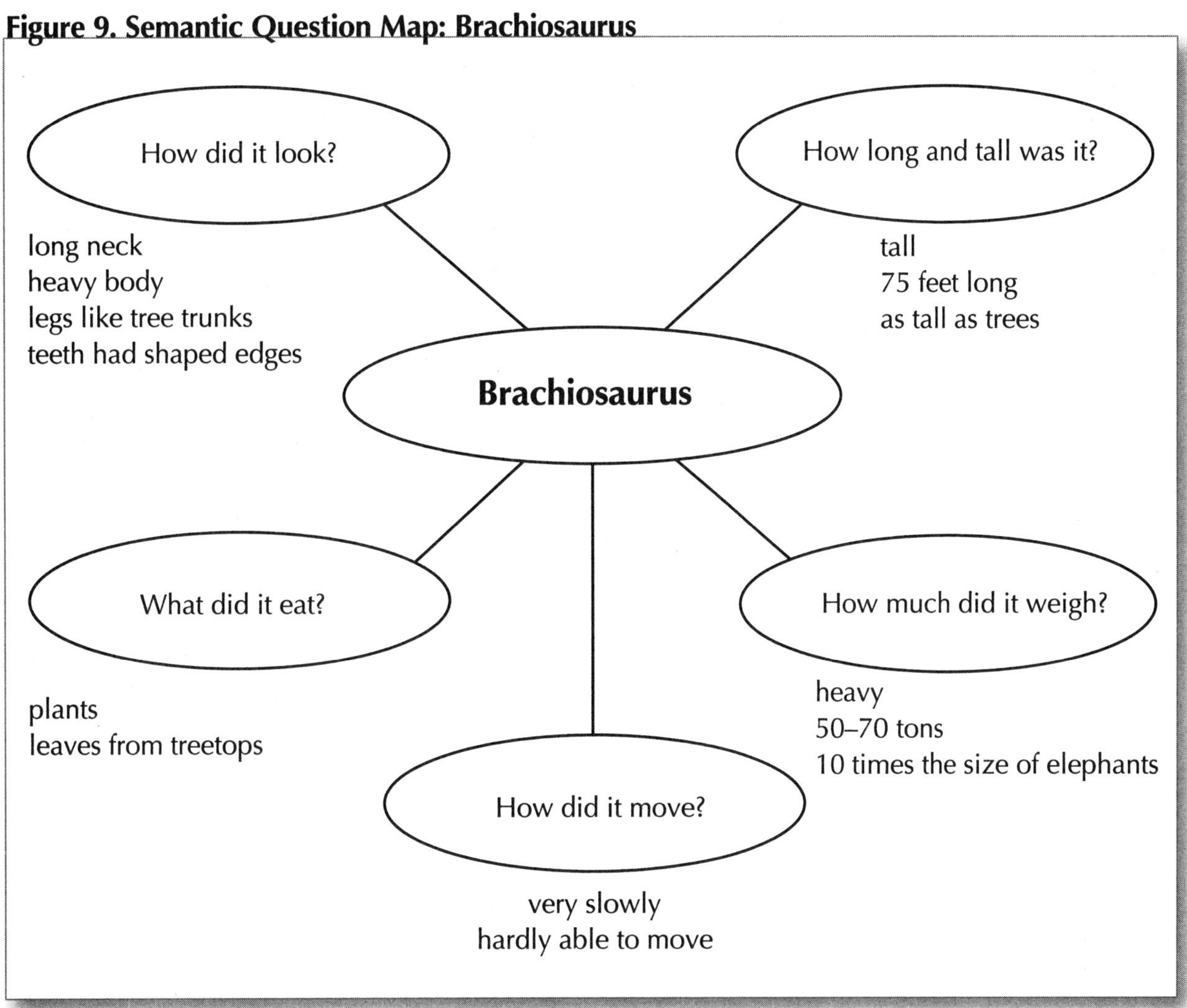

Guide: We briefly discussed what we already knew about this type of dinosaur. Students' responses generally focused on *Tyrannosaurus rex* being huge and eating meat. We wrote those descriptors on our map and decided to read to verify this information and find out more detailed information about this and other kinds of dinosaurs. Students read silently and I offered support as requested. Because the book offered information about a variety of dinosaurs, we decided to read it in sections and record information as we read it. Students noted that *Tyrannosaurus rex* means "king of tyrant lizards," so we added that to the center of our map. They also suggested that we include information about the weight of its skull. We added that to *How did it look?*

Practice: Students practiced by continuing to read the text. They were pleased that the author had included more information about *Tyrannosaurus rex* at the end of the book. We learned that we were correct about *Tyrannosaurus rex* being a meat eater. We also added the dinosaur's length and weight to the map.

Retell and Reflect: Rather than reread this text, students suggested we check texts we had already read for more information about *Tyrannosaurus rex*. So students reread segments of *The*

Ultimate Dino-pedia: The Most Complete Dinosaur Reference Ever (Lessem, 2010) and other theme-related texts (see the Theme Resources at the end of this chapter), and then we added additional descriptors to our map. Throughout the small group, the English learners partnered with a native English speaker and whisper read the text segments together. Our Semantic Question Map about *Tyrannosaurus rex*, as it appeared at the end of our guided small-group lesson, appears in Figure 10.

Student-Facilitated Comprehension Centers

A number of general accommodations were made for English learners when they engaged in the comprehension centers. These included the following:

- Including dinosaur books written in Spanish among the texts available in the centers
- Making other culturally relevant texts available in the centers
- Integrating multiple modes of representing thinking in student responses (sketching, singing, dramatizing)

Figure 10. Semantic Question Map: Tyrannosaurus Rex

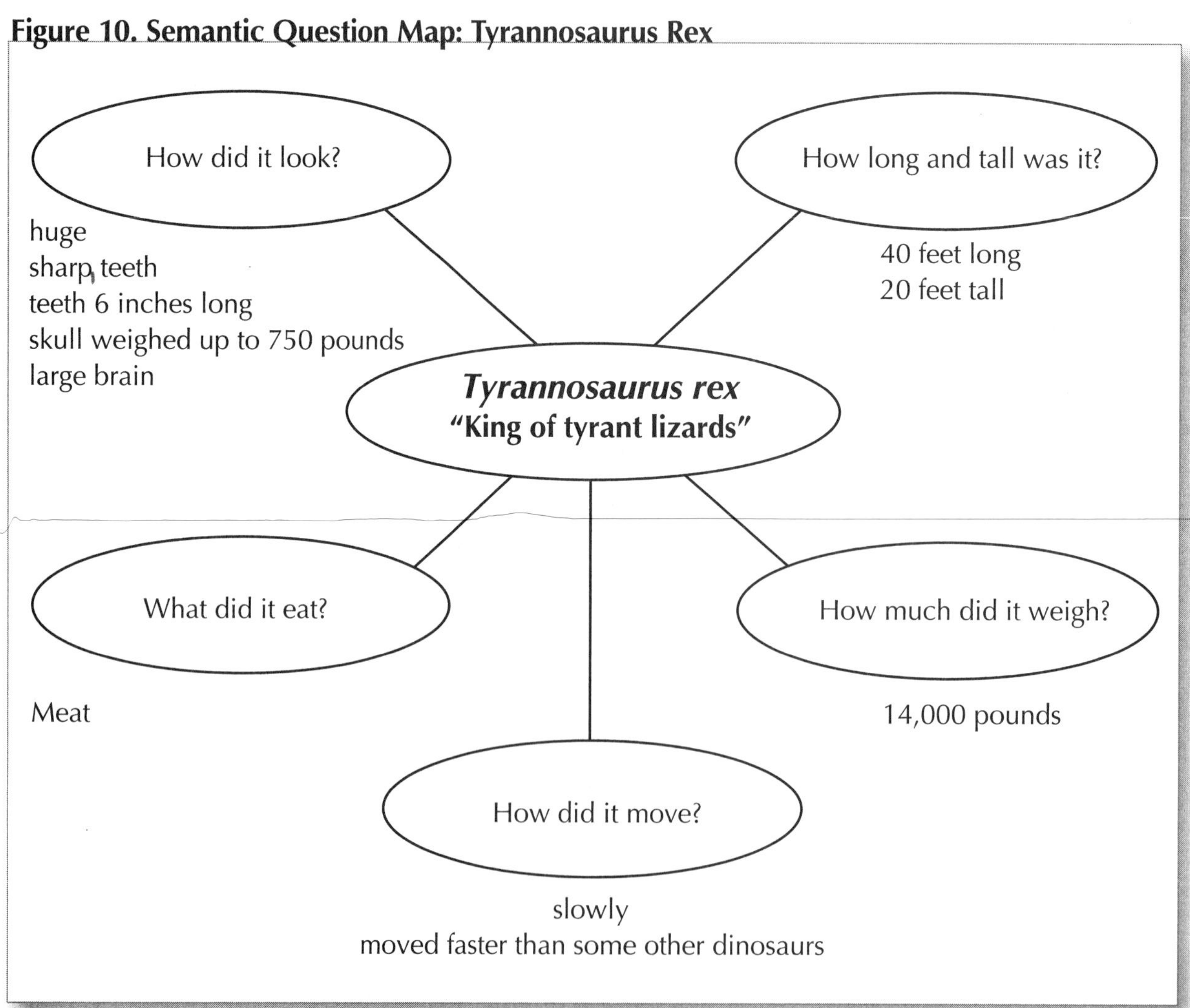

- Inviting students to work with other English learners of the same culture when reading texts in their native languages
- Encouraging English learners to partner with native English speakers when working in centers such as fluency, question and answer, vocabulary, and other centers focused on fluency and language development.

Art Center: Students worked in pairs on the computer to create a page for our class dinosaur alphabet book. When this project was complete, we shared the alphabet book in class, exhibited it during our theme celebration, and then placed it in our classroom library.

Poetry Center: Students used completed Semantic Question Maps to write and illustrate definition poems (see Appendix B, page 316) either about dinosaurs in general or about a particular type. Here is a definition poem written by Maria and Alejandro:

What are dinosaurs?
Prehistoric animals
Who lived a long time ago
Who ate plants or meat
Who were very big and very small
Who died 65 million years ago
They are dinosaurs!

Theme Center: Students self-selected texts from a large selection I had left at the theme center and worked either individually or with a partner to complete a Semantic Question Map.

Writing Center: Students used a Semantic Question Map they had completed previously to write and illustrate a paragraph or story about dinosaurs.

Student-Facilitated Comprehension Routines

A number of general accommodations were made for English learners when they engaged in the comprehension routines. These included the following:

- Making culturally relevant texts available
- Integrating multiple modes of representing thinking in student responses (sketching, singing, dramatizing)
- Encouraging English learners to choose to partner with native English speakers when working in Literature Circles
- Encouraging English learners to choose to partner with native language speakers or English language speakers when working in Cross-Age Reading Experiences

Literature Circles: Students used the Semantic Question Map to take notes as they read the text(s) the group had selected. After reading the text and completing the maps, students used them to facilitate discussion.

Cross-Age Reading Experiences: Students either read along with a text on tape or CD or read with a peer and a cross-age partner. They began completing a Semantic Question Map prior to reading and added information as necessary during and after reading. Then they used the completed map to create an oral summary.

STAGE FOUR: Teacher-Facilitated Whole-Group Reflection and Goal Setting

Share: Students shared their completed Semantic Question Maps from Stage Three in small groups and then shared selected maps, poems, paragraphs, and stories with the whole group.

Reflect: We reflected on how completing Semantic Question Maps helped to guide our reading and how well we could use them. The students seemed to take great pride in the super-sized Semantic Question Maps we had created for each type of dinosaur.

Set New Goals: We all felt very comfortable using the Semantic Question Map. The students were especially pleased that the completed maps could be used as the basis of discussion and writing. We decided to extend our goal of previewing and knowing how words work by learning how to use Concept of Definition Maps.

Assessment Options

I used a variety of assessments, including observation, running records, students' strategy applications, student writing, student self-assessments, and a variety of other formative assessments during this lesson.

Reflection on Teaching the English Learners in Our Class

I am pleased to note that the English learners were actively engaged throughout the lesson. I felt the key to their success was that they were highly motivated from the very beginning. I credit the dinosaur topic for part of that, but I should also note that our Engaging Prereading Sequence was great. It was a very relaxed, informative conversation in which the students readily engaged. Providing wait time was a challenge for me at first. I was very accustomed to students raising their hands quickly to respond, but now I can see all of my students benefiting from having a few moments to think. I can still see the expressions on their faces when they learned that all the land masses used to be joined together. It was also clear that the English learners enjoy expressing their thoughts in multiple ways. They seemed to particularly enjoy the sketching, working with partners, and learning in small groups. All the students seemed to enjoy learning together. It feels as if we have created our own community here.

Animals of the Past...Animals of the Present
Guided Comprehension Strategy: Summarizing
Teaching Idea: Lyric Summary/Lyric Retelling

STAGE ONE: Engaging Prereading Sequence for English Learners

We began our Engaging Prereading Sequence by meeting around the table I often use for Guided Reading. I had previously met with the students in this small group to explain the Engaging Prereading Sequence. I had told them that we would be having a conversation that would help them to more actively participate in reading when the class met in whole group. I had explained that they would know about some of the topics we discussed and that other topics would be new to them. I also told them that we would be using a lot of the ideas we discussed in small group when we met in whole group.

When we began our conversation, I revealed to the students that our topic would be dinosaurs. Then I was careful to share some pictures of dinosaurs I had gathered from the Internet and books in our classroom library. I realized right away that all the students had background knowledge about dinosaurs. They were all smiling as they talked about their favorite types and why they liked them. The discussion was quite rich, and the students were very enthusiastic. I knew it was time to teach the students how to create Lyric Summaries. I used explicit instruction.

Explain: I began by explaining summarizing as a strategy we use to help us remember the important information when we read. I asked the students if they had watched any television last night. When they said they had, I asked volunteers to share what had happened during the programs. Edward said he had watched *The Big Bang Theory.* Everyone in the group knew the show. Then Edward told us what had happened from beginning to end. Other students who had also watched added a few details. When Edward had finished, I said,

> Edward, you and the others who contributed ideas just did a good job summarizing what happened on *The Big Bang Theory* last night. You told us all the important information from the story. Now, let's remember that stories are different from informational text, which focuses on facts. Today we are going to be reading informational text about dinosaurs that contains important facts that we will want to include in our summary.

Then I explained we would be learning how to complete the Lyric Summary. I invited the students to talk to each other about what they thought a song's *lyrics* were. After waiting a few moments to provide time for students to think, I asked for volunteers. Everyone wanted to answer, so I said, "Let's all say it together. Lyrics are the song's...." "Words!" they all responded. After sharing a few examples of song lyrics, I explained that when we complete a Lyric Summary, we list all the facts we learned from our reading, choose a song we all know, and write the facts we learned as new lyrics—or words—to the song. I concluded by noting that the only way to share a Lyric Summary is for the group that writes it to sing it. The students were surprised by this, but they were also eager to begin.

Demonstrate: The students knew we were studying dinosaurs and they were happy when I noted we would be focusing on triceratops, a dinosaur that had roamed the United States and Canada millions of years ago. I used a read-aloud, a Think-Aloud, and a smartboard as I demonstrated how to complete a Lyric Summary. I introduced pictures and text selections about

Guided Comprehension: Animals of the Past…Animals of the Present
Summarizing: Lyric Summary/Lyric Retelling

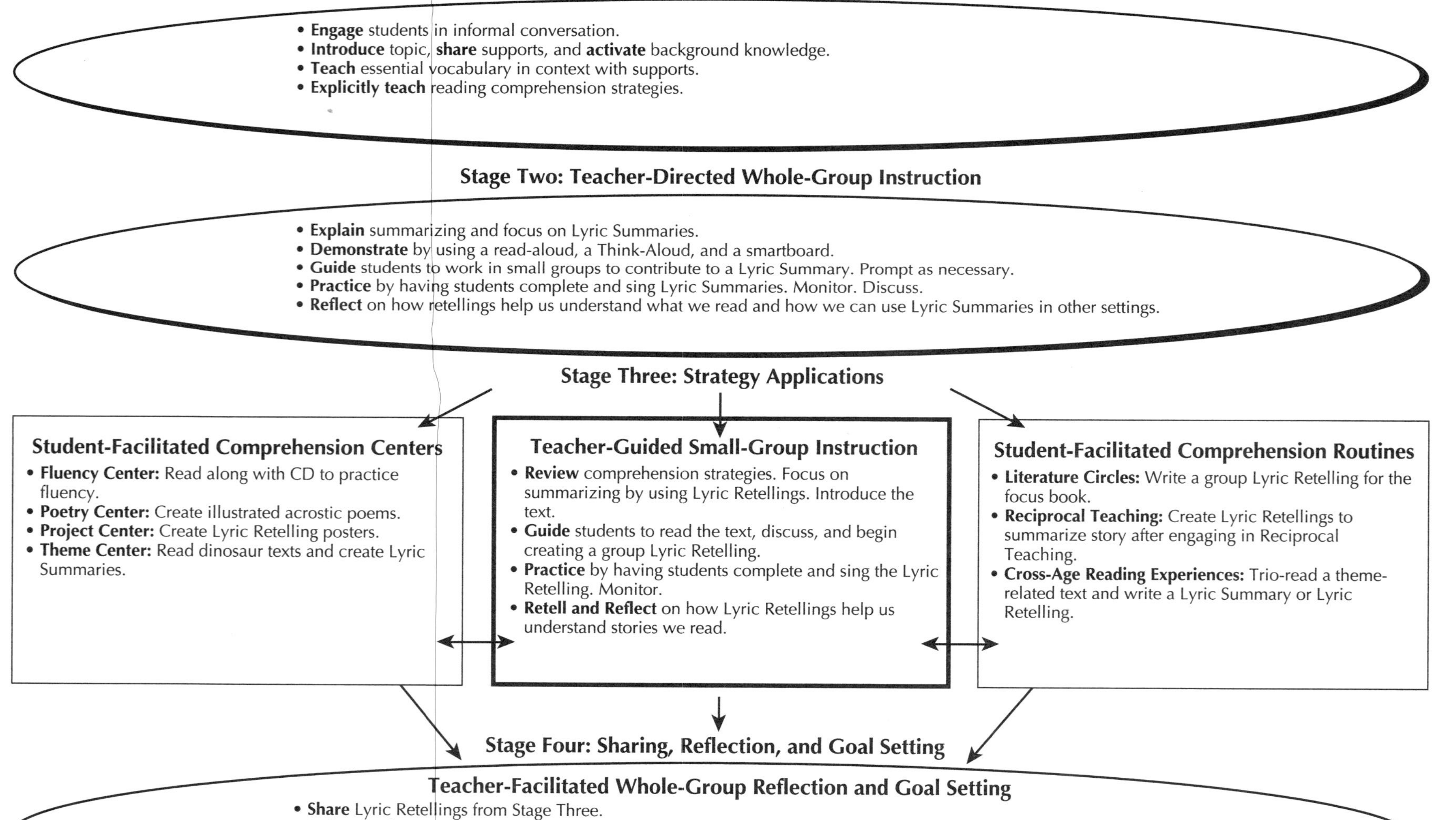

triceratops that I had downloaded from websites such as kids-dinosaurs.com (www.kids-dinosaurs.com/different-types-of-dinosaurs.html) and DinoDictionary (www.dinodictionary.com). At this point, the students contributed some information they already knew about triceratops to our conversation. Meeli said, "That is the dinosaur that looks like a rhino," and Edward said, "I think a triceratops has three horns." We used those comments to begin our conversation, which we continued as I read additional passages about triceratops. One of the segments noted that the triceratops was often thought to be like a rhino or an elephant. One of the passages included a detailed, labeled diagram of the triceratops, so we used the visual aid to discuss how the dinosaur was similar to and different from rhinos and elephants. Then I invited the students to work with a partner to sketch the triceratops and write one interesting fact they had learned about it.

Next, I focused on the dinosaur's name—*triceratops*—which means "three-horned face" in the text. I made a connection to what Edward had said about the triceratops having three horns. I used our prefix–suffix–root wall to explain that *tri* means "three." I provided examples of how *tri* is used in a variety of words: *tricycle*—a bike that has three wheels; *triangle*—a geometric figure that has three sides; and *triplets*—three children born during one birth. I used photos to support the words' meanings. The students knew the words. Geoffrey said, "Our neighbors have triplets. They are in second grade," and Rachel noted that everyone in the group had studied about triangles in math. Next, we examined a picture of a triceratops. When we first looked at it, we noticed only two long horns. Then we noticed the third, shorter horn located closer to the dinosaur's nose. At that point, we realized that the triceratops does indeed have a three-horned face, so its name is appropriate. Finally, I turned our conversation back to what we had learned about the triceratops. I prompted the students as they made a list of facts we had learned. Next, I reminded the students that we would use our list of facts to write new lyrics to the song we chose. I explained that everyone would need to know the song because we would all need to be able to sing it and write new lyrics for it. I was amazed when they chose "I'm a Believer," a song I knew was popular in the 1960s. I asked the students to sing a little of it, and it was the same song I knew. When I asked how they knew it, they all had the same answer: "It's from *Shrek* [the movie]." After that, we visited a website that had the lyrics to "I'm a Believer." We sang the song through once using the original lyrics. I was surprised that all the students knew the tune very well. I left the original lyrics on the screen as I thought aloud about how I would begin our Lyric Summary. I said, "Our Lyric Summary is about the triceratops, so I think I should mention that in the first line." I thought for a moment. Next, I sang the opening lines to "I'm a Believer," first with the original lyrics, then with my new opening lines: "I thought triceratops was just another kind of dinosaur...a big animal that ate a lot of food." I sang it again with one slight change: "We thought triceratops was just another kind of dinosaur...a big animal that ate a lot of food." I said, "I changed from 'I thought' to 'we thought' because this is our group's Lyric Summary, not just mine." Then we all sang the first two lines I had written. We all liked them.

Guide: I guided students to work with partners within the small group to use our list of facts to write the next two lines of the song. We went back to the original lyrics and sang just the first four lines. Then the students worked in pairs to think about lines 3 and 4. The students started humming the song and trying out their suggestions for new lyrics. Soon everyone was smiling and singing. Edward and Marta suggested that line 3 should be "Triceratops had three horns on his face" but quickly noted, "It's too many words. How can we fix it?" I suggested that we think about using a pronoun because we had just used *triceratops* in the first sentence. Edward and Marta decided we could use *he*. Then Geoffrey and Angelia said, "We can change our line, too. We think line 4 should be 'He had a large skull.'" Everyone sang the song to that point with our new lyrics. They worked! We were all happy. I asked the students to decide which fact we should include next. They suggested that we talk about how triceratops looked like rhinos and elephants. We went back and sang the song with the original lyrics up to the end of line five. Then we figured out our fifth line: "He looked like rhinos and elephants, too."

Practice: Students practiced by writing the remaining lines with their partners. The group members discussed each suggestion as we put our new lyrics together and finally sang our Triceratops Lyric Summary. Following is the shortened "verse and chorus" version of the Lyric Summary that we created about the triceratops.

Triceratops Lyric Summary

We thought triceratops was just another dinosaur,
A big animal that ate a lot of food
He had three horns on his face
He had a large skull
He looked like rhinos and elephants, too

He was 30 feet long. He was a herbivore
He ate green plants all of the time
He had a small brain. He weighed 5 tons
He lived 65 million years ago!

Reflect: There was a great deal of laughter, singing, humming, and fun as we composed our Lyric Summary. Students remarked that they did not know (a) that summarizing could be so much fun, (b) that the lists of things we learned could become words for songs, and (c) that singing lyrics we had written could be so enjoyable. The students were proud of their work, and I knew we were all ready to begin whole-group instruction.

STAGE TWO: Teacher-Directed Whole-Group Instruction

Text: *The Ultimate Book of Dinosaurs: Everything You Always Wanted to Know About Dinosaurs—But Were Too Terrified to Ask* (Dowswell, Malam, Mason, & Parker, 2002)

Explain: I began by reminding students about what we had already learned about summarizing—that we needed to include the important information from the text and that we summarized different kinds of text in different ways. Next, I explained that the Lyric Summary would be different from other summaries we had done because each small group would be choosing music—a song that everyone in the group knew—and writing our summaries as lyrics, or words, for that song. I noted that we would be keeping lists of facts we learned and using that information to write new lyrics for each group's songs. Then we would sing the songs we had written.

Demonstrate: I demonstrated by using a read-aloud, a Think-Aloud, the smartboard, pictures, and selected text segments about *Tyrannosaurus rex*, a dinosaur the students and I called by its more familiar name, T-rex. I shared the pictures, and the students were enthralled. The discussion was lively and engaging. I read aloud about T-rex, stopping periodically to make connections and discuss the text with students. I thought aloud as I wrote. I began by saying, "To start our summary, I need to think about which facts I want to include." I read the title of the book, showed the cover, and reread the first page about T-rex. I said,

> There are several important facts in what I just read. For example, *dinosaur* means "terrible lizard" and *Tyrannosaurus rex* means "king of tyrant lizards." Think for a moment about another fact that you think we should add to our list. Then share it with a partner.

After taking a few moments to think, the students talked to their partners. Then I invited them to share with the whole group. The students suggested that we add the following to our lists:

- T-rex had really big teeth.
- T-rex had a large brain.
- Its flexible neck allowed it to adjust its angle of attack.
- It had tiny arms and powerful hind legs.

As I continued to read, we made more connections and discussed the new information. The students suggested that we add the following to our lists:

- T-rex was a meat eater.
- It lived in North America and Asia.
- It was 40 feet long.
- It weighed 7 tons (14,000 pounds).
- Its tail helped it to balance.
- Sue the dinosaur was a female *Tyrannosaurus rex*.

Guide: I prompted pairs of students to discuss the selection of the song for our Lyric Summary. Then, when they were ready, I invited them to share their ideas. The students offered several titles, but not everyone in the class knew them, so I suggested that they keep those titles for their small group Lyric Summaries. The one song that everyone knew was the theme from *The Brady Bunch*. It seemed that students were watching this series in reruns on cable television, and I had watched the show when I was growing up. I found the lyrics online and brought them up on a screen. The students and I sang the original song together. Then I explained that we would be singing and humming it several times as we wrote our new lyrics. I thought aloud as I began to write our new lyrics for the Brady Bunch theme. I said, "I think we should mention *Tyrannosaurus* very early in our song. What if we keep part of the original first line and change the rest: 'Here's a story of Tyrannosaurus, a very powerful tyrant lizard.'" The students liked it, and we talked about what I might add for the next line. I suggested that we begin to physically describe T-rex. I suggested, "He had a big brain and very sharp teeth. He could twist his neck." The students approved, and I invited them to sing the song with the new lyrics we had so far. After that I encouraged the students to work with their partners to develop subsequent lines. These are the two verses that we wrote as a whole group, before students began working in small groups:

Here's a story of Tyrannosaurus
A very powerful tyrant lizard
He had a big brain and very sharp teeth
And he could twist his neck.
Here's a story of an extinct animal
Who was a meat eater who had really tiny arms
He had strong back legs and a long tail
And was 40 feet long

Tyrannosaurus lived in North America and in Asia
That was 65 million years ago
He was the strongest of the meat-eating dinosaurs
That's something that we know.
Till the one day when a mystery killed all the dinosaurs
He died even though he weighed 14,000 pounds
A meteorite may have hit Earth and changed the climate
Or it could have been volcanoes—no one really knows
T-rex fossils! T-rex fossils!
That's how our T-rex became fossils!!!

Practice: The students practiced by working in small groups to create Lyric Summaries about other dinosaurs. To facilitate this process, I provided a variety of texts, including books and websites. I also reminded the students about their need to read the information about the dinosaur they selected, discuss it, make lists of important facts, and use that information to write their new lyrics. I noted that it was very important to choose a song that everyone knew. I further explained that after they finished their Lyric Summaries, they would share them with the whole group by singing. I monitored this segment by visiting with each group to discuss their dinosaur choice and inquire about their song choices.

Reflect: We reflected on how writing summaries helped us understand what we were reading and how much fun it was to use Lyric Summaries. We all had a great time using this strategy application. The students seemed to especially enjoy working together and singing the Lyric Summaries.

STAGE THREE: Teacher-Guided Small-Group Instruction

Text: *Mama Rex & T: Homework Trouble* (Vail, 2001) (Texts varied according to students' abilities.)

Review: I began by reviewing the strategies good readers use and focusing on summarizing. Then I reviewed the process for creating Lyric Retellings and distributed the organizer to the students. I explained that we had read informational text in whole-group instruction, so we had included the important information in a Lyric Summary. I further noted that in small group we would be reading a story, so we would be creating a Lyric Retelling. I reminded the students that when we retell a story, we want to be sure to include the characters, setting, problem, attempts to resolve the problem, and resolution in our retelling. The students were familiar with the difference in text types because they had previously created Draw and Write Retellings.

Guide: I introduced the text by sharing the cover and title and reading aloud the first three pages of Chapter 1. We discussed the dinosaurs as characters in the story and what homework trouble might mean. We also discussed the setting of the story. Then I guided the students in reading the text, prompting as necessary. They paused when they finished reading each of the very brief chapters so we could discuss the story, note the narrative elements in that section, and jot them down.

Practice: The students practiced by creating a Lyric Retelling. The song they chose was "Are You Sleeping?" What follows is the Lyric Retelling of *Mama Rex & T: Homework Trouble* that the students wrote and sang.

> Little T,
> Little T,
> Where's your homework?
> Did you forget?
> You need a diorama,
> One that is about pigs,
> But you haven't done it,
> You haven't done it.
> To the library
> To the museum
> You and your mom went
> You and your mom went.
> Then you made the diorama
> You put a pink pig in mud
> In a cottage cheese tub
> Now your homework's done.

Retell and Reflect: We did a choral rereading of the text and revisited our retelling. Then we reflected on how to create Lyric Retellings and how they helped us understand stories that we read. Throughout our small group, students who were English learners whisper read with partners. Everyone seemed to enjoy creating the retelling. Alysia said, "Writing a Lyric Retelling is like writing a story in a song." Everyone agreed that writing Lyric Retellings was fun.

Student-Facilitated Comprehension Centers

A number of general accommodations were made for English learners when they engaged in the comprehension centers. These included the following:

- Including dinosaur books written in Spanish among the texts available in the centers
- Making other culturally relevant texts available in the centers
- Integrating multiple modes of representing thinking in student responses (sketching, singing, dramatizing)
- Inviting students to work with other English learners of the same culture when reading texts in their native languages
- Encouraging English learners to partner with native English speakers when working in centers such as fluency, question and answer, vocabulary, and other centers focused on fluency and language development

Fluency Center: Students either read along with a book on CD or read with a partner to practice their fluency. They were also able to record themselves reading.

Poetry Center: Students worked with a partner to write and illustrate acrostic poems about their favorite dinosaurs.

Project Center: Students worked in trios to create Lyric Retelling posters. They selected a book, wrote the title and author, discussed the story elements, and chose the music. Then they wrote the Lyric Retelling on a poster-size sticky note and illustrated it. Finally, they practiced singing it so they would be ready to perform it in Stage Three.

Theme Center: Students made selections from a variety of titles I had placed at the center and worked with a partner to create Lyric Summaries. They partner-read the book, using the read–pause–discuss pattern, and recorded information about the story elements. Then they chose their music and wrote their Lyric Summaries.

Student-Facilitated Comprehension Routines

A number of general accommodations were made for English learners when they engaged in the comprehension routines. These included the following:

- Making culturally relevant texts available
- Integrating multiple modes of representing thinking in student responses (sketching, singing, dramatizing)
- Encouraging English learners to choose to partner with native English speakers when working in Literature Circles or engaging in Reciprocal Teaching
- Encouraging English learners to choose to partner with native language speakers or English language speakers when working in Cross-Age Reading Experiences

Literature Circles: Students had just finished discussing a book, so they used their Lyric Retelling as an extension activity. They began by discussing the elements of the story. They used notes about the book that they had recorded in their Guided Comprehension Journals to facilitate this process. Then they created a group Lyric Retelling of the book and sang it for the class.

Reciprocal Teaching: Students engaged in Reciprocal Teaching and recorded information about the story elements after they summarized each section. After reading, they created a Lyric Retelling of the story.

Cross-Age Reading Experiences: Students listened to a theme-related audio book or trio-read with a cross-age partner. The students recorded information about the story elements as they read. Then they selected the music and wrote a Lyric Retelling, which they sang for the class.

STAGE FOUR: Teacher-Facilitated Whole-Group Reflection and Goal Setting

Share: Students sang their Lyric Retellings from Stage Three to the class. It was a fun sharing session because the students enjoyed singing as well as being audience members.

Reflect: We reflected on our understanding of summarizing and our ability to create Lyric Retellings.

Set New Goals or Extend Existing Ones: We decided that we all felt very comfortable creating Lyric Summaries and Lyric Retellings, so we extended our goal to learn how to summarize using Questions Into Paragraphs.

Assessment Options

I observed students throughout the Guided Comprehension process and reviewed and commented on their Lyric Summaries and Lyric Retellings. I also used the students' self-assessments as information sources and completed running records with several students.

Reflection on Teaching the English Learners in Our Class

Teaching this lesson to the English learners in our class was especially interesting for me. I have known for a while that these students respond well when they can use an alternative mode such as sketching, but today when we were all singing, they were really engaged. Everyone was laughing, singing, and repeatedly humming the tunes for the Lyric Summaries and Lyric Retellings. It was interesting to watch how partners negotiated language to make the lyrics work with the music. Learning today was genuinely a good time for all. I am happy to note that the English learners seem to be more comfortable every day. They were totally engaged in the lesson and everyone in the class worked well together. This was a relaxed, fun, and informative learning experience.

Animals of the Past...Animals of the Present
Guided Comprehension Strategy: Knowing How Words Work
Teaching Idea: Concept of Definition Map

STAGE ONE: Engaging Prereading Sequence for English Learners

We began our Engaging Prereading Sequence by meeting in our conversation circle. We had engaged in this segment of Guided Comprehension on several previous occasions, so the students in the small group were familiar with the conversation we would be having. For example, they knew that we would be having a conversation that would help them to actively participate when the class met in whole group. They also knew that we would be focusing on information they already knew and some that would be new to them. I noted that we would be using the ideas we discussed later in whole group.

When we began our conversation, I explained that we would be continuing our animal theme by talking about dogs. That was really all I needed to say. The students were eager to share everything they knew about dogs. Some of the students had dogs as pets. Next, I shared photos and other information about dogs that I had gathered from a variety of sources. The visuals included pictures of breeds such as beagles, German shepherds, and labs, as well as mixed varieties. We talked about what dogs look like, what they eat, and what they can do. As we discussed what they knew, I continued to share pictures and read interesting fun facts about dogs that I had gleaned from Good Dog Training Advice (gooddogtrainingadvice.com/10-Fun-Facts-About-Dogs.html) and FunnyFidos.com (www.funnyfidos.com/fun-dog-facts). Following are a few of the fun facts I shared:

- The United States has more dogs than any other country in the world.
- Dogs circle before lying down because in the wild the circling flattens the grass and creates a comfortable space for the dogs to rest.
- Dogs can hear 10 times better than people.
- Dogs can smell about 1,000 times better than people.

As our discussion drew to a close, I focused on using explicit instruction to teach the students how to use the Concept of Definition Map.

Explain: I began by explaining why it is important for us to know about how words work. Then I explained that the Concept of Definition Map is a graphic organizer that we can use to learn about words. I showed the students the organizer on the smartboard and provided them with individual copies. I explained that it had a focus word and that we would be providing more information about that word from our background knowledge, our discussion, and what we would learn from a short text I would be reading. I asked the students if they could guess what focus word I would write on our Concept of Definition Map. They all replied, "Dogs!"

Demonstrate: I demonstrated using a Think-Aloud, a read-aloud, and the smartboard. I began by briefly introducing the text, *Dogs* (Simon, 2009). I shared the title and cover, and the students and I made connections. Next, I read a short segment and the students and I discussed it. Then I referred to the Concept of Definition Map and the first information we would need to include. It was question one: *What is it?* I thought aloud as I answered the question. I said, "The map is asking what

Guided Comprehension: Animals of the Past...Animals of the Present
Knowing How Words Work: Concept of Definition Map

Stage One: Engaging Prereading Sequence for English Learners

- **Engage** students in informal conversation.
- **Introduce** topic, **share** supports, and **activate** background knowledge.
- **Teach** essential vocabulary in context with supports.
- **Explicitly teach** reading comprehension strategies.

Stage Two: Teacher-Directed Whole-Group Instruction

- **Explain** knowing how words work and focus on Concept of Definition Maps.
- **Demonstrate** by using a read-aloud, a Think-Aloud, and a smartboard.
- **Guide** small groups of students to contribute to Concept of Definition Maps.
- **Practice** by having students complete remaining segments of the maps. Summarize.
- **Reflect** on how knowing how words work helps us understand what we read and how we can use Concept of Definition Maps in other settings.

Stage Three: Strategy Applications

Student-Facilitated Comprehension Centers

- **Making Books Center:** Create a page for the class PowerPoint book.
- **Theme Center:** Complete Concept of Definition Maps and read theme-related texts.
- **Vocabulary Center:** Complete Vocabulary Bookmarks. Write stories using words from the animal word wall.
- **Writing Center:** Use completed Concept of Definition Maps as bases for creative stories.

Teacher-Guided Small-Group Instruction

- **Review** comprehension strategies and focus on knowing how words work using Concept of Definition Maps.
- **Guide** students to begin completing the Concept of Definition Map with partners, to discuss the maps, and to read the text.
- **Practice** by having students discuss the text and review the Concept of Definition Map, changing and adding information as necessary.
- **Retell and Reflect** by discussing how knowing how words work and Concept of Definition Maps help us understand what we read.

Student-Facilitated Comprehension Routines

- **Literature Circles:** Read a variety of books about the same animal and use Concept of Definition Maps to facilitate discussion and summarizing.
- **Cross-Age Reading Experiences:** Use the Concept of Definition Map while listening to audio books or trio-reading with a peer and a cross-age partner.

Stage Four: Sharing, Reflection, and Goal Setting

Teacher-Facilitated Whole-Group Reflection and Goal Setting

- **Share** completed Concept of Definition Maps from Stage Three.
- **Reflect** on how knowing how words work and Concept of Definition Maps help us comprehend and how well we can use the mapping technique.
- **Set new goals** or extend existing ones.

do

gs are. I know that dogs are animals, so I am going to write *animals* in that space." Then I wrote the word and read another segment, which the students and I discussed.

Guide: I guided the students to answer question two: *How would you describe dogs?* I invited the students to think about how they would describe dogs and to share their ideas with a partner. I showed them that there are three spaces for answers on the Concept of Definition Map, so we would be able to write three ideas. After providing a few moments for students to think and discuss, I asked for volunteers to share their thinking. Katrin and Arik suggested we write *furry*, because dogs they knew were furry. Everyone agreed that was a good suggestion and I wrote *furry* in the first space. Then Hannis and Carlos suggested we write *big and small* in the second space. I asked why we should write both words, and they said because some dogs like huskies are big and some dogs like chihuahuas and beagles are small. I said, "That is true!" Then I wrote those words in the second space. Finally, Cira and Vincente suggested that we write *friends* in the next space because dogs are like friends we play with. I wrote the word and read what we had on our map so far. I said, "Dogs are animals. They are furry, big and small. Dogs are like friends." When I finished reading the information on the Concept of Definition Map, I wrote it on the smartboard. Then I invited the students to read it with me.

Practice: The students practiced by completing the next section of the map: *What are some examples?* I noted that in this case the question meant, *What are some kinds of dogs?* They again took time to think and discuss with a partner. Then the partners made three suggestions: *labs*, *beagles*, and *poodles*. I praised their responses and added them to our map and our summary. Then I invited the students to read the Concept of Definition Map Summary with me. We read,

> Dogs are animals. They are furry, big and small. Dogs are like friends.
> Labs, beagles, and poodles are three kinds of dogs.

Reflect: The students smiled as we read. I could see that they were proud of our completed map. I praised the students for their good work and we wrapped up our conversation. When discussing our completed Concept of Definition Map, Hannis said, "We know things. We talk about things. We learn things. We write things. We tell important ideas. This is our map. It is a map of what we know about dogs." Everyone agreed, and they all seemed happy. I said, "That is a wonderful summary of what we have done today, Hannis. Let's move to whole group and think about your ideas as we complete our next map." Figure 11 features the Concept of Definition Map and Summary that the students and I completed about dogs.

STAGE TWO: Teacher-Directed Whole-Group Instruction

Text: *Do Penguins Get Frostbite? Questions and Answers About Polar Animals* (Berger & Berger, 2000)

Explain: I explained knowing how words work and focused on the Concept of Definition Map. I explained that we use Concept of Definition Maps to make connections between words and ideas we already know and information we discover in texts. I also noted that we could record what we already know about the topic on the Concept of Definition Map before reading, and after reading we could add new information we learned from the text. Next, I explained that we would use our completed maps to write a brief summary of the focus topic.

Figure 11. Concept of Definition Map: Dogs

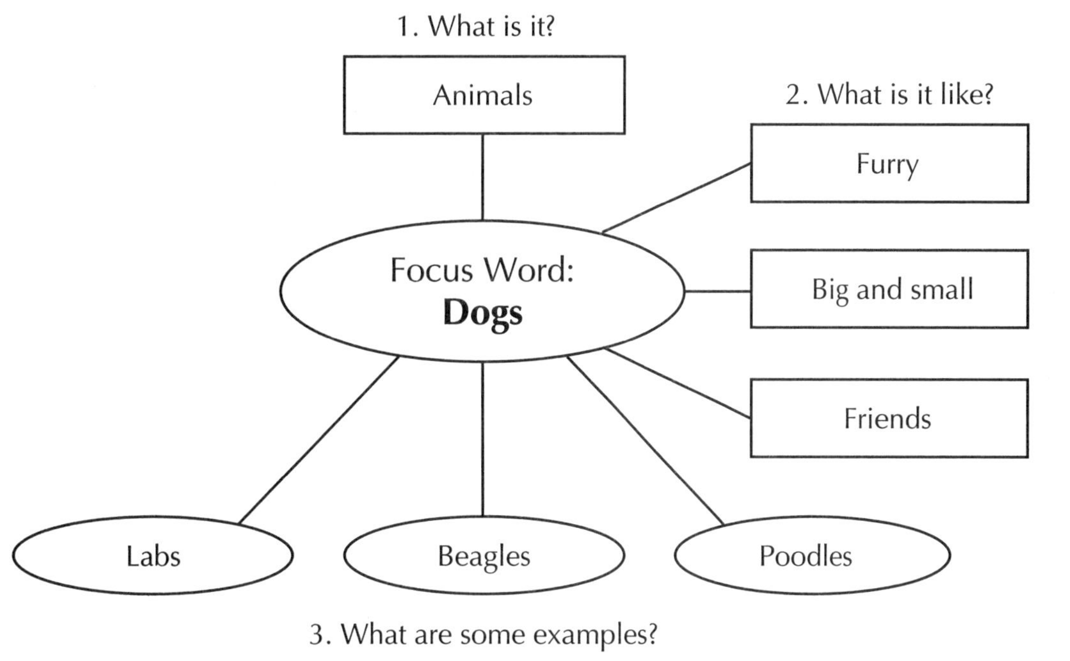

Concept of Definition Map Summary

Dogs are animals. They are furry, big and small. Dogs are like friends. Labs, beagles, and poodles are three kinds of dogs.

Demonstrate: I demonstrated by using a Think-Aloud, a smartboard, and a read-aloud of the section about polar bears in *Do Penguins Get Frostbite? Questions and Answers About Polar Animals.* I began by introducing the Concept of Definition Map, which appeared on the smartboard (see Appendix A, page 363). I read aloud the various categories of information we would need to complete it. I wrote *polar bear,* the topic for our Concept of Definition Map, in the center oval and explained that I would need to provide information for each category on the map. I shared photos and other information about polar bears I had gathered from a variety of sources. The photos included pictures of Knut, the polar bear at the Berlin Zoo that I had photographed when I was in Germany. We talked about how cuddly the cub looked close up and whether he seemed to be more ferocious or playful. The students had been engaged throughout our animals theme, and the polar bears seemed to continue to motivate them. They all had some background knowledge about these animals. For example, they knew it was a type of bear that was white and that it lived in places that were very cold. I read aloud the next category of information: "What is it?" I thought aloud and said, "I know that polar bears are animals because all bears are animals. I have also seen polar bears at zoos, so I know they are animals." Then I wrote *animal* in the space provided on the poster board. I continued my demonstration by writing what I already knew about polar bears in each section of the organizer. I examined the section labeled *How would you describe it?* and thought aloud about what I see when I visualize a polar bear, and then I wrote three words to describe polar bears in the boxes: *big, white*, and *furry*. I prompted students to complete the next part of the Concept of Definition Map by thinking aloud about three things a polar bear does. (I had adapted this section from the part of the map usually labeled *three examples*.) Students suggested writing *lives where it is very cold* in a space provided at the bottom of the graphic organizer. We decided that we would complete the other two sections as we learned more about polar bears. Then we discussed all the information we knew about polar bears at that point.

Guide: I began by reminding students that as I read aloud we should be listening for new information about polar bears. I noted that I would record new information on the poster board, and we would add some of that information to our Concept of Definition Map. I explained that when I recorded the information we had learned from the text on the map, I would use a different color marker. That way we would be able to easily distinguish between what we knew before reading and what we learned from reading the text. I introduced *Do Penguins Get Frostbite?* to the students by sharing the cover, providing a brief overview of the text, and sharing the title of the section on polar bears: "Polar Bears and Other Land Animals." We summarized what we had already written about polar bears on the Concept of Definition Map, and I noted that the section title in the text had already confirmed that polar bears are animals. When I finished reading the first section of the text, I prompted the students to share new information about polar bears. First, they suggested we add *eats seals* and *swims* to our list of things a polar bear does on our Concept of Definition Map. Then they offered the following information, which I recorded on the bottom section of the poster board:

- Polar bears travel alone.
- There is fat underneath their fur that keeps them warm.
- Polar bears live about 33 years.
- A running polar bear is faster than a swimming polar bear.

Stuart asked about the word *Arctic* because the text said that is where polar bears live. We went to our wall map to see where the Arctic is located and had a discussion about what we knew about the Arctic. Then we decided that it gave more specific information about where polar bears live. So we changed *lives where it is very cold* to *lives in the Arctic* on our map.

Practice: I continued to read aloud the rest of the text as students worked with partners to jot down new information about polar bears. This time students suggested the following:

- Only one polar bear cub is born at a time.
- Newborn polar bear cubs are tiny enough to stay between their mothers' toes.
- Polar bear mothers teach the cubs to hunt and search for berries and plants.

I recorded these suggestions, and we decided that we didn't need to include any of this information on our Concept of Definition Map. Because our map was complete, the students and I wrote a summary of what we knew about polar bears. Our completed Concept of Definition Map, Concept Map Summary, and list of other things we learned appear in Figure 12.

Reflect: We reflected on how we used the Concept of Definition Map to help us understand how words work and comprehend what we read. The students were excited about learning information about real animals. We also talked about how we could use the completed Concept

Figure 12. Concept of Definition Map: Polar Bears

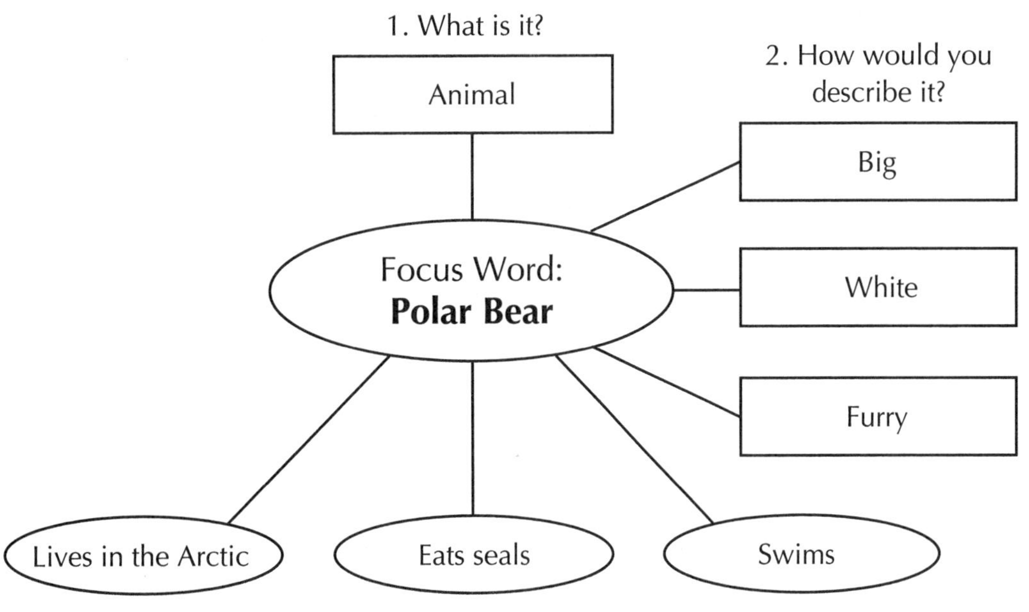

Concept Map Summary:
A polar bear is an animal that is big, white, and furry. A polar bear lives in the Arctic, eats seals, and swims.

We also learned:

- Polar bears travel alone.
- There is fat underneath their fur that keeps them warm.
- Polar bears live about 33 years.
- A running polar bear is faster than a swimming polar bear.
- Only one polar bear cub is born at a time.
- Newborn polar bear cubs are tiny enough to stay between their mothers' toes.
- Polar bear mothers teach the cubs to hunt and search for berries and plants.

of Definition Map and Concept Map Summary to review what we know about different animals. Finally, we talked about how we could use the maps with other texts in other settings.

STAGE THREE: Teacher-Guided Small-Group Instruction

Text: *Wolves* (Simon, 2009) (Texts varied according to students' abilities.)

Review: I reminded students about comprehension strategies active readers use and focused on knowing how words work and on using Concept of Definition Maps.

Guide: I gave the small group of students Concept of Definition Map graphic organizers and explained that our focus word was *wolves.* I shared photos of wolves and we briefly discussed some things we knew about wolves. Next, I guided the students to work with a partner to provide information about wolves for the first two categories. We discussed each group's responses, which included that wolves were animals and that they were similar to dogs, such as Akitas and German shepherds. I continued to guide the students as they completed the map. When they had recorded what they already knew about wolves, we had a brief discussion. They had described wolves with adjectives such as *furry, mean,* and *fast,* and with the phrase *have big teeth. Gray wolf* was the only response offered in the section labeled *different kinds,* so I reminded the students that we would add information we learned from the book to that and other sections of our maps. Next, I introduced the book *Wolves* and read aloud the first few sections. We stopped briefly so we could discuss the information in the book and record new information about wolves on the Concept of Definition Maps.

Practice: Students practiced by continuing to read to the end of the text and by revisiting their maps as necessary. For example, in the section of the map labeled *different kinds,* they recorded a variety of responses that included *arctic wolves, red wolves, Mexican wolves,* and *Rocky Mountain wolves.* When the students finished reading and revising, we discussed the maps and other information we had learned from the text. Then the students completed their Concept Map Summaries.

Retell and Reflect: Because our text was informational, the students read their summaries to a partner rather than reread and retell. Next, we reflected on how Concept of Definition Maps help us to understand how words work and to make connections between what we know and what we have read. Todd said, "Before today, most of what I knew about wolves happened in stories." Cristiana said, "The pictures of wolves in this book were beautiful. They don't look that way in a lot of stories." Finally, we discussed how we could use Concept of Definition Maps and Concept Map Summaries to help us understand other texts in other settings.

Student-Facilitated Comprehension Centers

A number of general accommodations were made for English learners when they engaged in the comprehension centers. These included the following:

- Including animal books and articles written in Spanish among the texts available in the centers
- Making other culturally relevant texts available in the centers
- Integrating multiple modes of representing thinking in student responses (sketching, singing, dramatizing)
- Inviting students to work with other English learners of the same culture when reading texts in their native languages
- Encouraging English learners to partner with native English speakers when working in centers such as fluency, question and answer, vocabulary, and other centers focused on fluency and language development

Making Books Center: Pairs of students created a page for our PowerPoint *Book of Our Favorite Animals.* A variety of books and articles were available as resources at the center, and several websites that I had bookmarked were also accessible.

Theme Center: I placed a variety of informational books and related Concept of Definition Maps at this center. I had also provided the focus word for each map. Students worked with partners to complete the maps and read the texts. After reading, students revisited the maps and added information they thought to be important. Next, they wrote Concept Map Summaries based on their completed maps. Some students then took their completed maps to the writing center.

Vocabulary Center: Pairs of students selected animal books and completed Vocabulary Bookmarks as they read. On the bookmarks, they wrote the word, what they thought the word meant, and the page on which they had found it. Students could also work together to write stories using vocabulary words from our Animal Word Wall.

Writing Center: Pairs of students used their completed Concept Map Summaries to write paragraphs or form poems about the animals they had learned about. Titles of their poems included "Wally the Whale," "The Wolf Goes to School," and "Ellie the Elephant."

Student-Facilitated Comprehension Routines

A number of general accommodations were made for English learners when they engaged in the comprehension routines. These included the following:

- Making culturally relevant texts available
- Integrating multiple modes of representing thinking in student responses (sketching, singing, dramatizing)
- Encouraging English learners to choose to partner with native English speakers when working in Literature Circles
- Encouraging English learners to choose to partner with native language speakers or English language speakers when working in Cross-Age Reading Experiences

Literature Circles: Students completed Concept of Definition Maps and Concept Map Summaries as they read a variety of books about the same animal. They worked with partners to record initial information and then individually read and completed the maps. They shared their map information and summaries during group discussion.

Cross-Age Reading Experiences: Students completed Concept of Definition Maps with a partner while listening to audio books or trio-reading about the animal of their choice with a peer and a cross-age partner. After revisiting and revising their maps, students wrote a Concept Map Summary.

STAGE FOUR: Teacher-Facilitated Whole-Group Reflection and Goal Setting

Share: Students shared their Concept of Definition Maps and Concept Map Summaries from Stage Three in small groups. Then we discussed selected examples as a whole class.

Reflect: We reflected on how knowing how words work and using Concept of Definition Maps helped us to understand what we read. We also talked about how well we could use the maps and that they seemed to work best with informational texts.

Set New Goals: We decided to continue working on knowing how words work by learning about Semantic Maps.

Assessment Options

I used observation, completed Concept of Definition Maps and Concept Map Summaries, discussion, and students' self-assessments during this lesson. I also completed a number of running records and retellings with individual students. The assessments were a natural part of each stage of the process.

Reflection on Teaching the English Learners in Our Class

Once again, I was reminded how critical background knowledge and motivation are when teaching all students, but especially English learners. When we began our conversation in our Engaging Prereading Sequence, I shared pictures of dogs with the students, and they were immediately talking about dogs—dogs they had known, dogs they had, and dogs they wanted to have. The discussion was robust, and when I shared information from the Internet, they were very excited. When I introduce new strategy applications, I always try to use a topic about which I think students will have some background knowledge. Dogs were perfect for this segment of our lesson. All the students were actively engaged not only throughout our Engaging Prereading Sequence but also throughout the lesson. They seemed to be very pleased with the fact that they had background knowledge about the comprehension strategies when they arrived in our whole-group setting. The Engaging Prereading Sequence has become a time of relaxed conversation during which the teaching is effortless and the students are eager to learn. I was thinking earlier today that the Engaging Prereading Sequence is the only time the English learners get to work alone with a teacher. They seem happy to have that time.

Animals of the Past...Animals of the Present
Guided Comprehension Strategy: Monitoring
Teaching Idea: Say Something

STAGE ONE: Engaging Prereading Sequence for English Learners

We began our Engaging Prereading Sequence by meeting in a section of the room where I had gathered a circle of chairs. We had engaged in Explicit Teaching Sequences before, so the students knew that we would be activating our background knowledge, having a conversation about what we know, and learning how to use a new strategy application. The students also knew that we were going to use what we learned in the Engaging Prereading Sequence to get ready to actively participate in whole-group instruction. The students liked the Engaging Prereading Sequence. They knew that what we were doing would be interesting and that they would be able to use what they learned. As Willem had said at the end of our previous meeting, "This is like the warm-up we have before basketball games."

As I was about to begin our conversation, Agacia asked what animal we would be talking about today. I said, "We are going to be talking about an animal from the ocean. Can you predict what it might be?" Agacia took a moment and then smiled and said, "I hope it is dolphins. They are my favorite ocean animals." I asked how many others liked dolphins, and everyone said yes. Then I told the students that Agacia's prediction had been correct. The students were very happy. I used my computer to show a short video I had made of dolphins when I was on vacation, and the students were entranced.

As our discussion continued, I shared photos of bottlenose dolphins from the Dolphin Picture Gallery at www.dolphins-world.com/Dolphin_Pictures.html. The students thoroughly enjoyed them. Then we took a few moments to sketch bottlenose dolphins on small pieces of paper I had provided. I left the photos on the computer screen as we sketched our dolphins. We shared our sketches with partners, and I read aloud a few interesting facts about bottlenose dolphins from Animal Planet: Dolphins Explored (animal.discovery.com/features/dolphins/facts/facts.html). Next, I focused on two words that would be helpful for students to know: *pods* and *echolocation*. When I introduced each word, I shared it in context so the students could see how it was used. I began by sharing *pods* in context and sharing a picture. I read the short segment of text, which explained that dolphins travel in groups and that the groups are called pods. Then I showed a photo of a group of dolphins traveling together through water and explained that while we would call people traveling together a group, we call dolphins traveling together a pod. Aisha said, "So this is a picture of a pod of dolphins." I said, "Yes, that is correct." I left the picture on the computer screen, and we taped all the dolphins we had sketched together and created a pod of dolphins on a large sheet of paper. The students enjoyed that. After that we talked about *echolocation*. I again introduced the word in context. I read the text that noted that echolocation is what dolphins use to figure out where things like food and other animals are located. I said,

> *Echolocation* is one word, but it has two little words inside it. It has *echo* and it has *location*. It involves echos of sounds the dolphins make and it helps the dolphins know where things, such as animals that could hurt them, are located. So, *echolocation* involves *echos* and *locations*. It is really two small words put together to form one big word. Whenever we are trying to figure out big words, we should look inside them for small words.

Guided Comprehension: Animals of the Past…Animals of the Present
Monitoring: Say Something

Stage One: Engaging Prereading Sequence for English Learners

- **Engage** students in informal conversation.
- **Introduce** topic, **share** supports, and **activate** background knowledge.
- **Teach** essential vocabulary in context with supports.
- **Explicitly teach** reading comprehension strategies.

Stage Two: Teacher-Directed Whole-Group Instruction

- **Explain** monitoring and Say Something and how this technique helps us monitor our understanding.
- **Demonstrate** by using a read-aloud, a Think-Aloud, and modeling with students.
- **Guide** students to Say Something to a partner after listening to a section of text read aloud.
- **Practice** by having students Say Something to partners as the read-aloud continues.
- **Reflect** on the importance of thinking about what we read while we are reading.

Stage Three: Strategy Applications

Student-Facilitated Comprehension Centers

- **Art Center:** Read student-authored stories and engage in Draw Something.
- **Fluency Center:** Engage in Patterned Partner Reading while reading books about animals.
- **Question and Answer Center:** Generate and respond to questions about animals.
- **Theme Center:** Read books about animals and engage in Write Something using stop-sign stickers and adapted Double-Entry Journals.
- **Writing Center:** Work with a partner to invent new animals and write and illustrate stories about them.

Teacher-Guided Small-Group Instruction

- **Review** strategies good students use. Focus on using Say Something to monitor understanding.
- **Guide** students to Say Something as they whisper read a text. Encourage a variety of responses.
- **Practice** by having students continue to Say Something as they finish reading the text.
- **Retell and Reflect** on the importance of monitoring as a way to check on understanding while reading.

Student-Facilitated Comprehension Routines

- **Literature Circles:** Select and read a group text, stopping periodically to Say Something.
- **Cross-Age Reading Experiences:** Read with upper-grade students or adult volunteers. Engage in Say Something while reading.

Stage Four: Sharing, Reflection, and Goal Setting

Teacher-Facilitated Whole-Group Reflection and Goal Setting

- **Share** applications of Say Something from Stage Three.
- **Reflect** on how Say Something helps us monitor our understanding of text.
- **Set new goals** or extend existing ones.

Next, I said "dolphin" and asked the students to echo what I said. Then I said it again and asked each of the students to say it after me, one after another. I explained that dolphin sounds travel quickly and then they bounce back to the dolphin. I showed a diagram about echolocation from Dolphin Ecolation (www.dolphins-world.com/Dolphin_Echolocation.html) and used it to explain how the sounds bounce back. The students thought this was a complex system for animals. Akiya said, "We are lucky that we can see our food and things that can hurt us. We don't need echolocation, but it is good that the dolphins can use it." After we finished our discussion, I began to explicitly teach how to use the comprehension application Say Something to help monitor understanding.

Explain: I explained that it is important that we understand what we are reading and that we often monitor or check on our understanding as we read. I noted that we had previously learned about Bookmark Technique, one way to check our understanding. I referenced the Bookmark Technique classroom examples to support students' thinking. Then I explained that Say Something is another way we can monitor our understanding. I explained that we could use Say Something when working with a partner or in a trio. I explained that when we use Say Something, we would read a section of the text, stop and Say Something—an idea based on what we have read—and then continue reading, stopping periodically to Say Something—share another idea.

Demonstrate: I began to demonstrate by noting that I needed to have a partner or be part of a small group to engage in Say Something. I asked if the students would like to be part of the small group and they all agreed. Next, I shared copies of *Dolphins* by Seymour Simon (2009) and introduced the text. I explained that we would be focusing on Simon's sections on pods and bottlenose dolphins, which began on page 17. I explained that I would be reading a short segment of text and then I would *say something* I found interesting. I would also need someone in the group to *say something* he or she found interesting in what we had read. Akiya volunteered to Say Something when the time came. I read about dolphins being social and traveling in pods. When I finished, I said, "I thought it was interesting that there could be anywhere from 2 to 12 dolphins in a pod." Akiya said, "I thought it was interesting that dolphins that are in a pod know each other even if they are away from each other for a very long time." I praised Akiya and asked who would like to be my next partner for Say Something. Willem said he would like to do it. So, I read another section about pods and said, "I think it is interesting that young adult male dolphins help each other when hunting." Willem said, "I think it is interesting that one of the dolphins becomes the leader in the pod." I praised Willem for his response.

Guide: I guided students to Say Something after I read aloud, and they whisper read a short segment about the bottlenose dolphin. Aisha and Agacia volunteered. When we finished reading, Aisha said, "I thought it was interesting that male bottlenose dolphins are bigger than females." Agacia said, "I thought it was interesting that bottlenose dolphins can be 12 feet long and weigh 1,400 pounds."

Practice: Students continued to practice Say Something after I read aloud, and they whisper read the final segment about bottlenose dolphins. Neema and Siti took turns saying something. Then pairs of students reread the section on bottlenose dolphins and engaged in Draw Something (a variation of Say Something) after reading each segment. Students shared their drawings and we talked about what we had read.

Reflect: We reflected by focusing on the facts we had learned about pods and bottlenose dolphins. Then we discussed how Say Something helped us to monitor or check on our understanding of what we read. Siti said, "I like Say Something and Draw Something. Sometimes after reading I am not sure what to say, but now I can Say Something I read and my partner can, too." Neema said, "I like it because deciding what to say helps me think about what I read." We finished our conversation and moved on to whole-group instruction.

STAGE TWO: Teacher-Directed Whole-Group Instruction

Text: *Bats* (Gibbons, 2000)

Explain: I began by explaining to the students the importance of monitoring our understanding while we are reading. I reminded them that our ultimate goal was to make sense of the text and that while we were reading, we should be asking ourselves if what we were reading is making sense. I described Say Something as a technique we could use to help us examine what we were reading to see if it does make sense. I noted that Say Something would help us think about our reading and share our ideas. I explained that we could use Say Something when working with a partner or in a trio. I explained that when using this technique, we would read a section of the text, stop and Say Something based on what we have read, and then continue reading, stopping periodically to Say Something.

Demonstrate: I demonstrated Say Something by using a read-aloud and a Think-Aloud. I also modeled the technique with two of my students. Billy, James, and I planned the demonstration a few days before the lesson. I began by introducing the text. I shared the cover and title and read the first three pages. I focused on the factual information about bats, and then Billy, James, and I engaged in Say Something. I said, "I didn't know that bats are shy and gentle animals. I think that's interesting because I always thought they were harmful." Billy said, "I didn't know that *nocturnal* meant that they were awake at night and asleep during the day." James said, "There are almost a thousand kinds of bats. I thought there was only one." I read the next two pages and said, "I didn't know that bats were the only mammals that could fly." Billy said, "I didn't know that baby bats are born—not hatched from eggs." James said, "I didn't know that bats are 50 million years old. That's really, really old."

Guide: Students worked with partners as I read the next four pages and stopped to guide the students to Say Something to their partners about what I had read. I suggested focusing on restating facts they already knew, revising ideas they had that now appeared to be incorrect, and learning new information. As I monitored, I heard a variety of responses including, "Bats have arms and fingers," "Bats can change direction quickly," "Bats can fly high and fast," and "I knew bats hung upside down, but I didn't know they held on by their toe claws."

Practice: I read the next section and stopped to provide the pairs of students with time to Say Something. I circulated around the room to monitor what students were saying and offer support as necessary. We continued this process throughout the reading of the book. Then we summarized what we had learned about bats. The book had in-depth information about bats, and the students enjoyed learning so many new things about them.

Reflect: We reflected on the importance of thinking about what we are reading and how using techniques like Say Something helped us engage with text and monitor our understanding. Richard said, "I need to think about what I will say when we're using Say Something." Gabrielle said, "I like Say Something because we can pick what we want to say."

STAGE THREE: Teacher-Guided Small-Group Instruction

Text: *Sea Turtles* (Gibbons, 2005) (Texts varied according to students' abilities.)

Review: First, I reviewed with students the strategies good readers use to make sense of text, and then I focused them on monitoring by using Say Something.

Guide: We briefly discussed what we knew about turtles in general and about sea turtles in particular. Next, I introduced the text by sharing the cover and reading the first few pages. Then I guided the students to read the text, stopping at designated points to Say Something. (I had placed stop-sign stickers in the texts to indicate where the students should stop.) Then they started to whisper read the book. I listened to each student whisper read a portion of the text to check for fluency. The students read two sections of text and stopped at designated points to Say Something to their partners. I encouraged a variety of responses, including predictions, connections, and questions. Students' comments included, "I didn't know that a bunch of sea turtle eggs were called a clutch," "I think it is interesting that sea turtles can lay 100 eggs at a time," and "I think it's sad that some people steal the sea turtles' eggs."

Practice: Students finished whisper reading *Sea Turtles*, stopping at designated points to Say Something to a partner. I continued to monitor throughout this process. When the students had finished reading, we discussed many new things we had learned about sea turtles.

Retell and Reflect: We did a choral rereading of the text and summarized what we had learned. Next, we discussed that what we say during Say Something can differ when we read different kinds of text. Then we reflected on how Say Something helped us make sense of what we were reading. Joaquin observed, "When we use Say Something, we get to say what we think is important about what we read."

Student-Facilitated Comprehension Centers

A number of general accommodations were made for English learners when they engaged in the comprehension centers. These included the following:

- Including animal books and articles written in Spanish among the texts available in the centers
- Making other culturally relevant texts available in the centers
- Integrating multiple modes of representing thinking in student responses (sketching, singing, dramatizing)
- Inviting students to work with other English learners of the same culture when reading texts in their native languages
- Encouraging English learners to partner with native English speakers when working in centers such as fluency, question and answer, vocabulary, and other centers focused on fluency and language development.

Art Center: Students read student-authored animal stories and engaged in Draw Something (see Appendix A, page 274). The completed organizers were displayed in our theme gallery.

Fluency Center: Pairs of students either read along with books on tape or CD or engaged in Patterned Partner Reading to practice their fluency.

Question and Answer Center: Students generated and responded to questions about animals of their choice. Question starters, based on Ciardiello's (1998, 2007) signal words (see Chapter 3, pages 33–34), were available for student use.

Theme Center: I placed a variety of animal books at this center and inserted stop-sign stickers at several points in each text. Pairs of students selected books to partner read. They used the partner-reading pattern Read–Pause–Say Something. They paused to Say Something each time they encountered a stop-sign sticker. Students recorded their responses on adapted Double-Entry Journal forms on which the column headings were replaced by the two students' names.

Writing Center: Pairs of students invented a new animal and wrote a story about it. Then each of them created an illustration of the new animal.

Student-Facilitated Comprehension Routines

A number of general accommodations were made for English learners when they engaged in the comprehension routines. These included the following:

- Making culturally relevant texts available
- Integrating multiple modes of representing thinking in student responses (sketching, singing, dramatizing)
- Encouraging English learners to choose to partner with native English speakers when working in Literature Circles
- Encouraging English learners to choose to partner with native language speakers or English language speakers when working in Cross-Age Reading Experiences

Literature Circles: Groups of students partner read animal books of their choice. One of the roles in our adapted Literature Circles was "the stopper." That student held up a stop sign and said, "Stop reading and Say Something at the end of page XXX." At that point, each student said something to the group. The stopper did this at points I had specified in the text he or she was reading. When the students finished reading the text, they engaged in discussion.

Cross-Age Reading Experiences: Upper-grade students and adult volunteers visited the class and paired with students from our class. Students read an animal book either to or with the cross-age literacy volunteer and engaged in Say Something. Then the students orally summarized what they had read.

STAGE FOUR: Teacher-Facilitated Whole-Group Reflection and Goal Setting

Share: Students shared and discussed their applications of Say Something in small groups. This included responses recorded in students' Guided Comprehension Journals and the Draw Something organizers displayed in our theme gallery. Then each group shared with the whole class.

Reflect: We reflected on how using Say Something helped us monitor our understanding of what we were reading. Students seemed to enjoy using this technique.

Set New Goals: Students thought that they did a good job of using Say Something to help monitor their understanding. We revisited the idea of how what we say in Say Something is influenced by the type of text we are reading. We decided to extend our goal and use Say Something when reading different types of text, including poetry.

Assessment Options

I observed students during all stages of Guided Comprehension and reviewed and commented on their responses in their Guided Comprehension Journals, their completed Double-Entry Journal forms, and their completed Draw Something graphic organizers. I also completed running records and retellings with selected students.

Reflection on Teaching the English Learners in Our Class

I am truly enjoying watching each of the English learners engage in conversation with just a little more confidence every time we meet in our Guided Comprehension lessons. I was a bit apprehensive about teaching Say Something because many of the other strategy applications involved writing, but the students were fine with it. I think that may have been because they are so accustomed to discussing what we read. Of course, Draw Something was even more popular because the students really enjoy sketching. I think we have reached a time when we are all very comfortable with each other. Our Engaging Prereading Sequence has turned out to be a very relaxing teaching and learning setting, and our classroom has turned into quite a learning community—one in which everyone is celebrated. We're all enjoying that.

Final Thoughts About the Animals of the Past...Animals of the Present Theme

Whether reading about dinosaurs, polar bears, wolves, bats, or sea turtles, students engaged in this theme reveled in learning about animals. The readers were equally captivated by information from books and websites, and all readily engaged in discussion.

It is important to acknowledge that lessons about a variety of skills that underpin comprehension strategies were taught during this theme. For example, aspects of language development and skills such as sequencing, generating questions, and distinguishing important from less important ideas were embedded in the theme. A variety of informational texts such as *Dinosaurs: The Most Complete, Up-to-Date Encyclopedia for Dinosaur Lovers of All Ages* (Holtz & Rey, 2007), *Dorling Kindersley Guide to Dinosaurs: A Thrilling Journey through Prehistoric Times* (Lambert & Hutt, 2000), and *The Ultimate Dino-pedia: The Most Complete Dinosaur Reference Ever* (Lessem, 2010) were used to teach text frames and generating questions at a variety of levels. Timelines of dinosaur discoveries were used to teach sequencing. Students also used Readers Theatre and repeated readings to improve fluency. Students' fascination with the dinosaur theme motivated them to read and promoted their engagement in learning. In addition, teachers engaged in read-alouds and encouraged students to use multiple modes of representing their thinking, including sketching, singing, and dramatizing.

Theme Resources

Books

Andreae, G. (2001). *Giraffes can't dance.* New York: Scholastic.

Arlon, P. (2004). *First animal encyclopedia* (DK reference series). New York: Dorling Kindersley.

Barner, B. (2001). *Dinosaur bones.* San Francisco: Chronicle.

Base, G. (2001). *The water hole.* New York: Abrams.

Benton, M.J. (2000). *The encyclopedia of awesome dinosaurs.* Brookfield, CT: Copper Beech.

Berger, M., & Berger, G. (2000). *Do penguins get frostbite? Questions and answers about polar animals.* New York: Scholastic.

Bingham, C. (2006). *First dinosaur encyclopedia.* New York: Dorling Kindersley.

Buckley, C. (2009). *Tarra & Bella: The elephant and dog who became best friends.* New York: Putnam.

Carle, E. (1989). *Eric Carle's animals, animals.* New York: Philomel.

Crotty, K.M. (2000). *Dinosongs: Poems to celebrate a T-rex named Sue.* New York: Scholastic.

Dixon, D. (2005). *Visual encyclopedia of dinosaurs.* New York: Dorling Kindersley.

Dorling Kindersley. (2006). *Encyclopedia of animals.* New York: Author.

Dorling Kindersley. (2011). *Animal: The definitive visual guide.* New York: Author.

Dowswell, P., Malam, J., Mason, P., & Parker, S. (2002). *The ultimate book of dinosaurs: Everything you always wanted to know about dinosaurs—but were too terrified to ask.* London: Parragon.

Florian, D. (2000). *Mammalabilia: Poems and paintings.* New York: Scholastic.

George, J.C. (1997). *Look to the north: A wolf pup diary.* New York: Scholastic.

Gibbons, G. (2000). *Bats.* New York: Holiday House.

Gibbons, G. (2002). *Polar bears.* New York: Holiday House.

Gibbons, G. (2005). *Sea turtles.* Pine Plains, NY: Live Oak Media.
Hatkoff, I., Hatkoff, C., & Kahumbu, P. (2006). *Owen & Mzee: The true story of a remarkable friendship.* New York: Scholastic.
Holland, J.S. (2011). *Unlikely friendships: 47 remarkable stories from the animal kingdom.* New York: Workman.
Holtz, T.R., & Rey, L.V. (2007). *Dinosaurs: The most complete, up-to-date encyclopedia for dinosaur lovers of all ages.* New York: Random House.
Hughes, C.D. (2010). *National Geographic little kids first big book of animals.* Washington, DC: National Geographic.
Lambert, D., & Hutt, S. (2000). *Dorling Kindersley guide to dinosaurs: A thrilling journey through prehistoric times.* New York: Dorling Kindersley.
Lauber, P. (1998). *The news about dinosaurs.* New York: Aladdin.
Lessem, D. (2010). *The ultimate dino-pedia: The most complete dinosaur reference ever.* Washington, DC: National Geographic.
Matthew, W.D. (2011). *Dinosaurs: With special reference to the American Museum Collections.* New York: Echo Library.
McGhee, K., & McKay, G. (2006). *National Geographic encyclopedia of animals.* Washington, DC: National Geographic.
McGough, K. (2001). *Fossils.* Washington, DC: National Geographic.
McKay, G. (2004). *The encyclopedia of animals: A complete visual guide.* Berkeley: University of California Press.
National Geographic Society. (2000). *National Geographic animal encyclopedia.* Washington, DC: Author.
National Geographic. (2010). *Nat Geo wild animal atlas: Earth's astonishing animals and where they live.* Washington, DC: Author.
Pallotta, J. (1990). *The dinosaur alphabet book.* Watertown, MA: Charlesbridge.
Paul, G.S. (2010). *The Princeton field guide to dinosaurs.* Princeton, NJ: Princeton University Press.
Pringle, L. (2000). *Bats! Strange and wonderful.* Honesdale, PA: Boyds Mills.
Pringle, L. (2001). *Scholastic encyclopedia of animals.* New York: Scholastic.
Quigley, S. (2008). *The dinosaur museum: An unforgettable, interactive virtual tour through dinosaur history.* Washington, DC: National Geographic.
Relf, P. (2000). *A dinosaur named Sue: The story of the colossal fossil.* New York: Scholastic.
Robinson, F. (1999). *A dinosaur named Sue: The find of the century.* New York: Scholastic.
Sabuda, R., & Reinhart, M. (2005). *Encyclopedia prehistorica dinosaurs: The definitive pop-up.* Somerville, MA: Candlewick.
Simon, S. (2001). *Crocodiles and alligators.* New York: HarperCollins.
Simon, S. (2002). *Animals nobody loves.* San Francisco: Chronicle.
Simon, S. (2002). *Baby animals.* San Francisco: Chronicle.
Simon, S. (2002). *Killer whales* (See more readers, level 1). San Francisco: Chronicle.
Simon, S. (2005). *Amazing bats* (See more readers, level 1). San Francisco: Chronicle.
Simon, S. (2006). *Horses.* New York: HarperCollins.
Simon, S. (2006). *Whales.* New York: Collins.
Simon, S. (2007). *Penguins.* New York: Collins.

Simon, S. (2007). *Snakes.* New York: Collins.
Simon, S. (2008). *Gorillas.* New York: Collins.
Simon, S. (2009). *Cats.* New York: Collins.
Simon, S. (2009). *Dogs.* New York: Collins.
Simon, S. (2009). *Dolphins.* New York: Collins.
Simon, S. (2009). *Wolves.* New York: Collins.
Thimmesh, C. (2011). *Friends: True stories of extraordinary animal friendships.* Boston: Houghton Mifflin.
Vail, R. (2001). *Mama Rex & T: Homework trouble.* New York: Scholastic.
Wilkes, A. (1994). *The big book of dinosaurs: A first book for young children.* New York: Dorling Kindersley.
Zimmerman, H., & Olshevsky, G. (2000). *Dinosaurs! The biggest baddest strangest fastest.* New York: Simon & Schuster.

Dinosaur Books: Spanish Editions

Barrett, P., Sanz, L., & Martin, R. (2008). *Larousse dinosaurios: Del inicio a la extinción* (Larousse dinosaurs: From the origin to extinction). London: Larousse Editorial.
Frost, H. (2008). *Estegosaurio/stegosaurus* (Dinosaurios y animales prehistoricos/Dinosaurs and prehistoric animals series). North Mankato, MN: Capstone.
Frost, H. (2006). *Mamut lanudo/Woolly mammoth* (Dinosaurios y animales prehistoricos/Dinosaurs and prehistoric animals series). North Mankato, MN: Capstone.
Frost, H. (2008). *Tiranosaurio rex/Tyrannosaurus rex* (Dinosaurios y animales prehistoricos/Dinosaurs and prehistoric animals series). North Mankato, MN: Capstone.
Frost, H. (2008). *Triceratops/triceratops* (Dinosaurios y animales prehistoricos/Dinosaurs and prehistoric animals series). North Mankato, MN: Capstone.
Lessem, D., & Bindon, J. (2005). *Dinosaurios cornudos/Horned dinosaurs* (Meet the dinosaurs). Minneapolis, MN: Lerner.
Lindeen, C.K. (2007). *Apatosaurio/apatosaurus* (Dinosaurios y animales prehistoricos/Dinosaurs and prehistoric animals series). North Mankato, MN: Capstone.
Mattern, J. (2007). *Tyrannosaurus rex/Tiranosaurio rex* (Let's read about dinosaurs/Conozcamos a los dinosaurios). Delran, NJ: Weekly Reader.
Nunn, D. (2007). *Velociraptor* (Dinosaurios/dinosaurs). Mankato, MN: Heinemann-Raintree.
Priddy Books. (2012). *Mi libro gigante de dinosaurios.* New York: Macmillan.
Riehecky, J. (2007). *Pteranodonte/pteranodon* (Dinosaurios y animales prehistoricos/Dinosaurs and prehistoric animals series). North Mankato, MN: Capstone.
Williams, J. (2007). *Descubriendo dinosaurios con un cazador de fósiles* (Discovering dinosaurs with a fossil hunter) (I like science! bilingual). Berkeley Heights, NJ: Enslow Elementary.

Websites

Animals

Animal Planet
animal.discovery.com

Animals.com
animals.com

Animals: Nat Geo Wild
animals.nationalgeographic.com/animals/

SeaWorld/Busch Gardens Animal Information Database
www.seaworld.org/animal-info/info-books/index.htm

South Washington County Schools: Animals
www.sowashco.k12.mn.us/virtualmedia/elementary/animals.htm

The Arctic and Its Animals
library.thinkquest.org/3500/animals.htm

Dinosaurs

DinoDictionary
www.dinodictionary.com

Dinorama
magma.nationalgeographic.com/ngexplorer/0203/adventures/

Dinosaur Fossils
www.enchantedlearning.com/subjects/dinosaurs/dinofossils/

Dinosaur Games and Puzzles
www.enchantedlearning.com/subjects/dinosaurs/fun/Games.html

Dinosaur Illustrations
www.search4dinosaurs.com/index.html

The Dinosauria
www.ucmp.berkeley.edu/diapsids/dinosaur.html

Discovery Dinosaur Central
dsc.discovery.com/dinosaurs

Kids-Dinosaurs.com
www.kids-dinosaurs.com/different-types-of-dinosaurs.html

Kids Domain Dinosaurs Links
www.kidsdomain.com/kids/links/Dinosaurs.html

Natural History Museum: The Dino Directory
www.nhm.ac.uk/nature-online/life/dinosaurs-other-extinct-creatures/dino-directory

Smithsonian National Museum of Natural History: Dinosaurs
paleobiology.si.edu/dinosaurs/

Sue at The Field Museum
archive.fieldmuseum.org/sue/#index

Dinosaurs: Facts and Fiction
pubs.usgs.gov/gip/dinosaurs/

Zoom Dinosaurs
www.enchantedlearning.com/subjects/dinosaurs/toc.shtml

Dogs

FunnyFidos.com
www.funnyfidos.com/fun-dog-facts

Good Dog Training Advice: 10 Fun Facts About Dogs
gooddogtrainingadvice.com/10-Fun-Facts-About-Dogs.html

Dolphins

Amazing Facts About Dolphins
www.ego4u.com/en/read-on/animals/dolphin/facts

Animal Planet: Dolphins Explored
animal.discovery.com/features/dolphins/facts/facts.html

Bottlenose Dolphin: Natural History and Ecology
www.dolphin-institute.org/resource_guide/nathistandecol.htm

Defenders of Wildlife: Dolphin
www.defenders.org/wildlife_and_habitat/wildlife/dolphin.php

Dolphin Facts and Information
www.dolphins-world.com

The Dolphin Institute
www.dolphin-institute.org

Animals: Nat Geo Wild: Bottlenose Dolphin
animals.nationalgeographic.com/animals/mammals/bottlenose-dolphin/

Scholastic Teachers Wild Animal Watch: Dolphins
teacher.scholastic.com/dolphin/index.htm

Science Kids Animal Facts: Dolphins
www.sciencekids.co.nz/sciencefacts/animals/dolphin.html

Polar Bears

Polar Bears International
www.polarbearsinternational.org/polar-bears/bear-essentials-polar-style

Animal Facts: The Polar Bear
www.kidzone.ws/sg/polarbear/polar_bear.htm

Seymour Simon

Reading Rockets: Seymour Simon
www.readingrockets.org/books/interviews/simon

Scholastic Biography: Seymour Simon
www2.scholastic.com/browse/contributor.jsp?id=2232

Seymour Simon Personal Website
www.seymoursimon.com

Whales

Facts on Whales for Kids
www.essortment.com/whales-kids-55761.html

Killer Whale
www.kidsplanet.org/factsheets/orca.html

Wolves

International Wolf Center: Teaching the World About Wolves
www.wolf.org/wolves/learn/justkids/kids.asp

KidsKonnect.com: Wolves
www.kidskonnect.com/subject-index/13-animals/56-wolves.html

National Geographic Kids: Gray Wolves
kids.nationalgeographic.com/Animals/CreatureFeature/Graywolf

Performance Extensions Across the Curriculum

Art/Drama/Music

- Students visit the local museum of natural history or virtual museums online to observe the appearance of different kinds of dinosaurs. Students can use the information gleaned from this experience, other websites, and texts to create different kinds of dinosaurs in a variety of mediums from sketching to an Eric Carle–style collage.
- Students write and perform a variety of songs about dinosaurs or other animals. As an alternative, students can create Lyric Summaries about animals by adapting classic melodies. They can also create posters to advertise their songs and use rhythm instruments while performing the songs.
- Students create class art projects to support their reading of books about animals. For example, they can create a sculpture of a whale or a drawing of a wolf. Provide materials to create in various mediums, including construction paper, paints, markers, crayons, clay, and so on. Students can use information they researched in science to help construct animals accurately.
- Students participate in a music class talent show in which groups sing songs they have written related to Seymour Simon animal books. Students play rhythm instruments while singing.

Mathematics

- Students create and solve dino-problems using the measurements and weights of a variety of dinosaurs. They base the problems on the mathematical operations currently being studied. They also design dino-math cards by writing the problem on one side of the card and a solution on the other.
- Students read a Seymour Simon book on the animal of their choice (*Penguins, Whales, Wolves*) and work with a partner to create math problems and solutions based on that topic. They use multiple mathematical operations, including the ones currently being studied.
- Students survey teachers and other students about their favorite animals and graph the results.
- Students use the Write and Draw math strategy (McLaughlin, Corbett, & Stevenson, 2000) to employ both words and symbols to make students' thinking about problem solving visible to themselves and others. They begin by posing a problem about animals. The students read or listen to the problem and paraphrase if desired. Next, the students record their thinking about how to solve the problem on a paper that has been divided in half vertically. On one side of the paper, students draw a picture to show how they would solve the problem. On the other side, they use words to describe how they solved the problem. Finally, the students share their Write and Draw applications with a partner.

Science

- Students explore how fossils are created and endure through such prolonged periods of time. They visit the local museum to examine plant or animal fossils that have been found in the community. They discuss what can be learned from fossils. They also create fossil-like imprints in class and write about them.
- Students investigate the work of paleontologists. They create an illustrated, interactive timeline of the process from fossil discovery to fossil exhibition by examining dinosaur discoveries such as the T-rex skeleton named Sue. (Sue is on display at The Field Museum. See archive.fieldmuseum.org/sue for more information.)
- Students visit any of the various animal websites and research animals of choice. Information can be placed on a mobile to be displayed in the theme gallery.
- Students work with a partner to create a PowerPoint presentation or an illustrated poster about the habitat of a particular animal, such as a polar bear, lion, or elephant.

Social Studies

- Students create a wall map of dino-discovery sites. Then small groups research each site to learn more about the type of dinosaur(s) discovered there, as well as information about the country, the culture, and the people who live there. Students include what they learn in an electronic class book.
- Students work with a partner to gather information about a meat-eating dinosaur and a planting-eating dinosaur. They compare and contrast characteristics of the two animals using a Venn Diagram. The students explain their similarities and differences to the class by writing a song about them or creating a painting or sculpture of them.
- Students explore animals in different habitats around the world (such as a desert or rainforest). They report what they learn in a Press Conference.
- Students read informational texts about animals. They create projects such as illustrated definition poems and Lyric Summaries to present what they have learned.

Culminating Activity

Animals, Animals! A Celebration of Past and Present. Students will create and deliver invitations to their families and friends to participate in this theme celebration. Students' performances across the curriculum from the animal theme will be displayed in the hallways approaching the classroom. Other performances such as self-authored books, a class alphabet book, Lyric Summaries, mobiles, and strategy applications will be displayed inside the classroom. Students and guests will wear nametags shaped liked a variety of animals. Students will wear animal masks that they created in art class and serve as guides, sharing their knowledge of animals of the past and present as they escort their guests on tours of the classroom. Some students will narrate videos of selected animals in their natural habitats. An expert from a local university or museum will speak briefly about dinosaurs and make connections to the students' performances. As desserts are served, a PowerPoint slideshow featuring the highlights of theme performances and field trips will be presented. During the course of the celebration, everyone will be invited to visit an interactive computer display titled *We Like Animals!* where students and guests will write their reactions to and comments about the Animals of the Past...Animals of the Present theme. Students will give their families autographed CDs of the class book *Our Poems About Animals* as thank-you gifts for attending the theme celebration.

CHAPTER 9

Favorite Authors: Eve Bunting, Doreen Cronin, Gary Soto, and Gary Paulsen

Authors are writers who share unique perspectives on a variety of topics. They may write to entertain, to persuade, or to inform. They may share life experiences, offer insights into social or historical issues, detail the humor of a situation, or serve as tour guides on imaginative journeys. Our favorite authors have engaging styles that motivate us to read. Eve Bunting, Doreen Cronin, Gary Soto, and Gary Paulsen are a few of the authors we and our students love to read.

Eve Bunting is a perennial favorite because she has written on a wide variety of topics with great expertise. Whether telling the emotional story of an adult's first reading experiences in *The Wednesday Surprise*, recounting the Los Angeles riots in *Smoky Nights*, relating a story of homeless life in *Fly Away Home*, acknowledging Vietnam veterans in *The Wall*, or telling a story about a young immigrant of Arab descent in *One Green Apple*, Bunting writes from a perspective of knowledge and candor.

From the moment we read *Click, Clack, Moo* and learned that cows could type, we and our students have been fans of Doreen Cronin's stories. They are engaging, funny tales that often focus on somewhat different views of life on a farm. Needless to say, in that setting the animals always seem to outsmart Farmer Brown. Beyond her cow and duck titles, Cronin has also provided us with humorous insights into the personal thoughts of the main characters in *Diary of a Worm*, *Diary of a Spider*, and *Diary of a Fly*. These books make it easy for us and our students to make connections to the characters' families, friends, and school lives. The unique photo album excerpts featured inside the front and back covers of the diaries serve as Connection Stems, and our students can relate to all of them.

Another favorite author, Gary Soto, writes short stories, books, poetry, and plays. He has also ventured into the biography genre by authoring *Jessie De La Cruz: A Profile of a United Farm Worker.* Although the themes of his works are universal, Soto draws heavily on his Mexican American heritage in his writing. In addition to being an author, he is a professor of creative writing at the University of California, Riverside. Some of the favorite Soto titles are *Baseball in April and Other Stories*, *The Skirt*, *Novio Boy*, *Taking Sides*, *Canto Familiar*, and *Neighborhood Odes*.

Gary Paulsen, our final favorite author, has written picture books, young adult novels, adult novels, and two autobiographical volumes: *Eastern Sun, Winter Moon* and *Guts*. Whenever Paulsen shares his literacy history, he is quick to note that his life changed one cold night when he went into a library to get warm. The librarian offered him a library card and that's what sparked his interest in reading. Paulsen frequently writes about his life experiences. For example, in *Winterdance* he chronicles his participation in the Iditarod, a grueling 1,180-mile dogsled race across Alaska.

The favorite author theme was of particular interest to English learners in the classes in which the lessons were taught. The teachers held high expectations for these students throughout the lessons, and their hopes were fulfilled. The teachers created culturally responsive classrooms in which diversity was appreciated by all. They valued all students' cultural heritages and used that information to support teaching and learning in an educational community. They also used the Guided Comprehension Model for English Learners, a structured lesson format, and appropriate supports, including visuals and adapted graphic organizers, to teach.

In conversations held during the Engaging Prereading Sequence, English learners displayed good background knowledge about stories. They knew how to tell a story and were aware of the narrative elements—characters, setting, problem, attempts to resolve the problem, and resolution. The English learners seemed happy to learn in this small-group setting and eager to engage in discussion. They were open to reading stories written by a wide variety of authors, but seemed especially interested when a book connected to their lives. The teachers were particularly attentive to motivating students, activating background knowledge, and sharing engaging read-alouds. During the Engaging Prereading Sequence, students actively participated as the teachers engaged them with interesting, accessible text; provided meaningful visual supports; invited students to respond in multiple modes (speaking, writing, sketching, dramatizing, and singing); provided sufficient wait time when questions were raised; taught essential vocabulary in context; and explicitly taught reading comprehension strategies.

When the English learners moved on to whole-group instruction, they were comfortable, well prepared, and eager to participate. In this setting, opportunities to work with partners and multiple modes of response were prevalent throughout explicit instruction. The comprehension strategy focus was the same one they learned to use during the Engaging Prereading Sequence, so they were always familiar with it. In addition, these lessons occasionally focused on the teaching of reading skills. A prime example of this focused on teaching students how to generate and respond to questions at multiple levels (see Chapter 3, page 22). Text supports and wait time were provided, and students actively engaged. In teacher-guided small-group instruction, students often had the opportunity to whisper read text with a partner or on their own. They also engaged in discussion and practiced using comprehension skills and strategies. Students were able to represent their thinking in multiple ways.

In Guided Comprehension Centers and Routines, English learners partnered with native language speakers or native English speakers, depending on the nature of the activity. For example, when reading theme-related texts in their native language to support their understanding in the theme center, they worked with native language speakers. Conversely, when engaging in activities at the fluency center, the students would typically work with native English speakers. In addition, culturally relevant texts, including titles published in native languages, were available in the centers. In these settings, multiple opportunities were provided for students to interact with text to make content more comprehensible.

The sample Theme-Based Plan for Guided Comprehension: Favorite Authors: Eve Bunting, Doreen Cronin, Gary Soto, and Gary Paulsen (see Figure 13), offers an overview of the thinking and resources that support the theme. It makes connections to the Common Core State Standards (CCSS; Common Core State Standards Initiative, 2010c) and presents a sampling of assessments, texts, technology resources, comprehension strategies, teaching ideas, comprehension centers, and comprehension routines. The plan begins by delineating examples of student goals and related Common Core College and Career Readiness Anchor Standards for Reading, Writing, Speaking and Listening, and Language. The student goals for this theme include the following:

- Use appropriate comprehension skills and strategies
- Interpret and respond to text in a variety of ways
- Write a variety of types of text
- Communicate effectively

The CCSS for English Language Arts (Common Core State Standards Initiative, 2010c) delineate grade-level expectations in reading, writing, speaking, and listening. They were designed to help teachers prepare all students to be college and career ready. This includes English learners.

The CCSS (Common Core State Standards Initiative, 2010c, p. 7) suggest that students who are college and career ready

- Demonstrate independence
- Build strong content knowledge
- Respond to the varying demands of audience, task, purpose, and discipline
- Comprehend as well as critique
- Value evidence
- Use technology and digital media strategically and capably
- Understand other perspectives and cultures

In this theme, the lessons are aligned with the Common Core College and Career Readiness Anchor Standards for Reading, Writing, Speaking and Listening, and Language. The key features of these standards include the following (Common Core State Standards Initiative, 2010c, p. 8):

- Reading: Text complexity and the growth of comprehension
- Writing: Text types, responding to reading, and research
- Speaking and Listening: Flexible communication and collaboration
- Language: Conventions, effective use, and vocabulary

The Common Core State Standards addressed in this theme follow. These standards are directly related to the College and Career Readiness Anchor Standards for Reading, Writing, Speaking and Listening, and Language. (For a complete listing of the Common Core State Standards for English Language Arts, see www.corestandards.org/assets/CCSSI_ELA%20Standards.pdf.)

Figure 13. Theme-Based Plan for Guided Comprehension: Favorite Authors: Eve Bunting, Doreen Cronin, Gary Soto, and Gary Paulsen

Goals and Common Core College and Career Readiness Anchor Standards for Reading, Writing, Speaking and Listening, and Language

Students will

- Use appropriate comprehension strategies
- Interpret literature
- Write retellings and reviews
- Communicate effectively

For related College and Career Readiness Standards and Common Core State Standards, see pages 145–148.

Assessment

The following measures can be used for a variety of purposes, including diagnostic, formative, and summative assessment:

Connection Stems
Draw and Write Retellings
Draw and Write Visualizations
Evaluative Questioning
Observation
Student Self-Assessments

Comprehension Strategies	Teaching Ideas
1. Visualizing 2. Making Connections 3. Summarizing 4. Evaluating	1. Draw and Write Visualizations 2. Connection Stems 3. Draw and Write Retellings 4. Evaluative Questioning

Text

1. *One Green Apple* (Bunting, 2006)
2. *Click, Clack, Moo: Cows That Type* (Cronin, 2000)
3. *Taking Sides* (Soto, 2003)
4. *Winterdance: The Fine Madness of Running the Iditarod* (Paulsen, 1994)

Comprehension Centers

Students will apply the comprehension strategies and related teaching ideas in the following comprehension centers:

Art Center
Fluency Center
Poetry Center
Project Center
Question and Answer Center
Theme Center
Vocabulary Center
Writing Center

Technology Resources

KidsReads.com: Eve Bunting
www.kidsreads.com/authors/au-bunting-eve.asp
Doreen Cronin Personal Website
www.doreencronin.com
The Official Gary Soto Website
www.garysoto.com
Random House Children's Books: Gary Paulsen
www.randomhouse.com/features/garypaulsen/about.html

Comprehension Routines

Students will apply the comprehension strategies and related teaching ideas in the following comprehension routines:

Literature Circles
Questioning the Author
Reciprocal Teaching

College and Career Readiness Standards for Reading

The categories of the College and Career Readiness Anchor Standards for Reading featured in these lessons include the following:

- Key Ideas and Details
- Craft and Structure
- Integration of Knowledge and Ideas
- Range of Reading and Level of Text Complexity

Key Ideas and Details

Examples of CCSS for Reading that support the anchor standards in this category include the following:

- Ask and answer questions to demonstrate understanding of a text, referring explicitly to the text as the basis for the answers
- Determine a theme of a story, drama, or poem from details in the text; summarize the text
- Describe in depth a character, setting, or event in a story or drama, drawing on specific details in the text (e.g., a character's thoughts, words, or actions)

Craft and Structure

Examples of CCSS for Reading that support the anchor standards in this category include the following:

- Read with sufficient accuracy and fluency to support comprehension
- Determine the meaning of words and phrases as they are used in a text, distinguishing literal from nonliteral language
- Refer to parts of stories, dramas, and poems when writing or speaking about a text, using terms such as *chapter, scene*, and *stanza*; describe how each successive part builds on earlier sections
- Describe how a narrator's or speaker's point of view influences how events are described

Integration of Knowledge and Ideas

Examples of CCSS for Reading that support the anchor standards in this category include the following:

- Make connections between the text of a story or drama and a visual or oral presentation of the text, identifying where each version reflects specific descriptions and directions in the text
- Compare and contrast stories in the same genre (e.g., mysteries and adventure stories) on their approaches to similar themes and topics

- Draw on information from multiple print or digital sources, demonstrating the ability to locate an answer to a question quickly or to solve a problem efficiently
- Integrate information from several texts on the same topic in order to write or speak about the subject knowledgeably

Range of Reading and Level of Text Complexity

Examples of CCSS for Reading that support the anchor standards in this category include the following:

- By the end of the year, read and comprehend literature, including stories, dramas, and poetry, at the high end of the grade-level text complexity band independently and proficiently

College and Career Readiness Standards for Writing

The categories of the College and Career Readiness Anchor Standards for Writing featured in these lessons include the following:

- Text Types and Purposes
- Production and Distribution of Writing
- Research to Build and Present Knowledge
- Range of Writing

Text Types and Purposes

Examples of CCSS for Writing that support the anchor standards in this category include the following:

- Write opinion pieces on topics or texts, supporting a point of view with reasons and information
- Write informative/explanatory texts to examine a topic and convey ideas and information clearly
- Write narratives to develop real or imagined experiences or events using effective technique, descriptive details, and clear event sequences

Production and Distribution of Writing

Examples of CCSS for Writing that support the anchor standards in this category include the following:

- Produce clear and coherent writing in which the development and organization are appropriate to task, purpose, and audience
- With guidance and support from peers and adults, develop and strengthen writing as needed by planning, revising, editing, rewriting, or trying a new approach

- With some guidance and support from adults, use technology, including the Internet, to produce and publish writing as well as to interact and collaborate with others
- Use technology, including the Internet, to produce and publish writing and present the relationships between information and ideas efficiently as well as to interact and collaborate with others

Range of Writing

Examples of CCSS for Writing that support the anchor standards in this category include the following:

- Write routinely over extended time frames (time for research, reflection, and revision) and shorter time frames (a single sitting or a day or two) for a range of discipline-specific tasks, purposes, and audiences

College and Career Readiness Anchor Standards for Speaking and Listening

The categories of the College and Career Readiness Anchor Standards for Speaking and Listening featured in these lessons include the following:

- Comprehension and Collaboration
- Presentation of Knowledge and Ideas

Comprehension and Collaboration

Examples of CCSS for Speaking and Listening that support the anchor standards in this category include the following:

- Engage effectively in a range of collaborative discussions (one-on-one, group, and teacher-led) with diverse partners on grade-appropriate topics and texts, building on others' ideas and expressing their own clearly

Presentation of Knowledge and Ideas

Examples of CCSS for Speaking and Listening that support the anchor standards in this category include the following:

- Report on a topic or text, tell a story, or recount an experience in an organized manner, using appropriate facts and relevant, descriptive details to support main ideas or themes; speak clearly at an understandable pace
- Include multimedia components (e.g., graphics, sound) and visual displays in presentations when appropriate to enhance the development of main ideas or themes
- Integrate multimedia and visual displays into presentations to clarify information, strengthen claims and evidence, and add interest

College and Career Readiness Anchor Standards for Language

The categories of the College and Career Readiness Anchor Standards for Language featured in these lessons include the following:

- Conventions of Standard English
- Knowledge of Language
- Vocabulary Acquisition and Use

Conventions of Standard English

Examples of CCSS for Language that support the anchor standards in this category include the following:

- Demonstrate command of the conventions of standard English grammar and usage when writing or speaking

Knowledge of Language

Examples of CCSS for Language that support the anchor standards in this category include the following:

- Use knowledge of language and its conventions when writing, speaking, reading, or listening

Vocabulary Acquisition and Use

Examples of CCSS for Language that support the anchor standards in this category include the following:

- Determine or clarify the meaning of unknown and multiple-meaning words and phrases based on grade-level reading and content, choosing flexibly from a range of strategies

Examples of assessments used in the theme-based Guided Comprehension lessons include observation, running records, strategy applications, student self-assessments, and student writing. The Guided Comprehension lessons, which were designed and taught by classroom teachers, are based on the following strategies and corresponding teaching ideas:

- Visualizing: Draw and Write Visualizations
- Making Connections: Connection Stems
- Summarizing: Draw and Write Retellings
- Evaluating: Evaluative Questioning

The Wednesday Surprise (Bunting, 1989), *Click, Clack, Moo: Cows That Type* (Cronin, 2000), *Taking Sides* (Soto, 2003), and *Winterdance: The Fine Madness of Running the Iditarod* (Paulsen, 1994) are the texts used in Stage Two for teacher-directed whole-group instruction. Numerous additional theme-related texts, including those used in teacher-guided small-group instruction and the student-facilitated comprehension centers and routines, are presented in the Theme Resources at the end of the chapter.

Examples of comprehension centers students use during Stage Three of Guided Comprehension include art, fluency, poetry, project, question and answer, theme, vocabulary, and writing. Students also engage in strategy applications in comprehension routines such as Literature Circles, Questioning the Author, and Reciprocal Teaching. Sample online resources—including websites for favorite authors Eve Bunting, Doreen Cronin, Gary Soto, and Gary Paulsen—complete the overview.

The four Guided Comprehension lessons that follow are presented through first-person teacher commentaries. Examples of student work are featured throughout the lessons.

Guided Comprehension Lessons

Favorite Author Eve Bunting
Guided Comprehension Strategy: Visualizing
Teaching Idea: Draw and Write Visualizations

STAGE ONE: Engaging Prereading Sequence for English Learners

We met for our Engaging Prereading Sequence in an informal sitting area I had organized for our conversations. I had previously met with the English learners in this small-group setting to explain what the Engaging Prereading Sequence was and what we would be doing when we met. I had told them that we would be having a conversation that would help them to take an active role in our reading when the class met in whole group. I had explained that we would be talking about some topics they already knew about and some that may be new to them. I told them that we would be talking about background knowledge and how to activate it. I also noted that we would be using the ideas we discussed later in whole group.

When we began our conversation, I reminded the students that we would be talking about another book written by Eve Bunting, a favorite author we had been studying. I told the students that the book we would be reading today was *The Wednesday Surprise* (Bunting, 1989). I introduced the book using Marie Clay's (1991) Storybook Introduction (see Appendix A) and began by sharing the title and cover and talking to the students about what they thought might happen in the book. They predicted it would be about a grandmother who reads books with her granddaughter. We talked about grandparents and what surprises are. The students made connections to grandparents living in the United States and in their native lands. Then we took a few minutes to think about a favorite time we had spent with grandparents. After that I invited the students to close their eyes and create a picture in their minds about a happy time they had spent with their grandparents. While their eyes were closed, I prompted the students to focus on their grandparents' faces, what they were wearing, and what they were doing. When the images were complete, I encouraged the students to sketch their *mind pictures* of their grandparents. We shared our drawings with partners and offered details about our favorite times with our grandparents. When we discussed surprises, the students talked about birthday presents, holiday gifts, and parties. Next, I read the first page of the book and did a brief picture walk, being careful not to reveal the ending. I noted that we could think about the illustrator's drawings as his mind pictures about the story. Figure 14 features Aldonza's mind picture about his grandparents.

Explain: I began by explaining visualizing and Draw and Write Visualizations. I made connections to the visualizing we had done with the images of our grandparents. Then I explained that as we read, we can visualize what we are reading. We can read a section of text, close our eyes, and create mind pictures about what we have read. Next, I explained that when we create mind pictures while we are reading, we often sketch what we see in our minds, so we can share our thoughts with a partner. We can also write a sentence telling about what appears in our mind pictures. I told the students that we call this Draw and Write Visualizations.

Demonstrate: I shared the Draw and Write Visualizations blackline (see Appendix A, page 273) and demonstrated how I would engage in Draw and Write Visualizations. I read the first section of the book and focused on the "breath pictures" Anna creates while waiting for her grandmother. It

Guided Comprehension: Favorite Author Eve Bunting
Visualizing: Draw and Write Visualizations

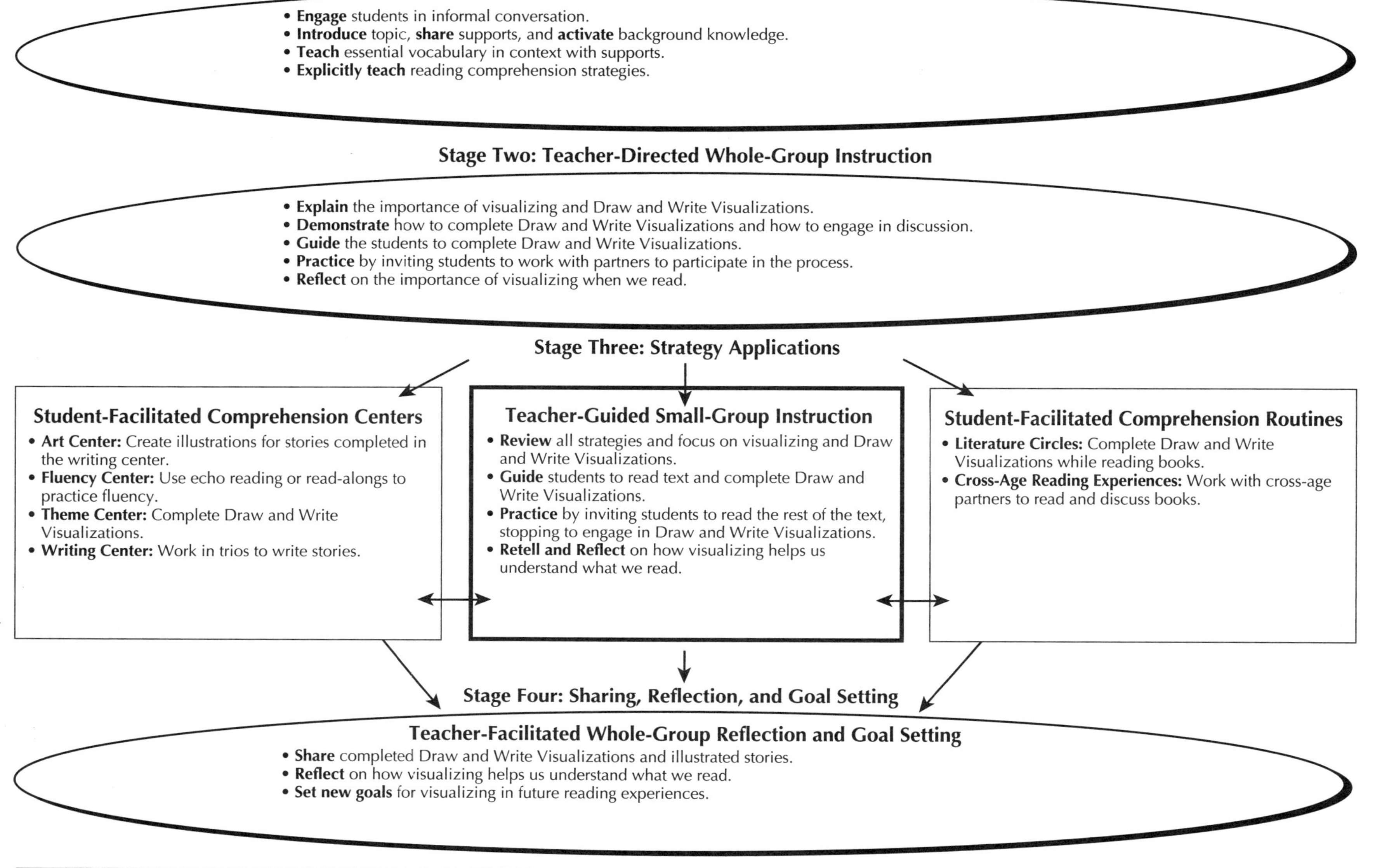

Figure 14. Aldonza's Mind Picture About His Grandparents

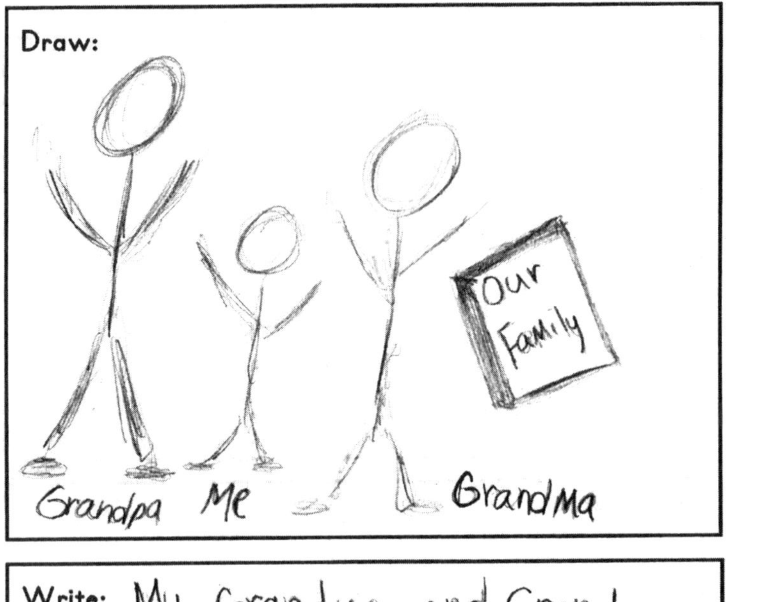

was winter and it was very cold outside. I invited the students to the window so they could watch me create a breath picture. They watched me as I huffed on the glass and then drew the big bag of books that Grandma was carrying. Then I invited the students to draw breath pictures related to the first part of the book and share them with a partner before we returned to our seats. The students found this to be a fun experience. Next, I explained that I still had the big bag of books as my mind picture. I sketched it on the blackline and wrote a sentence underneath it: "Grandma's bag of books is very big and heavy." I explained to the students that we did not need to be very good at drawing because we could use simple lines and shapes to draw our mind pictures.

Guide: I read another section of the text and guided the students to listen closely, close their eyes, and create mind pictures. A few of the students focused on Anna's father being a truck driver and drew a truck. They also wrote sentences; for example, Benito wrote, "Her father drives a truck. My father drives a truck. When I close my eyes, I can see them drive trucks."

Practice: I read aloud the last segment of the story and we once again engaged in Draw and Write Visualizations. This time, students created different images, including a birthday party for Anna's father and Grandma reading to him. We discussed the students' responses and they shared their sketches with a partner. Figure 15 features Carlos's Draw and Write Visualization for the final section of *The Wednesday Surprise*.

Figure 15. Carlos's Draw and Write Visualization

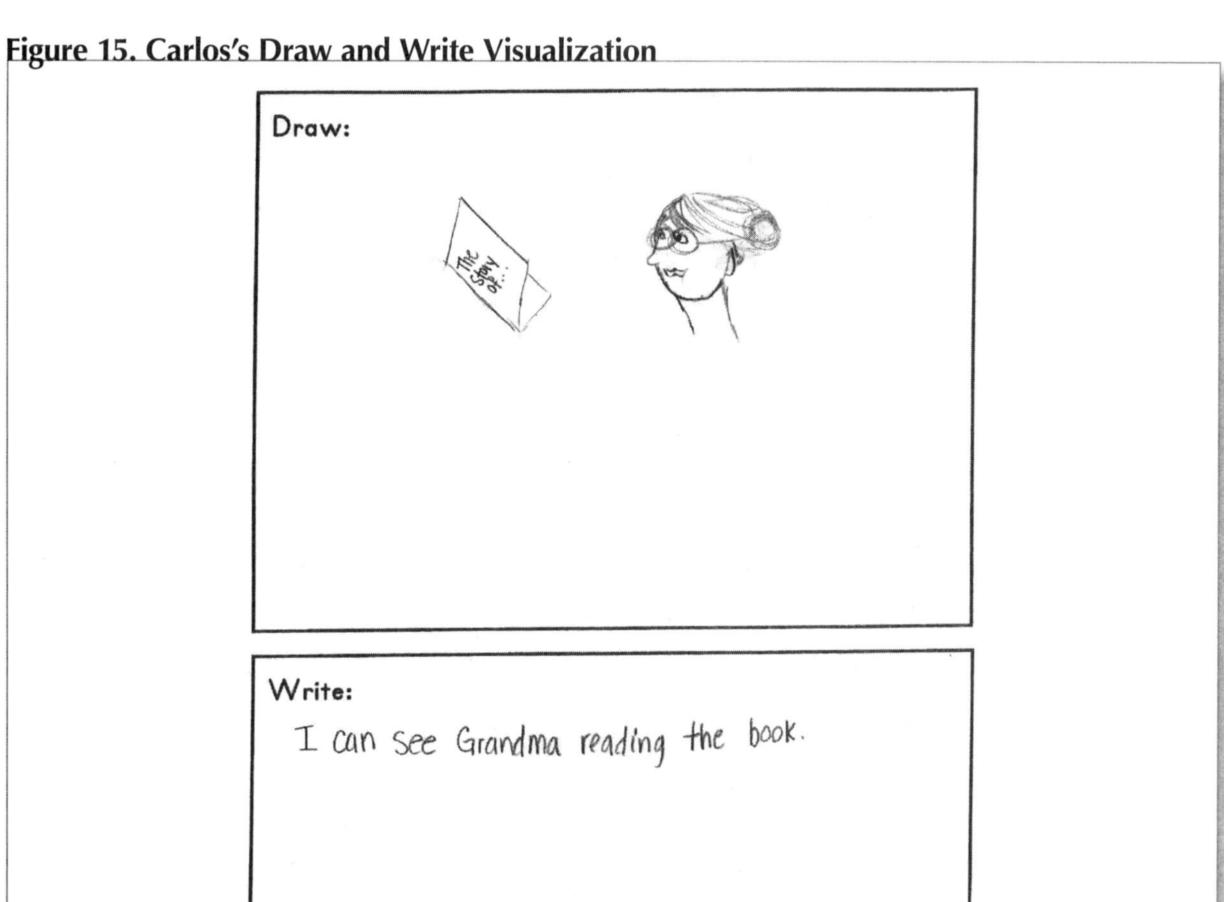

Reflect: We reflected on how we can create mind pictures as we read, draw them, and write about them in Draw and Write Visualizations. The students talked about how picturing what the author is saying helped them to understand what they read. Delfina said, "I know I will remember my mental pictures," and Elena said, "I like that we can all have different pictures and write about them."

After we discussed the story and how surprised we all were when Grandma began reading, we talked about how important it is for everyone to be able to read. Then we moved on to whole-group instruction.

STAGE TWO: Teacher-Directed Whole-Group Instruction

Text: *One Green Apple* (Bunting, 2006)

Explain: I explained to the students that visualizing was an important reading strategy. I also explained that as we read, we can create pictures in our mind—or mind pictures—of the text and that we can share our visualizations by sketching them and discussing them with a partner.

Demonstrate: I introduced the book by inviting students to think about and then quick-write about what it is like to be a student from a different country in a school in the United States. The students shared their views and I started reading the book aloud. I read the first segment and stopped to engage in Draw and Write Visualizations. I thought aloud as I began sketching. I said,

"As I was reading, I was picturing Farah and how she felt being a student of Arab descent in a school in the United States. So, I am going to sketch Farah alone, because based on the story so far, I think that is how she felt." When I had completed my visualization and sentence, the students and I talked about what I had read.

Guide: I guided the students to think about creating a Draw and Write Visualization as I read the next two segments of text. When I stopped reading, the students and I engaged in the strategy application and discussed our work.

Practice: Students practiced by partner reading the final segment of the text and creating a Draw and Write Visualization. They shared with their partners, and then volunteers shared with the class. After that, we talked about Farah's story and what we could learn from its message about welcoming people from all countries to our schools and classrooms. Figure 16 features Michael's Draw and Write Visualization.

Reflect: We reflected on visualizing and how using Draw and Write Visualizations helped us to understand what we read. The students said that it was fun to use this teaching idea because they got to draw what they could see in their minds and share it with a partner. Finally, we talked about how and when we could use this idea in other settings, including Guided Comprehension centers and routines.

Figure 16. Michael's Draw and Write Visualization

STAGE THREE: Teacher-Guided Small-Group Instruction

Text: *Fly Away Home* (Bunting, 1991)

Review: I reviewed the comprehension strategies good readers use and then focused on visualizing and Draw and Write Visualizations.

Guide: I introduced the new book we were going to read, *Fly Away Home*. I shared the title and the cover of the book and invited the students to predict what they thought would happen in the story. They saw a young boy and his father. The students thought they were in an airport and might be getting ready to travel. I read the first segment of the book aloud, and we talked about part of their prediction being verified: The boy and his father were in an airport. Then we discussed that the boy and his dad were not traveling. They were homeless and living at the airport because they didn't have a house or apartment. The students were very sensitive to the characters' circumstances. I guided them to read the next two segments of text, stopping where indicated to engage in Draw and Write Visualizations and share their sketches with a partner. English learners read these segments with a partner. Next, we discussed what the students had read. They weren't surprised that there were people in the world who were homeless, but they were impressed that Eve Bunting had written a book about the homeless.

Practice: The students practiced by reading the final segment and completing one more Draw and Write Visualization. We shared our visualizations and discussed the remainder of the story.

Reflect: We reflected on how visualizing helped us think about the text in a personal way and understand the text.

Student-Facilitated Comprehension Centers

A number of general accommodations were made for English learners when they engaged in the comprehension centers. These included the following:

- Ensuring that favorite-author books written in the students' native languages were among the texts available in the centers
- Making other culturally relevant texts available in the centers
- Integrating multiple modes of representing thinking in student responses (sketching, singing, dramatizing)
- Inviting students to work with other English learners of the same culture when reading texts in their native languages
- Encouraging English learners to partner with native English speakers when working in centers such as fluency, question and answer, vocabulary, and other centers focused on fluency and language development

Art Center: Students created one new illustration for their favorite Eve Bunting book. They shared their creative endeavors with the class in Stage Four of Guided Comprehension.

Fluency Center: I placed a variety of Eve Bunting books, including culturally relevant texts, at this center. These books were also at a variety of levels. Pairs of students either used echo reading to practice reading texts fluently or read along with books on tape or CD.

Theme Center: I placed several Eve Bunting books about a variety of topics at this center. Pairs of students completed two Draw and Write Visualizations as they read the books. Then they discussed them with their partners.

Writing Center: Students worked in trios to write stories. They used Eve Bunting titles and created new stories. For example, Marlena wrote *The Wednesday Surprise*, but in her story the surprise was the family getting a new puppy.

Student-Facilitated Comprehension Routines

A number of general accommodations were made for English learners when they engaged in the comprehension routines. These included the following:

- Making culturally relevant texts available
- Integrating multiple modes of representing thinking in student responses (sketching, singing, dramatizing)
- Encouraging English learners to choose to partner with native English speakers when working in Literature Circles
- Encouraging English learners to choose to partner with native language speakers or English language speakers when working in Cross-Age Reading Experiences

Literature Circles: Students read *Smoky Nights* and other titles by Eve Bunting. They used Draw and Write Visualizations when discussing their books.

Cross-Age Reading Experiences: Pairs of students read and discussed Eve Bunting books and other relevant titles with cross-age partners.

STAGE FOUR: Teacher-Facilitated Whole-Group Reflection and Goal Setting

Share: Students shared their completed Draw and Write Visualizations from the Guided Comprehension centers and routines in small groups. Then they discussed the stories they wrote based on Eve Bunting book titles.

Reflect: We reflected on how visualizing helped us to make connections with the text. Students also noted that visualizing and sketching helped them to share what they were thinking.

Set New Goals: Everyone felt good about using Draw and Write Visualizations, so we decided to extend our goal of visualizing by learning how to use Guided Imagery.

Assessment Options

I observed students in all stages of Guided Comprehension, and I reviewed their performances from the centers and routines. I also used running records, strategy applications, and a variety of other formative measures to assess students.

Reflection on Teaching the English Learners in Our Class

We had been working quite a bit with informational text, so I was happy to observe the English learners actively engaged with stories. Eve Bunting seemed to be the perfect author for this, primarily because she has written about so many meaningful topics. *The Wednesday Surprise* was a great book for making connections to grandparents. I knew that all the students had grandparents either in this country or their family's native land. It was wonderful to hear the students talking about their grandparents and their family lives. Making connections to background knowledge is always the best. The students appeared to enjoy the focuses of our Engaging Prereading Sequence a great deal. When raising questions, I was careful to provide sufficient wait time for the students. I also often elaborated on responses they provided. I am pleased to note that the English learners were actively engaged throughout the lesson. They were highly motivated from the very beginning. In whole group, when we were reading and discussing *One Green Apple*, the students shared openly about what it is like to be in a school when you are from another country. They noted that unlike Farah, the character in the story, they felt welcome in our school from their first day. They recounted a variety of ways in which they had been welcomed and those who had been friends from the beginning. They talked about our buddy program and how much they appreciated having a student in the class to help them acclimate. I have strived to create a classroom community, so it was good to hear such comments from the students. Although the English learners still seem to appreciate small-group and paired settings, they are becoming more and more active and relaxed in whole group as well.

Favorite Author Doreen Cronin
Guided Comprehension Strategy: Making Connections
Teaching Idea: Connection Stems

STAGE ONE: Engaging Prereading Sequence for English Learners

We began our Engaging Prereading Sequence by meeting in an informal area where I had gathered some comfortable chairs around a table. This was not our first Engaging Prereading Sequence, so the students knew what it was and the kinds of things we would be doing. For example, they knew that we would be having a conversation that would help them to take a more active role in our reading when the class met in whole group. They also knew that we would be focusing on background knowledge and how it helps us to construct meaning.

When we began our conversation, I explained that we would be reading another book written by Doreen Cronin and that much like her other texts, this one was going to be funny. In fact, I told them, we would be reading a story about talking farm animals and some problems the animals were having with the farmer. The students were smiling.

Before we began reading *Click, Clack, Moo: Cows That Type* (Cronin, 2000), I invited the students to watch as I shared a wordless picture book, Alexandra Day's *Carl Goes to Daycare*. I spoke briefly about Day and her series of books about a dog named Carl. I reminded the students that I often use pictures at the start of our Engaging Prereading Sequence to help activate our background knowledge, provide additional information, and stimulate discussion. Then I said that I was going to be using pictures for an additional reason today—to help us understand all the elements we needed to include when we are writing our own stories. I showed the students the cover of the book and read the title. Then I asked them what they thought would happen in the story, and their responses centered on Carl visiting a school for young children. A few of the students also made connections to younger siblings they had who were attending day care. Then I began telling the story as I saw it in the author's illustrations. As I "read" the first several illustrations, I wrote information about the narrative elements on a very large Story Map blackline I had sketched on the whiteboard (see Appendix A, page 283). I noted that Carl, Madeline, and the children were the main characters and that the story took place at a day care. Then I described the problem by noting that Carl had accidentally locked the door when the teacher was outside, and she was not able to get back in the classroom. Of course, we all thought this was a funny problem to have. The students and I reviewed the next segment of illustrations. I explained that when we said what was happening in the illustrations, we were actually telling the story. Next, I invited the students to examine the next few illustrations with a partner and volunteer to share what was happening in one of them. After a few moments, Carl and Robert volunteered to tell us what was happening in the first picture. Then the other students talked about the other illustrations in that segment. We learned that Carl did many fun activities with the children, including play practice, arts and crafts, and snack time, while the teacher tried many different ways to get back into the classroom. When I asked the students about attempts to resolve the problem, they suggested that I write the ways the teacher tried to get back into the classroom. They ranged from climbing up to the skylight to tying her car to the door handle. Next, I paused to ask the students if they thought the teacher would get into the classroom. They all said yes. Then I asked them to talk with a partner about how that might happen. The students had many great ideas that ranged from the teacher jumping up and down to get Carl's attention to Carl's

Guided Comprehension: Favorite Author Doreen Cronin
Making Connections: Connection Stems

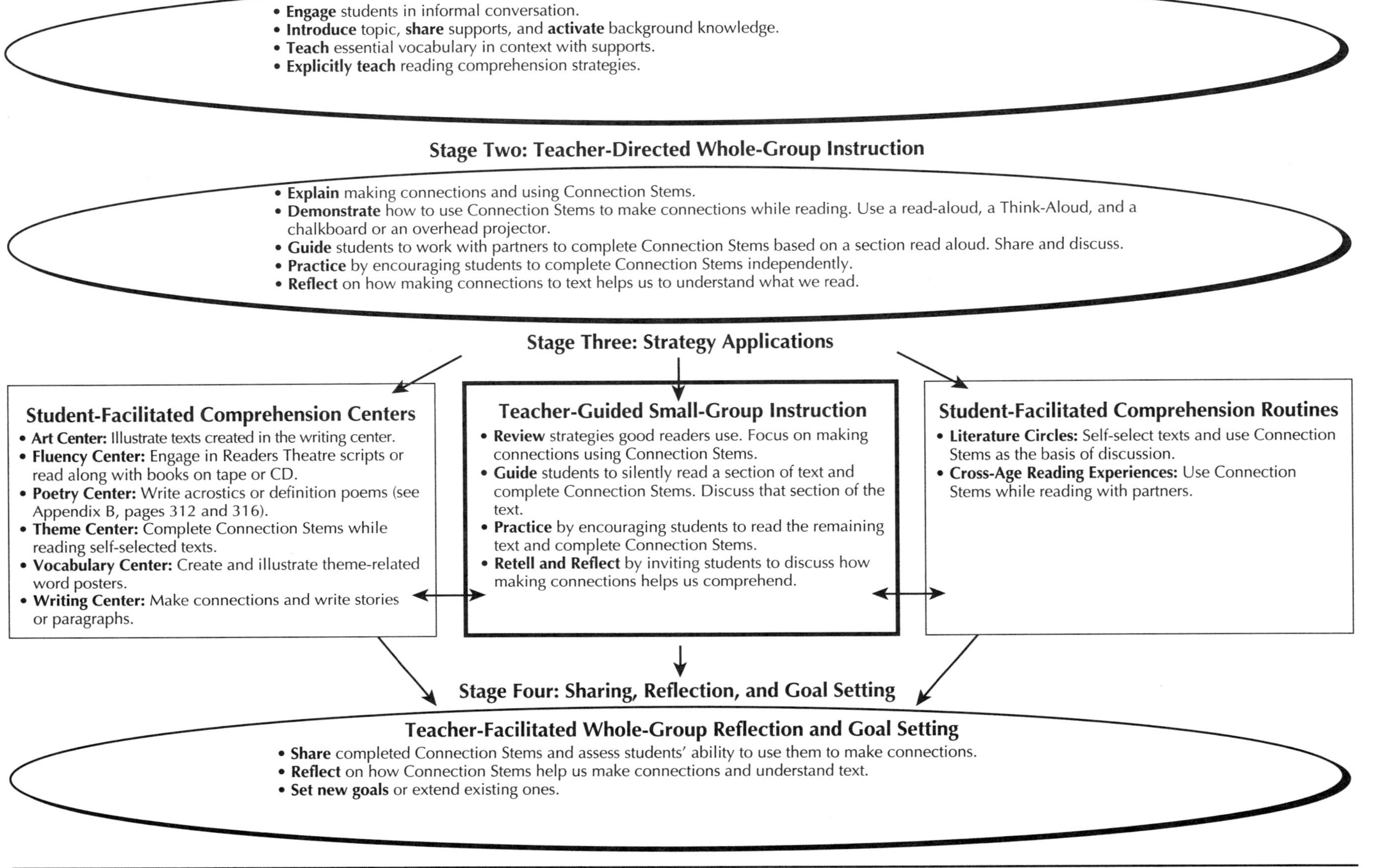

Stage One: Engaging Prereading Sequence for English Learners

- **Engage** students in informal conversation.
- **Introduce** topic, **share** supports, and **activate** background knowledge.
- **Teach** essential vocabulary in context with supports.
- **Explicitly teach** reading comprehension strategies.

Stage Two: Teacher-Directed Whole-Group Instruction

- **Explain** making connections and using Connection Stems.
- **Demonstrate** how to use Connection Stems to make connections while reading. Use a read-aloud, a Think-Aloud, and a chalkboard or an overhead projector.
- **Guide** students to work with partners to complete Connection Stems based on a section read aloud. Share and discuss.
- **Practice** by encouraging students to complete Connection Stems independently.
- **Reflect** on how making connections to text helps us to understand what we read.

Stage Three: Strategy Applications

Student-Facilitated Comprehension Centers

- **Art Center:** Illustrate texts created in the writing center.
- **Fluency Center:** Engage in Readers Theatre scripts or read along with books on tape or CD.
- **Poetry Center:** Write acrostics or definition poems (see Appendix B, pages 312 and 316).
- **Theme Center:** Complete Connection Stems while reading self-selected texts.
- **Vocabulary Center:** Create and illustrate theme-related word posters.
- **Writing Center:** Make connections and write stories or paragraphs.

Teacher-Guided Small-Group Instruction

- **Review** strategies good readers use. Focus on making connections using Connection Stems.
- **Guide** students to silently read a section of text and complete Connection Stems. Discuss that section of the text.
- **Practice** by encouraging students to read the remaining text and complete Connection Stems.
- **Retell and Reflect** by inviting students to discuss how making connections helps us comprehend.

Student-Facilitated Comprehension Routines

- **Literature Circles:** Self-select texts and use Connection Stems as the basis of discussion.
- **Cross-Age Reading Experiences:** Use Connection Stems while reading with partners.

Stage Four: Sharing, Reflection, and Goal Setting

Teacher-Facilitated Whole-Group Reflection and Goal Setting

- **Share** completed Connection Stems and assess students' ability to use them to make connections.
- **Reflect** on how Connection Stems help us make connections and understand text.
- **Set new goals** or extend existing ones.

opening the door because he needed to go outside to go to the bathroom. I praised the students' responses and then they "read" the final few pages. They all laughed when they saw that the teacher had written a big note telling Carl to open the door and he did. Marena said, "Dogs can't read, but Carl can! We should have known. He was reading the teacher's list of things to do while she was outside." I agreed, but noted that the first time I had "read" the book, I was just as surprised as they were. Then we wrote what Carl did in the space for the resolution of the problem, and the students and I read the completed Story Map together. The students thought it was fun that Alexandra Day had made the illustrations, but we actually told the story in our words. I explained that when we would be writing stories, it would be very important to include all the elements on the Story Map in our stories. I also told the students that I would be placing other wordless picture books and Story Maps at the writing center during this lesson and that they could choose to do this activity with other titles. The students were happy about that.

Next, I turned my attention to making connections and using Connection Stems. I used explicit instruction to teach the students about this strategy and teaching idea.

Explain: I began by explaining making connections, noting that we make connections when we read something that relates to something we know—information we already have in our background knowledge. As an example, I referred to the students who had mentioned that they had younger siblings who go to day care, when we were reading *Carl Goes to Daycare*. I said that those students were making text-to-self connections because something that they were reading about in the text (the book) related—or connected—to something in their lives. I explained that the connections we would be making would be text-to-self and text-to-text. Next, I explained that Connection Stems are sentence starters that help us to connect something that happened in the story with background knowledge that we have. Then I read selected Connection Stems: That reminds me of.... I remember when.... I have a connection to.... An experience I have had like that is.... That character reminds me of.... This book reminds me of another book I have read..... I demonstrated examples of each stem and asked the students to work with a partner to write one connection they could make to their lives or a book they had read. I reminded them that they could use *Carl Goes to Daycare* to create their connections, if they would like. After providing sufficient wait time, I invited volunteers to share. Carl and Tomas suggested, "We have a connection to *Carl Goes to Daycare* because we both have dogs," and Gina and Marena said, "We have a connection to *Carl Goes to Daycare* because our little sisters go to day care."

Demonstrate: I introduced *Click, Clack, Moo* by using Marie Clay's Storybook Introduction (see Appendix A, page 232). I shared the cover and the title. Then the students and I talked about the farm animals and what they were looking at. It was somewhat humorous to need to explain what the typewriter was. We did a brief picture walk and paused when we got to the illustration of Farmer Brown typing on his typewriter. I said, "Farmer Brown is sending a note to the farm animals. He is using his typewriter to type the note. Let's look at the illustration very closely and see if we can guess what a typewriter is." After a few moments of intense scrutiny, Marena said, "It looks like a funny-looking keyboard. He is typing on a keyboard," and Edward said, "I think I have seen one of these at my grandparents' house. They told me that my mother used it when she was in school. I think it is what people had before they had computers." We discussed both responses and then I brought out my really old typewriter. It was all set to be used, so I encouraged the students to type their names. They thought it was a wonderfully funny machine. Most had never seen one before, but it made sense to them that this was how people created written communications before we had computers. Then I said, "I can make a connection to the typewriter. This is what I used to use when I was writing my papers when I was in college." They gasped and smiled because my students had never known life without computers.

Guide: I read aloud a section of text and guided pairs of students to make connections using the Connection Stem "We have a connection to…." When I finished reading, we stopped to discuss students' connections. They included "We have a connection to the cows because we like milk" and "We have a connection to the hens because we like eggs."

Practice: As I read the final segment of the book, I paused occasionally to encourage the students to make connections. This time I suggested they continue using the connection stem "We have a connection to..." and also using "That reminds us of another book we have read...." When the students were ready to share, Edward and Domenico said, "That reminds us of Dav Pilkey's books, because it is funny and his books are funny, too." Gina and Marena said, "That reminds us of *Meteor!* [Polacco, 1996] because both stories happened on farms."

Reflect: We reflected on how Connection Stems helped us to make connections and how making connections to our background knowledge helped us understand what we were reading. Domenico said, "It is like the more we know, the more connections we can make." We all agreed. Finally, we reflected on how we could use Connection Stems in other settings to help us understand what we read.

STAGE TWO: Teacher-Directed Whole-Group Instruction

Text: *Diary of a Worm* (Cronin, 2003)

Explain: I began by engaging in direct explanation of making connections. I explained that the connections we make are usually text–self, text–text, and text–world, and that today we would be focusing on text–self connections and text–text connections. I explained that a Connection Stem is part of a sentence that connects something in the story with our background knowledge. Then I introduced the Connection Stems and read each one aloud:

- That reminds me of...
- I remember when...
- I have a connection to...
- An experience I have had like that is...
- That character reminds me of...
- This book reminds me of another book I've read...

Demonstrate: I introduced *Diary of a Worm* by sharing the cover and reading the title. We talked about worms and diaries. Then I asked pairs of students what they thought the story would be about. Julianna and Olivia said that they thought it would be about a worm that writes in a diary like we write in our journals. Ryan and Michael said they thought it would be about a worm that lives underground and keeps a diary. Next, I used a Think-Aloud, a read-aloud, and a whiteboard to share my connections to *Diary of a Worm.* I began by thinking aloud about the cover, the title, and the first few pages of the story. As I spoke, I noted that on the book cover the worm is sitting at a table or desk. So I said, "Seeing the worm sitting at the table or desk and writing reminds me of when we sit at our desks and write." Then I noticed that the worm is sitting on a bottle cap. I said, "Seeing the worm sitting on a bottle cap reminds me of how small worms are." Finally, after reading the first two pages aloud, I said, "An experience I have had like Worm's mother giving him advice is when my mother gives me advice." Then I asked the students if their moms, dads, or other family members gave them advice. Many of the students replied that they did. Jordyn said, "My mom is always telling me to be careful crossing the street." Xavier said, "My dad is always telling me to take care of Earth by recycling."

Guide: I guided the students to work with a partner to think of a connection they could make to the section I was about to read aloud. I encouraged the students to use the stem "We have a connection to..." when sharing their connections. Then I read aloud. Here are some examples of the students' connections:

- Sasha and Angie: "We have a connection to...the girls the worm scared in the park. We would run away if we saw a worm where we were playing, too."
- Marc and Domenico: "We have a connection to...Worm's mother telling him not to eat so much garbage before going to bed. Our moms tell us not to eat so much junk before going to bed."
- Melanie and Gina: "We have a connection to...the dance the worms were doing. They could only do part of it because they don't have arms and legs, but we do all of it when we go to weddings."

As students shared their connections, we discussed them and determined if they were text–self or text–text connections.

Practice: I continued reading aloud to the end of the book, and the students practiced by continuing to create connections with a partner and share them with the class. Most of their connections focused on Worm's never getting cavities and never needing to take a bath.

Reflect: We reflected on how making connections helped us to understand what we read. Students observed that the more they knew about the topic of the story, the more connections they could make. They especially liked the text–self connections because they could make connections to their life experiences. Finally, we reflected on how we could use Connection Stems in other settings to help us understand what we read.

STAGE THREE: Teacher-Guided Small-Group Instruction

Text: *Diary of a Spider* (Cronin, 2005) (Texts varied according to students' abilities.)

Review: I reminded the students about the comprehension strategies good readers use and focused on using Connection Stems. We reviewed how to make text–self and text–text connections. We noted the examples of Connection Stems from Stage Two that were still on display.

Guide: I introduced *Diary of a Spider* by sharing the cover and reading the opening pages. Students immediately noted connections to the pencil the spider used to write in his diary and that he was using a leaf as a sail. I asked the students if they could make a connection between this book and another book, and they made connections to *Diary of a Worm* and *Spiders*, a book by Seymour Simon (2007) that we had previously read. Then I guided the students as they silently read *Diary of a Spider*. English learners whisper read with partners during this time. The students stopped at predetermined points to make and share connections, and we discussed their ideas.

Practice: Students continued to use Connection Stems to make connections until they finished reading the text. They shared their connections and we discussed the story.

Retell and Reflect: Students whisper read the story with a partner and we completed a group oral retelling. We reflected on how Connection Stems helped us to understand what we read and talked about how we could use making connections with informational texts.

Student-Facilitated Comprehension Centers

A number of general accommodations were made for English learners when they engaged in the comprehension centers. These included the following:

- Ensuring that favorite-author books written in the students' native languages were among the texts available in the centers
- Making other culturally relevant texts available in the centers
- Integrating multiple modes of representing thinking in student responses (sketching, singing, dramatizing)
- Inviting students to work with other English learners of the same culture when reading texts in their native languages
- Encouraging English learners to partner with native English speakers when working in centers such as fluency, question and answer, vocabulary, and other centers focused on fluency and language development

Art Center: Students illustrated stories or texts they wrote in the writing center. When completed, the stories were displayed in the classroom where others could read them.

Fluency Center: Students practiced their fluency by either working in small groups to read Readers Theatre scripts based on animal books or by reading along with Doreen Cronin books on tape or CD.

Poetry Center: Students worked in pairs to read short informational texts about topics such as cows, ducks, hens, farmers, worms, spiders, and flies that relate to Doreen Cronin's books. Students stopped periodically to make connections as they read. Then they wrote definition poems (see Appendix B, page 316, for a blackline) based on the informational text they read and posted them in our poetry corner where we displayed student-authored poems.

Theme Center: Students chose from a variety of Doreen Cronin books or related informational texts and completed Connection Stems as they read. They recorded their connections on a response sheet I provided.

Vocabulary Center: Pairs of students chose vocabulary from our theme word wall and used it to create word posters, which included the word, an illustration of the word, and a sentence in which the word was used.

Writing Center: Students worked either on their own or with a partner to make connections to one of Doreen Cronin's farm and diary books or related informational texts. Then they wrote a story or an informational paragraph. Story titles included *Diary of a Dog*, *Duck for Principal*, and *Click, Clack, Ta-da: Kids That Type!* Next, students illustrated their writing in the Writing Center. When they finished writing, students completed Center Student Self-Assessments (see Appendix B, page 295).

Student-Facilitated Comprehension Routines

A number of general accommodations were made for English learners when they engaged in the comprehension routines. These included the following:

- Making culturally relevant texts available
- Integrating multiple modes of representing thinking in student responses (sketching, singing, dramatizing)
- Encouraging English learners to choose to partner with native English speakers when working in Literature Circles
- Encouraging English learners to choose to partner with native language speakers or English language speakers when working in Cross-Age Reading Experiences

Literature Circles: Students selected theme-related books and read them in Literature Circles. As they read, the students completed at least three Connection Stems. They also completed Literature Circle Bookmarks (see Appendix B, page 306). When they finished reading their books, students engaged in extension projects, such as creating an acrostic retelling of the story they illustrated, an illustrated book review in which they presented their thoughts about the book, and a Lyric Retelling. The students presented their completed projects to the class in Stage Four. Students also completed Literature Circle Group Assessments (see Appendix B, page 307).

Cross-Age Reading Experiences: Students worked with cross-age partners to read Doreen Cronin books or related informational texts. As they read, students completed Connection Stems. After reading, they completed Cross-Age Reading Experience Self-Assessments (see Appendix B, page 298).

STAGE FOUR: Teacher-Facilitated Whole-Group Reflection and Goal Setting

Share: We began by sharing Connection Stems and projects from Stage Three. The students enjoyed sharing the connections they had made. All the students seemed confident in their abilities, and their applications from Stage Three supported their thinking.

Reflect: We reflected on how Connection Stems helped us to understand what we read. Students also talked about how we can use Connection Stems with many different kinds of text, including poetry, song lyrics, newspaper articles, and what we read on the Internet.

Set New Goals: We decided to extend our goal about making connections to learning how to use Draw and Write Connections.

Assessment Options

I observed students in all settings during Guided Comprehension, focusing on topics such as student responses, comprehension strategy applications, fluency, student–text matches, and ability to work with others. I reviewed and commented on students' written connections and projects. During teacher-guided small groups, I did occasional fluency checks and running records. I used the assessment results to inform future teaching.

Reflection on Teaching the English Learners in Our Class

The conversational tone, high level of student engagement, and humorous text combined to make our Engaging Prereading Sequence a wonderful learning experience. I should also mention that the wordless picture book and my old typewriter emerged as great motivators. The students seemed quite happy to learn how to "read" a wordless picture book and use it to create stories. They also successfully made connections to their background knowledge and readily participated in the Engaging Prereading Sequence, as well as the remainder of the Guided Comprehension lesson. Having opportunities to learn in paired, small-group, and whole-group settings seems to be working well for the students. I can see the pride on their faces every time they realize that they already have knowledge of what we are studying in whole group. The English learners' contributions in that stage are also increasing.

Favorite Author Gary Soto
Guided Comprehension Strategy: Summarizing
Teaching Idea: Draw and Write Retellings

STAGE ONE: Engaging Prereading Sequence for English Learners

We began our Engaging Prereading Sequence in an area of the classroom I had designated for our conversations. This was not our first meeting, so the students knew what the Engaging Prereading Sequence was and what we would be doing during our session. I reminded them that we would be talking about background knowledge and how to activate it. I also noted that we would be using the ideas we discussed later in the lesson.

As we began our conversation, I noted the comfortable, casual atmosphere. I reminded the students that we would be talking about Gary Soto, a well-known author of Mexican American heritage, and his book *Mercy on These Teenage Chimps* (2007). I explained that it was a book about students who were middle school-aged, just as they were. I provided an overview of the novel and explained that usually we would be completing a Draw and Write Retelling of the entire novel, but because of our limited time, we would practice completing a retelling of just Chapter 2. Then I would place copies of the text in the classroom library, and the students could finish reading it at their leisure.

Next, we talked about how teenage boys change as they grow older. I explained that Ronnie Gonzalez and Joey Rios were two good friends who went to Washington Middle School. Ronnie believed that they are turning into chimpanzees because they were getting hair on their faces, their arms were growing longer, and they could juggle fruit. We talked about whether middle school boys really turn into chimpanzees as they grow older, and we decided that Gary Soto was trying to be funny when he wrote this story. David pointed out, "Sometimes I tell my older brother he is an ape, and he tells me I am one, too. Then we laugh and walk around swinging our arms like apes." We concluded that Gary Soto was writing a funny story, and the boys were just getting older and feeling different.

Explain: I explained summarizing and the Draw and Write Retelling. I noted that when we are summarizing stories, we need to think about the characters (who is in the story), the setting (where the story is happening), what happened (what the problem is), and how it ended (how the problem is resolved).

Demonstrate: I read Chapter 1 to further introduce the book to the students. We talked about Ronaldo (Ronnie) and Joey's friendship and made connections to friends that we had. We also talked about how they called the coach Coach Bear because he was hairy and growled a lot.

Guide: I guided students to think about the information we needed for our Draw and Write Retellings. I also shared copies of the Draw and Write Retelling blackline (see Appendix A, page 272). I began reading Chapter 2, stopping periodically to encourage the students to make connections. Next, I thought aloud and said, "I am going to start thinking about who the characters are in this chapter because we need to add that information to our Draw and Write Retelling." In the spaces provided for information about who is in the story, I used simple lines and shapes to draw four people and wrote, "Ronnie, Joey, Coach Bear, and Jessica are the characters in Chapter 2." I pointed out that we should write about our drawings in complete sentences. Next, I thought aloud about the second question—where the story took place. I said, "Chapter 2 takes place at Lincoln High School.

Guided Comprehension: Favorite Author Gary Soto
Summarizing: Draw and Write Retellings

Stage One: Engaging Prereading Sequence for English Learners

- **Engage** students in informal conversation.
- **Introduce** topic, **share** supports, and **activate** background knowledge.
- **Teach** essential vocabulary in context with supports.
- **Explicitly teach** reading comprehension strategies.

Stage Two: Teacher-Directed Whole-Group Instruction

- **Explain** summarizing and Draw and Write Retellings.
- **Demonstrate** how to use Draw and Write Retellings.
- **Guide** students to use Draw and Write Retellings.
- **Practice** by inviting students to complete retellings.
- **Reflect** on how visualizing helps us understand what we read.

Stage Three: Strategy Applications

Student-Facilitated Comprehension Centers

- **Art Center:** Illustrate self-authored form poems.
- **Fluency Center:** Read along with Gary Soto's stories on tape or CD.
- **Poetry Center:** Write acrostic poems or definition poems about Gary Soto and his writings.
- **Project Center:** Use the Internet to complete a Press Conference about Gary Soto and his books.
- **Theme Center:** Read and complete Draw and Write Retellings.

Teacher-Guided Small-Group Instruction

- **Review** all strategies; focus on summarizing using Draw and Write Retellings.
- **Guide** students through reading and summarizing.
- **Practice** by inviting students to discuss and summarize narrative elements.
- **Retell and Reflect** on visualizing and using Draw and Write Retellings.

Student-Facilitated Comprehension Routines

- **Literature Circles:** Read *Pacific Crossing* and create group Draw and Write Retellings using the information discussed.
- **Reciprocal Teaching:** Create Draw and Write Retellings during the summary phase of this routine.

Stage Four: Sharing, Reflection, and Goal Setting

Teacher-Facilitated Whole-Group Reflection and Goal Setting

- **Share** individual performances in small groups and with the whole group.
- **Reflect** on how summarizing and Draw and Write Retellings improved understanding.
- **Set new goals** or revise existing goals.

The boys meet the coach there to help him with the banquet." I drew a building and wrote "Lincoln High School" on it. Then I wrote my sentence: "Lincoln High School is the setting of Chapter 2."

Practice: I read more of Chapter 2 and invited the students to think about what happened in that chapter. What, specifically, was the problem Ronnie and Joey encountered in Chapter 2? Then I encouraged them to share with a partner. When they were ready to respond, Marietta and Samuel said, "We think the problem was that the balloon on Jessica's table floated to the top of the room." Everyone agreed. I suggested that the students draw that and write a sentence describing what happened on the blacklines I had shared with them. Then I turned and drew a table and a balloon in the space for *What happened?* on the Draw and Write Retelling that I was completing. The sentence I wrote was "Jessica's balloon floated to the top of the room." Next, the students worked together to develop the final part of the Draw and Write Retelling. Everyone agreed that Joey solved the problem by climbing up to get the balloon. I drew Joey holding the balloon and wrote, "Joey climbed up very high to get the balloon for Jessica." The students also shared what they drew and wrote in the final section. Then we took a moment to read the class Draw and Write Retelling. Next, I read the first two sections and the students read the final two sections from the blacklines they had completed. We talked about the chapter and about Gary Soto's Mexican American heritage.

Reflect: We reflected on how we could retell the essential components of a story, or in this case a chapter, through drawing and writing. The students noted that they liked the Draw and Write Retelling because they could draw what they were thinking about and then write about it.

The students were looking forward to reading the copies of the book I had placed in our classroom library, and I knew we were ready to engage in whole-group instruction.

STAGE TWO: Teacher-Directed Whole-Group Instruction

Text: *Taking Sides* (Soto, 2003)

Explain: I began by reminding students about how to summarize a story. Then I explained Draw and Write Retellings. I displayed the blackline for this strategy application (see Appendix A, page 272) on the smartboard and explained the information we would need to know to complete it. Then I made connections to the narrative elements (characters, setting, problem, attempts to resolve the problem, and resolution) and Story Maps. I also reminded students that we didn't need to be expert artists to complete the Draw and Write Retelling; we could use simple lines and shapes to draw.

Demonstrate: I used a Think-Aloud, the smartboard, and a blackline to demonstrate the Draw and Write Retelling. I reminded the students that we would be using Gary Soto's *Taking Sides*, a book we had used for our most recent novel read-aloud, for the Draw and Write Retelling. I suggested that we begin by retelling the story because we would need to include essential information about the story in our Draw and Write Retelling. I ensured that the students had their own copies of *Taking Sides* and invited them to meet with a partner and engage in a retelling. I shared blacklines of Story Maps (see Appendix A, page 283) to facilitate students' thinking. After providing sufficient time, we reviewed the essentials of the story:

> Lincoln Mendoza was a great basketball player when he was at Franklin Junior High, but when his house was robbed, his mother decided they should move to a nicer neighborhood. That meant Lincoln had to go to a new school. At first, he liked his new school, but then he started missing his old friends and his other school. He has a fight with Tony, his best friend from his old school; he

doesn't like Roy, the white man his mother is dating; his basketball coach doesn't like him; he hurts his knee; and his new house is robbed. Lincoln can't play in the big game between his new school and his old school, but when the game is over, he celebrates with his old team, even though they didn't win the game.

Next, we began completing the Draw and Write Retelling.

Guide: I guided pairs of students to begin completing the Draw and Write Retelling. I thought aloud and said, "We should begin by completing part 1 of the retelling: who was in the story. So, let's think about who the main characters were in the story." Then I encouraged the students to discuss who those characters might be. A few minutes later, we decided the main characters were Lincoln, his mom, Roy, Tony, and the coach. I began drawing these five people in the space provided. Then I wrote, "Lincoln, his mom, Roy, Tony, and the coach were the main characters in the story." The students created their own drawings and wrote their own sentences about the characters. Then we discussed part 2 of the retelling. It focused on the setting—where the story took place. I asked the students where they thought most of the story took place. They discussed this, and after having some time to think, they said most of the story took place in Lincoln's new home and new school. They drew the settings and wrote their sentences. I did the same.

Practice: The students practiced by completing parts 3 and 4 of the Draw and Write Retelling: what happened in the story and how it ended. Then they shared each part with the class. Most students agreed that what happened in the story was that Lincoln moved to a new town and encountered new challenges. They had drawn pictures to support their thinking. Then they shared part 4. They noted that Lincoln figured out how he could live his new life and drew corresponding pictures. Melinda and Sam's Draw and Write Retelling of *Taking Sides* is featured in Figure 17.

Figure 17. Melinda and Sam's Draw and Write Retelling of *Taking Sides*

Reflect: When we finished our Draw and Write Retellings, everyone felt we had done a good job. We discussed the book and posted our strategy applications so everyone could see them. Several students commented about how much fun it was to draw and retell.

STAGE THREE: Teacher-Guided Small-Group Instruction

Text: *Buried Onions* (Soto, 2006) (Texts varied according to students' abilities.)

Review: I reviewed the strategies good readers use and focused our lesson on summarizing using Draw and Write Retellings.

Guide: I guided my students through their reading of the conclusion of *Buried Onions*, a book we had been reading as a group during our study of Gary Soto's works. Then I encouraged them to discuss the story with a partner and offer ideas that would be important to include in a retelling. I recorded their suggestions about parts 1 and 2, characters, and setting, and guided students to use those ideas to begin completing the Draw and Write Retelling.

Practice: The pairs of students practiced by continuing to discuss, draw, and write sentences about the important events in the story. They completed parts 3 and 4: what happened and how did it end. I monitored student progress throughout the completion of the Draw and Write Retelling. David and Nancy's Draw and Write Retelling of *Buried Onions* is featured in Figure 18.

Retell and Reflect: We reread our completed retellings and shared them with the group. Then we reflected on how Draw and Write Retellings helped us to summarize what we had read and talked about how we could use them in other settings.

Figure 18. David and Nancy's Draw and Write Retelling of *Buried Onions*

Who?
Draw:
Write: The story is about Eddie And people he knows.

Where?
Draw: Welcome to Fresno, CA
Write: The book takes place in and near Fresno.

What happened?
Draw: Just Say No; RIP
Write: Eddie's dad, uncles, and best friend die. He tries not to take drugs or be in gangs.

How did it end?
Draw: USA
Write: Eddie joins the military to try to have a better future.

Student-Facilitated Comprehension Centers

A number of general accommodations were made for English learners when they engaged in the comprehension centers. These included the following:

- Ensuring that favorite-author books written in the students' native languages were among the texts available in the centers
- Making other culturally relevant texts available in the centers
- Integrating multiple modes of representing thinking in student responses (sketching, singing, dramatizing)
- Inviting students to work with other English learners of the same culture when reading texts in their native languages
- Encouraging English learners to partner with native English speakers when working in centers such as fluency, question and answer, vocabulary, and other centers focused on fluency and language development

Art Center: Students illustrated form poems they wrote in the poetry center.

Fluency Center: Students read along with Gary Soto's stories on tape or CD.

Poetry Center: Students either wrote acrostic poems or definition poems about Gary Soto and his writings.

Project Center: Pairs of students visited this center and used computers to search for information about Gary Soto and his books. Then they created a Press Conference or added information to our Gary Soto class mural.

Theme Center: Students visited this center and created Draw and Write Retellings of self-selected Gary Soto novels or poems they had read previously. Among the works available were *The Skirt* (novel), *Neighborhood Odes* (poetry collection), *Canto Familiar* (poetry collection), *Crazy Weekend* (novel), and *Novio Boy* (play).

Student-Facilitated Comprehension Routines

A number of general accommodations were made for English learners when they engaged in the comprehension routines. These included the following:

- Making culturally relevant texts available
- Integrating multiple modes of representing thinking in student responses (sketching, singing, dramatizing)
- Encouraging English learners to choose to partner with native English speakers when working in Literature Circles and Reciprocal Teaching

Literature Circles: Students read other books by Gary Soto, such as *Pacific Crossing*, and used them as the basis of their discussions. Then they created group Draw and Write Retellings based on the books.

Reciprocal Teaching: Students created Draw and Write Retellings during the summary phase.

STAGE FOUR: Teacher-Facilitated Whole-Group Reflection and Goal Setting

Share: At the conclusion of the lesson, students shared their performances from centers and routines in small groups. Then each group shared a few items with the class. This seemed to work well.

Reflect: We reflected on the engagement and enjoyment Draw and Write Retellings provided for all students, including those who struggled with traditional writing assignments. We also reflected on how summarizing improved understanding by providing an opportunity to synthesize the important information about the story.

Set New Goals: Feeling confident with our ability to use Draw and Write Retellings, we decided to extend our goal about summarizing to using Lyric Summaries.

Assessment Options

I used observation, students' completed strategy applications, and informal writing as assessments. I also periodically conducted fluency checks and administered running records.

Reflection on Teaching the English Learners in Our Class

The English learners in our class were actively engaged throughout our Engaging Prereading Sequence. They enjoyed our reading of a segment from Gary Soto's book about middle school boys, and because several of the students are of Mexican American heritage, they seemed to take special pride in our studying a writer who shares their background. They were especially pleased to be able to use a strategy application in which sketching was involved. I was careful to provide appropriate wait time and elaborate on the responses the students offered. The students were active throughout the Guided Comprehension lesson and engaged in paired, small-group, and whole-group settings. They also partnered with native language speakers and native English speakers on several occasions. All the students appeared to enjoy working with each other. It looks and feels as if our community-building efforts have been successful. I should further note that the entire group honors diversity, and we build on that whenever we can.

Favorite Author Gary Paulsen
Guided Comprehension Strategy: Evaluating
Teaching Idea: Evaluative Questioning

STAGE ONE: Engaging Prereading Sequence for English Learners

We met for our Engaging Prereading Sequence conversation in an area of the classroom where I had gathered some comfortable chairs I had set aside for our conversations. We had already met several times, so the students were familiar with what the Engaging Prereading Sequence was and what we would be doing during our session. I noted that we would be talking about background knowledge and a new strategy application.

As we began our conversation, I told the students that we would be focusing on Gary Paulsen's book *Hatchet*. We had already read this novel earlier in our author study of Paulsen, so I explained to the students that today I would reread parts of the novel to teach Evaluative Questioning. Then I made connections to Ciardiello's (1998, 2007) levels of questioning and reviewed asking and answering questions at different levels (see Chapter 3, pages 33–34). I noted that we would be structuring our evaluative questions to include the format Ciardiello had suggested. We took a few minutes to summarize *Hatchet* and then began discussing Evaluative Questioning. Then I began engaging in explicit instruction.

Explain: I explained evaluating as a reading comprehension strategy and then focused on Evaluative Questioning. I explained that when we were engaging in Evaluative Questioning, we would be asking readers what they thought. We would also be asking the readers to defend or justify their responses. So, we would be engaging in a two-part process: (1) asking readers what they think and (2) asking them to defend or justify their answers.

Demonstrate: I demonstrated by making connections to the students' everyday lives. I asked which fast-food business they thought had the best French fries. I provided time for the students to think and then listened to their responses. It was pretty much a tie between McDonalds and Burger King. Then I asked the students to justify their responses—to provide reasons for the choices they made. I invited them to share their reasons with a partner. A few moments later, I encouraged the students to share their thinking. Their reasons for choosing a particular restaurant included the best taste and best price for the largest serving. After our French fry discussion, we turned to our text. I again reminded the students that we can engage in Evaluative Questioning as we read. I further noted that when we were providing reasons for our responses to evaluative questions, some might appear in the text and some might be in our background knowledge. Sometimes we might find reasons in both places.

Guide: I guided pairs of students to listen as I read selected passages from *Hatchet*. The first was about the crash of the plane after the pilot had a heart attack. My question was, "Do you think it is important for everyone to learn to swim? Justify your response." I provided sufficient wait time and then I asked for volunteers to respond. Matthew and Diego said,

> We hadn't thought about that question before reading the book, but now we think they should. If Brian had not been able to swim, he probably would have died when the plane landed in the lake. So, it is something everyone should know how to do.

Everyone agreed.

Guided Comprehension: Favorite Author Gary Paulsen
Evaluating: Evaluative Questions

Stage One: Engaging Prereading Sequence for English Learners

- **Engage** students in informal conversation.
- **Introduce** topic, **share** supports, and **activate** background knowledge.
- **Teach** essential vocabulary in context with supports.
- **Explicitly teach** reading comprehension strategies.

Stage Two: Teacher-Directed Whole-Group Instruction

- **Explain** evaluating and how to use Evaluative Questions.
- **Demonstrate** how to create and use Evaluative Questions.
- **Guide** students in pairs to use Evaluative Questions.
- **Practice** by finishing reading and inviting students to work in pairs to create additional Evaluative Questions. Share and respond to the questions.
- **Reflect** on how evaluating and Evaluative Questions help us make judgments about text and how we can use them in other settings.

Stage Three: Strategy Applications

Student-Facilitated Comprehension Centers

- **Fluency Center:** Practice fluency by engaging in Readers Theatre or reading along with texts.
- **Project Center:** Select a topic and create a PowerPoint slide presentation.
- **Question and Answer Center:** Use Gary Paulsen's biography and autobiographies to generate and respond to questions.
- **Theme Center:** Revisit texts to create and respond to Evaluative Questions.

Teacher-Guided Small-Group Instruction

- **Review** the comprehension strategies that good readers use and focus on evaluating and Evaluative Questions.
- **Guide** students to read *The Monument* (Paulsen, 1991) and create and respond to Evaluative Questions.
- **Practice** by inviting students to read to the end of the chapter and create Evaluative Questions. Encourage group members to respond to the questions raised.
- **Retell and Reflect** on how using Evaluative Questions helps us understand text.

Student-Facilitated Comprehension Routines

- **Literature Circles:** Create and respond to Evaluative Questions while reading.
- **Cross-Age Reading Experiences:** Work with cross-age partners to read and discuss stories written by Gary Paulsen.

Stage Four: Sharing, Reflection, and Goal Setting

Teacher-Facilitated Whole-Group Reflection and Goal Setting

- **Share** completed Evaluative Questions, reviews, rubrics, and the class PowerPoint slide show.
- **Reflect** on why evaluating is important for understanding text.
- **Set new goals** or extend existing ones.

Practice: The next segment that I read was about all that Brian experienced for the 54 days he was in the wilderness. My question was "Do you think the hatchet helped Brian survive?" All the students agreed that it did, and to document their reasoning they cited the various occasions when Brian used the hatchet, including to get food and to protect himself.

Next, I read a short segment in which Brian debates whether to drink the water in the lake. He chooses to drink it but then becomes ill. My question was, "If you crashed in a lake and had no food or water, would you drink the lake water? Justify your response." After waiting a few minutes, I asked for volunteers. Marilyn and Jeff responded by saying,

> It would be better to know if the lake water was clean, but if there was no other water, we would drink the lake water. We would drink it, because if we had no water for a long time in hot weather, we could die. Our bodies need water to live.

Finally, I read the segment toward the end of the book in which Brian finds the survival pack. My question was, "If you had found the survival pack, what would you have valued the most? Justify your response." The students' responses and rationales differed for this question. Some valued the soap so they could finally feel clean, some the food because they would be so hungry, some the rifle because they could use it to hunt food.

Reflect: We reflected on how to generate and respond to Evaluative Questioning. I explained that eventually we would learn to use evaluative questions as we read. We would question what the author wrote and if the author's message was consistent, but we would begin by learning how to ask and answer evaluative questions related to the content of our reading.

We concluded our discussion. Jerreh said, "I like that we need to tell the reasons. It makes me think about why I answer the way I do." Everyone agreed. Then we moved on to whole-group instruction.

STAGE TWO: Teacher-Directed Whole-Group Instruction

Text: *Winterdance: The Fine Madness of Running the Iditarod* (Paulsen, 1994)

Explain: I began by explaining how using Evaluative Questioning helps us to make judgments about the text. I reminded students that when we evaluate, we make judgments, and we need to support our thinking with sound reasoning. Then I explained how to structure evaluative questions by asking "What do you think?" and then using signal words such as *defend*, *judge*, and *justify*, as in "justify your thinking."

Demonstrate: I demonstrated how to create and use Evaluative Questioning by reading aloud the first chapter of *Winterdance*. Before reading I shared the title with the students, and they immediately made connections to what we had already learned about Gary Paulsen's life, especially his participation in the Iditarod. As I read, I stopped periodically to think aloud about evaluative questions that I had and displayed them on the whiteboard. For example, I paused after reading "I grabbed, snatched with my hand as the wind hit, but it was too sudden, too wild, and I was torn from the sled, taken by the wind, tumbling end over end down the mountain" on page 6. I thought aloud about an evaluative question I had: "How could Gary Paulsen justify risking his life and the dogs' lives for this grueling Iditarod training?" I wrote the question on the whiteboard and underlined the signal word *justify*. Next, I demonstrated that responding to evaluative questions involved what I had already read in this book, what I already knew about Gary Paulsen and his life experiences, and any prior knowledge I had about such circumstances. We discussed possible responses and I continued to read. I stopped again on page 14 after reading about the author's use of math: "If you broke trail with snowshoes at half a mile an hour and it was eighty miles to camp—where there was food for the dogs—it would take 160 hours." My evaluative question this time was, "What do I think Gary's chances of surviving would be if he chose to break trail?" We discussed possible responses and decided that based on weather, lack of food, time, and distance, his chances were nonexistent.

Guide: I continued to read aloud and guided students to work in pairs to use the signal words to structure evaluative questions. I asked them to structure one question based on the next section I read. Many of their questions focused on the last paragraph in Chapter 1:

> and I thought that any sane man who was in his forties and had a good career going would quit now, would leave the dogs, end it now and go back to the world and sanity and I knew what scared me wasn't the canyon and wasn't the hook hanging by one prong but the knowledge, the absolute fundamental knowledge that I could not stop, would not stop, would never be able to stop running dogs of my own free will. (p. 18)

Students structured questions requiring the author and them to defend why he should quit or why he should continue. We shared and discussed all their questions and possible answers, which resulted in quite a lively debate.

Practice: I read aloud the beginning sections of Chapter 2 and the students continued to work in pairs to create additional evaluative questions and to formulate possible responses. The students liked creating their own questions, and I found that even struggling readers were able to create and respond to evaluative questions.

Reflect: I asked the students to reflect on how using Evaluative Questioning helped them to make judgments about text. Shelby responded, "I like these questions because what I think matters, and I have a lot of sources I can use to think of a response. It's not like when the answer is right there in the book."

STAGE THREE: Teacher-Guided Small-Group Instruction

Text: *The Monument* (Paulsen, 1991) (Texts varied according to students' abilities.)

Review: I reviewed the comprehension strategies that all good readers use, such as previewing and visualizing. Then I focused on evaluating and Evaluative Questioning.

Guide: I previewed *The Monument* and guided students' reading of the opening chapter. English learners whisper read with partners during this time. I asked them to create one evaluative question and think about possible responses. Several of the students focused on the passage from page 4 when Rocky (Rachel Ellen Turner) says, "I mean I want to know every little thing that's going to happen and not have any surprises. But I can't and that sometimes makes me mad." Students' questions focused on justifying Rocky's perspective. Other students questioned the author's use of the name Rocky for the girl in the story and asked that he and they defend his choice. They also made personal connections to his thinking.

Practice: The students continued to read Chapters 2 and 3 of *The Monument*, creating two evaluative questions as they read. We discussed their evaluative questions and possible answers. Questions included, "What do you think it was like for Rocky to be an abandoned orphan?" "How would you defend Rocky's feelings of rejection when she was not selected for adoption?" "How would you justify Rocky's feelings when she learned that her adoptive parents were alcoholics?" "How would Gary Paulsen (or you) justify his use of his life circumstance (alcoholic parents) in this book?" The students' queries resulted in a lively discussion.

Retell and Reflect: The students engaged in partner retellings. Then I asked the students how creating and responding to evaluative questions helped them to understand text. Deron said that creating evaluative questions reminded him of predicting because he wanted to read ahead to see if his ideas and the author's were similar.

Student-Facilitated Comprehension Centers

A number of general accommodations were made for English learners when they engaged in the comprehension centers. These included the following:

- Ensuring that favorite-author books written in the students' native languages were among the texts available in the centers
- Making other culturally relevant texts available in the centers
- Integrating multiple modes of representing thinking in student responses (sketching, singing, dramatizing)
- Inviting students to work with other English learners of the same culture when reading texts in their native languages
- Encouraging English learners to partner with native English speakers when working in centers such as fluency, question and answer, vocabulary, and other centers focused on fluency and language development

Fluency Center: Students practiced their oral reading fluency by engaging in Readers Theatre or reading along with texts on CD.

Project Center: Pairs of students selected a related topic, such as Gary Paulsen's life or the Iditarod, and researched it using a variety of sources. Then they used the information to create a PowerPoint presentation using clip art, sound, and animation. They saved their presentations and shared them in Stage Four.

Question and Answer Center: Pairs of students used Gary Paulsen's biography and his two autobiographies to generate and respond to questions at the four levels suggested by Ciardiello (1998, 2007; see Chapter 3, pages 33–34).

Theme Center: The students chose a book by Gary Paulsen that they had already read. They revisited the text to create and respond to four evaluative questions. Then they used their knowledge of the book and the responses to the evaluative questions to write a critique. They posted the completed reviews in our critics' corner.

Student-Facilitated Comprehension Routines

A number of general accommodations were made for English learners when they engaged in the comprehension routines. These included the following:

- Making culturally relevant texts available
- Integrating multiple modes of representing thinking in student responses (sketching, singing, dramatizing)

- Encouraging English learners to choose to partner with native English speakers when working in Literature Circles
- Encouraging English learners to choose to partner with native language speakers or English language speakers when working in Cross-Age Reading Experiences

Literature Circles: The students finished reading the last two chapters of *Hatchet* individually. Then they wrote and responded to two evaluative questions. When all the group members had completed these tasks, they met and used their evaluative questions as the basis of discussion. Finally, they used what they learned to write a group book review.

Cross-Age Reading Experiences: Students worked with cross-age partners to read and discuss stories written by Gary Paulsen. The partners also engaged in Evaluative Questioning.

STAGE FOUR: Teacher-Facilitated Whole-Group Reflection and Goal Setting

Share: Students shared their performances from Stage Three in small groups and then each group shared a few performances with the whole class.

Reflect: We reflected on what we had learned and how Evaluative Questioning helped us to think through text.

Set New Goals: Students assessed their abilities to use Evaluative Questioning, and we decided to stay with this goal and learn how to use journal entries, another technique for evaluating.

Assessment Options

I observed students in all stages of the process, focusing on their ability to create and respond to evaluative questions. I also reviewed students' applications during Stage Three, including their contributions to the PowerPoint presentation.

Reflection on Teaching the English Learners in Our Class

As I was listening to the students' responses to evaluative questions, I thought about how much more clearly several of them are expressing their ideas. It's as if they have gained confidence in their own thinking. They seemed to enjoy that we were interacting with *Hatchet*. All the students enjoyed that book when we read it at the start of the theme. The English learners were actively engaged throughout the lesson. They learned in a variety of settings, including paired, small group, and whole group. I was careful to provide sufficient wait time and to encourage elaboration of their responses when appropriate.

Final Thoughts About the Favorite Authors: Eve Bunting, Doreen Cronin, Gary Soto, and Gary Paulsen Theme

Favorite authors invite us in. They create wonderful stories and invite us to partake. We are fortunate, indeed, to be able to read the works produced by these creative minds. During this theme, it was clear the students shared our thinking. They appreciated the diversity of Eve Bunting's topics, the humorous works of Doreen Cronin, the culturally relevant titles of Gary Soto, and the adventure-driven texts of Gary Paulsen.

It is important to acknowledge that lessons about a variety of skills that underpin comprehension strategies were taught during this theme. For example, aspects of language development and skills such as sequencing, generating questions, and distinguishing important from less important ideas were embedded in the theme. A variety of informational texts were used to teach text frames and generating questions at a variety of levels. Students also frequently used Readers Theatre, repeated readings, and read-alongs to improve fluency. Students' fascination with the favorite authors promoted their engagement in learning. In addition, teachers engaged in read-alouds and encouraged students to use multiple modes of representing their thinking, including sketching, singing, and dramatizing.

Theme Resources

Books

Bunting, E. (1989). *The ghost children.* Boston: Houghton Mifflin.
Bunting, E. (1989). *The Wednesday surprise.* New York: Clarion.
Bunting, E. (1990). *The wall.* New York: Clarion.
Bunting, E. (1991). *Fly away home.* New York: Clarion.
Bunting, E. (1991). *The hideout.* Orlando, FL: Harcourt Brace Jovanovich.
Bunting, E. (1994). *Smoky nights.* Orlando, FL: Harcourt Brace Jovanovich.
Bunting, E. (1994). *Terrible things: An allegory of the Holocaust.* New York: Harper and Row.
Bunting, E. (2000). *Train to somewhere.* Boston: Sandpiper.
Bunting, E. (2001). *Dandelions.* Boston: Sandpiper.
Bunting, E. (2005). *Sunshine home.* Boston: Sandpiper.
Bunting, E. (2006). *One green apple.* New York: Clarion.
Bunting, E. (2009). *So far from the sea.* New York: Clarion.
Bunting, E. (2012). *Ballywhinney girl: An Irish mummy.* New York: Clarion.
Cronin, D. (2000). *Click, clack, moo: Cows that type.* New York: Simon & Schuster.
Cronin, D. (2002). *Giggle, giggle, quack.* New York: Atheneum.
Cronin, D. (2003). *Diary of a worm.* New York: HarperCollins.
Cronin, D. (2004). *Duck for president.* New York: Simon & Schuster.
Cronin, D. (2005). *Diary of a spider.* New York: HarperCollins.
Cronin, D. (2005). *Wiggle.* New York: Atheneum.
Cronin, D. (2006). *Click, clack, splish, splash.* New York: Simon & Schuster.
Cronin, D. (2007). *Bounce.* New York: Atheneum.
Cronin, D. (2007). *Diary of a fly.* New York: HarperCollins.

Cronin, D. (2008). *Click, clack, quackity-quack: A typing adventure.* New York: Little Simon.
Cronin, D. (2008). *Farmer Brown's barnyard: A bestselling board book gift set.* New York: Little Simon.
Cronin, D. (2008). *Thump, quack, moo: A whacky adventure.* New York: Atheneum.
Cronin, D. (2009). *A busy day at the farm.* New York: Little Simon.
Cronin, D. (2009). *Dooby dooby moo.* New York: Atheneum.
Cronin, D. (2009). *Stretch.* New York: Atheneum.
Paulsen, G. (1987). *Hatchet.* New York: Bradbury Press.
Paulsen, G. (1990). *Woodsong.* New York: Bradbury Press.
Paulsen, G. (1991). *The monument.* New York: Dell.
Paulsen, G. (1993). *Eastern sun, winter moon: An autobiographical odyssey.* New York: Harcourt Brace Jovanovich.
Paulsen, G. (1994). *Winterdance: The fine madness of running the Iditarod.* Toronto: Harcourt Brace Jovanovich.
Paulsen, G. (1995). *The tortilla factory.* New York: Harcourt Brace.
Paulsen, G. (1995). *Dogsong.* New York: Aladdin.
Paulsen, G. (1996). *Brian's winter.* New York: Delacorte.
Paulsen, G. (2001). *Brian's return.* New York: Laurel Leaf.
Paulsen, G. (2001). *Guts: The true stories behind* Hatchet *and the* Brian *books.* New York: Delacorte.
Paulsen, G. (2005). *Brian's hunt.* New York: Laurel Leaf.
Paulsen, G. (2007). *Tracker.* New York: Simon & Schuster.
Paulsen, G. (2011). *Woods runner.* New York: Wendy Lamb.
Soto, G. (1992). *Neighborhood odes.* New York: Scholastic.
Soto, G. (1992). *The skirt.* New York: Delacorte.
Soto, G. (1993). *Too many tamales.* New York: Putnam.
Soto, G. (1994). *Crazy weekend.* New York: Scholastic.
Soto, G. (1995). *Canto familiar.* San Diego, CA: Harcourt Brace.
Soto, G. (1995). *Chato's kitchen.* New York: Putnam.
Soto, G. (1996). *Boys at work.* New York: Yearling.
Soto, G. (1997). *Novio boy.* San Diego, CA: Harcourt Brace.
Soto, G. (2000). *Baseball in April and other stories.* Boston: Sandpiper.
Soto, G. (2000). *Chato and the party animals.* New York: Putnam.
Soto, G. (2003). *Taking sides.* Boston: Sandpiper.
Soto, G. (2006). *Buried onions.* Boston: Graphia.
Soto, G. (2006). *Jesse.* Boston: Mariner.
Soto, G. (2007). *Help wanted: Stories.* Boston: Graphia.
Soto, G. (2007). *Mercy on these teenage chimps.* New York: Harcourt.

Websites

Eve Bunting

Reading Rockets: Eve Bunting Biography
www.readingrockets.org/books/interviews/bunting/

Book Page: A Talk With Eve Bunting
bookpage.com/interview/a-talk-with-eve-bunting

Doreen Cronin

HarperCollins Children's, Authors & Illustrators: Doreen Cronin
www.harpercollinschildrens.com/Kids/AuthorsAndIllustrators/ContributorDetail.aspx?CId=21225

Love to Know Children's Books: Doreen Cronin Bio
childrens-books.lovetoknow.com/Doreen_Cronin_Bio

Doreen Cronin Personal Website
www.doreencronin.com

Scholastic Teachers Biography: Doreen Cronin
www2.scholastic.com/browse/contributor.jsp?id=2887

Web English Teacher: Doreen Cronin
www.webenglishteacher.com/cronin.html#

Gary Soto

Gary Soto Personal Website
www.garysoto.com

Poets.org: Gary Soto
www.poets.org/poet.php/prmPID/230

Scholastic Teachers Biography: Gary Soto
www.scholastic.com/teachers/contributor/gary-soto

Gary Paulsen

Gary Paulsen: A Writer of His Time
scholar.lib.vt.edu/ejournals/ALAN/fall94/Schmitz.html

Iditarod: The Last Great Race: A Interview With Gary Paulsen
www.iditarod.com/learn/dailyarchives/story_6.html

Learning About Gary Paulsen
comminfo.rutgers.edu/professional-development/childlit/paulsen.html

Scholastic Teachers: Meet Gary Paulsen
teacher.scholastic.com/activities/iditarod/top_mushers/index.asp?article=gary_paulsen

Random House Children's Books: Gary Paulsen
www.randomhouse.com/features/garypaulsen/about.html

Performance Extensions Across the Curriculum

Social Studies

- Students use Eve Bunting books to explore social issues (*Fly Away Home*—homelessness, *The Wednesday Surprise*—illiteracy). Gather additional information and develop an action plan to help a community organization that supports the issue.
- Students use the book *Dandelions* to introduce the settling of the plains. Investigate the hardships the settlers faced, the motives that drew them to the plains, and how people such as Native Americans affected and were affected by the settlers.

- Students use Gary Soto's books to explore cultures, traditions, and lifestyles of Mexican Americans. Celebrate a World Cultures Day with food, art, music, and traditions from multiple countries, including Mexico.
- Students use Gary Paulsen's experiences and novels to make connections to and research Alaska, including the Iditarod.

Science

- Students use Gary Paulsen's *Hatchet* and *Brian's Winter* to explore factors needed for survival in various environments and climates. Choose additional climates and environments and record information needed to live there. Use this information as the basis of a *Survivor* episode.

Art

- Students investigate various art techniques used in picture books—painting, sketching, paper cutting, collage, and so on. They explore how to use a technique employed by their favorite illustrator and create additional illustrations for the book.

Drama

- Students become their favorite author or illustrator and share information about life and works with the class at an Author Celebration Night.

Music

- Students work with partners or in small groups to present a musical talent show based on Doreen Cronin's *Dooby Dooby Moo*. They can sing songs, write their own songs, play instruments, create their own instruments, and choose to be in other creative acts during the show.

Culminating Activity

Author Celebration Night: Students will design, create, and deliver invitations for their families to attend this celebration. Students will share with their families selected projects, including poems they have written and books the class has created. Refreshments will be served, and the entire event will take only one hour. Photos of students reading, writing, dramatizing, and working with their cross-age partners will be featured. The classroom computers will be available so parents, siblings, and friends can provide feedback on the celebration. The students will give one of the class books to their families as a gift.

CHAPTER 10

Biographies: The Stories of Our Lives

Perhaps because we all have life stories, biographies seem to fascinate us. We read about the goals, successes, and failures of people we know only in a very general way. This often leads to our writing biographies about the lives of others and creating autobiographies about our own experiences. A biography about Barack Obama, Hillary Clinton, Bruce Springsteen, J.K. Rowling, or John Adams may have been the one that drew us to this genre, but it is the biographies and autobiographies that we have yet to read that keep us coming back.

The Biographies: The Stories of Our Lives theme captured the interest of the English learners in the classes in which the lessons were taught. The teachers held high expectations for these students throughout the lessons, and their hopes were fulfilled. The teachers created culturally responsive classrooms in which diversity was appreciated by all. They valued all students' cultural heritages and used that information to support teaching and learning in an educational community. They also used the Guided Comprehension Model for English Learners, a structured lesson format, and appropriate supports, including visuals and adapted graphic organizers, to teach.

In conversations held during the Engaging Prereading Sequence for English Learners, it was clear that these English learners had background knowledge about a variety of biography subjects and that they were comfortable discussing it in this small-group setting. The teachers were particularly attentive to motivating students, activating background knowledge, and sharing engaging read-alouds. During the Engaging Prereading Sequence, students actively participated as the teachers engaged them with interesting, accessible text; provided meaningful visual supports; invited students to respond in multiple modes (speaking, writing, sketching, dramatizing, and singing); provided sufficient wait time when questions were raised; taught essential vocabulary in context; and explicitly taught reading comprehension strategies.

When the English learners moved on to whole-group instruction, they were comfortable, well prepared, and eager to participate. In this setting, opportunities to work with partners and multiple modes of response were prevalent throughout explicit instruction. The comprehension strategy focus was the same one they learned to use during the Engaging Prereading Sequence, so they already had background knowledge about it. In addition, these lessons occasionally focused on the teaching of reading skills. A prime example of this focused on teaching students how to generate and respond to questions at multiple levels (see Chapter 3). Text supports and wait time were provided, and students actively engaged. In teacher-guided small-group instruction, students often had the opportunity to read text with a partner or on their own. They also engaged in discussion and practiced using comprehension skills and strategies. Students were also able to represent their thinking in multiple ways.

In Guided Comprehension centers and routines, English learners partnered with native language speakers or native English speakers, depending on the nature of the activity. For example, when reading theme-related texts in their native language to support their understanding in the theme center, they worked with native language speakers. Conversely, when engaging in activities at the fluency center, the students would typically work with native English speakers. In addition, culturally relevant texts, including titles published in native languages, were available in the centers. In these settings, multiple opportunities were provided for students to interact with text to make content more comprehensible.

The sample Theme-Based Plan for Guided Comprehension: Biographies: The Stories of Our Lives (see Figure 19) offers an overview of the thinking and resources that support the theme. It makes connections to the Common Core State Standards (CCSS; Common Core State Standards Initiative, 2010c) and presents a sampling of assessments, texts, technology resources, comprehension strategies, teaching ideas, comprehension centers, and comprehension routines. The plan begins by delineating examples of student goals and related Common Core College and Career Readiness Anchor Standards for Reading, Writing, Speaking and Listening, and Language. The student goals for this theme include the following:

- Use appropriate comprehension skills and strategies
- Interpret and respond to text in a variety of ways
- Write a variety of types of text
- Communicate effectively

The CCSS for English Language Arts (Common Core State Standards Initiative, 2010c) delineate grade-level expectations in reading, writing, speaking, and listening. Their purpose is to prepare all students to be college and career ready. This includes English learners.

The CCSS (Common Core State Standards Initiative, 2010c, p. 7) suggest that students who are college and career ready

- Demonstrate independence
- Build strong content knowledge
- Respond to the varying demands of audience, task, purpose, and discipline
- Comprehend as well as critique
- Value evidence
- Use technology and digital media strategically and capably
- Understand other perspectives and cultures

In this theme, the lessons are aligned with the Common Core College and Career Readiness Anchor Standards for Reading, Writing, Speaking and Listening, and Language. The key features of these standards include the following (Common Core State Standards Initiative, 2010c, p. 8):

- Reading: Text complexity and the growth of comprehension

Figure 19. Theme-Based Plan for Guided Comprehension: Biographies: The Stories of Our Lives

Goals and Common Core College and Career Readiness Anchor Standards for Reading, Writing, Speaking and Listening, and Language

Students will
- Use appropriate comprehension skills and strategies
- Interpret and respond to text
- Write a variety of types of text
- Communicate effectively

For related College and Career Readiness Standards and Common Core State Standards, see pages 186–189.

Assessment

The following measures can be used for a variety of purposes, including diagnostic, formative, and summative assessment:

Bio-Impression
Double-Entry Journal
Observation
Projects
QuIP
Running Records
Self-Assessments
Student Writing
Thick and Thin Questions

Text

1. *A Picture Book of Jackie Robinson* (Adler, 1997)
2. *Knots in My Yo-Yo String* (Spinelli, 1998)
3. *Satchel Paige* (Cline-Ransome, 2000)
4. *Rosa* (Giovanni, 2007)

Technology Resources

Biography
   www.biography.com
Scholastic: Biography Writer's Workshop
   teacher.scholastic.com/writewit/biograph/index.htm
Encyclopedia of World Biography
   www.notablebiographies.com

Comprehension Strategies	Teaching Ideas
1. Previewing	1. Bio-Impression
2. Making Connections	2. Double-Entry Journal
3. Summarizing	3. Thick and Thin Questions
4. Summarizing	4. Questions Into Paragraphs (QuIP)

Comprehension Centers

Students will apply the comprehension strategies and related teaching ideas in the following comprehension centers:

Art Center
Fluency Center
Making Books Center
Poetry Center
Project Center
Question and Answer Center
Theme Center
Vocabulary Center
Writing Center

Comprehension Routines

Students will apply the comprehension strategies and related teaching ideas in the following comprehension routines:

Literature Circles
Reciprocal Teaching
Cross-Age Reading Experiences

- Writing: Text types, responding to reading, and research
- Speaking and Listening: Flexible communication and collaboration
- Language: Conventions, effective use, and vocabulary

The Common Core State Standards addressed in this theme follow. These standards are directly related to the College and Career Readiness Anchor Standards for Reading, Writing, Speaking and Listening, and Language. (For a complete listing of the Common Core State Standards for English Language Arts, see www.corestandards.org/assets/CCSSI_ELA%20Standards.pdf.)

College and Career Readiness Standards for Reading

The categories of the College and Career Readiness Anchor Standards for Reading featured in these lessons include the following:

- Key Ideas and Details
- Craft and Structure
- Integration of Knowledge and Ideas
- Range of Reading and Level of Text Complexity

Key Ideas and Details

Examples of CCSS for Reading that support the anchor standards in this category include the following:

- Ask and answer questions to demonstrate understanding of a text, referring explicitly to the text as the basis for the answers
- Refer to details and examples in a text when explaining what the text says explicitly and when drawing inferences from the text
- Determine two or more main ideas of a text and explain how they are supported by key details; summarize the text
- Cite the textual evidence that most strongly supports an analysis of what the text says explicitly as well as inferences drawn from the text

Craft and Structure

Examples of CCSS for Reading that support the anchor standards in this category include the following:

- Read with sufficient accuracy and fluency to support comprehension
- Determine the meaning of general academic and domain-specific words or phrases in a text relevant to a topic or subject area
- Compare and contrast the overall structure (e.g., chronology, comparison, cause/effect, problem/solution) of events, ideas, concepts, or information in two or more texts

Integration of Knowledge and Ideas

Examples of CCSS for Reading that support the anchor standards in this category include the following:

- Draw on information from multiple print or digital sources, demonstrating the ability to locate an answer to a question quickly or to solve a problem efficiently
- Integrate information from several texts on the same topic in order to write or speak about the subject knowledgeably
- Evaluate the advantages and disadvantages of using different mediums (e.g., print or digital text, video, multimedia) to present a particular topic or idea

Range of Reading and Level of Text Complexity

Examples of CCSS for Reading that support the anchor standards in this category include the following:

- By the end of the year, read and comprehend informational texts at the high end of the grade-level text complexity band independently and proficiently

College and Career Readiness Standards for Writing

The categories of the College and Career Readiness Anchor Standards for Writing featured in these lessons include the following:

- Text Types and Purposes
- Production and Distribution of Writing
- Research to Build and Present Knowledge
- Range of Writing

Text Types and Purposes

Examples of CCSS for Writing that support the anchor standards in this category include the following:

- Write opinion pieces on topics or texts, supporting a point of view with reasons and information
- Write informative/explanatory texts to examine a topic and convey ideas and information clearly
- Write narratives to develop real or imagined experiences or events using effective technique, descriptive details, and clear event sequences

Production and Distribution of Writing

Examples of CCSS for Writing that support the anchor standards in this category include the following:

- Produce clear and coherent writing in which the development and organization are appropriate to task, purpose, and audience
- With guidance and support from peers and adults, develop and strengthen writing as needed by planning, revising, editing, rewriting, or trying a new approach
- With some guidance and support from adults, use technology, including the Internet, to produce and publish writing as well as to interact and collaborate with others
- Use technology, including the Internet, to produce and publish writing and present the relationships between information and ideas efficiently as well as to interact and collaborate with others

Research to Build and Present Knowledge

Examples of CCSS for Writing that support the anchor standards in this category include the following:

- Conduct short as well as more sustained research projects based on focused questions, demonstrating understanding of the subject under investigation

Range of Writing

Examples of CCSS for Writing that support the anchor standards in this category include the following:

- Write routinely over extended time frames (time for research, reflection, and revision) and shorter time frames (a single sitting or a day or two) for a range of discipline-specific tasks, purposes, and audiences

College and Career Readiness Anchor Standards for Speaking and Listening

The categories of the College and Career Readiness Anchor Standards for Speaking and Listening featured in these lessons include the following:

- Comprehension and Collaboration
- Presentation of Knowledge and Ideas

Comprehension and Collaboration

Examples of CCSS for Speaking and Listening that support the anchor standards in this category include the following:

- Engage effectively in a range of collaborative discussions (one-on-one, group, and teacher-led) with diverse partners on grade-appropriate topics and texts, building on others' ideas and expressing their own clearly

Presentation of Knowledge and Ideas

Examples of CCSS for Speaking and Listening that support the anchor standards in this category include the following:

- Report on a topic or text or present an opinion, sequencing ideas logically and using appropriate facts and relevant, descriptive details to support main ideas or themes; speak clearly at an understandable pace
- Include multimedia components (e.g., graphics, sound) and visual displays in presentations when appropriate to enhance the development of main ideas or themes
- Integrate multimedia and visual displays into presentations to clarify information, strengthen claims and evidence, and add interest

College and Career Readiness Anchor Standards for Language

The categories of the College and Career Readiness Anchor Standards for Language featured in these lessons include the following:

- Conventions of Standard English
- Knowledge of Language
- Vocabulary Acquisition and Use

Conventions of Standard English

Examples of CCSS for Language that support the anchor standards in this category include the following:

- Demonstrate command of the conventions of standard English grammar and usage when writing or speaking

Knowledge of Language

Examples of CCSS for Language that support the anchor standards in this category include the following:

- Use knowledge of language and its conventions when writing, speaking, reading, or listening

Vocabulary Acquisition and Use

Examples of CCSS for Language that support the anchor standards in this category include the following:

- Determine or clarify the meaning of unknown and multiple-meaning words and phrases based on grade-level reading and content, choosing flexibly from a range of strategies

Examples of assessments used in the theme-based Guided Comprehension lessons include observation, running records and retellings, skill and strategy applications, and other formative assessments. The Guided Comprehension lessons, which were designed and taught by classroom teachers, are based on the following strategies and corresponding teaching ideas:

- Previewing: Bio-Impression
- Self-Questioning: Thick and Thin Questions
- Making Connections: Double-Entry Journal
- Summarizing: Questions Into Paragraphs (QuIP)

The texts used in teacher-directed whole-group instruction include *A Picture Book of Jackie Robinson* (Adler, 1997), *Knots in My Yo-Yo String* (Spinelli, 1998), *Satchel Paige* (Cline-Ransome, 2000), and *Rosa* (Giovanni, 2007). Numerous additional theme-related resources—including texts, websites, performance extensions across the curriculum, and a culminating activity—are presented in the Theme Resources at the end of the chapter.

In this theme, students' independent strategy applications occur in the comprehension centers and comprehension routines. The centers include art, fluency, making books, poetry, project, question and answer, theme, vocabulary, and writing. The routines include Literature Circles, Reciprocal Teaching, and Cross-Age Reading Experiences. Sample websites complete the overview.

The four Guided Comprehension lessons that follow are presented through first-person teacher commentaries.

Guided Comprehension Lessons

Biographies: The Stories of Our Lives
Guided Comprehension Strategy: Previewing
Teaching Idea: Bio-Impression

STAGE ONE: Engaging Prereading Sequence for English Learners

We began our Engaging Prereading Sequence by meeting in a sitting area I had created for our conversations. I had previously met with the students in this small group to explain what the Engaging Prereading Sequence was and what we would be doing when we met. I had told them that we would be having a conversation that would help them to take an active role in our reading when the class met in whole group. I had explained that we would be talking about some topics they already knew about and some that may be new to them. I told them that we would be talking about background knowledge we have and how to activate it. I also noted that we would be using the ideas we discussed later in whole group.

When we began our conversation, I reminded the English learners that our topic today would be biographies. We had been working on our biography theme, so the students had already learned the terms *biography* and *autobiography*. They also knew the word *chronological* and why it is important when reading this genre. These words were on our theme word wall, and the prefix and root meanings for *biography* and *autobiography* were on display on another word wall that focused on using prefixes, suffixes, and roots. The students were eager to know the subject of today's biography, so I began by telling them it would be Roberto Clemente. Then I shared photos and other information about Clemente. We discussed the photos I had shared, as well as those that appeared on Biography.com. The students smiled as Elizabetta said, "I know who he is! Roberto Clemente was my grandfather's favorite baseball player when he was a little boy in Puerto Rico." The students were immediately interested. They knew Clemente was an athlete and that he was Hispanic, a culture he shared with most of the students. I knew the students were motivated, so I thought it was time to transition to explicit instruction of the Bio-Impression.

Explain: I explained previewing, a comprehension strategy with which the students were already familiar. I noted that when we preview, we activate background knowledge, predict what the text will be about, and set purposes for reading. I explained that we would be using a Bio-Impression to share clues about Clemente's life, activate our background knowledge, and set purposes for reading Clemente's life story on Biography.com. Next, I adapted Marie Clay's Storybook Introduction (see Appendix A, page 232) to the information on the website. I chose to use the website because I needed to access a reasonably short biography, and I knew Biography .com would provide quality information. The students also seemed more motivated when we used the Internet.

Demonstrate: I demonstrated using a read-aloud, a Think-Aloud, and a whiteboard. I shared a Bio-Impression about Roberto Clemente's life with the students. I explained that the Bio-Impression was about people's life stories and the Story Impression we had learned about earlier was about stories. I reminded them that the Story Impression clues included the narrative elements and that the Bio-Impression clues would appear in chronological order. I showed them the clues about

Guided Comprehension: Biographies: The Stories of Our Lives
Previewing: Bio-Impression

Stage One: Engaging Prereading Sequence for English Learners

- **Engage** students in informal conversation.
- **Introduce** topic, **share** supports, and **activate** background knowledge.
- **Teach** essential vocabulary in context with supports.
- **Explicitly teach** reading comprehension strategies.

Stage Two: Teacher-Directed Whole-Group Instruction

- **Explain** previewing and how to create a Bio-Impression. Focus on using clues to predict information contained in biographies.
- **Demonstrate** a Bio-Impression by introducing the sequential clues for *A Picture Book of Jackie Robinson.* Think aloud about how to use the first two clues to create an opening sentence for the predictive paragraph.
- **Guide** students to contribute to the prediction by looking at the next two clues and creating the next sentence in the impression. Guide students to use the following two words.
- **Practice** using the Bio-Impression to continue predicting the content for the text.
- **Reflect** on how using the Bio-Impression helped to create predictions about text.

Stage Three: Strategy Applications

Student-Facilitated Comprehension Centers

- **Fluency Center:** Read along with books on CD or echo read.
- **Making Books Center:** Create a slide for the class electronic Autobiography Book.
- **Question and Answer Center**: Create a question about biographies at each of Ciardiello's (1998, 2007) levels.
- **Theme Center:** Create Bio-Impressions for a variety of biographies at different levels. Invite students to use the sequential clues to write the predictive paragraph and then read to learn which predictions are verified.
- **Vocabulary Center:** Use our word wall that focuses on using prefixes, suffixes, and roots to create words, write meanings, verify meanings, use in a sentence, and create an illustration.
- **Writing Center:** Encourage students to learn more about the people featured in the biographies they have read and to write about them. Encourage students to write autobiographies.

Teacher-Guided Small-Group Instruction

- **Review** all strategies and focus on using Bio-Impressions.
- **Guide** students to complete a Bio-Impression.
- **Practice** by inviting students to finish reading the text and compare and contrast the Bio-Impression with what they learned from the reading.
- **Retell and Reflect** on how previewing using the Bio-Impression helps us understand what we read.

Student-Facilitated Comprehension Routines

- **Literature Circles:** Write Bio-Impressions while reading biographies.
- **Reciprocal Teaching:** Use Bio-Impressions to predict while engaging in Reciprocal Teaching.

Stage Four: Sharing, Reflection, and Goal Setting

Teacher-Facilitated Whole-Group Reflection and Goal Setting

- **Share** insights about previewing using the Bio-Impression; assess students' ability to make meaningful predictions.
- **Reflect** on how previewing and using the Bio-Impression help prepare for reading the text.
- **Set new goals** or extend existing ones.

Clemente's life and then read the list, noting that the downward arrows that connected the clues showed the order in which the events had occurred. I read the six clues connected by downward arrows:

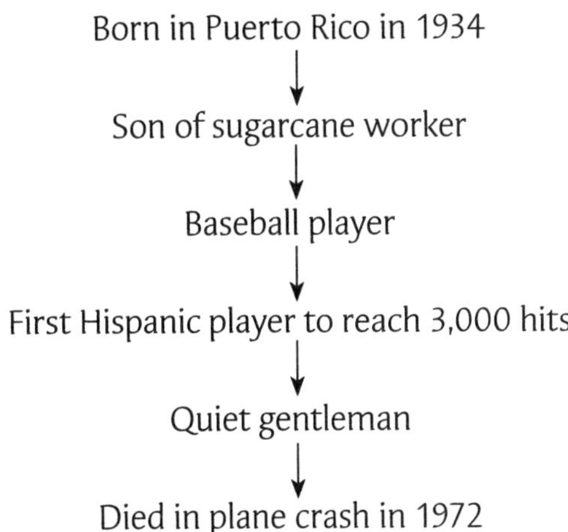

Guide: Next, I invited the students to read the clues with a partner. Then I invited the students to join me in using the Bio-Impression clues to tell the story of Clemente's life. I encouraged the students to make suggestions as I used the Bio-Impression to write Clemente's biography. They suggested several sentences. Each included a clue from the list. I wrote our impression of Clemente's life on the whiteboard:

> Roberto Clemente was born in Puerto Rico in 1934. He was the son of a sugarcane worker. Clemente was the first Hispanic baseball player to reach 3,000 hits. He was a quiet gentleman. He died in a plane crash in 1972.

As we read what we had written, we noticed that we had started a lot of sentences with *he*. I encouraged the students to think of how we could change that. Alicia and David suggested we use his last name to start a sentence. So, we changed the *he* to *Clemente* in the third sentence. Then we read our Bio-Impression again. After we read what we had written, I guided the students to listen carefully as I read aloud the short biography of Roberto Clemente. I also told them that I would stop occasionally so we could make connections. Then I reminded the students that we could use Connection Stems such as "That reminds me of..." to begin our connections. I read the short piece and stopped to make connections. I made sure to provide sufficient wait time and elaborated on student responses as needed. The students were actively engaged and made connections to baseball, Clemente's Puerto Rican heritage, and his being killed in a plane crash trying to help victims of an earthquake in Nicaragua. The students related that earthquake to the one in Haiti, in which some of their relatives had been involved.

Practice: After discussing Clemente's life, we talked about how our Bio-Impression was like Clemente's biography on the website and how it was different. We decided our Bio-Impression was good and it helped us to predict what we would read on the website. It contained the essential information, but the biography on the website provided more details. We talked for a few more minutes about Bio-Impressions and then moved on to whole-group instruction.

STAGE TWO: Teacher-Directed Whole-Group Instruction

Text: *A Picture Book of Jackie Robinson* (Adler, 1997)

Explain: I began by explaining the importance of previewing a text before reading, and I thought aloud about what I would read. I said, "Previewing involves activating prior knowledge, predicting, and setting purposes for reading." I reminded students about the Story Impressions we had created previously (see Appendix A, page 282, for a blackline master). I explained that we used sequential clues about published stories to write Story Impressions—what we predicted the story was about. I reminded students that the clues we used in Story Impressions included the narrative elements: characters, setting, problem, attempts to resolve the problem, and resolution. Then I explained that Bio-Impressions were very similar, but this time the sequential clues would be about facts from a person's life instead of story elements. I told the students that thinking about the content of a biography and predicting what we would read about would help get our minds ready to read and understand the text. It would also help us set purposes for reading. I explained that we would be previewing the text by reading a list of clues that would help us predict what we would read about. Then we would write our impression or prediction of what would happen in the biography.

Demonstrate: I shared the title and showed the students the cover of the book. I asked them what they knew about Jackie Robinson. I also showed the students a variety of photos of Robinson, including several in his baseball uniform. Then I showed students the clues—words and phrases from the biography—that we would use to preview the text and create a Bio-Impression. I reminded students that the clues were connected by arrows and that we would need to use the clues in the order in which they appeared in the list. The clues, which represented events in Jackie Robinson's life, were as follows:

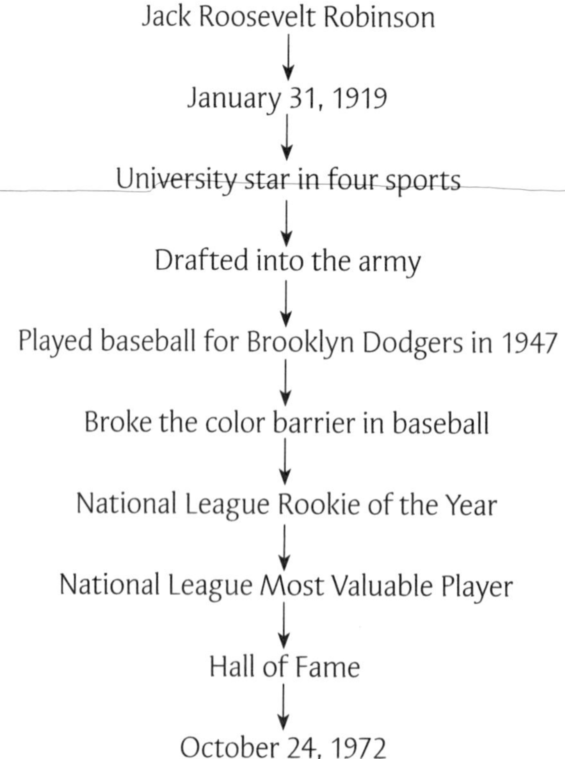

I read through each of the clues and discussed them with the students. Next, I modeled how to start the predictive paragraph by thinking aloud and saying, "I think that the date listed must be when he was born, so I am going to start my prediction by writing, '*Jack Roosevelt Robinson was born on January 31, 1919.*'" I wrote this on the Bio-Impression chart and invited the students to write it on their copies of the blackline I had provided. Then I said, "The next phrase says *university star in four sports*. So for my next sentence, I will write, '*He attended college and was a star in four different sports. One of them was baseball.*'" I explained that the clue didn't mention baseball but that I was predicting that was one of the four sports because Jackie Robinson was such an excellent baseball player. I wrote the sentence on the chart, and the students wrote it, too.

Guide: I guided the students to help me write the next sentence. We discussed what *drafted* meant, and then we wrote, "*Jackie Robinson didn't volunteer to go into the Army. He was drafted.*" I guided the students to think about the next two phrases, *played baseball for Brooklyn Dodgers in 1947* and *broke the color barrier*. Then they suggested we write, "*He played for the Brooklyn Dodgers in 1947 and broke the color barrier, because black people weren't allowed to play in the major leagues at that time.*"

Practice: The students continued to write the Bio-Impression in pairs, using the rest of the words and phrases. I guided them as needed, and when they finished, they shared their impressions. Next, I read aloud *A Picture Book of Jackie Robinson* and we discussed the similarities and differences between our Bio-Impressions and the book David Adler had authored about Jackie Robinson's life. Alyson said, "Our impression was pretty similar, but there were more details about his family in the book." Alejandro said that he liked writing the Bio-Impression because it gave him an idea of what happened in Jackie Robinson's life before he learned everything that was in the book. Steffie said that when we write Story Impressions and Bio-Impressions, we get to write our predictions based on the clues we have. They also noted that my predictions about baseball being one of the sports in which Robinson excelled in college was verified in the text. Here is the Bio-Impression that I started and Steve and Aurora completed on their own:

> Jack Roosevelt Robinson was born on January 31, 1919. He attended college and was a star in four different sports. One of them was baseball. Jackie Robinson didn't volunteer to go into the Army. He was drafted. He played for the Brooklyn Dodgers in 1947 and broke the color barrier, because black people weren't allowed to play in the major leagues at that time. While he was playing for the Brooklyn Dodgers, he was named the National League Rookie of the Year and Most Valuable Player. Later he was elected to the Baseball Hall of Fame. Jackie Robinson died on October 24, 1972.

Reflect: We engaged in a discussion about how the clues helped us predict what we knew about Jackie Robinson. Then we talked about how previewing a text this way helped prepare us for reading and made us want to read to find out if our predictions were accurate. We also talked about how previewing vocabulary ahead of time helped make the words easier to know when we encountered them in the text.

STAGE THREE: Teacher-Guided Small-Group Instruction

Text: *The Real McCoy: The Life of an African-American Inventor* (Towle, 1993) (Texts varied according to students' abilities.)

Review: I reviewed with students that as good readers we can preview a text to get our minds ready to read. I also reviewed how we could use sequential clues from a text to create a predictive paragraph called a Bio-Impression. I introduced the book and asked students what they noticed on the cover of the book. I also asked them if they had ever heard the expression "the real McCoy" and what they thought it meant. Several students suggested that it meant "the real thing or the genuine item." Then I shared the list of sequential clues—words and phrases from the biography—that we would use and reviewed them with the students.

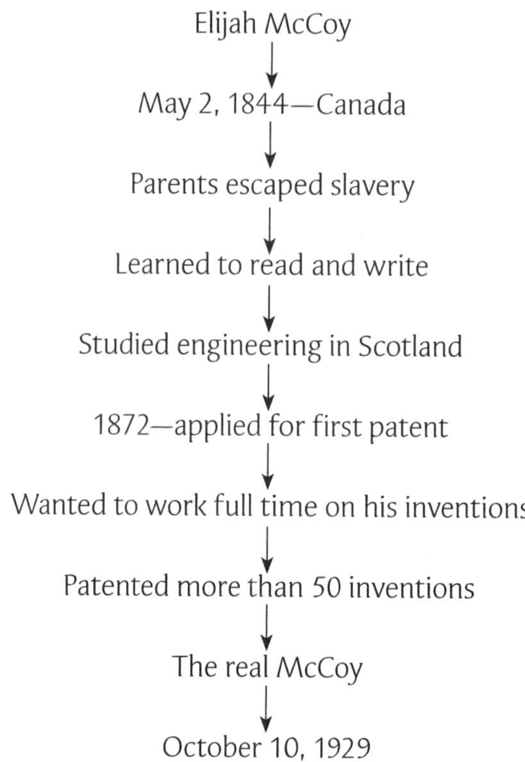

Guide: I guided the students to look at the first two phrases and think of the first sentence of our predictive paragraph. Because it was similar to the Jackie Robinson example, they had no trouble predicting that the date was probably when he was born. They wrote, "*Elijah McCoy was born on May 2, 1844, in Canada.*" Then we discussed how his parents could have been slaves if they lived in Canada. The students realized that Elijah was born in Canada, but his parents must have escaped slavery in the United States. The students knew that slaves in the United States were not allowed to read and write, but Elijah was. They wrote, "*His parents were slaves from the United States who were able to escape to Canada. In Canada, Elijah was free to learn to read and write.*"

Practice: The students continued to create their predictive paragraphs with partners. When they were finished, each pair read their Bio-Impression and we used their predictions to set purposes for reading. Students read the biography and then we compared and contrasted the Bio-Impressions with the original text.

Reflect: I asked the students how using the Bio-Impression helped them to preview. They said it helped them learn a little about Elijah McCoy's life even before they read the book. Maria remarked that she and her partner were able to make connections to the clues based on information they had learned about slavery in their social studies class. Robert said that he and his partner enjoyed reading about Elijah, because as they read they learned which of their predictions were verified and which were not.

Student-Facilitated Comprehension Centers

A number of general accommodations were made for English learners when they engaged in the comprehension centers. These included the following:

- Ensuring that biographies and other books written in the students' native languages were among the texts available in the centers
- Making other culturally relevant texts available in the centers
- Integrating multiple modes of representing thinking in student responses (sketching, singing, dramatizing)
- Inviting students to work with other English learners of the same culture when reading texts in their native languages
- Encouraging English learners to partner with native English speakers when working in centers such as fluency, question and answer, vocabulary, and other centers focused on fluency and language development

Fluency Center: Pairs of students either read along with a biography on tape or CD or echo read short selections.

Making Books Center: Each student used a computer to create a page for the class Autobiography Book. Students used the project checklist, the Autobiography Organizer, and PowerPoint. Students' slides were combined into the class book.

Question and Answer Center: Pairs of students chose a biography I had printed from Biography.com and generated four questions, one at each of Ciardiello's (1998, 2007) four levels (see Chapter 3, pages 33–34). Then they responded to each question. They wrote each question on the front of a large index card and wrote the answer on the back.

Theme Center: I provided sequential clue lists for each biography and autobiography. Students wrote their Bio-Impressions, read the text, and then wrote journal entries about how their impressions and the original biographies were similar and different.

Vocabulary Center: Pairs of students used our word wall that focused on using prefixes, suffixes, and roots to create words. They wrote the word and what they thought the word meant. Next, they checked the word's meaning in an online dictionary and used it in a sentence. Then they created an illustration to represent the word.

Writing Center: Students used Bio-Impressions they had already written to learn more about the people featured in biographies and autobiographies they had read. For example, Jacquelyn used her Bio-Impression of Jackie Robinson to learn more about his life. She used two bookmarked websites to complete a Questions Into Paragraphs (QuIP) graphic organizer about Jackie Robinson. Then she used the completed organizer to write a paragraph about Jackie Robinson's life.

Student-Facilitated Comprehension Routines

A number of general accommodations were made for English learners when they engaged in the comprehension routines. These included the following:

- Making culturally relevant texts available
- Integrating multiple modes of representing thinking in student responses (sketching, singing, dramatizing)

- Encouraging English learners to choose to partner with native English speakers when working in Literature Circles or Reciprocal Teaching

Literature Circles: I provided Bio-Impression clues for the biographies students read in Literature Circles. Students in each group wrote Bio-Impressions and shared their predictions before reading the text. Then they used their impressions to compare and contrast their ideas with the original text.

Reciprocal Teaching: I provided Bio-Impression clues for biographies students read in Reciprocal Teaching. Students used their completed Bio-Impressions to share predictions about the text. They also created questions they had about the books. The list of clues helped them to summarize the important information in the text.

STAGE FOUR: Teacher-Facilitated Whole-Group Reflection and Goal Setting

Share: Students shared their work from Stage Three, first in small groups and then with the class. They shared their Bio-Impressions and discussed examples of when their predictions had been confirmed and when they needed to be adjusted.

Reflect: We discussed why previewing is important and how it helps us prepare to read and understand. Cody said that creating Bio-Impressions motivated him to read because he wanted to find out if his predictions were verified. The other students agreed and decided they were comfortable using Bio-Impressions on their own.

Set New Goals: The students enjoyed writing Bio-Impressions. They thought adapting Bio-Impressions for use with other types of informational text would be helpful when reading their social studies and science textbooks. The students thought this would help them think about the content before reading. We decided we would create some Text Impressions for future content area chapters.

Assessment Options

I used observation during whole-group and small-group instruction. I used the checklist I had provided to review students' book pages. I reviewed their completed Bio-Impressions to see if what the students wrote was a reasonable predictive paragraph. This helped me when planning future previewing and writing lessons. I also read and provided feedback on students' self-assessments.

Reflection on Teaching the English Learners in Our Class

I noticed today that our Engaging Prereading Sequence is becoming more and more conversational. I am thoroughly enjoying watching each of the English learners actively engage. They are often genuinely happy that they can make connections and comment in meaningful ways about the text. The Bio-Impression worked well for us, and the biography of Roberto Clemente turned out to be a really good motivational choice. The English learners worked in pairs, small groups, and whole group. They still seem more comfortable in the first two settings, but they are also actively involved in the whole group. I have been careful about providing sufficient wait time in all settings, and I must note that all the students seem to appreciate it. It gives them just a few extra moments to think. Some of my favorite moments are when the English learners contribute to whole-group learning. They are truly using what they learn in the Engaging Prereading Sequence to their advantage.

Biographies: The Stories of Our Lives
Guided Comprehension Strategy: Making Connections
Teaching Idea: Double-Entry Journals

Engaging Prereading Sequence for English Learners

We began our Engaging Prereading Sequence by meeting in a comfortable corner I had created in our classroom. My students had been learning in this setting for a while, so they knew what the Engaging Prereading Sequence was and what we would be doing when we met. I had told them that we would be having a conversation that would help them to take an active role in our reading when the class met in whole group. I had explained that we would be talking about some topics they already knew about and some that may be new to them. I told them that we would be talking about background knowledge and how to activate it. I also noted that we would be using the ideas we discussed later in whole group.

I told the students that we would be focusing on our biography theme again today and that we would be making connections using an idea called Double-Entry Journals. I explained that the focus of our work would be the life of Nelson Mandela. When I asked if anyone knew anything about Nelson Mandela, Edward said, "He was born in my country, South Africa, and he did a lot to help people there." I said that Edward was correct and we would use what he had told us as a foundation for other things we would learn. Then I shared pictures of Mandela and we listened to Edward share some additional information about his country. He made a point of noting that South Africa is a country on the continent of Africa. He said a lot of people think Africa is a country, but it is a continent that has a lot of countries. The students were quite interested in this information. Next, I suggested that we engage in explicit instruction of the Double-Entry Journal.

Explain: I began by introducing the text, which was a brief biography of Nelson Mandela from Biography.com. I chose to use biographies from this website because they are short and would work well—especially as text for the Engaging Prereading Sequence. I reviewed making connections, which the students had already been using, and introduced Double-Entry Journals. I gave the students the blacklines (see Appendix A, page 367–368) and explained that when we find information to which we can make connections, we write the information from the text in column 1 and then we write our connection in column 2. I reminded students that using Connection Stems such as "That reminds me of..." was a good way to make connections.

Demonstrate: I read a short section of text and thought aloud about making connections. I said,

> When I was reading that Nelson Mandela was from South Africa, I was thinking that Edward made a connection to that. So, I am going to write *Nelson Mandela is from South Africa* in column 1 because that is where we are writing ideas from the text. Then I am going to write *Edward is also from South Africa* in column 2 because that is where we are writing our connections.

Then I asked for a volunteer to read what I had written, and Edward read it.

Guide: I guided students to make connections to Nelson Mandela. I read another segment of text and encouraged students to talk with a partner to make a connection to something in the text about Nelson Mandela's life. After a few moments, Arid and Tomas said, "We can make a connection to Nelson Mandela becoming president of South Africa because we live in the United

Guided Comprehension: Biographies: The Stories of Our Lives
Making Connections: Double-Entry Journals

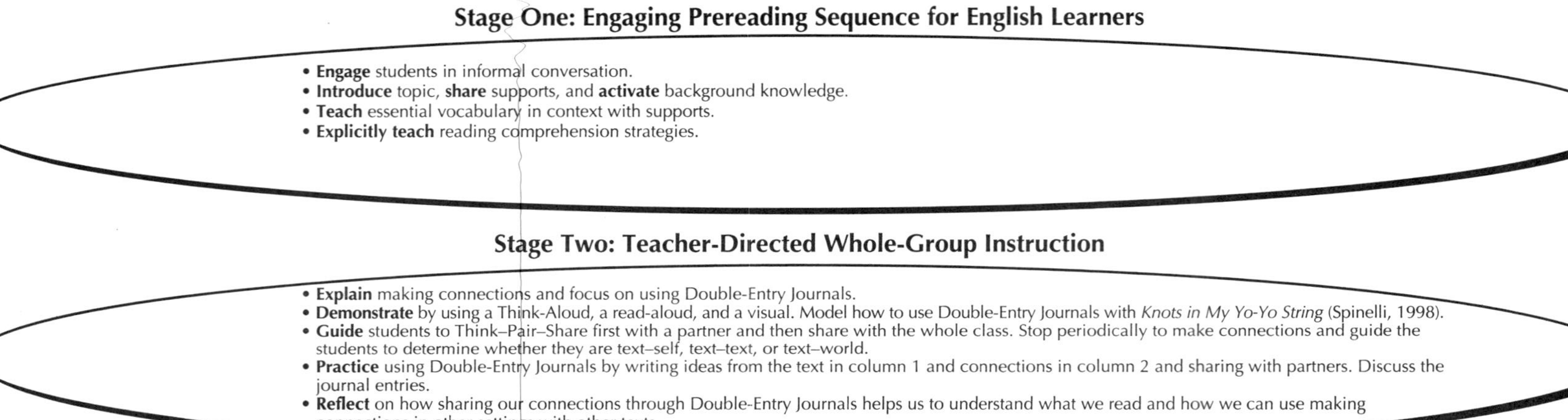

Stage One: Engaging Prereading Sequence for English Learners

- **Engage** students in informal conversation.
- **Introduce** topic, **share** supports, and **activate** background knowledge.
- **Teach** essential vocabulary in context with supports.
- **Explicitly teach** reading comprehension strategies.

Stage Two: Teacher-Directed Whole-Group Instruction

- **Explain** making connections and focus on using Double-Entry Journals.
- **Demonstrate** by using a Think-Aloud, a read-aloud, and a visual. Model how to use Double-Entry Journals with *Knots in My Yo-Yo String* (Spinelli, 1998).
- **Guide** students to Think–Pair–Share first with a partner and then share with the whole class. Stop periodically to make connections and guide the students to determine whether they are text–self, text–text, or text–world.
- **Practice** using Double-Entry Journals by writing ideas from the text in column 1 and connections in column 2 and sharing with partners. Discuss the journal entries.
- **Reflect** on how sharing our connections through Double-Entry Journals helps us to understand what we read and how we can use making connections in other settings with other texts.

Stage Three: Strategy Applications

Student-Facilitated Comprehension Centers

- **Art Center:** Illustrate acrostics created in the poetry center.
- **Fluency Center:** Engage in Readers Theatre to practice fluency.
- **Poetry Center:** Place a variety of biographies and autobiographies at various levels at this center. Students choose a book to read and then write an acrostic poem about that person. As an alternative, students write acrostics or bio-poems about themselves.
- **Question and Answer Center:** Create and respond to questions about self-selected biographies.
- **Theme Center:** Engage in Patterned Partner Reading to read a biography with a partner. Use the pattern Read–Pause–Make a Connection while reading.
- **Writing Center:** Students interview partners and write their biographies. Then they reverse roles.

Teacher-Guided Small-Group Instruction

- **Review** the comprehension strategies and focus on using Double-Entry Journals when making connections. Introduce the text.
- **Guide** students to silently read a segment of *Maya Angelou: More Than a Poet,* stopping periodically to make connections. Provide support as needed.
- **Practice** by encouraging students to continue to read the text, to stop to make connections, and to record connections in Double-Entry Journals. Discuss the connections.
- **Reflect** on how making connections and Double-Entry Journals help us understand what we are reading.

Student-Facilitated Comprehension Routines

- **Literature Circles:** Use Double-Entry Journals to make connections while reading text. Share and discuss connections.
- **Reciprocal Teaching:** Use making connections in the portion of the routine that focuses on clarifying.

Stage Four: Sharing, Reflection, and Goal Setting

Teacher-Facilitated Whole-Group Reflection and Goal Setting

- **Share** applications of making connections using Double-Entry Journals from Stage Three.
- **Reflect** on how making connections promotes engagement and guides our thinking during reading.
- **Set new goals** or extend existing ones.

States, and we have a president, too." I said, "That is a very good connection. How shall we write it?" Then Arid and Tomas explained that the statement about Mandela would be in column 1 and the statement about the United States would be in column 2. Everyone agreed.

Practice: To practice, I continued reading the text and inviting pairs of students to make connections. The connections the students made included the following:

Column 1: Idea from the text	Column 2: My connection
Mandela made his own toys.	My brothers and I make some of our own toys.
Mandela ate things his family grew.	My family eats things that we grow.
Mandela did what he thought was right.	I try to do what I think is right.
Mandela was his country's first black president.	President Obama is our first black president.

Reflect: We reflected on how making connections helped us understand what we read. We also talked about the fact that to use Double-Entry Journals, we needed to write an idea from the text and then write a connection that we knew about it. We felt good that we knew how to use the journals. We finished our discussion about Nelson Mandela and moved on to whole-group instruction.

STAGE TWO: Teacher-Directed Whole-Group Instruction

Text: *Knots in My Yo-Yo String* (Spinelli, 1998)

Explain: I began by reminding the students that making connections is a strategy good readers use while reading. I noted that we can make text–self, text–text, and text–world connections between ideas in what we are reading and our background knowledge. I explained that Double-Entry Journals is one way that we can make connections. Then I focused on how these connections help us understand what we are reading.

Demonstrate: I organized students into pairs and introduced Jerry Spinelli's autobiography, *Knots in My Yo-Yo String*. I reminded students that autobiographies are life stories people write about themselves and that Jerry Spinelli was the author of several books in our classroom library. I demonstrated making connections by reading aloud the title and showing the students the cover of the book. I said, "The title and illustration remind me of how much I enjoyed playing with a yo-yo when I was younger. My aunt bought me a Duncan yo-yo for my 10th birthday." Then I asked the students what they knew about yo-yos. I was surprised that so many of them were familiar with the simple toy. We also discussed what students liked to do to have fun. Their responses included playing baseball. They had noticed Jerry Spinelli was wearing a baseball uniform on page 4 of the book. Students also mentioned that they had fun dancing, going to the movies, and playing games on the computer. Next, I looked at the book cover and read the title again. I said, "Knots. I hated when my yo-yo string would get knots. We also used to fly kites down in Ocean City, Maryland, on the beach. That string sometimes got knotted, too." I read the first page aloud to the class and said, "Jerry seems to be really upset because Lucky, his dog, was hit by a car. When my dog died, I cried and we buried her in our yard." When I read a few more pages, I made another connection. I said, "We also loved to ride our bikes outside every day." Then I demonstrated how to use Double-Entry Journals. I said, "I will write an idea or quote from the book in the first column, and I will write my connection to the idea in the second column." I continued reading aloud. When I stopped, I said,

> Jerry lived in a row house in the West End of Norristown near a park and a creek. I am going to write that in column 1. I will write my connection in column 1. My connection is that I also lived in a row house but in a smaller town. We had a community park where we spent every day in the summer, either at the pool or the creek, doing arts and crafts, or playing tennis.

Next, I said,

> When we are making connections using Double-Entry Journals, we choose an idea from the text that we think we can make a connection to. We write that idea in column 1. Then we make a connection and write that in column 2. It's important to remember that we can make connections to ourselves, other texts, and the world.

Guide: As I continued to read aloud the next chapter of the book, I invited students to work with partners to make connections with the story. I guided students to listen for ideas that they could relate to their own experiences and to which they could make connections. I encouraged students to write an idea in column 1 and to write their connection in column 2. Then the students worked with partners to create two connections. Some of their connections included "I felt sad and guilty like Jerry Spinelli when I played war with my friend and I accidentally broke his collarbone," and "Jerry talks about being a captive and being tortured during a real war. I can make a connection to Senator John McCain, who was a prisoner of war during the Vietnam War."

Practice: I continued to read the next chapter of the book while students practiced recording their ideas and their connections in their Double-Entry Journals. The students shared their connections and discussed whether they were text–self, text–text, or text–world. Samples of their connections included the following:

Column 1: Idea from the text	Column 2: My connection
Jerry enjoyed being a cowboy when he was little. (page 18)	My little brother has a cowboy outfit and he wore it last year to the county fair. (text–self connection)
Jerry is a "sports nut" including baseball, football, and basketball. (page 22)	Jerry lived near Philadelphia and the Philadelphia Phillies won the 2008 World Series. (text–world connection)
Jerry won a medal for the 50-yard dash. (page 28)	I won a medal for placing first in our gymnastics competition. (text–self connection)
Jerry felt sorry for himself when he made an error playing shortstop for the "Greensox." (page 30)	In "Casey at the Bat," Casey feels sorry for himself because he struck out. (text–text connection)

Reflect: We began our reflection by discussing how making connections was helping us to relate to Jerry Spinelli's life. The students made many connections to his early life. We had an interesting discussion about how things are different from when Jerry was growing up in the 1950s and about how many things are still the same. Then we reflected on the importance of using Double-Entry Journals to make connections. Marita and Kathy said they liked Double-Entry Journals because they could pick an idea from the text and make a connection. Everyone decided that making connections keeps us interested in what we are reading and helps us to understand biographies and autobiographies.

STAGE THREE: Teacher-Guided Small-Group Instruction

Text: *Maya Angelou: More Than a Poet* (Lisandrelli, 1996) (Texts varied according to students' abilities.)

Review: I reminded students about the reading strategies good readers use and reviewed how to make connections using Double-Entry Journals.

Guide: I introduced the biography *Maya Angelou: More Than a Poet* by showing the cover, reading the title, and asking students to make connections. Samples of their statements included "Maya is at a podium speaking. This reminds me of when we see the President speak," and "I remember seeing Maya doing an interview on television." After everyone shared, students silently read segments of the text, stopping periodically to make connections using Double-Entry Journals. They shared their connections with a partner.

Practice: Students silently read Chapter 2 and made connections using Double-Entry Journals. After each chapter, we discussed their connections. We continued this process until the end of Chapter 5. Examples of the connections students shared in their Double-Entry Journals included the following:

Column 1: Idea from the text	Column 2: My connection
Maya pretended to be a character from the books. (page 28)	I often do this after I read a story. I enjoyed pretending to be "Julie" in *Julie of the Wolves.* (text–self connection)
After the bombing of Pearl Harbor, West Coast Japanese-Americans, two-thirds of whom were American citizens, were subjected to much hatred. Many were uprooted from their homes and taken to detention camps. (pages 38–39)	I remember reading about the Japanese internment camps last year. Our teacher read Eve Bunting's book *So Far From the Sea* to us. (text–text connection)
Maya went to Big Mary's to pick up her son, but Big Mary and Clyde were not there. (page 59)	In the news, babies are taken all the time. (text–world connection)

Reflect: We engaged in a group summary of what we had learned about Maya Angelou's life. Next, we discussed her life so far and how we can make connections to it. One student observed how difficult Maya's life has been and compared it with her own. Then we discussed how making connections helped us understand what we read.

Student-Facilitated Comprehension Centers

A number of general accommodations were made for English learners when they engaged in the comprehension centers. These included the following:

- Ensuring that biographies and other books written in the students' native languages were among the texts available in the centers
- Making other culturally relevant texts available in the centers
- Integrating multiple modes of representing thinking in student responses (sketching, singing, dramatizing)

- Inviting students to work with other English learners of the same culture when reading texts in their native languages
- Encouraging English learners to partner with native English speakers when working in centers such as fluency, question and answer, vocabulary, and other centers focused on fluency and language development

Art Center: Students illustrated the acrostics they created in the poetry center.

Fluency Center: I placed a variety of Readers Theatre scripts at this center. Pairs of students practiced their fluency by reading the scripts.

Poetry Center: Students read a biography or autobiography and wrote an acrostic about that person. Students could also choose to write a bio-poem about themselves or use their first names to write acrostic poems about themselves. This is the acrostic Adriah created:

A student who loves to read

D evoted to my parents and friends

R egrets making some bad decisions

I nterested in going to college

A positive attitude and determination will bring me success

H appy

Question and Answer Center: I placed a wide variety of short biographies of famous heroes, musicians, sports figures, and political leaders at this center. Students worked with a partner to generate and respond to questions about their self-selected subject.

Theme Center: I placed a variety of biographies and autobiographies at various levels at this center. Students read in pairs, using Patterned Partner Reading with the read–pause–make a connection pattern. They wrote or sketched their connections in their Double-Entry Journals. They shared and discussed their connections with a partner.

Writing Center: Students worked with a partner to write each other's biographies. They began by interviewing each other. When the biographies were complete, each partner made connections to the other's life story.

Student-Facilitated Comprehension Routines

A number of general accommodations were made for English learners when they engaged in the comprehension routines. These included the following:

- Making culturally relevant texts available
- Integrating multiple modes of representing thinking in student responses (sketching, singing, dramatizing)
- Encouraging English learners to choose to partner with native English speakers when working in Literature Circles and Reciprocal Teaching

Literature Circles: One group of advanced-level readers chose to read *All God's Children Need Traveling Shoes* (1986) by Maya Angelou. They made connections as they read and shared their thoughts through their Double-Entry Journals. This is an example of Melanie's work:

> Column 1: "Hope for the best; be prepared for the worst. You may not get what you pay for, but you will definitely pay for what you get."
>
> Column 2: "When my Mom and me have talks, she says pretty much the same thing." (text–self connection)

Reciprocal Teaching: The students made connections using Double-Entry Journals and shared them during the portion of the routine that focuses on clarifying.

STAGE FOUR: Teacher-Facilitated Whole-Group Reflection and Goal Setting

Share: Students shared their connections from Stage Three in small groups. Then we discussed their applications as a whole class.

Reflect: We reflected on how making connections can promote engagement and guide our reading. We also talked about how we can make all three different types of connections: text–self, text–text, and text–world.

Set New Goals: Students felt confident with their ability to make connections with biographies and autobiographies, so we extended our goal to using Double-Entry Journals with poetry. We decided to make connections with Maya Angelou's "On the Pulse of Morning" as well as other poems.

Assessment Options

I observed students and listened carefully as they made connections throughout this lesson. I also reviewed their performances from Stage Three and checked for understanding during their discussions. Students used a graphic organizer and a checklist when writing their autobiographies. I reviewed the organizer and used the checklist to assess what they had written.

Reflection on Teaching the English Learners in Our Class

The English learners seem to be very comfortable in their learning, especially in paired and small-group settings. They also seem to particularly enjoy our time in the Engaging Prereading Sequence. Edward's face was absolutely beaming as he talked about his homeland when making connections to Nelson Mandela. The other students appeared equally engaged as they made connections. I try when teaching the Engaging Prereading Sequence to use culturally relevant text to which the students can make personal connections. The students also actively participated in whole-group instruction. They partnered with native English speakers in that setting. A few of the students still choose to read in their native languages when that is an option in centers, but all are making efforts to read more and speak more in English.

Biographies: The Stories of Our Lives
Guided Comprehension Strategy: Self-Questioning
Teaching Idea: Thick and Thin Questions

Engaging Prereading Sequence for English Learners

We began our Engaging Prereading Sequence by gathering in a relaxed sitting area I had created for our conversations. I had previously met with the students in this small group to explain what the Engaging Prereading Sequence was and what we would be doing when we met. I had told them that we would be having a conversation that would help them to take an active role in our reading when the class met in whole group. I told them that we would be talking about background knowledge and how to activate it. I also noted that we would be using the ideas we discussed later in whole group.

When we began our conversation, I reminded the students our topic today was biography—specifically, the life story of Sandra Cisneros, a Latina author and poet. I shared photos and explained that we would be reading more about Sandra in a few minutes during the explicit instruction of Thick and Thin Questions. In the interim, we talked about some authors and poets we had studied and discussed a few examples of each.

Explain: I explained self-questioning to students, noting that this strategy, like all the others, required us to think in depth. Then I made connections to Ciardiello's (1998, 2007) questioning levels (see Chapter 3, pages 33–34), which we had learned earlier. I also explained Thick and Thin Questions. I said,

> Thin questions are usually short questions that have one-, two-, or three-word answers. These are like Ciardiello's memory level questions. You can put your finger on the answer, because it is in the book. Thick questions have longer answers. Those answers may require a few sentences. Some of that information may be in our minds, but some may also be in the text. Thick questions are like Ciardiello's *why* questions (convergent level), *creative thinking* questions (divergent level), and *what do you think/justify your response* questions (evaluative levels).

I referred to a wall poster in our classroom that featured Ciardiello's levels of questioning and examples of each. I also reminded the students that good readers engage in self-questioning before, during, and after reading. Then I distributed blacklines for Thick and Thin Questions, on which students could record their questions and answers.

Demonstrate: I told the students that it was always a good idea to have questions about the topic in our minds before we start reading. Then I shared copies of Sandra Cisneros's biography. After reading the first few sentences aloud, I said, "I have two questions. My first question is 'Where was Cisneros born?' My second question is 'Why is she famous?'" Then I thought aloud about whether the questions were thick or thin. I said, "The first question is short and probably has a one- or two-word answer. Is it a thick question or a thin question?" The students said that it was a thin question because it was a short question that would have a short answer. Then I said, "I notice that the second question starts with the word *why*. According to Ciardiello's signal words, that makes it a convergent question. Are convergent questions thick or thin?" The students indicated it was a thick question because the answer would be more than a few words and would come from the book and my mind. I confirmed that was correct.

Guided Comprehension: Biographies: The Stories of Our Lives
Self-Questioning: Thick and Thin Questions

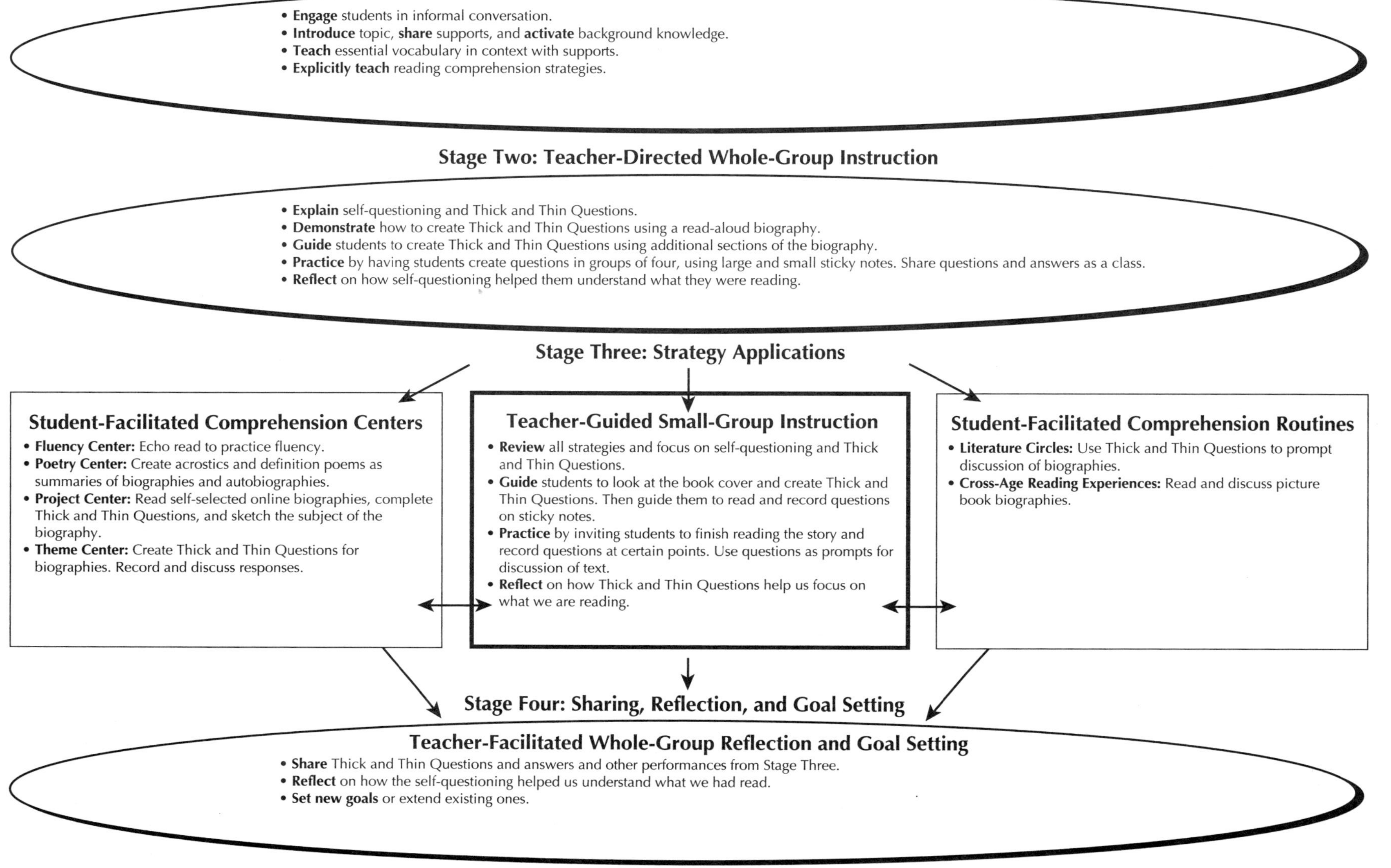

Guide: I guided the students to read along as I read the remainder of the brief biography of Sandra Cisneros. Then I asked the students to discuss the questions I had raised about Sandra Cisneros. After a few moments, I asked, "What do you think the answer to the first question is?" Marta responded, "Chicago. I think the answer is Chicago. It is a one-word answer, and I can put my finger on it in the text, so I think it is a thin question." I said that was correct. Then I asked about the answer to "What made Sandra Cisneros famous?" Johnny said, "I think it is a thick question, and the answer is that she is famous because she wrote books and poems."

Arid said, "That sounds right, and the answer is longer than an answer to a thin question." Everyone agreed that it was a thick question and the answer was correct. We generated a few more questions and labeled each thick or thin.

Practice: To practice, pairs of students reread the brief Cisneros biography. I encouraged the students as they read to create one thick question and one thin question, record them on the blackline, and write an answer to each. I provided sufficient time and engaged with the pairs of students as requested. After a few minutes, the students shared their questions and responses. Here are some examples of their ideas:

Thin Questions:

1. What does Cisneros write about? The Latina experience.
2. How many copies of *The House on Mango Street* have been sold? 2 million.

Thick Questions:

1. Why did so many people buy Cisneros's book? We think people bought the book because it was about a Latina girl and there weren't a lot of books about Latinas then.
2. If Cisneros writes another book, what do you think it will be about? We think it will be about Latino families, because she grew up in one.

We discussed the students' questions and responses. Then we talked about how important it was to question before, during, and after reading.

Reflect: The students reflected on how the questions helped them to think about what they were reading. Arid said, "It is like we should always have questions in our head about what we are reading." I said, "Yes, we should. We should also make sure that some of our questions are thick questions because they will require us to think at high levels." Marietta smiled and said, "Thin questions are OK, but thick questions make us think more." I smiled. I knew the students were fine using Thick and Thin Questions, so we moved on to whole-group instruction.

STAGE TWO: Teacher-Directed Whole-Group Instruction

Text: *Satchel Paige* (Cline-Ransome, 2000)

Explain: I explained self-questioning to students, noting that this strategy, like all the others, required us to think in depth. I explained the concept of Thick and Thin Questions using the biography *Satchel Paige*, which I read aloud to the students. I told them that thin questions had short answers that required just a word or phrase. I explained that thick questions had larger answers that required several phrases or sentences and usually needed a combination of information from the text and their own minds. I reminded the students that good readers engage in self-questioning before, during, and after reading and that we would use this process in other texts we read.

Demonstrate: I put the Thick and Thin Questions blackline (see Appendix A, page 284) on the smartboard so I could show the students how to record their questions and answers. I showed the students the cover of the book and thought aloud about how important it is to have questions in my mind before I start reading because it helps to focus my reading and gives me purposes for reading. I said, "One question I have as I look at the cover of this book is 'What made Satchel Paige famous?'" I wrote this question in the Thin Question column and told the students that it was a thin question because the answer is probably short and evident in the text. Next, I asked aloud, "What impact did Satchel Paige have on African Americans and baseball?" I recorded this question in the Thick Question column and explained to the students that the answer was probably larger than a word or two. I explained that I knew from prior experience that Satchel Paige pitched a long time ago and that black men were not always welcome in the major leagues then. I also told them that I knew that Satchel was famous so I think that he did influence blacks in baseball. I explained that this is a thick question because it would take information from the text and my mind to answer it.

Guide: I read the first two pages of text to the students and then prompted them to think of a question that had a small answer. They suggested "Where did Satchel grow up?" and "How did Satchel help his mother?" I recorded these in the Thin Question column. I then guided the students to think of some larger questions that could be answered from the information in the text and from their minds or in other parts of the text. They were having trouble thinking of these because they were so focused on the direct recall questions. I gave them another example—"What evidence is there that Satchel had an 'early gift for throwing'?"—and explained that this question had a bigger answer than just one word or phrase. I then read the next two pages and prompted the students with guiding questions, such as "What do you know about Satchel?" and "What more do you want to know?" They came up with "Why did Satchel need to earn money?" and "What kind of worker is Satchel? How do you know?" I recorded these in the Thick Question column. I then repeated this process with the next two pages of text. The students were able to create Thick and Thin Questions. I felt they were able to try this on their own, so I gave each group of four students a stack of large and small sticky notes. I demonstrated how to record thin questions on the small sticky notes and thick questions on the larger notes.

Practice: I read the next two pages of text aloud and asked each group to create one thin question and one thick question. Each group shared questions and possible answers. Other students contributed additional responses to the thick questions. I continued this process throughout the reading of Satchel Paige's biography.

Reflect: The students reflected on how the questions really helped to focus them as they listened to the story. They also shared that the thick questions made them think about larger connections within the text and their own minds. We talked about ways they could use self-questioning when they read, and they set goals for using questioning when they read on their own.

STAGE THREE: Teacher-Guided Small-Group Instruction

Text: *Helen Keller: Courage in Darkness* (Berne, 2009) (Texts varied according to students' abilities.)

Review: I reviewed the comprehension strategies good readers use and then focused on self-questioning and Thick and Thin Questions.

Guide: I provided some background information about Helen Keller. The students were very motivated. I showed the students the cover of *Helen Keller: Courage in Darkness.* I encouraged them to think of a thin question and a thick question to give them a focus for reading. I started by asking, "What was Helen Keller's disability?" I explained that was a thin question because it had a short answer. Then I asked, "What kinds of hardships did Helen Keller face because of her disability?" I explained why that was a thick question and we used the questions to set purposes for reading. I asked the students to read the first chapter silently. The English learners whisper read with a partner at this time. When they finished, we discussed that the text had provided the answer to the thin question I had raised, but not the thick question. We decided we would keep that question in mind as we continued to read the book. We created new Thick and Thin Questions and students read the next chapter.

Practice: The students created responses to the questions as they read the next two chapters. They also created new Thick and Thin Questions on sticky notes. We used these questions as prompts to discuss the biography the next time we met in small groups. I continued this process as a way to prompt discussion and monitor students' understanding as they completed this biography. These are some of the Thick and Thin Questions students raised:

Thick Questions

- How will Annie get Helen to learn self-control?
- Why was Helen so difficult toward Annie?
- What might Annie try next?

Thin Questions

- What is Annie's job?
- Why was Helen angry with Annie?
- What caused the worst fight Helen and Annie had?

Reflect: I encouraged the students to reflect on the importance of self-questioning when they read and on the difference between questions with small and large answers. We discussed how this helped them think and understand what they were reading. They agreed that it helped to give them a purpose for wanting to read more.

Student-Facilitated Comprehension Centers

A number of general accommodations were made for English learners when they engaged in the comprehension centers. These included the following:

- Ensuring that biographies and other books written in the students' native languages were among the texts available in the centers
- Making other culturally relevant texts available in the centers
- Integrating multiple modes of representing thinking in student responses (sketching, singing, dramatizing)
- Inviting students to work with other English learners of the same culture when reading texts in their native languages

- Encouraging English learners to partner with native English speakers when working in centers such as fluency, question and answer, vocabulary, and other centers focused on fluency and language development

Fluency Center: Pairs of students echo read picture book biographies to practice fluency.

Poetry Center: Students created acrostic poems and definition poems as creative ways to summarize the information in biographies autobiographies.

Project Center: Students visited bookmarked websites such as www.biography.com. They read a biography of special interest to them, completed Thick and Thin Questions, and drew a sketch about the subject of the biography.

Theme Center: I placed a variety of biographies and autobiographies at different levels at this center. Students chose a book to read and generated and responded to Thick and Thin Questions.

Student-Facilitated Comprehension Routines

A number of general accommodations were made for English learners when they engaged in the comprehension routines. These included the following:

- Making culturally relevant texts available
- Integrating multiple modes of representing thinking in student responses (sketching, singing, dramatizing)
- Encouraging English learners to choose to partner with native English speakers when working in Literature Circles
- Encouraging English learners to choose to partner with native language speakers or English language speakers when working in Cross-Age Reading Experiences

Literature Circles: Students read the same biography and used Thick and Thin Questions recorded on sticky notes as the prompts for their discussions. Students took turns posing questions to and getting answers from the group before they shared their own answers. They continued this process throughout the reading of the biography. They placed their sticky notes and answers in their Guided Comprehension Journals.

Cross-Age Reading Experiences: Students worked with cross-age partners to read picture book biographies. Subjects ranged from Martin Luther King to President Barack Obama to Amelia Earhart.

STAGE FOUR: Teacher-Facilitated Whole-Group Reflection and Goal Setting

Share: In small groups, students shared examples of Thick and Thin Questions and other performances they had created in Stage Three.

Reflect: In whole group, I reminded the students about the importance of self-questioning while reading and asked them to think about how it helped them understand the text. They agreed that the questions helped give them a reason to continue reading and in many instances clarified ideas for them as they shared answers. They got into a discussion on the value of thin questions and we came to a consensus that thin questions were valuable, but they should not be the only kind of question we think about. Then I invited the students to think about how they could use this questioning technique in other reading settings.

Set New Goals: We engaged in self-assessment and decided to extend our current goal by learning about Evaluative Questioning.

Assessment Options

I observed students during all stages of Guided Comprehension and made notes about their contributions and interactions. I also read their Guided Comprehension Journals to gather evidence about their ability to create Thick and Thin Questions. The students' self-assessments during comprehension centers and routines provided additional information about their understanding.

Reflection on Teaching the English Learners in Our Class

The English learners are still highly engaged in the Engaging Prereading Sequence. They seem to genuinely enjoy the relaxed, conversational tone of our sessions. They also seem to take pride in their many successes. Today when we were in whole group, they were particularly active when we formed the groups of four. The English learners whisper read with native English speakers in Stage Three and worked with both native language speakers and native English speakers when working in centers and routines. They are also reading books I have been recommending based of the results of their interest inventories. It is very rewarding to see their confidence growing.

Biographies: The Stories of Our Lives
Guided Comprehension Strategy: Summarizing
Teaching Idea: Questions Into Paragraphs (QuIP)

STAGE ONE: Engaging Prereading Sequence for English Learners

We began our Engaging Prereading Sequence by meeting in a quiet sitting area I had created for our conversations. I had previously met with the students in this small group, so they knew what the Engaging Prereading Sequence was and what we would be doing when we met. I had told them that we would be having a conversation that would help them to take an active role in our reading when the class met in whole group. I had explained that we would be talking about some topics they already knew about and some that may be new to them. I told them that we would be talking about background knowledge and how to activate it. I also noted that we would be using the ideas we discussed later in whole group.

When we began our conversation, I reminded the students that we would be continuing our work in our biography theme. I told the students that the subject of our biography today would be Cesar Chavez, a person of Mexican American descent who worked in peaceful ways to make life better for farm workers. Then I shared some photos and news stories about Chavez. I further noted that Chavez had grown up in a family of migrant farm workers. The students and I talked about what migrant farmer workers were. I shared the phrase in context in Chavez's biography, and Inez predicted that *migrant* meant "traveling." Marcus agreed. He said, "I think they moved from farm to farm so they could work." I noted that Inez and Marcus were correct and shared some photos showing the farm workers on trucks moving on to the next farm. Next, I explained that we would be using Chavez's biography to learn how to use Questions Into Paragraphs (QuIP). I followed this by engaging in explicit instruction of QuIP.

Explain: I began by reminding students that when we summarize informational text, we include the important ideas from the text. Then I explained QuIP to students as a way to summarize informational text.

Demonstrate: I demonstrated QuIP by using a read-aloud, a Think-Aloud, the QuIP graphic organizer (see Appendix A, page 278), and the text. I showed the students a completed QuIP and pointed out that, as we had discussed, we would be creating two questions about Cesar Chavez's life and using two sources to answer each question. I noted that there are typically three questions on a QuIP organizer but that we would only use two. I read aloud the Chavez information from Biography.com in segments, pausing to make connections and discuss with students. Prior to reading, I encouraged them to think about questions that we could use on our QuIP.

Guide: When I finished reading, the students and I talked about the questions we would like to use on our QuIP organizer. We decided to use these two questions and I wrote them on the QuIP:

1. What did Chavez do for the farm workers?
2. Why did Chavez help the farm workers?

I noted that we would read two sources to find answers to each question. I explained that Biography .com (www.biography.com) would be one source and Hispanic Heritage in the Americas (www .britannica.com/hispanic_heritage/article-9022718) would be the other. Both websites appeared on class computers. I encouraged the students to listen for information that might help us respond to

Guided Comprehension: Biographies: The Stories of Our Lives
Summarizing: Questions Into Paragraphs (QuIP)

Stage One: Engaging Prereading Sequence for English Learners

- **Engage** students in informal conversation.
- **Introduce** topic, **share** supports, and **activate** background knowledge.
- **Teach** essential vocabulary in context with supports.
- **Explicitly teach** reading comprehension strategies.

Stage Two: Teacher-Directed Whole-Group Instruction

- **Explain** summarizing as a reading comprehension strategy and using Questions Into Paragraphs (QuIP) as a way to summarize what we have read.
- **Demonstrate** summarizing using QuIP, a Think-Aloud, and the QuIP graphic organizer.
- **Guide** students to generate questions and use the first source to respond to them.
- **Practice** by responding to the questions using the second source and writing a paragraph based on the information that has been gathered.
- **Reflect** on how QuIP helps us to generate questions, research, and summarize informational text.

Stage Three: Strategy Applications

Student-Facilitated Comprehension Centers

- **Fluency Center:** Read along with books on CD.
- **Making Books Center**: Create your autobiography or a biography of the subject of your choice. Create an electronic book.
- **Project Center:** Create transmediations. Working with a partner, choose a biography in book format and change it into a poem or song lyrics.
- **Theme Center:** Work with a partner. Choose two biographies about the same person and use the QuIP research process to question, research, and summarize information about that person's life.

Teacher-Guided Small-Group Instruction

- **Review** the comprehension strategies and focus on generating questions, researching, and summarizing information using QuIP.
- **Guide** students to generate questions about Martin Luther King Jr.'s life. Provide support as needed. Discuss the questions and responses.
- **Practice** by asking students to research responses to their questions from two sources. Remind students to record their responses on the QuIP graphic organizer. Discuss responses.
- **Reflect** on how QuIP helps us to question before reading, guides us to understand text while we are reading, and provides organized information to help us summarize after reading.

Student-Facilitated Comprehension Routines

- **Literature Circles:** Read biographies and autobiographies. Complete a QuIP graphic organizer as an extension activity.
- **Reciprocal Teaching:** Read biographies and autobiographies using Reciprocal Teaching strategies.
- **Cross-Age Reading Experiences**: Work with cross-age partners to read biographies and other texts.

Stage Four: Sharing, Reflection, and Goal Setting

Teacher-Facilitated Whole-Group Reflection and Goal Setting

- **Share** applications of QuIP and other performances from Stage Three and assess students' abilities to use them.
- **Reflect** on how QuIP promotes engagement, guides our reading, and helps us organize information to help us summarize.
- **Set new goals** or extend existing ones.

the questions and then I read the first selection aloud. I discussed it with the students. Then we read question 1: What did Chavez do for the farm workers? We decided that Chavez worked for equality in nonviolent ways and he founded the National Farm Workers Association. I was careful to provide sufficient time for students to think before they began sharing. Then I listened carefully as the students talked. I was pleased to note that several focused on similar ideas.

Guide: After reviewing question 1, I guided students to listen as I read the second selection. As I read it, I stopped periodically for students to discuss the text. When I finished, I again repeated the question. This time, David said, "I think we should include that Chavez worked as a community organizer and that he helped form the United Farm Workers." Renaldo said, "Should we include the year? It was 1972." Everyone agreed that we had good information.

We used the same process to respond to question 2. We decided that source one had ideas that indicated that Chavez helped the farm workers because he grew up in a migrant farm worker family and served as a community organizer. Then we decided that source two had similar information. It noted that Chavez lived in many migrant worker camps as a child and was a general director of a community organization before founding the union. We wrote that in the correct space and our questions and responses were complete.

Practice: We practiced by using the information on the QuIP to write a summary:

> Cesar Chavez worked for equality in nonviolent ways. He helped the farm workers and was a community organizer who founded the National Farm Workers Association. Chavez grew up in a migrant farm worker family. The National Farm Workers Association joined with another group to become the United Farm Workers of America in 1972.

Reflect: We began by discussing how generating our own research questions and taking notes from more than one source made writing summaries easier. We all agreed that QuIP provided a good way for us to organize information.

We reviewed all that Cesar Chavez did for the farm workers and then we moved on to whole-group instruction.

STAGE TWO: Teacher-Directed Whole-Group Instruction

Text: *Rosa* (Giovanni, 2007)

Explain: I began by explaining summarizing to the students, noting that when we summarize, we include the important ideas from the text. I pointed out that summarizing informational text is very different from summarizing or retelling stories because retellings include the story elements: characters, setting, problem, attempts to resolve the problem, and resolution. Then I explained QuIP to students as a way to summarize informational text. I focused on how we use questioning, research, and summarizing to understand new information while we are reading.

Demonstrate: I demonstrated QuIP by using a Think-Aloud, the QuIP graphic organizer (see Appendix A, page 278), and the text. I began by reading aloud the title and showing the students the cover of the book *Rosa*. I showed the cover of the book and thought aloud, "The title tells me this book is about a woman named Rosa. I think it is about Rosa Parks. The illustration made me wonder why the man is looking down at her." Then I asked students what they knew about Rosa Parks. We discussed their responses, which included that she was arrested for not giving up her seat to white people on a bus.

Guide: I guided students to generate ideas by raising a question I had about Rosa Parks. I said, "I have a question about Rosa Parks that I would like to research. My question is, 'Why is Rosa Parks considered to be the mother of the modern-day Civil Rights movement in the United States?'" I wrote the question in the box labeled 1 on the graphic organizer. Next, I quickly reviewed the levels of questioning we had previously learned (see Chapter 3, page 22) and suggested that students generate questions at higher thinking levels. Then I asked the students to work with partners to generate questions they might have about Rosa Parks. After a few minutes, we discussed their ideas. The students generated a variety of questions and we decided to add two of them to our QuIP graphic organizers. I added them to the organizer on the overhead projector, and students added them to their copies. The three questions were as follows:

1. Why is Rosa Parks considered to be the mother of the modern-day Civil Rights movement in the United States?
2. How were Rosa Parks's refusal to give up her seat and the Montgomery Bus Boycott connected?
3. In what ways has the U.S. government acknowledged Rosa Parks's contributions to our world?

I guided students to use two websites about Rosa Parks to gather responses to the questions. I modeled the process by using the first website to respond to question 1. Then I wrote the response in the space provided on the graphic organizer. Students worked with partners to find responses to questions 2 and 3 from the first website. These were the websites I bookmarked for student use:

- Rosa and Raymond Parks Institute for Self-Development: www.rosaparks.org
- Biography.com—Rosa Parks: www.biography.com/search/article.do?id=9433715

Figure 20 shows the QuIP organizer and paragraph Sadie and Max completed in response to the three questions.

Practice: Students practiced by responding to the three questions using information from the second website. We discussed the responses and then the students worked on their own to write QuIP summaries. When they finished and we shared a few examples, I invited students to relax as I read aloud *Rosa*. Then we discussed the book and compared and contrasted it to the information we found on the websites.

Reflect: We began our reflection by discussing how important good questions are when we need to find information. Then we discussed using more than one research source and how easy it was to write summaries based on our completed QuIP organizers. Michael said that the QuIP made it very easy to write a paragraph because all the information was important enough to include. Louis remarked that he will remember the information about Rosa Parks for a long time because he found it in response to our own questions. Students agreed that QuIP provides a good way for us to organize the information we want to learn.

Figure 20. Sadie and Max's QuIP Organizer and Summary Paragraph

Topic: Rosa Parks

	Answers	
Questions	**Source A:** Rosa and Raymond Parks Institute for Self-Development www.rosaparks.org	**Source B:** Biography.com—Rosa Parks www.biography.com/people/rosa-parks-9433715
1. Why is Rosa Parks considered to be the mother of the modern-day Civil Rights movement in the United States?	She stood up for herself and her people by not giving up her seat on a bus for a white person.	Rosa Parks and three other black people were asked to give up their seats on a bus so a white man could sit down. The others moved. Rosa Parks refused to give up her seat and the bus driver had her arrested.
2. How were Rosa Parks's refusal to give up her seat and the Montgomery Bus Boycott connected?	After Rosa Parks was arrested, the black people who lived in Montgomery organized a bus boycott that lasted 381 days. Martin Luther King Jr. was the spokesperson for the boycott.	The Montgomery Bus Boycott began after Rosa Parks was convicted of violating a local law. 40,000 people boycotted the buses.
3. In what ways has the United States government acknowledged Rosa Parks's contributions to our world?	President Clinton awarded Rosa Parks the Medal of Freedom.	Rosa Parks was awarded the Congressional Gold Medal of Honor.

Rosa Parks is considered to be the mother of the Civil Rights movement because she refused to give up her seat to a white person when the bus driver asked her to. The bus driver told the police and Rosa Parks was arrested for disorderly conduct. Black people in Montgomery organized a bus boycott after Rosa Parks was convicted. The boycott lasted for 381 days and the spokesperson was Martin Luther King, Jr. When President Clinton was in office, Rosa Parks was awarded the Medal of Freedom and the Congressional Gold Medal of Honor for her courage.

STAGE THREE: Teacher-Guided Small-Group Instruction

Texts: *M.L.K.: Journey of a King* (Bolden, 2007) and *Who Was Martin Luther King Jr.?* (Bader & Harrison, 2007) (Texts varied according to students' abilities.)

Review: I reminded students about the strategies good readers use and focused on questioning and summarizing using QuIP.

Guide: I introduced the texts about Martin Luther King Jr. and guided the students to work with partners to generate questions they would like to include on our QuIP graphic organizer. English learners worked with native English speakers during this time. We discussed their suggestions and added three questions to our QuIP:

1. What is known about Martin Luther King's education?
2. Why is Dr. King's "I Have a Dream" speech so famous?
3. How would you describe Martin Luther King Jr.'s contributions to our world?

Practice: Students read the texts silently and used them to respond to the QuIP questions. After our small-group time ended, students went to the writing center and wrote paragraphs based on their completed QuIPs. This is Jenny's QuIP paragraph:

> Martin Luther King, Jr. became a minister after he went to a theological seminary and earned his doctorate at Boston University. Many people think that his "I Have a Dream" speech contained a very powerful message of hope for America. He led a peaceful march on Washington, DC and gave the speech to 250,000 people. Martin Luther King, Jr. contributed to our world by leading a nonviolent civil rights movement. He received the Nobel Peace Prize in 1964 and was assassinated in 1968.

Reflect: We discussed what we had learned about Martin Luther King. Jesse pointed out that there was a timeline in the back of one of the texts that helped us to understand the events of King's life in chronological order. We reflected on the role good questions play when we are completing QuIPs. We discussed how questioning and recording the information we researched helped us learn new information and organize it so we remember what we have read. Then students moved on to the writing center to write paragraphs based on their completed QuIPs.

Student-Facilitated Comprehension Centers

A number of general accommodations were made for English learners when they engaged in the comprehension centers. These included the following:

- Ensuring that biographies and other books written in the students' native languages were among the texts available in the centers
- Making other culturally relevant texts available in the centers
- Integrating multiple modes of representing thinking in student responses (sketching, singing, dramatizing)
- Inviting students to work with other English learners of the same culture when reading texts in their native languages
- Encouraging English learners to partner with native English speakers when working in centers such as fluency, question and answer, vocabulary, and other centers focused on fluency and language development

Fluency Center: Pairs of students either read along with picture book biographies on tape or CD or read the information chorally to practice oral reading fluency.

Making Books Center: Students either wrote their autobiography or wrote a biography of a self-selected subject. Students used their writings as text for an electronic book.

Project Center: I provided a checklist at this center for students to follow as they created their transmediations. Students worked with partners to select a biography or autobiography in picture book format and change it into a poem or song lyrics. If time permitted, students illustrated their transmediations.

Theme Center: Students worked in pairs to read two biographies of the same person. Students generated their questions together on the QuIP graphic organizer and then read the books together to find the information. They recorded their answers on the QuIP and wrote summary paragraphs.

Student-Facilitated Comprehension Routines

A number of general accommodations were made for English learners when they engaged in the comprehension routines. These included the following:

- Making other culturally relevant texts available
- Integrating multiple modes of representing thinking in student responses (sketching, singing, dramatizing)
- Encouraging English learners to choose to partner with native English speakers when working in Literature Circles and Reciprocal Teaching
- Encouraging English learners to choose to partner with native language speakers or English language speakers when working in Cross-Age Reading Experiences

Literature Circles: Students read their biographies and completed QuIPs as an extension activity. They discussed their completed QuIPs and wrote their paragraphs in their Guided Comprehension Journals.

Reciprocal Teaching: The students used their questions and summaries during the portion of the routine that focuses on these strategies.

Cross-Age Reading Experiences: Pairs of students worked with cross-age partners to read biographies and other texts. Partners made connections and completed QuIPs.

STAGE FOUR: Teacher-Facilitated Whole-Group Reflection and Goal Setting

Share: Students shared their QuIPs and projects from Stage Three in small groups. Then we discussed examples as a whole class.

Reflect: We reflected on how QuIP questions guide our research and reading and how the organizer makes it easier to write a summary.

Set New Goals: Students felt confident with their ability to use QuIPs to question and summarize research, so we extended our goal to using this technique with other forms of expository text. We decided to use QuIPs to learn about endangered species for our upcoming science unit on animals.

Assessment Options

I used observation throughout the lesson. I listened carefully to students' questions and reviewed their responses and paragraphs. I used checklists, which I provided at the centers, when assessing students' transmediations and research projects. I also read and provided feedback on students' center self-assessments.

Reflection on Teaching the English Learners in Our Class

The English learners in our class were fascinated by the fact that we were reading life stories and we each had one. We read published biographies but wrote our autobiographies. The English learners enjoyed talking to their families about ancestors and other relatives who had interesting life histories and brought photos to class to share what they learned. They were totally relaxed and engaged in our Engaging Prereading Sequence and were actively engaged throughout the lesson. They seemed to especially enjoy the transmediations in the project center. They appear to be thinking about themselves as readers, writers, speakers, listeners, and creative thinkers. I can't resist saying it was a pleasure to be able to make that observation.

Final Thoughts About the Biographies: The Stories of Our Lives Theme

Whether reading biographies about others or writing their autobiographies, the students were thoroughly absorbed by the life stories they encountered in this theme. The students were equally captivated by information from books and websites, and all readily engaged in discussion.

It is important to acknowledge that lessons about a variety of skills that underpin comprehension strategies were taught during this theme. For example, aspects of language development and skills such as sequencing, generating questions, and distinguishing important from less important ideas were embedded in the theme. A variety of informational texts were used to teach text frames and generating questions at a variety of levels. The chronological nature of biographies was used to teach sequencing. Students also used ideas such as Readers Theatre, choral reading, and CD read-alongs to improve fluency. Students' fascination with the biography theme motivated them to read and promoted their engagement in learning. In addition, teachers engaged in read-alouds and encouraged students to use multiple modes of representing their thinking, including sketching, singing, and dramatizing.

Theme Resources

Books

Adams, M.M. (2005). *The life and times of Cleopatra.* Hockessin, DE: Mitchell Lane.

Adler, D.A. (1997). *A picture book of Jackie Robinson.* New York: Holiday House.

Atalay, B., & Wamsley, K. (2009). *Leonardo's universe: The Renaissance world of Leonardo da Vinci.* Washington, DC: National Geographic.

Bader, B., & Harrison, N. (2008). *Who was Martin Luther King, Jr.?* New York: Grosset & Dunlap.

Bankston, J. (2003). *Venus Williams.* Bear, DE: Mitchell Lane.

Berne, E.C. (2009). *Helen Keller: Courage in darkness.* New York: Sterling.

Bolden, T. (2007). *M.L.K.: Journey of a king.* New York: Abrams.

Brophy, D.B. (2009). *Michelle Obama: Meet the First Lady.* New York: Collins.

Carpenter, A.S. (2003). *Lewis Carroll: Through the looking glass.* Minneapolis, MN: Lerner.

Christopher, M. (1998). *On the field with...Mia Hamm.* New York: Little, Brown.

Christopher, M. (2004). *On the court with...Yao Ming.* New York: Little, Brown.

Cline-Ransome, L. (2000). *Satchel Paige.* New York: Simon & Schuster.

Cobb, V. (2005). *Harry Houdini.* New York: Dorling Kindersley.

Collins, K. (2004). *Sojourner Truth: Equal rights advocate.* New York: Rosen.

DeMauro, L. (2006). *Presidents of the United States.* New York: HarperCollins.

Denenberg, D., & Roscoe, L. (2006). *50 American heroes every kid should meet.* Minneapolis, MN: Millbrook.

Foster, F.S. (2007). *T: An auto-biography.* Farmington, NH: River Road.

Fradin, D.B. (2002). *Who was Ben Franklin?* New York: Grosset & Dunlap.

Gibson, K.B. (2006). *The life and times of Catherine the Great.* Hockessin, DE: Mitchell Lane.

Giovanni, N. (2007). *Rosa.* New York: Square Fish.

Glass, M. (2004). *Benjamin Franklin: Early American genius.* New York: Rosen.

Gunderson, J. (2007). *Sacagawea: Journey into the west.* Mankato, MN: Capstone.
Humphrey, S.M. (2005). *Dare to dream! 25 extraordinary lives.* Amherst, NY: Prometheus.
Kaplan, H.S. (2004). *John F. Kennedy.* New York: Dorling Kindersley.
King, D.C. (2006). *Charles Darwin.* New York: Dorling Kindersley.
Lisandrelli, E.S. (1996). *Maya Angelou: More than a poet.* Springfield, NJ: Enslow.
McPherson, S.S. (1995). *Ordinary genius: The story of Albert Einstein.* Minneapolis, MN: Carolrhoda.
Márquez, H. (2005). *Roberto Clemente: Baseball's humanitarian hero.* Minneapolis, MN: Carolrhoda.
Mattern, J. (2006). *Princess Diana.* New York: Dorling Kindersley.
Mattern, J. (2007). *Peyton Manning.* Hockessin, DE: Mitchell Lane.
O'Connor, B. (2003). *Leonardo da Vinci: Renaissance genius.* Minneapolis, MN: Carolrhoda.
Olmstead, K. (2008). *Jacques Cousteau: A life under the sea.* New York: Sterling.
Pastan, A. (2004). *Martin Luther King, Jr.* New York: Dorling Kindersley.
Spinelli, J. (1998). *Knots in my yo-yo string.* New York: Knopf.
Sterling biographies series. New York: Sterling.
Thomas, G. (2008). *Yes we can: A biography of Barack Obama.* New York: Feiwel & Friends.
Time for Kids biography series. New York: HarperCollins.
Towle, W. (1993). *The real McCoy: The life of an African-American inventor.* New York: Scholastic.
Whiting, J. (2006). *Aristotle.* Hockessin, DE: Mitchell Lane.
Who was...? book series. New York: Grosset & Dunlap.
Wilkinson, P. (2005). *Gandhi: The young protester who founded a nation.* Washington, DC: National Geographic.
Woog, A. (2003). *Bill Gates.* San Diego, CA: KidHaven.

Websites

Biography
www.biography.com

Biography Base
www.biographybase.com

BiographyBiography.com: How to Write a Biography
www.biographybiography.com/howtowriteabiography.html

Biography Shelf
www.biographyshelf.com

Encyclopedia of World Biography
www.notablebiographies.com

Leonardo Da Vinci: Artist, Inventor, and Universal Genius of the Renaissance
www.leonardo-history.com

Nobelprize.org
nobelprize.org/nobel_prizes/peace/laureates/1964/king-bio.html

The Official Website of The British Monarchy
www.royal.gov.uk/output/page151.asp

Scholastic: Biography Writer's Workshop
teacher.scholastic.com/writewit/biograph/index.htm

Scholastic Teachers: Biography Writer's Workshop
www2.scholastic.com/browse/lessonplan.jsp?id=24

Smithsonian.com Biography: Who Was Cleopatra?
www.smithsonianmag.com/history-archaeology/biography/cleopatra.html

The White House: Our Presidents
www.whitehouse.gov/history/presidents/jk35.html

Performance Extensions Across the Curriculum

Social Studies

- Students choose a person who has played a prominent role in U.S. or world history and research that person's biography. They share what they learn through a presentation mode such as a picture book, poem, or PowerPoint slideshow.
- Students work with a partner and read two biographies about a great military leader of their choice. They create interview questions and responses based on what they learned from their reading. Then they digitally record and share the interview in a *Meet the Press* or press conference format.
- Students write biographies of grandparents or other relatives, focusing on changing lives and times.
- Students create oral histories of family and community members.

Science

- Students visit a website that focuses on biographies of great scientists, such as World of Biography (www.worldofbiography.com/Scientists-inventors-biography.asp). They choose one scientist from the 18th, 19th, and 20th centuries and read their biographies. Then they add information about each to a Scientists of the Past descriptive timeline/mural.
- Students select a scientist, and using a total of three library and online sources, create a page for him or her in a class *Scientists of the Ages* PowerPoint book.

Math

- Students use at least two bookmarked website sources, such as Biographies of Women Mathematicians (www.agnesscott.edu/lriddle/women/women.htm), to create a biography for a woman mathematician of their choice. Then they select a presentation mode for the information they gather.
- Students work in a small group to create a trifold presentation about a mathematician associated with a current topic of study. They use a minimum of three sources.

Art

- Students research using a minimum of three sources and then create a picture book biography of their favorite author.
- Students create and illustrate their autobiographies.

Music

- Students choose a familiar tune and write lyrics based on their autobiography.

- Students create a PowerPoint presentation for a biography they have read or written and integrate music to enhance the information.
- Students write original songs based on biographies or autobiographies.
- Students work with a partner to create a transmediation by changing a biography picture book into song lyrics.

Culminating Activity

Our Lives, Our Stories: Students design, create, and deliver invitations to their families to participate in a theme celebration titled *Our Lives, Our Stories*. Students' projects from the biography theme will be displayed in the classroom. Students will create a variety of stations where they can explain their biography projects to the visitors. Students can serve as tour guides for their projects or become the subjects of biographies they have read and tell participants about that person's life. Electronic versions of students' autobiographies, as well as biographies they have written about family or community members, will be posted as a volume on the school's website. A PowerPoint slideshow of the volume will be featured during the celebration, and the students will give special printed copies to the subjects of the biographies they wrote. Parents, community members, and students will be invited to share their favorite life memories. Refreshments will be provided and visitors will be afforded opportunities to give feedback on the celebration, such as writing comments on the class mural or e-mailing comments to students on class computers. Students will autograph copies of the class book *Our Awesome Autobiographies* and give them as gifts to their families.

APPENDIXES

Guided Comprehension Resources

Focus: Resources that underpin the Guided Comprehension Model for English Learners and facilitate its use.

Comprehension Strategy Applications and Blacklines (see page 227): Appendix A offers a wide variety of ideas for teaching comprehension strategies that can be used before, during, and after reading. Organized by comprehension strategy, the teaching ideas are presented in an explicit, step-by-step instructional format. Teaching examples and reproducible blackline masters complete this appendix.

Resources for Organizing and Managing Comprehension Centers and Routines (see page 286): A wide variety of reproducible blackline masters to facilitate classroom organization and management, as well as graphic organizers that support a number of comprehension centers and routines, are presented in Appendix B.

Informal Assessments (see page 325) and Sources of Leveled Texts (see page 344): Informal assessments, ranging from attitude and motivation surveys to observation guides, are featured in Appendix C. Sources of leveled texts, including websites and publishers' materials, are presented in Appendix D.

Ideas for Creating Home–School Connections (see page 347): A variety of activities that are easily adaptable to the themes presented in Chapters 8–10 are described in Appendix E.

Guided Comprehension Planning Forms (see page 349): Reproducible forms for planning Guided Comprehension themes and lessons are included in Appendix F. A sample schedule form for Guided Comprehension lessons is also included in this section.

APPENDIX A

Comprehension Strategy Applications and Blackline Masters

TEACHING IDEAS AT A GLANCE

Teaching Idea	When to Use	Comprehension Strategy	Text
Previewing			
Semantic Map	Before After	Previewing Knowing How Words Work Summarizing	Narrative Informational
Semantic Question Map	Before After	Previewing Knowing How Words Work Summarizing	Narrative Informational
Story Impressions	Before	Previewing Making Connections	Narrative
Storybook Introductions	Before	Previewing Making Connections Knowing How Words Work	Narrative
Self-Questioning			
Paired Questioning	During After	Self-Questioning Making Connections Monitoring	Narrative Informational
Question–Answer Relationships (QAR)	During After	Self-Questioning Making Connections Monitoring	Narrative Informational
Thick and Thin Questions	Before During After	Self-Questioning Making Connections	Narrative Informational
Making Connections			
Connection Stems	After	Making Connections	Narrative Informational
Double-Entry Journal	Before During After	Making Connections Monitoring Summarizing	Narrative Informational
Draw and Write Connections	During After	Making Connections Visualizing	Narrative Informational
Visualizing			
Draw and Write Visualizations	During After	Making Connections Visualizing Summarizing	Narrative Informational
Graphic Organizers/Visual Organizers	Before During After	Making Connections Visualizing Summarizing	Narrative Informational
Guided Imagery	Before After	Making Connections Visualizing	Narrative Informational
Knowing How Words Work			
Concept of Definition Map	Before After	Knowing How Words Work	Narrative Informational
Context Clues	During	Knowing How Words Work	Narrative Informational
Semantic Feature Analysis	Before After	Making Connections Knowing How Words Work	Narrative Informational
Vocabulary Bookmark	During After	Knowing How Words Work Monitoring	Narrative Informational

TEACHING IDEAS AT A GLANCE

Teaching Idea	When to Use	Comprehension Strategy	Text
		Monitoring	
Bookmark Technique	During After	Making Connections Knowing How Words Work Monitoring	Narrative Informational
Patterned Partner Reading	During	Making Connections Monitoring Evaluating	Narrative Informational
Say Something	During	Making Connections Monitoring	Narrative Informational
Think-Alouds	Before During After	All	Narrative Informational
		Summarizing	
Lyric Retelling/Lyric Summary	After	Summarizing	Narrative Informational
Paired Summarizing	After	Making Connections Monitoring Summarizing	Narrative Informational
QuIP (Questions Into Paragraphs)	Before During After	Self-Questioning Summarizing	Informational
Retelling	After	Summarizing	Narrative
Story Map	After	Monitoring Summarizing	Narrative
		Evaluating	
Evaluative Questioning	During After	Self-Questioning Evaluating	Narrative Informational
Journal Responses	During After	Making Connections Summarizing Evaluating	Narrative Informational
Persuasive Writing	Before During After	Evaluating	Narrative Informational
Venn Diagram	During After	Making Connections Summarizing Evaluating	Informational
		Comprehension Routines	
Cross-Age Reading Experiences	Before During After	All	Narrative Informational
Directed Reading–Thinking Activity/Directed Listening–Thinking Activity	Before During After	Previewing Making Connections Monitoring	Narrative Informational
Literature Circles	Before During After	All	Narrative Informational
Reciprocal Teaching	Before During After	Previewing Self-Questioning Monitoring Summarizing	Narrative Informational

TEACHING IDEAS

Semantic Map

Purposes: To activate and organize knowledge about a specific topic.

Comprehension Strategies: Previewing, Knowing How Words Work, Summarizing

Text: Narrative, Informational **Use:** Before and After Reading

Procedure: (Begin by explaining and demonstrating Semantic Maps.)

1. Select a focus word that relates to the main idea or topic of a text; write it on a chart, overhead, or chalkboard; and draw an oval around it.
2. Ask students what comes to mind when they think of the focus word. Write students' responses.
3. Invite students to review the list of responses and suggest subtopics that emerge.
4. Add the subtopics to the Semantic Map, draw ovals around them, and use lines to connect them to the focus word.
5. Visit each subtopic and ask students which of their original responses support each subtopic. Record these ideas beneath each subtopic.
6. Read the text and revise the Semantic Map to reflect new knowledge.

Example: Deedy, C.A. (2009). *14 cows for America*. Atlanta, GA: Peachtree.

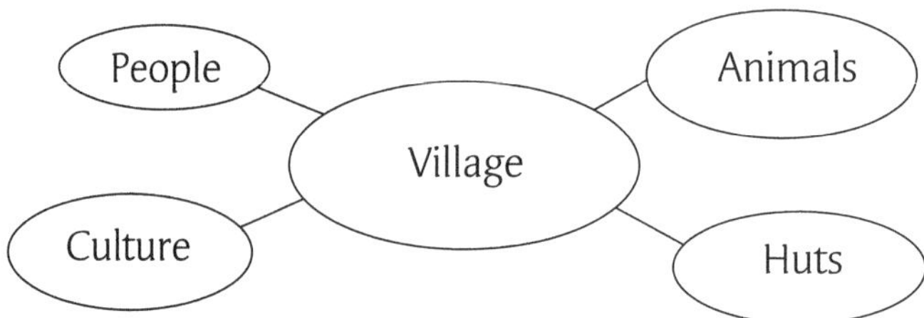

Source: Johnson, D.D., & Pearson, P.D. (1984). *Teaching reading vocabulary* (2nd ed.). New York: Holt, Rinehart and Winston.

Semantic Question Map

(See blackline, page 280.)

Purposes: To use specific questions to activate and organize knowledge about a particular topic.

Comprehension Strategies: Previewing, Knowing How Words Work, Summarizing

Text: Narrative, Informational **Use:** Before and After Reading

Procedure: (Begin by explaining and modeling Semantic Question Maps.)

1. Select the main idea or topic of the passage; write it on a chart, overhead, or chalkboard; and draw an oval around it.
2. Draw four arms that extend from the oval. At the end of each arm, draw another oval. Write a specific question about the topic in each of the four ovals. Number the questions.

3. Discuss the topic with the students and share the four questions. Then, beginning with question one, invite the students to share whatever information they may already know to respond to the question. Record student responses beneath each question.
4. Read the text and revise the Semantic Question Map to reflect new knowledge.
5. Use the questions and responses to summarize what students know about the topic.

Example: Reynolds, J. (2009). *Cycle of rice, cycle of life: A story of unsustainable farming.* New York: Lee & Low.

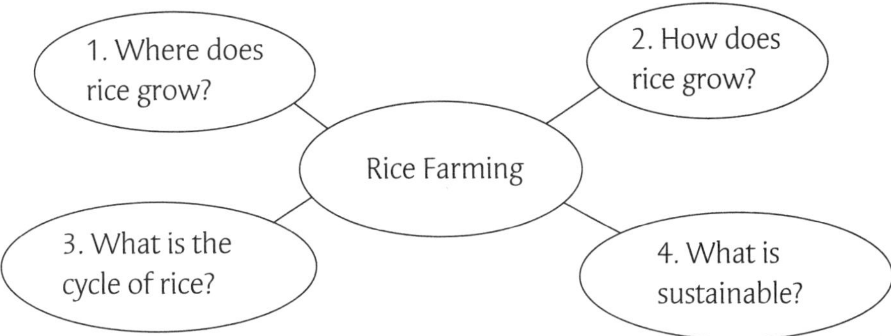

Source: McLaughlin, M. (2010). *Guided Comprehension in the primary grades* (2nd ed.). Newark, DE: International Reading Association.

Story Impressions

(See blackline, page 282.)

Purposes: To provide a framework for narrative writing; to encourage predictions about the story; to make connections between story vocabulary and story structure.

Comprehension Strategies: Previewing, Making Connections

Text: Narrative **Use:** Before Reading

Procedure: (Begin by explaining and demonstrating Story Impressions.)

1. Provide students with a list of words that provide clues about the story. Choose words that relate to the narrative elements—characters, setting, problem, attempts to resolve the problem, and resolution. Clues may be up to 5 words long. The maximum number of clues is 10.
2. List the clues in the order in which they appear in the story. Connect them with downward arrows. Share the list of sequential clues with the students.
3. Ask students to work in small groups to use the sequential clues to write Story Impressions.
4. Invite small groups to share their Story Impressions with the class and discuss them.
5. Read the original story to the class and ask students to compare and contrast their Story Impressions with the original story.

Example: Wild, M., & Argent, K. (2000). *Nighty night!* Atlanta, GA: Peachtree.

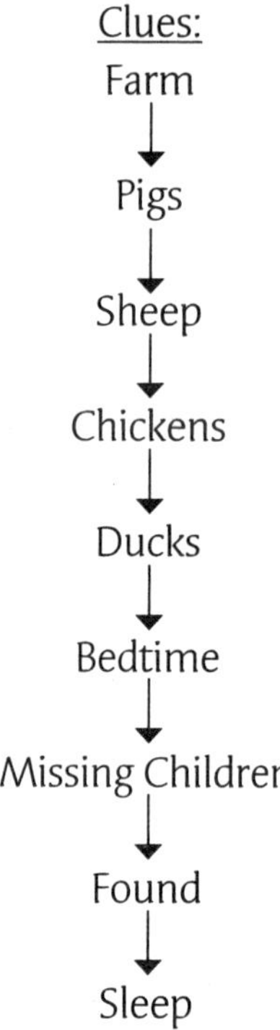

Story Impression: Once there was a farm. Pigs, sheep, chickens, and ducks lived there. When the animals went to tuck in their children at bedtime, they found them missing. They searched all over the farm and found the children playing a game of hide and seek. The animals took their children home to get some sleep.

Adaptations: Create Poem Impressions using story poems. Create Bio-Impressions or Text Impressions using informational text.

Source: McGinley, W., & Denner, P. (1987). Story impressions: A prereading/prewriting activity. *Journal of Reading, 31*, 248–253.

Storybook Introductions

Purposes: To introduce story, characters, vocabulary, and style of a book prior to reading; to promote prediction and anticipation of a story; to make new texts accessible to readers.

Comprehension Strategies: Previewing, Making Connections, Knowing How Words Work

Text: Narrative **Use:** Before Reading

Procedure: (Begin by explaining and modeling Storybook Introductions.)

1. Preview the text and prepare the introduction. Focus on those points that will help make the text accessible to students. These may include text structure, specific vocabulary, language patterns, plot, or difficult parts.
2. Introduce the text (topic, title, and characters).

TEACHING IDEAS

3. Encourage students to respond to the cover and text illustrations by making connections to personal experiences or other texts.
4. Do a picture walk with the text. While browsing through the illustrations, introduce the plot up to the climax (if possible, not giving away the ending). Throughout this process, encourage students to make connections to personal experiences or other texts, and make predictions about what will happen next.
5. Choose to introduce some literary language, vocabulary, or repetitive sentence patterns that will be helpful to the readers.
6. Invite students to read the text, or a section of the text. Then engage in discussion and other activities, such as retelling.

Note: It is important to make decisions about the introduction based on the text and the students' competency and familiarity with the text type.

Adaptation: Use with informational texts, focusing on text elements.

Examples: Numeroff, L. (1998). *If you give a pig a pancake.* New York: HarperCollins. (English version)
Numeroff, L. (2008). *Si le das un panqueque a una cerdita.* New York: Scholastic. (Spanish version)

- Introduce the text (topic, title, and characters): For example, "The title of this book is *If You Give a Pig a Pancake*. The characters are a pig and a young girl. This book is about giving a pig a pancake and what happens to that pig."
- Ask the students to make connections: Encourage students to respond to the cover and text illustrations by making connections to personal experiences or other text.
  Student One: "The cover and title remind me of when my dad made pancakes and we gave one to my dog. He ate the pancake so fast, and I could tell he wanted another one. I think that after the pig eats a pancake he will want to eat another one, just like my dog." (Text–Self Connection)
- Do a Picture Walk and invite students to make connections and predictions: Browse the text and illustrations with the students, and introduce the plot up to the climax (if possible, without giving away the ending). Browse the text up until the last three pages, encourage students to make connections to personal experiences or other texts, and make predictions about what they think will happen next.
  Student Two: "I think that the pig is going to turn the house into a mess and get syrup from the pancakes everywhere. The whole house will be sticky." (Prediction)
- Choose to introduce some literacy language or repetitive sentence patterns that will be helpful to the readers. For this text, you may bring up the repetitive fashion of giving the pig something, which builds on the pig wanting something else.
- Invite students to read the text or a section of the text. For example, "Now it is time for us to read the story. Let's remember the connections and predictions we made. We'll discuss *If You Give a Pig a Pancake* when we finish reading."

Source: Clay, M.M. (1991). Introducing a new storybook to young readers. *The Reading Teacher, 45*, 264–273.

TEACHING IDEAS

Paired Questioning

Purpose: To engage in questioning and active decision making during the reading of a narrative or informational text.

Comprehension Strategies: Self-Questioning, Making Connections, Monitoring

Text: Narrative, Informational **Use:** During and After Reading

Procedure: (Begin by explaining and demonstrating Paired Questioning.)

1. Introduce a text and encourage students to read the title or subtitle of a manageable section, put the reading material aside, and ask a question related to the title or subtitle. Each partner provides a reasonable answer to the question.
2. Encourage students to silently read a predetermined (by teacher or students) section of text and take turns asking a question about the reading. If needed, they can use the text when asking or responding to the question. Students reverse roles and continue reading and asking questions until the text is finished.
3. After the text is read, invite each partner to explain what he or she believes to be the important and unimportant ideas in the text. Encourage the students to share their reasoning. Then the partner agrees or disagrees with the choices and offers support for his or her thinking.

Example: Demi. (2001). *Gandhi*. New York: Simon & Schuster.

Student 1: Were you surprised that Gandhi slept with the lights on?
Student 2: No, because a lot of people are afraid of the dark. I know I am.

Student 2: Do you think Gandhi was treated unfairly in South Africa?
Student 1: Yes, I think he was not treated fairly because of his culture.

Student 1: I think the important idea in this book is that you have to remember who you are and not try to please others.

Student 2: I agree. I think people should have their own goals and live their own lives—not live to please others.

Source: Vaughn, J., & Estes, T. (1986). *Reading and reasoning beyond the primary grades*. Boston: Allyn & Bacon.

Question–Answer Relationships (QAR)

(See blackline, page 277.)

Purposes: To promote self-questioning; to answer comprehension questions by focusing on the information source needed to answer the question.

Comprehension Strategies: Self-Questioning, Making Connections, Monitoring

Text: Narrative, Informational **Use:** During and After Reading

TEACHING IDEAS

Procedure: (Begin by explaining and demonstrating QAR.)

1. Introduce the QAR concept and terminology. Explain that there are two kinds of information:

    In the Book: The answer is found in the text.
    In My Head: The answer requires input from the student's understandings and background knowledge.

    Explain that there are two kinds of QARs for each kind of information:

    In the Book

    Right There: The answer is stated in the passage.
    Think and Search: The answer is derived from more than one sentence or paragraph but is stated in the text.

    In My Head

    On My Own: The answer is contingent on information the reader already possesses in his or her background knowledge.
    Author and Me: The answer is inferred in the text, but the reader must make the connections with his or her own prior knowledge.

2. Use a Think-Aloud to practice using QAR with a text. Model choosing the appropriate QAR, giving the answer from the source, and writing or speaking the answer.
3. Introduce a short passage and related questions. Ask groups or individuals to work through the passages and the questions. Students answer the questions and tell the QAR strategy they used. Any justifiable answer should be accepted.
4. Practice QAR with additional texts.

Principles of Teaching QAR: Give immediate feedback; progress from shorter to longer texts; guide students from group to independent activities; provide transitions from easier to more difficult tasks.

Example: Johnson, D. (2002). *Substitute teacher plans.* New York: Henry Holt.

In the Book

Right There: What did Miss Huff forget to write on the top of her list?
Substitute teacher plans.

Think and Search: Why did Miss Huff stay up all night writing a list of fun things to do instead of going to bed?
She had to write her substitute teacher plans and then her list of fun things to do. She was having so much fun thinking of fun things to do that she lost track of time.

In My Head

Author and Me: Did Miss Huff really dislike her job?
No, she was happy doing all the things she had planned for her class to do. She didn't even know that she had mixed up her lists.

On My Own: Why does Miss Huff invite the principal to join the class on tomorrow's trip?
She invites him because he needs a day away from school, too.

Source: Raphael, T. (1986). Teaching Question Answer Relationships, revisited. *The Reading Teacher, 39*, 516–522.

Thick and Thin Questions

(See blackline, page 284.)

Purposes: To create questions pertaining to a text; to help students discern the depth of the questions they ask and are asked; to use questions to facilitate understanding a text.

Comprehension Strategies: Self-Questioning, Making Connections

Text: Narrative, Informational **Use:** Before, During, and After Reading

Procedure: (Begin by explaining and demonstrating Thick and Thin Questions.)

1. Teach the students the difference between thick questions and thin questions. Thick questions deal with the big picture and large concepts. Answers to thick questions are involved, complex, and open-ended. Thin questions deal with specific content or words. Answers to thin questions are short (often one, two, or three words) and close-ended. Thick questions usually require higher order thinking; thin questions require literal responses.
2. Guide students to work with partners to create Thick and Thin Questions. Read a portion of text, and prompt students with stems such as "Why..." or "What if..." for thick questions and "How far..." and "When..." for thin questions.
3. Encourage students to create Thick and Thin Questions for the texts they are reading. They can use the blackline master, write the questions in their Guided Comprehension Journals, or write their thick questions on larger sticky notes and their thin questions on smaller sticky notes.
4. Share questions and answers in small and large groups.

Example: Wise, B. (2009). *Louis Sockalexis: Native American baseball pioneer.* New York: Lee & Low.

Before Reading

Thick Question: Why is Louis Sockalexis considered a baseball pioneer?
Thin Question: Who is Louis Sockalexis?

During Reading

Thick Question: Why is Louis determined to stay calm?
Thin Question: When Louis played baseball with the boys, how did it make him feel?

After Reading

Thick Question: Why didn't Louis have the same rights as white Americans?
Thin Question: When did Louis feel the magic of baseball just like he did in the summer of 1884?

Source: Lewin, L. (1998). *Great performances: Creating classroom-based assessment tasks*. Alexandria, VA: Association for Supervision and Curriculum Development.

TEACHING IDEAS

Connection Stems

Purposes: To provide a structure to make connections while reading; to encourage reflection during reading.

Comprehension Strategy: Making Connections

Text: Narrative, Informational **Use:** After Reading

Procedure: (Begin by explaining and demonstrating Connection Stems.)

1. After reading a section of text aloud, show students a sentence stem, and think aloud about the process you use for completing it. Use text support and personal experiences to explain the text–self, text–text, or text–world connection.
2. Read another section of text aloud and guide the students to complete the stem orally with a partner.
3. Invite students to read a short text in pairs and work together to complete Connection Stems.
4. Discuss the completed stems.

Connection Stems

- That reminds me of...
- I remember when...
- I have a connection to...
- An experience I have had like that...
- I felt like that character when...
- If I were that character, I would...

Example: Weston, M. (2008). *Honda: The boy who dreamed of cars.* New York: Lee & Low.

This book reminds me of when I wanted to learn to make ice cream. I always watched my grandfather make the ice cream. I really wanted to make it myself, and after watching him a couple times he gave me a chance. Now, I make ice cream almost every weekend for family dinner on Sunday.

Source: Adapted from Harvey, S., & Goudvis, A. (2000). *Strategies that work: Teaching comprehension to enhance understanding.* York, ME: Stenhouse.

Double-Entry Journal

(See blacklines, pages 267–268.)

Purposes: To provide a structure for reading response; to make decisions about significant aspects of text and reflect on personal connections to the text.

Comprehension Strategies: Making Connections, Monitoring, Summarizing

Text: Narrative, Informational **Use:** Before, During, and After Reading

Procedure: (Begin by explaining and demonstrating Double-Entry Journals.)

1. Provide students with a Double-Entry Journal blackline.

2. Model the procedure by writing a quote, phrase, or idea in the left column and providing corresponding examples of reflective comments in the right column. (Encourage text–self, text–text, or text–world connections.)
3. Invite students to read (or listen to) a text or part of a text.
4. Ask students to select a key event, idea, word, quote, or concept from the text and write it in the left column.
5. In the right column, ask students to write their response or connection to the item in the left column.
6. Use Double-Entry Journals as a springboard for discussion of text.

Adaptation: Use a different Double-Entry Journal format and ask students to create a summary and reflection.

Example: Medina, T. (2001). *DeShawn days.* New York: Lee & Low.

Idea/Text From Story	My Connection
They laugh when Jonny sneezes.	Every time my dad sneezes, we giggle. When he sneezes, it is very loud and kind of scary. We are always afraid he might sneeze on us.

Source: Tompkins, G.E. (2006). *Literacy for the 21st century: A balanced approach* (4th ed.). Upper Saddle River, NJ: Prentice Hall.

Draw and Write Connections

(See blacklines, pages 269–271.)

Purposes: To provide a structure to make connections while reading; to use visual representations to express connections.

Comprehension Strategies: Making Connections, Visualizing

Text: Narrative, Informational **Use:** During and After Reading

Procedure: (Begin by explaining and modeling Drawing Connections.)

1. Demonstrate how to draw visual representations (pictures, shapes, lines) to communicate connections with text.
2. Read a section of text and think aloud about a connection you can make. Demonstrate sketching a visual representation of your thoughts. Then think aloud as you write a sentence explaining the connection you made.
3. Read another section of text to the students and ask them to create visual representations of their connections to the text. Next, ask students to write a sentence explaining their connections. Finally, invite students to share their drawings and explain their connections in small groups.
4. Encourage students to create visual representations of texts they are reading on their own and write a sentence explaining their connection.

Example: Elliott, Z. (2008). *Bird.* New York: Lee & Low.

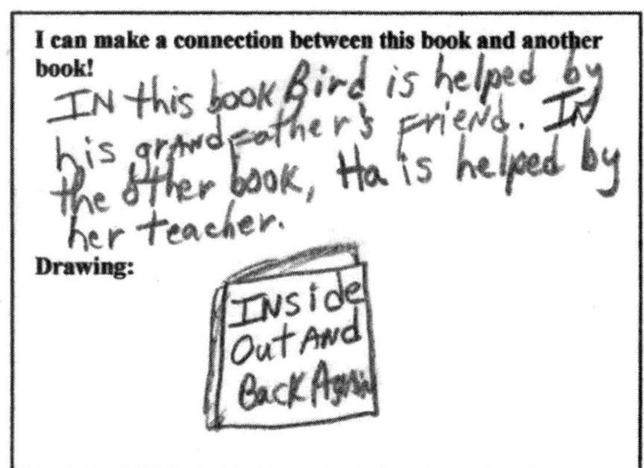

Source: McLaughlin, M., & Allen, M.B. (2009). *Guided Comprehension in grades 3–8* (2nd ed.). Newark, DE: International Reading Association.

Draw and Write Visualizations

(See blackline, page 273.)

Purposes: To provide a structure to encourage students to create mental images while reading; to encourage students to use artistic representations to express visualizations.

Comprehension Strategies: Making Connections, Visualizing, Summarizing

Text: Narrative, Informational **Use:** During and After Reading

Procedure: (Begin by explaining and modeling Draw and Write Visualizations.)

1. Demonstrate how to use visual representations (pictures, shapes, lines) to express the pictures made in your head while reading.
2. Think aloud about the visualization and the sketch. Then write a sentence about it.
3. Invite students to listen to a selection and ask them to draw their visualizations. Next, encourage students to write a sentence about their drawing. Then ask them to share their drawings in small groups, explaining how their drawings show the pictures they created in their heads.
4. Encourage students to create visual representations of texts they are reading on their own. Remind them to write sentences explaining their visualizations.

Example: Silverstein, S. (1974). "Sarah Cynthia Sylvia Stout" in *Where the sidewalk ends.* New York: HarperCollins.

Source: McLaughlin, M., & Allen, M.B. (2009). *Guided Comprehension in grades 3–8* (2nd ed.). Newark, DE: International Reading Association.

Graphic Organizers/Visual Organizers

Purposes: To provide a visual model of the structure of text; to provide a format for organizing information and concepts.

Comprehension Strategies: Making Connections, Visualizing, Summarizing

Text: Narrative, Informational **Use:** Before, During, and After Reading

Procedure: (Begin by explaining and demonstrating Graphic Organizers/Visual Organizers.)

1. Introduce the Graphic Organizer to students. Demonstrate how it works by reading a piece of text and noting key concepts and ideas on the organizer.
2. Ask students to work with partners to practice using the Graphic Organizer with ideas from an independently read text. Share ideas with the class.
3. Choose organizers that match text structures and thinking processes.
4. Encourage students to use graphic organizers to help them think through text.

Examples: Concept of Definition Map and QuIP

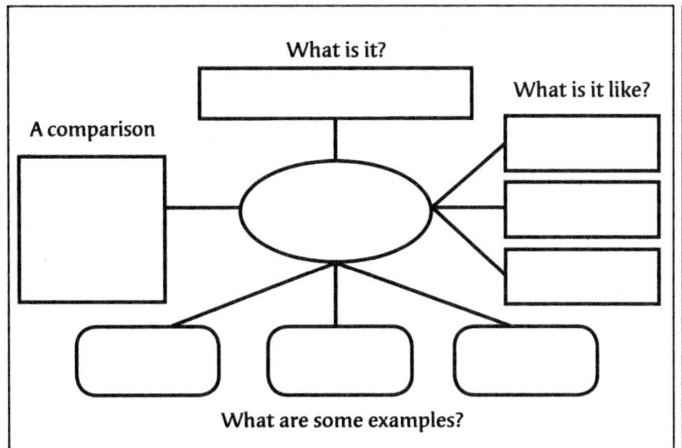

Topic: ______________________

Questions	Answers	
	Source A:	Source B:
1.		
2.		
3.		

Guided Imagery

Purposes: To create mental images; to provide opportunities to discuss visualizations.

Comprehension Strategies: Making Connections, Visualizing

Text: Narrative, Informational **Use:** Before and After Reading

Procedure: (Begin by explaining and demonstrating Guided Imagery.)

1. Ask students to turn to partners and describe to each other the mental images they create when you provide a verbal stimulus of things with which the students are familiar—a birthday party, a favorite pet, or a fireworks display. Provide time for students to elaborate on their mental pictures.
2. Introduce the text students will be reading next. Invite them to preview the text by focusing on illustrations, charts, or any other graphics.
3. Explain to students that they should close their eyes, breathe deeply, and relax. Guide the students to think more deeply about the topic they will read about. Provide a detailed description of the setting, the action, sensory images, emotions, and so on.
4. Ask students to open their eyes and work with partners to share the pictures they made in their minds. Monitor and respond to any questions.
5. Invite students to write or draw information gleaned from Guided Imagery.
6. Finally, ask students to read the text and modify or enhance their writing or sketching as necessary.

Example: Russell, C.Y. (2009). *Tofu quilt.* New York: Lee & Low.

When I was reading the poem "My New Name," I could see in my mind each new action the author described. It began as I visualized the girl's bedroom, where she read Tom Sawyer and wrote her story about the quilts. I could feel the privacy and the feeling of being an author she felt as she wrote and checked the newspaper to see if her story had been printed. I could also clearly imagine her receiving the money and her family praising her story when she was not around. I felt her sadness when she wrote about her uncle saying it was too bad she was not a boy. She used her words to paint these pictures. It reminded me of when I was in 4th grade and wrote a poem for the newspaper poetry contest. We wrote the poems at school and our teacher mailed them to the local paper. I never told my Mom and Dad because I did not think I had a chance of winning, but I won and my poem was printed in the paper. Like the girl in the story, I was really happy to see my poem in print and so was my family.

Source: Lasear, D. (1991). *Seven ways of teaching: The artistry of teaching with multiple intelligences.* Palatine, IL: Skylight.

Concept of Definition Map

(See blackline, page 263.)

Purposes: To make connections with new words and topics and build personal meanings by connecting the new information with prior knowledge.

Comprehension Strategy: Knowing How Words Work

Text: Narrative, Informational **Use:** Before and After Reading

Procedure: (Begin by explaining and demonstrating a Concept of Definition Map.)

1. Select or have student(s) select a word to be explored and place the word in the center of the map. (Example: *culture*)
2. Ask students to determine a broad category that best describes the word and write it in the *What is it?* section. (Example: *shared values and beliefs*)
3. Encourage student(s) to provide some words that describe the focus word in the *What is it like?* section. (Examples: *celebrations, food, music*)
4. Have students provide some specific examples of the word in the *What are some examples?* section. (Examples: *Chinese, Greek, Italian*)
5. Ask students to determine a comparison. (Example: *society*)
6. Discuss the Concept of Definition Map.
7. Read the text. Revisit the map. Make modifications or additions.
8. Encourage students to write a Concept of Definition Map summary after completing the map.

Example: Reynolds, J. (2010). *Celebrate! Connections among cultures.* New York: Lee & Low.

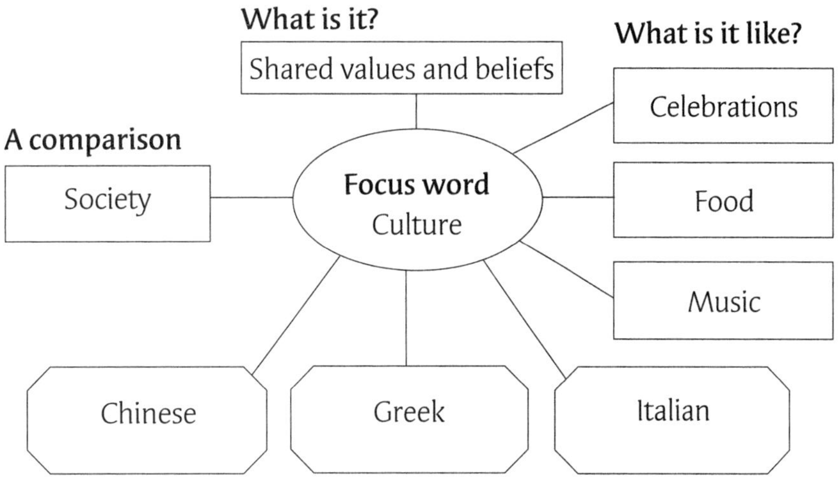

Source: Schwartz, R., & Raphael, T. (1985). Concept of definition: A key to improving students' vocabulary. *The Reading Teacher, 39*, 198–205.

Context Clues

Purposes: To use semantics and syntax to figure out unknown words; to use a variety of cueing systems to make sense of text.

Comprehension Strategy: Knowing How Words Work

Text: Narrative, Informational **Use:** During Reading

Procedure: (Begin by demonstrating how to use Context Clues to figure out word meanings.)

1. Explain to students the eight types of Context Clues and give examples of each:

    Definition: provides a definition that often connects the unknown word to a known word
    Example/Illustration: provides an example or illustration to describe the word
    Compare/Contrast: provides a comparison or contrast to the word
    Logic: provides a connection (such as a simile) to the word
    Root Words and Affixes: provides meaningful roots and affixes that the reader uses to determine meaning
    Grammar: provides syntactical cues that allow for reader interpretation
    Cause and Effect: cause and effect example allows the reader to hypothesize meaning
    Mood and Tone: description of mood related to the word allows readers to hypothesize meaning

2. Read aloud and think aloud to demonstrate using one or more of the clues to determine the meaning of a difficult or unfamiliar word in the text. (Use a Think-Aloud to demonstrate the most effective type of clue based on the context of the sentence.) Readers use several of the clues to figure out unknown words.

3. If the context does not provide enough information, demonstrate other strategies for figuring out the meaning of the word.

Example: Lewin, T., & Lewin, B. (2009). *Balarama: A royal elephant.* New York: Lee & Low.

Example/Illustration Clue: The illustration of India in which Karapur Forest is marked is a clue.

Definition Clue: From the 1880s until about 1970, roundups were used to capture elephants in pit traps called *kheddas*. A very large, deep pit was dug and covered with a thin layer of branches and leaves. (Definition Context Clue)

Source: McLaughlin, M. (2010). *Content area reading: Teaching and learning in an age of multiple literacies.* Boston: Allyn & Bacon.

Semantic Feature Analysis

(See blackline, page 279.)

Purposes: To make predictions about attributes related to specific vocabulary words or concepts; to set a purpose for reading or researching; to confirm predictions.

Comprehension Strategies: Making Connections, Knowing How Words Work

Text: Narrative, Informational **Use:** Before and After Reading

Procedure: (Begin by explaining and demonstrating Semantic Feature Analysis.)

1. Select a topic and some words or categories that relate to that topic. List the words in the left-hand column of the Semantic Feature Analysis chart.
2. Choose characteristics that relate to one or more of the related words. List those across the top row of the chart.
3. Ask students to make predictions about which characteristics relate to each word by placing a + if it is a characteristic, a – if it is not, and a ? if they are not sure.
4. Discuss students' predictions. Have them explain why they chose the characteristics.
5. Introduce the text and ask students to read about the topic and modify their charts as necessary.
6. Encourage students to share completed charts in small groups and then discuss as a class.

Example: Vogt, G. (2001). *Solar system.* New York: Scholastic.

	Characteristics			
Categories	Has its own moon	Has rings	Has clouds	Is a planet
Mercury	–	–	–	+
Venus	–	–	+	+
Earth	+	–	+	+
Mars	+	–	+	+
Jupiter	+	+	+	+

Source: Johnson, D.D., & Pearson, P.D. (1984). *Teaching reading vocabulary* (2nd ed.). New York: Holt, Rinehart and Winston.

Vocabulary Bookmark

(See blackline, page 261.)

Purposes: To expand vocabularies; to motivate students to learn new words.

Comprehension Strategies: Knowing How Words Work, Monitoring

Text: Narrative, Informational **Use:** During and After Reading

Procedure: (Begin by explaining and demonstrating Vocabulary Bookmark.)

1. Select a word from a current narrative or informational text that you think the whole class needs to discuss.
2. Write the word, what you think it means, and the page number on which it appears on the Vocabulary Bookmark.
3. Read the word in context. Then share what you think the word means and discuss the word and its meaning with the students. Verify the meaning in a dictionary if needed.
4. Invite the students to work with a partner to choose a word from a current narrative or informational text that they think the whole class needs to discuss.
5. Guide the students to write the word, what they think the word means, and the page on which it is located.
6. Invite the pairs of students to share their word choices, read them in context, explain what they think the words mean, and discuss them with the class. Verify word meanings in a dictionary as needed.
7. Invite students to complete their own Vocabulary Bookmarks when they have had sufficient practice working with a partner.

Example: Malaspina, A. (2010). *Yasmin's hammer.* New York: Lee & Low.

Vocabulary Bookmark

A word I think the whole class needs to talk about is...

dinghy

I think it is a kind of really small boat.

Page number 27

TEACHING IDEAS

Bookmark Technique

(See blacklines, pages 261–262.)

Purposes: To monitor comprehension while reading; to make evaluative judgments about aspects of text.

Comprehension Strategies: Making Connections, Knowing How Words Work, Monitoring

Text: Narrative, Informational **Use:** During and After Reading

Procedure: (Begin by explaining and demonstrating the Bookmark Technique.)

1. As students read, ask them to make decisions and record specific information on each bookmark, including the page and paragraph where the information is located.

   Bookmark 1: Write and/or sketch about the part of the text that you found most interesting.
   Bookmark 2: Write a word you think the whole class needs to discuss.
   Bookmark 3: Write and/or sketch something you found confusing.
   Bookmark 4: Choose a chart, map, graph, or illustration that helped you to understand what you were reading.

2. Use the completed bookmarks to promote discussion about the text.

Example: Cronin, D. (2000). *Click, clack, moo: Cows that type.* New York: Simon & Schuster. (English version)
Cronin, D. (2001). *Clic clac muu: Vacas escritoras.* Lyndhurst, NJ: Lectorum. (Spanish version)

Bookmark 1	Bookmark 2	Bookmark 3	Bookmark 4
The part I found most interesting was when the duck used the typewriter to get something he wanted. He did what the cows did. p. 24	*Impossible* I think it means it can't be done. p. 6	I am confused about what a typewriter is. Is it like a computer? p. 10	The picture of the chickens holding up the sign that reads, "Closed. No milk. No eggs." helped me understand. p. 16

Source: McLaughlin, M., & Allen, M.B. (2009). *Guided Comprehension in grades 3–8* (2nd ed.). Newark, DE: International Reading Association.

Patterned Partner Reading

Purposes: To provide a structure for reading interactively with another; to promote strategic reading.

Comprehension Strategies: Making Connections, Monitoring, Evaluating

Text: Narrative, Informational **Use:** During Reading

Procedure: (Begin by explaining and demonstrating Patterned Partner Reading.)

1. Invite students to select a text and a partner with whom they will read, or assign partners yourself.
2. Partners should determine the amount of text to be read and choose a pattern such as the following to use as they engage in the reading:

   <u>Read–Pause–Ask Questions</u>: Partners read a page silently and then ask each other a question about that page before moving on.
   <u>Predict–Read–Discuss</u>: Partners make predictions about material, read to confirm or disconfirm their predictions, discuss the outcome, and renew the cycle.
   <u>Read–Pause–Retell</u>: Partners read, stop to think, and take turns retelling what they have read to a given point.
   <u>Read–Pause–Make Connections</u>: Partners read a predetermined amount and then tell the text–self, text–text, or text–world connections they have made.
   <u>Read–Pause–Visualize</u>: Partners read a portion of the text and describe the pictures they have created in their minds.
   <u>You Choose Days</u>: Partners select which pattern to use.

Example: Mora, P. (2009). *Gracias/thanks* (English and Spanish edition). New York: Lee & Low.

<u>Read–Pause–Make Connections</u>:
pp. 1–10
The child is thankful for his Abuelita, who always winks and gives him a dollar when nobody is looking. I can make a connection to this because my great-grandmother used to give me bottles of pennies and tell me not to tell my mother. It was our little secret.

Source: Adapted from Cunningham, P., & Allington, R. (1999). *Classrooms that work: They can all read and write* (2nd ed.). New York: Addison-Wesley.

Say Something

Purposes: To make connections with texts during reading; to enhance comprehension of written material through short readings and oral discussion.

Comprehension Strategies: Making Connections, Monitoring

Text: Narrative, Informational **Use:** During Reading

Procedure: (Begin by explaining and demonstrating Say Something.)

1. Instruct pairs of students to select text to read.
2. Designate a stopping point for reading.
3. Ask students to read to the stopping point and then "Say Something" about the text to their partner.
4. Allow pairs to choose the next stopping point. (If the text has subheadings, these make good stopping points.)
5. Students repeat steps 3 and 4 until they have finished reading the text.

Example: Wolf, B. (2003). *Coming to America: A Muslim family's story.* New York: Lee & Low.

Student 1: I have always wanted to be a doctor when I grow up, just like Rowan's sister, Dina. pp. 1–3

Student 2: Rowan wants to become a teacher when she grows up. It's neat that she already knows what she wants to do when she grows up. pp. 1–8

Student 1: The students in Rowan's class make Father's Day cards. They celebrate holidays just like American students do.

Student 2: Amir's school has students from 49 nations. That's a lot of different places. He must learn a lot about other cultures from his classmates.

Student 1: Amir and his classmates play handball. From the picture, it looks like handball is kind of like dodgeball.

Student 2: Amir has 45 minutes for lunch and recess, just like we do! His school is a lot like our school.

Student 1: I think it's great that they moved to America and are enjoying the culture.

Student 2: I am glad that their classmates welcomed them and taught them new things about American culture.

Source: Adapted from Short, K.G., Harste, J.C., & Burke, C. (1996). *Creating classrooms for authors and inquirers.* Portsmouth, NH: Heinemann.

Think-Alouds

Purpose: To provide a model for active thinking during the reading process.

Comprehension Strategies: Previewing, Visualizing, Monitoring, Self-Questioning, Making Connections, Knowing How Words Work, Summarizing, Evaluating

Text: Narrative, Informational **Use:** Before, During, and After Reading

Procedure: (Begin by explaining and demonstrating Think-Alouds.)

1. Introduce the text. Select a passage to read aloud to the students. The passage should require some strategic thinking in order to clarify understandings.
2. Before reading, encourage students to work with partners to make predictions for the story or chapter and explain their reasoning. (For example, "From the title [or cover], we can predict... because....")
3. During reading, encourage students to think aloud to demonstrate strategies such as the following:
    - Making/confirming/modifying predictions ("We were thinking ________, but now we predict ____________."; "We thought that was what was going to happen because ____________.")

- Visualizing—making pictures in our minds ("What we are seeing in our minds right now is ________________.")
- Making connections ("This reminds us of ____________________."; This is like a __________________.")
- Monitoring ("This is confusing. We need to reread or read on or ask someone for help."; "This is not what we expected.")
- Figuring out unknown words ("We don't know that word, but it looks like _________."; "That word must mean ______________ because _________.")

4. After guiding them to practice with partners several times, encourage students to use this technique on their own.

Example: Simon, S. (1998). *The universe.* New York: Scholastic.

Visualizing: After reading this passage, what are you seeing in your mind right now?
What I am seeing in my mind right now is the creation of our solar system. I see a big ball of dust and gases swirling around together like a tornado. In the center of the swirling disk I see the sun. As things slow down, the particles and gases form planets, and that is how our solar system came to be.

Source: Davey, B. (1983). Think-aloud—Modeling the cognitive processes of reading comprehension. *Journal of Reading, 27,* 44–47.

Lyric Retelling/Lyric Summary

(See blackline, page 275.)

Purposes: To provide an alternative format for narrative text retellings or informational text summaries; to provide opportunities to use multiple modalities when creating summaries; to link content learning and the arts.

Comprehension Strategy: Summarizing

Text: Narrative, Informational **Use:** After Reading

Procedure: (Begin by explaining and demonstrating Lyric Retellings/Lyric Summaries.)

1. Review summarizing with the students. Ask them to note the types of information that make up narrative or informational summaries. Choose a topic and brainstorm a list of related information.
2. Introduce the musical aspect of Lyric Retellings/Lyric Summaries by explaining to students that summaries can also be written as song lyrics to familiar tunes (rock, easy listening, children's songs).
3. Choose a melody with which students are familiar and use the brainstormed list to write lyrics. Write the first line and then encourage pairs of students to suggest subsequent lines. When the Lyric Retelling/Lyric Summary is completed, sing it with the class.

4. Ask small groups of students to brainstorm a list of facts they know about a story they have read or a content area topic they have studied. Invite them to choose a melody everyone in the group knows and create their own Lyric Retellings/Lyric Summaries.
5. Invite the students to sing their completed summaries for the class.

Example: Simon, S. (2006). *The heart: Our circulatory system.* New York: Collins.

Sung to the tune of "Twinkle Twinkle Little Star"

The heart pumps blood through our bodies.
It is a muscle that works very hard.
The heart, blood, and blood vessels
Provide our cells with food and oxygen.
The heart pumps blood through our bodies.
It is a muscle that works very hard.

Source: McLaughlin, M. & Allen, M.B. (2009). *Guided Comprehension in grades 3–8* (2nd ed.). Newark, DE: International Reading Association.

Paired Summarizing

Purposes: To provide a format for pairs to summarize narrative or informational text and to articulate understandings and confusions.

Comprehension Strategies: Making Connections, Monitoring, Summarizing

Text: Narrative, Informational **Use:** After Reading

Procedure: (Begin by explaining and demonstrating Paired Summarizing.)

1. Ask pairs of students to read a selection, and invite each student to write a summary or retelling. They may refer to the text to help cue their memory, but they should not write while they are looking at the text.
2. Ask partners to trade the retellings or summaries that they wrote and read each other's work. Encourage each student to write a summary of the other partner's paper.
3. Encourage students to compare and contrast their summaries. The discussion should focus on
    - Articulating what each reader understands
    - Identifying what they collectively cannot come to understand
    - Formulating clarification questions for classmates and the teacher
4. Invite students to share understandings and questions in a small-group or whole-class discussion.

Example: Battle-Lavert, G. (2003). *Papa's mark.* New York: Holiday House.

<u>Student 1 Summary</u>: In this story, Simms and his Papa rode along the bumpy road from town to the general store. While at the store, the storekeeper talked to Papa about the upcoming election. Also when they were at the store, Simms's Papa had to sign his name, but he only put an X because he didn't know how to write his name. Simms tells Papa he will show him, but his Papa tells Simms he

has enough work of his own. When they get home, there is a discussion about the election and Simms makes a poster for all the homes. Simms's Papa really wants to learn to write his name before voting day, so he practices with Simms every day. Papa learns to write his name, and on Election Day he writes his name when he casts his ballot for the very first time.

Student 2 Summary of First Summary: Simms and his Papa were close like really good friends. Simms wanted his Papa to learn to write his name before Election Day, and they practiced every day. When Election Day came, Papa was able to write his own name.

Source: Vaughn, J., & Estes, T. (1986). *Reading and reasoning beyond the primary grades*. Boston: Allyn & Bacon.

QuIP (Questions Into Paragraphs)

(See blackline, page 278.)

Purpose: To provide a framework for initiating research and structuring writing.

Comprehension Strategies: Self-Questioning, Summarizing

Text: Informational **Use:** Before, During, and After Reading

Procedure: (Begin by explaining and demonstrating QuIP.)

1. Invite students to choose a topic to explore and write the topic at the top of the QuIP grid.
2. Ask students to generate and write on the grid three broad questions related to the topic.
3. Students should locate and read two sources to find the answers to their questions. They write the titles of the sources in spaces provided on the grid.
4. Students record answers to the questions in the spaces provided on the grid.
5. Students synthesize information into a paragraph. (Demonstrating synthesizing and paragraph writing facilitates this process.)
6. Students share their paragraphs in pairs or small groups.

Examples: Berger, M., & Berger, G. (2003). *Whales.* New York: Scholastic.
Milton, J. (1989). *Whales: The gentle giants.* New York: Random House.

TOPIC: Whale

Questions	*Answers*	
	Source 1: Berger, M., & Berger, G. (2003). *Whales.* New York: Scholastic.	Source 2: Milton, J. (1989). *Whales: The gentle giants.* New York: Random House.
A. What is the biggest animal in the world?	The blue whale is the biggest animal ever to live on land or sea.	The blue whale is the biggest animal in the world.
B. How does a whale breathe?	A whale breathes through its blowhole.	A whale breathes through a hole in its head called a blowhole.
C. How does a whale catch its dinner?	A whale catches tiny sea plants and animals using its baleen.	A whale uses its baleen to catch food. It grows in long strips and works like a strainer.

The biggest animal on land and sea is a type of whale called a blue whale. Whales breathe through a small hole on their heads called a blowhole. Whales catch their food by capturing small plants and animals with their baleen. Baleen grows in long strands and works like a big strainer for capturing food.

Source: McLaughlin, E.M. (1987). QuIP: A writing strategy to improve comprehension of informational structure. *The Reading Teacher, 40*, 650–654.

Retelling

(See blackline, page 272.)

Purposes: To promote reflection about narrative text; to provide a format for summarizing narrative text structure.

Comprehension Strategy: Summarizing

Text: Narrative **Use:** After Reading

Procedure: (Begin by explaining and demonstrating Retelling.)

1. Explain to the students the purpose of retelling a story and the major elements that are included (characters, setting, problem, attempts to resolve the problem, resolution).
2. Demonstrate a Retelling after reading a story aloud. Discuss the components you included. (A story map or other graphic organizer may help.)
3. Read another story to the students, and then ask them to form groups and retell the story. (You may want to give each student in the group a card listing a specific story element, such as characters, setting, problem, attempts to resolve the problem, resolution.)

4. Share information with the class and record it on a chart or overhead. Review the Retellings to ensure all elements are addressed.
5. Encourage students to do Retellings orally, in writing, or through sketching or dramatization to demonstrate understanding of a narrative text.

Adaptation: Invite students to complete Draw and Write Retellings.

Example: Fine, E.H., & Josephson, J.P. (2007). *Armando and the blue tarp school.* New York: Lee & Low.

After Armando and his dad picked through the trash, they heard a truck horn. It belonged to Señor David, a man who had taught Armando and his friends the previous summer. They called his school the Blue Tarp School, because there was no building, just a blue tarp. Señor David came back to teach the children again this summer. Armando's father said he could go to the school once, but he would need to work with his father the other days. Armando was sad, because he really wanted to go to Señor David's school. His friend Isabella started teaching Armando what she learned in school while he was working, but it was not the same as being there. Finally, his father said he could leave work early every day and go to the school. Then there was a very bad fire and many homes burned. Armando's was one of them. A few days later, Señor David started teaching again. Armando was turning into a really good artist, and a newspaper published a story about the fire and used one of his paintings. Then the community rebuilt their homes and worked on building a real school where the Blue Tarp School had been.

Source: Morrow, L.M. (1985). Retelling stories: A strategy for improving children's comprehension, concept of story, and oral language complexity. *The Elementary School Journal*, *85*(5), 647–661.

Story Map

(See blackline, page 283.)

Purposes: To promote understanding of the narrative elements; to encourage summarizing using narrative text structure.

Comprehension Strategies: Monitoring, Summarizing

Text: Narrative **Use:** After Reading

Procedure: (Begin by explaining and modeling a Story Map.)

1. Explain to the students the purpose of summarizing and the narrative (story) elements that are included (characters, setting, problem, attempts to resolve the problem, solution) when summarizing a story.
2. Demonstrate completing a Story Map after reading a story aloud. Think aloud about who was in the story, where the story took place, and so on. Discuss the components as you complete each. (A Story Map or other visual cues may help.) Use the completed Story Map to briefly summarize the story.
3. Read another story to the students and invite them to complete a Story Map in small groups. (Be sure students have the Story Map blackline master, which includes the narrative elements.)

4. Share and discuss the completed Story Maps. Use them to summarize the story.

    Ideas for using Story Maps
    - Summarize key events in a story.
    - Predict key events in a story.
    - Plan story elements when writing a story.
    - Increase students' understanding of story structure when reading and writing original stories.

Example: Slonim, D. (2003). *Oh, Ducky! A chocolate calamity*. San Francisco: Chronicle.

Title: *Oh, Ducky! A Chocolate Calamity*

Setting: Chocolate factory

Characters:
Mr. Peters, Johnny, Ducky, Pauline.

Problem: The machine stopped making candy.

Events:
- The machine stops making candy.
- Mr. Peters puts on a rubber suit and goes into the chocolate machine to fix it.
- Ducky had fallen into the machine and caused it to stop working.

Solution:
Mr. Peters is inspired by Ducky and decides to make chocolate ducks. Everyone loves them, and there is a big parade.

Evaluative Questioning

Purpose: To promote self-questioning and evaluative thinking.

Comprehension Strategies: Self-Questioning, Evaluating

Text: Narrative, Informational **Use:** During and After Reading

Procedure: (Begin by explaining and demonstrating Evaluative Questioning.)

1. Explain the importance of multiple levels of questioning, focusing on evaluative questions. (See Chapter 3.)
2. Model creating and responding to evaluative questions using a read-aloud and Think-Aloud. Explain the signal words and cognitive operations used to form and respond to evaluative questions.

    Signal words: *defend, judge, justify*
    Cognitive operations: valuing, judging, defending, justifying

3. Using a common text, guide small groups of students to read the text and create an evaluative question. One at a time, ask groups to share their question and encourage other students to respond. Discuss the cognitive processes students used to answer each question.
4. Provide opportunities for students to use evaluative questions to engage in reflection and conversations about the texts they read.

Example: Gill, S. (2007). *Alaska*. Watertown, MA: Charlesbridge.

How do you think global warming will affect us in the future? How do you think it will affect Alaska in the future? Defend your responses.

Source: Ciardiello, A.V. (1998). Did you ask a good question today? Alternative cognitive and metacognitive strategies. *Journal of Adolescent & Adult Literacy*, 42, 210–219.

Journal Responses

Purposes: To provide opportunities for reflection and critical thinking; to encourage students to respond in writing to what they are reading.

Comprehension Strategies: Making Connections, Summarizing, Evaluating

Text: Narrative, Informational **Use:** During and After Reading

Procedure: (Begin by explaining and demonstrating Journal Responses.)

1. Provide students with a journal or a system for keeping their responses.
2. Show students examples of good responses to texts. Help students identify aspects of thoughtful reading responses.
3. Read aloud a portion of text and think aloud through a thoughtful response. Discuss with students why it was thoughtful.
4. Read aloud another portion of text and encourage students to write a thoughtful response and share it with partners.
5. For independent reading, ask students to write the date and the title of the text or chapter at the top of the page or in the left margin.
6. After reading a text or listening to one, use Journal Responses as one of many methods students use to respond to what they read. Journal Responses can include reactions, questions, wonderings, predictions, connections, or feelings.

   Possible Journal Response prompts
   - What was the most interesting part of what you read? Explain.
   - What was important in the chapter? How do you know?
   - What is something new you learned? Explain.
   - What connection(s) did you make? Explain.
7. Encourage students to share responses in groups or with the whole class.

Example: Boyden, L. (2002). *The blue roses*. New York: Lee & Low.

What was the most interesting part of the story? Why?

The most interesting part of the story for me was when Papa tells Rosalie how he got his first wrinkle. He tells Rosalie that he was at sea when a fierce storm rolled in and he clutched the wheel and squeezed his face tight. I think it is funny how he just looked in the mirror and discovered the wrinkle and he has a story to go along with it. I don't think most people have a story to go along with their wrinkles.

Persuasive Writing

Purposes: To express points of view with supporting ideas; to foster understanding of multiple perspectives on a topic.

Comprehension Strategy: Evaluating

Text: Narrative, Informational **Use:** Before, During, and After Reading

Procedure: (Begin by explaining and demonstrating Persuasive Writing.)

1. Introduce a topic by reading an article that contains two points of view about the same issue.
2. Use a Think-Aloud to share the different perspectives about the topic.
3. Choose a side and write persuasively to defend your choice. Think aloud throughout this process. Be certain to support your argument with facts.
4. Discuss your writing with the students and encourage them to express their ideas about the topic.
5. Guide the students to engage in Persuasive Writing by sharing a different article and scaffolding their ability to write persuasively.
6. Provide additional opportunities for students to engage in practice by using current events, character choices, and historical events in other instructional settings.

Example: Van Allsburg, C. (2011). *Just a dream*. Boston: Sandpiper.

This book reminds me that we need to take care of our planet. Everyone can do something to help. We can plant trees, recycle garbage, and save water. If everyone helps, the world will be a better place for all of us.

Source: McLaughlin, M., & Allen, M.B. (2009). *Guided Comprehension in grades 3–8* (2nd ed.). Newark, DE: International Reading Association.

Venn Diagram

(See blackline, page 285.)

Purpose: To compare and contrast two topics.

Comprehension Strategies: Making Connections, Summarizing, Evaluating

Text: Informational **Use:** During and After Reading

TEACHING IDEAS

Procedure: (Begin by explaining and modeling a Venn Diagram.)

1. Explain that we use Venn Diagrams to show what is similar and what is different about two topics.
2. Read aloud a brief text that includes information about two topics.
3. Demonstrate how to complete a Venn Diagram. Use the blackline and label the diagram with the topics to be discussed. Next, think aloud as you list the similarities the topics share in the section where the circles overlap. Then think aloud as you list what is unique about each topic in the section of the diagram directly below where that topic is listed. Use the completed Venn Diagram to summarize and discuss how the topics are similar and how they are different.
4. Read aloud another brief text that includes information about two topics. Distribute copies of the Venn Diagram blackline to students.
5. Invite students to work with a partner to list similarities in the overlapped section of the circles. Discuss the ideas that students record.
6. Encourage students to write what is unique about each topic in the outer portion of the circle that appears below each topic. Discuss the ideas that students record.
7. Invite the students to use the completed Venn Diagram to summarize similarities and differences about the topics.

Example: Simon, S. (2008). *Gorillas.* New York: HarperCollins.

COMPREHENSION ROUTINES

Cross-Age Reading Experiences

(See Chapter 5; blackline in Appendix B, page 298; and observation guide in Appendix C, page 336.)

Purposes: To provide a structure for reading strategically with a more experienced partner; to promote discussion and negotiation of meaning in a social setting.

Comprehension Strategies: All

Text: Narrative, Informational **Use:** Before, During, and After Reading

Procedure: (Begin by explaining and modeling Cross-Age Reading Experiences.)

1. Meet with the coordinator of cross-age volunteers or the teacher of the partner class to discuss organizational issues such as meeting time, materials, and matching students with buddies.
2. Meet with the cross-age volunteers and discuss the goals of the Cross-Age Reading Experience. Focus on the students' needs and introduce or review the Guided Comprehension strategies and teaching ideas. Model cross-age reading—including fluency and strategy use—for the volunteers. Discuss the process.
3. Begin the Cross-Age Reading Experience with an introductory activity such as "Getting to Know You," in which the students and volunteers have time to learn about each other. Provide appropriate theme-related texts for reading. Respond to any questions participants may have.
4. Integrate Cross-Age Reading Experiences as a routine in Stage Two of Guided Comprehension. Remember to ensure that students have access to appropriate theme-related texts, that students and cross-age volunteers are aware of the strategy focus, and that they engage in reflection and sharing at the close of the experience.
5. Provide opportunities for students to engage in Cross-Age Reading Experiences in Stage Two of Guided Comprehension on a regular basis.

Directed Reading–Thinking Activity (DR–TA)/ Directed Listening–Thinking Activity (DL–TA)

Purposes: To encourage students to make predictions about a story or text; to use the author's clues to make meaningful connections and predictions; to foster active reading of or listening to a text.

Comprehension Strategies: Previewing, Making Connections, Monitoring

Text: Narrative, Informational **Use:** Before, During, and After Reading

Procedure: (Begin by explaining and demonstrating DR–TA or DL–TA.)

1. Invite students to look at the title and/or cover of a book and ask them, "What do you think this story (or book) is about? Explain your thinking." Students respond with predictions and reasons for their thinking. This helps activate prior knowledge.
2. Ask students to read to a designated stopping point in the text, review their predictions, make new predictions, and explain the reasons for the new predictions.
3. Repeat Step 2 until the text is finished.

4. Encourage students to reflect on their predictions, stating what was helpful, what was surprising, and what was confusing.

   Other ideas for using DR–TA:
   - Students can predict orally, in writing, or by illustrating.
   - For DL–TA, students listen to the story. The reader stops at various preselected places and asks students to review predictions, make new ones, and explain their reasoning.

Source: Stauffer, R. (1975). *Directing the reading–thinking process*. New York: Harper & Row.

Literature Circles

(See Chapter 3; blacklines in Appendix B, pages 306–308; and observation guide in Appendix C, page 337.)

Purposes: To provide a structure for student talk about texts from a variety of perspectives; to provide opportunities for social learning.

Comprehension Strategies: All

Text: Narrative, Informational **Use:** Before, During, and After Reading

Procedure: (Begin by explaining and demonstrating Literature Circles.)

1. Invite students to select books to read and to join groups based on their text selections.
2. Ask groups to meet to develop a schedule—how much they will read, when they will meet, and so on.
3. Encourage students to read the predetermined amount of text independently, taking notes as they read. Students can keep their notes in their Guided Comprehension Journals. The notes can reflect the students' role in the Literature Circle or their personal connections to the text. Roles within the Literature Circles should vary from meeting to meeting.
4. Encourage students to continue to meet according to the group schedule to discuss ideas about the text until the book is completed.
5. Provide opportunities for students to participate in Literature Circles in Stage Two of Guided Comprehension.

Source: Daniels, H. (2002). *Literature circles: Voice and choice in the student-centered classroom* (2nd ed.). York, ME: Stenhouse.

Reciprocal Teaching

(See Chapter 3; blacklines in Appendix B, pages 319–321; and observation guide in Appendix C, page 338.)

Purposes: To provide a format for using comprehension strategies—predicting, self-questioning, monitoring, and summarizing—in a small-group setting; to facilitate a group effort to bring meaning to a text; to monitor thinking and learning.

Comprehension Strategies: Previewing, Self-Questioning, Monitoring, Summarizing

Text: Narrative, Informational **Use:** Before, During, and After Reading

Procedure: (Begin by explaining and demonstrating Reciprocal Teaching.)

1. Explain the procedure and each of the four reading comprehension strategies: predicting, self-questioning, monitoring, and summarizing.
2. Model thinking related to each of the four strategies by using an authentic text and thinking aloud.
3. With the whole class, guide students to engage in similar types of thinking by providing responses for each of the strategies. Sentence stems, such as the following, facilitate this:

Predicting:
- I think...
- I bet...
- I imagine...
- I suppose...

Questioning:
- What connections can I make?
- How does this support my thinking?

Clarifying:
- I did not understand the part where...
- I need to know more about...

Summarizing:
- The important ideas in what I read are...

4. Place students in groups of four and provide each group with copies of the same text to use as the basis for Reciprocal Teaching.
5. Assign each student one of the four strategies and the suggested prompts.
6. Invite students to engage in Reciprocal Teaching using the process that was modeled.
7. Ask students to reflect on the process and their comprehension of the text.
8. Provide opportunities for the students to engage in Reciprocal Teaching in Stage Two of Guided Comprehension as an independent comprehension routine.

Source: Palincsar, A.S., & Brown, A.L. (1986). Interactive teaching to promote independent learning from text. *The Reading Teacher, 39*, 771–777.

BOOKMARK TECHNIQUE (4)

Bookmark 1	Bookmark 2
Name: ________	Name: ________
Date: ________	Date: ________
The most interesting part was...	A word I think the whole class needs to talk about is...
Page number: ______	Page number: ______

BOOKMARK TECHNIQUE (4)

Bookmark 3

Name: ______________________

Date: ______________________

Something that confused me was...

____

____

____

____

____

____

Page number: ________

Bookmark 4

Name: ______________________

Date: ______________________

A picture or map that helped me understand what I read was...

____

____

____

____

____

____

Page number: ________

CONCEPT OF DEFINITION MAP

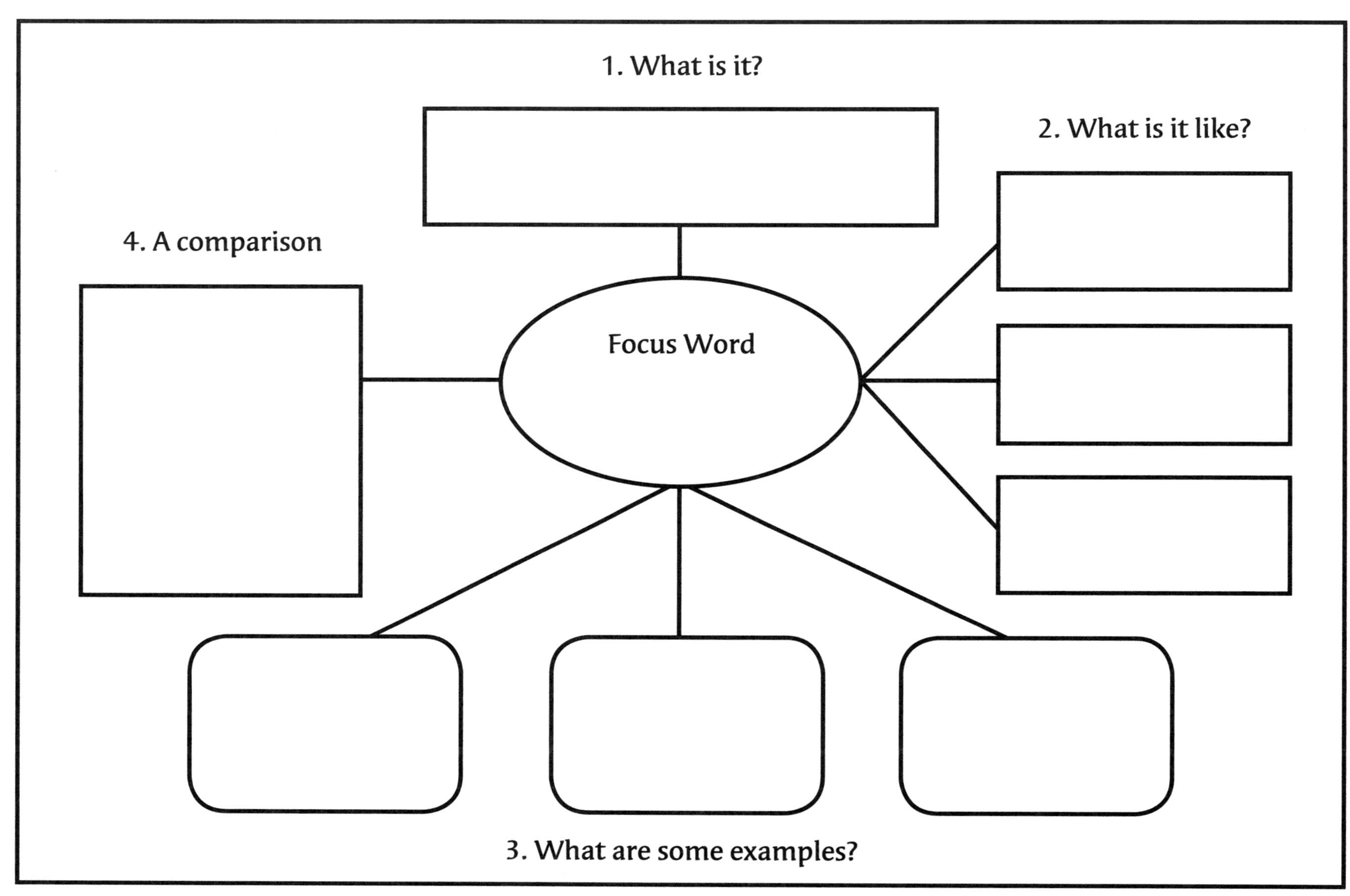

CONNECTION STEMS (2)

Name: ______________________ Date: ______________

1. I have a connection...

to ______________________________

____

because ______________________________

____

2. I have a connection...

to ______________________________

____

because ______________________________

____

CONNECTION STEMS (2)

Name: ______________________________ Date: ________________

1. That reminds me of...

____

____

because ____

____

2. That reminds me of...

____

____

because ____

____

CONTRAST CHART

Name: ____________________ Date: __________

1. ________	1. ________
2. ________	2. ________
3. ________	3. ________
4. ________	4. ________
5. ________	5. ________

DOUBLE-ENTRY JOURNAL (2)

Name: ______________________________ Date: ________________

Idea	Reflection/Reaction
1.	1.
2.	2.
3.	3.
4.	4.

DOUBLE-ENTRY JOURNAL (2)

Name: ______________________________ Date: ________________

Idea/Text From Story	My Connection
1.	1.
2.	2.
3.	3.
4.	4.

DRAW AND WRITE CONNECTIONS (3)

Name: ______________________________ Date: ________________

Book Title: ____

1. Drawing:

2. I have a connection to this book!

____

____

____

____

____

DRAW AND WRITE CONNECTIONS (3)

Name: ______________________________ Date: ________________

Book Titles: ____

1. Drawing:

2. I can make a connection between this book and another book!

____

____

____

____

____

DRAW AND WRITE CONNECTIONS (3)

Name: ______________________________ Date: ________________

Book Title: ____

1. Drawing:

2. I felt like the character when...

____

____

____

____

____

DRAW AND WRITE RETELLING

Name: ______________________ Date: __________

DRAW AND WRITE RETELLING FOR ______________________

1. Who?

   Draw:

   Write:

2. Where?

   Draw:

   Write:

3. What happened?

   Draw:

   Write:

4. How did it end?

   Draw:

   Write:

DRAW AND WRITE VISUALIZATIONS

Name:________________________________ Date:________________

1. Draw:

2. Write:

DRAW SOMETHING

Name: ______________________________ Date: ______________

1	2
3	4

LYRIC RETELLING/LYRIC SUMMARY

Name: ______________________________ Date: _________________________

Text: ____

Tune: ____

Verse 1:

____

____

____

____

____

Verse 2:

____

____

____

____

____

Refrain (or Verse 3):

____

____

____

____

____

MAIN IDEA TABLE

Name: ______________________ Date: __________

Main Idea		
1.	2.	3.

Supporting Details

QUESTION–ANSWER RELATIONSHIPS (QAR)

Name:______________________________________ Date:____________________

1. In the text

   - Right There–the answer is within one sentence in the text.

   - Think and Search–the answer is contained in more than one sentence from the text.

2. In my head

   - Author and You–the answer needs information from the reader's background knowledge and the text.

   - On Your Own–the answer needs information from only the reader's background knowledge.

QuIP RESEARCH GRID

Topic: ____________________________________

Questions	Answers	
	Source A:	Source B:
1.		
2.		
3.		

SEMANTIC FEATURE ANALYSIS

Name: ______________________________ Date: __________

Categories	Characteristics						
1.							
2.							
3.							
4.							
5.							
6.							
7.							
8.							

SEMANTIC QUESTION MAP

Name: ______________________ Date: ______________

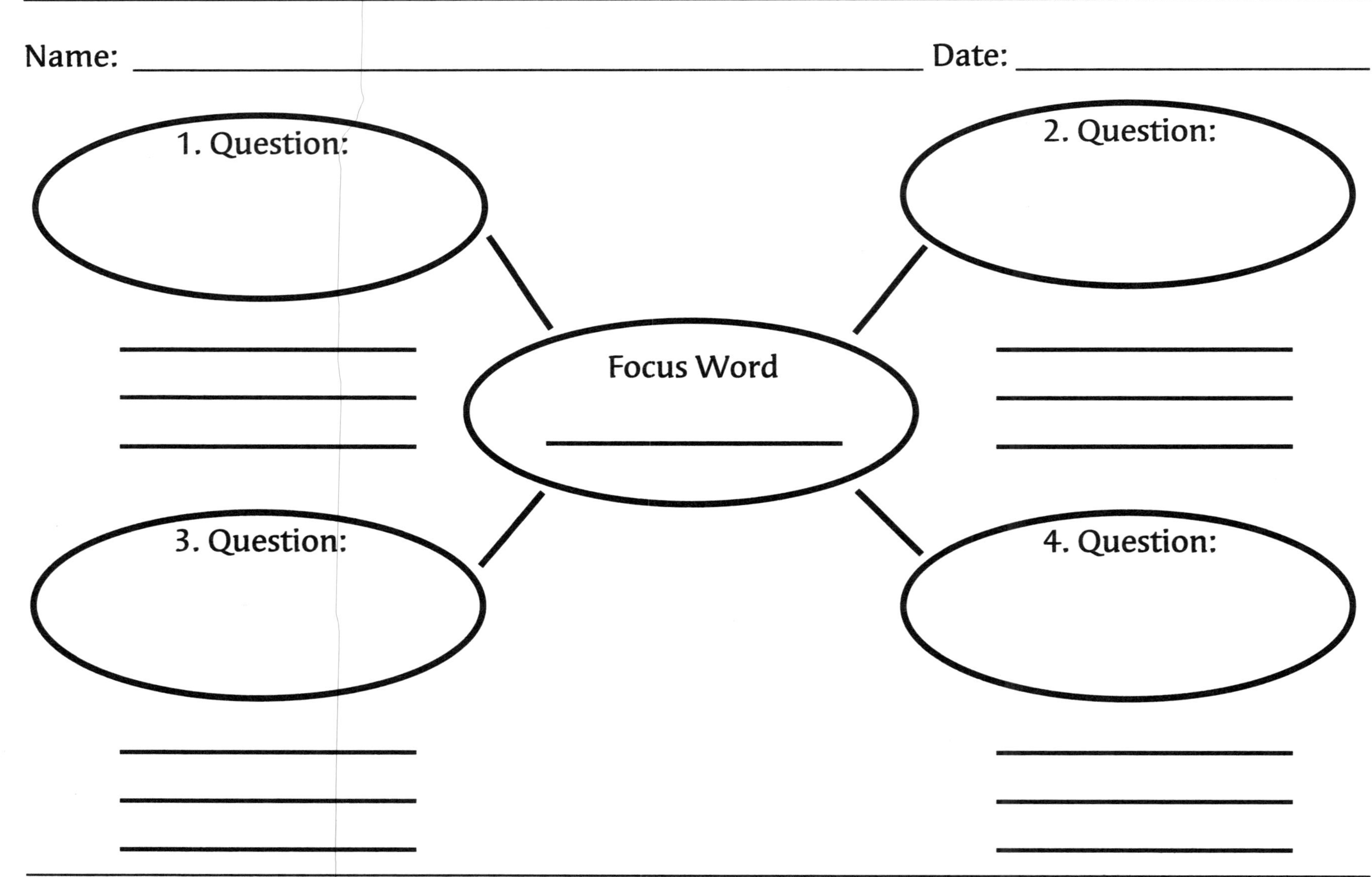

SEQUENCE CHAIN

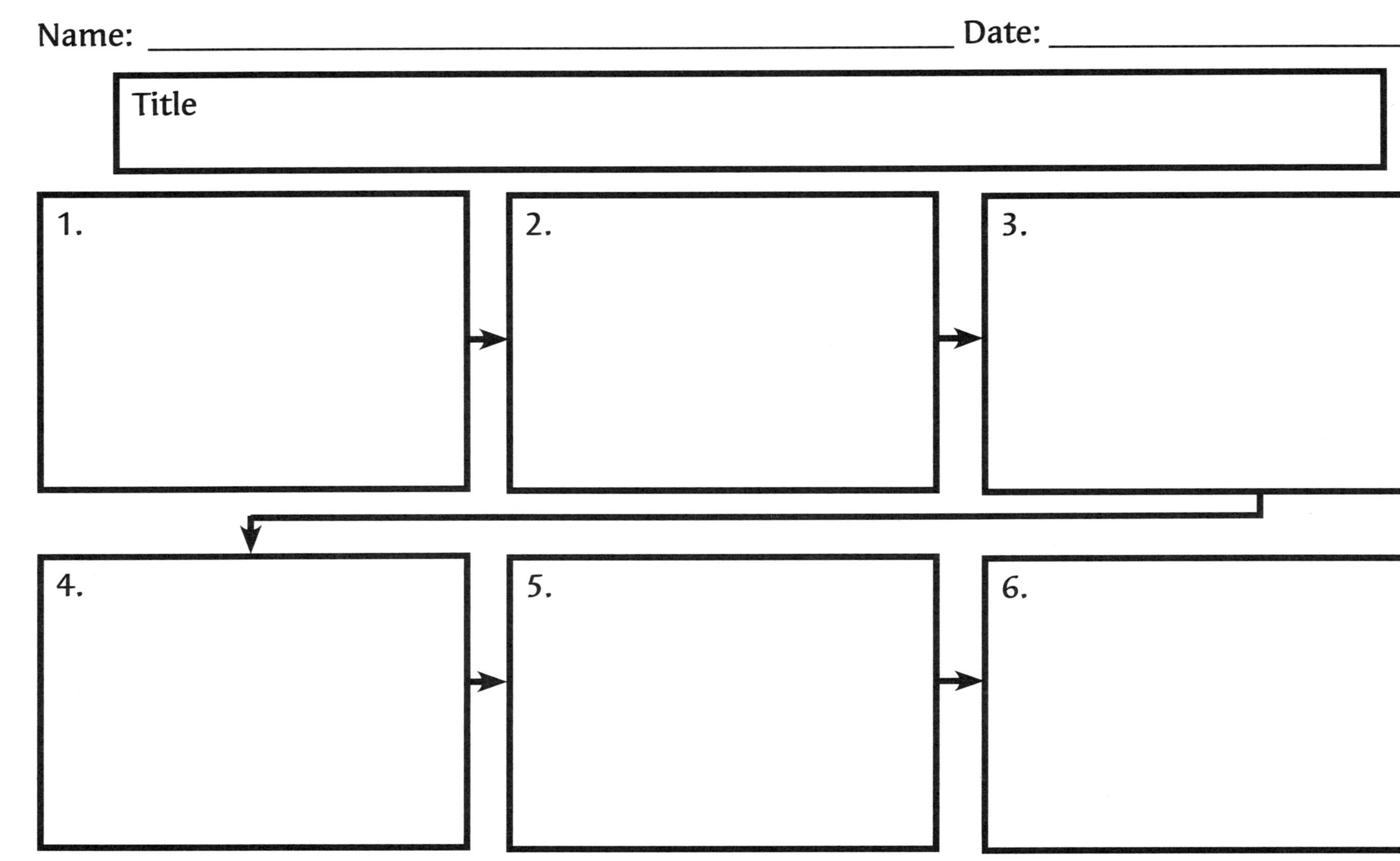

STORY IMPRESSIONS

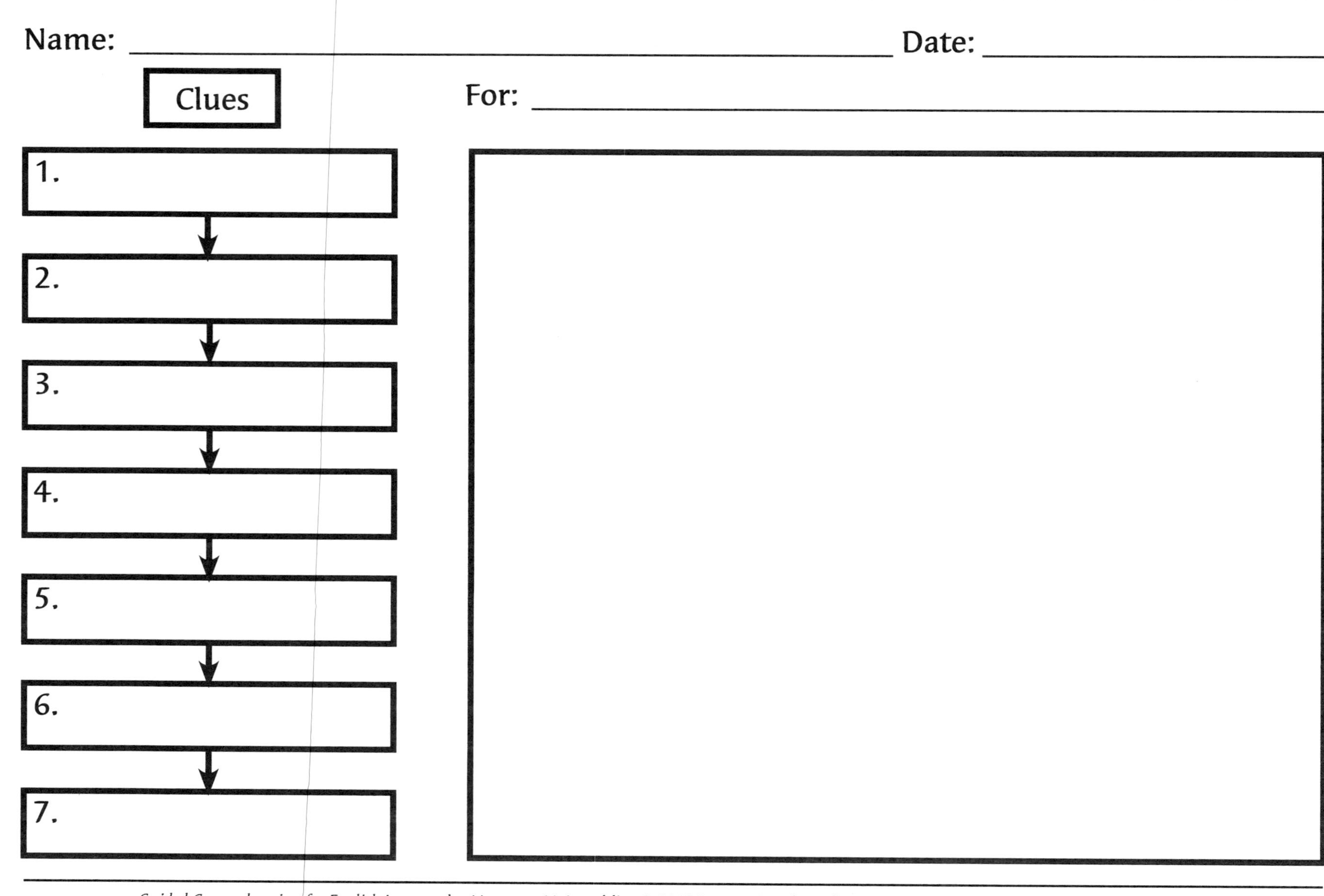

STORY MAP

Name: ______________________ Date: ______________

Title/Chapter: ______________________________

Setting	Characters

Problem

Event 1

Event 2

Event 3

Solution

THICK AND THIN QUESTIONS

Name:______________________________ Date:______________________

Page	Thin Questions	Thick Questions

VENN DIAGRAM

Name: ______________________ Date: ______________

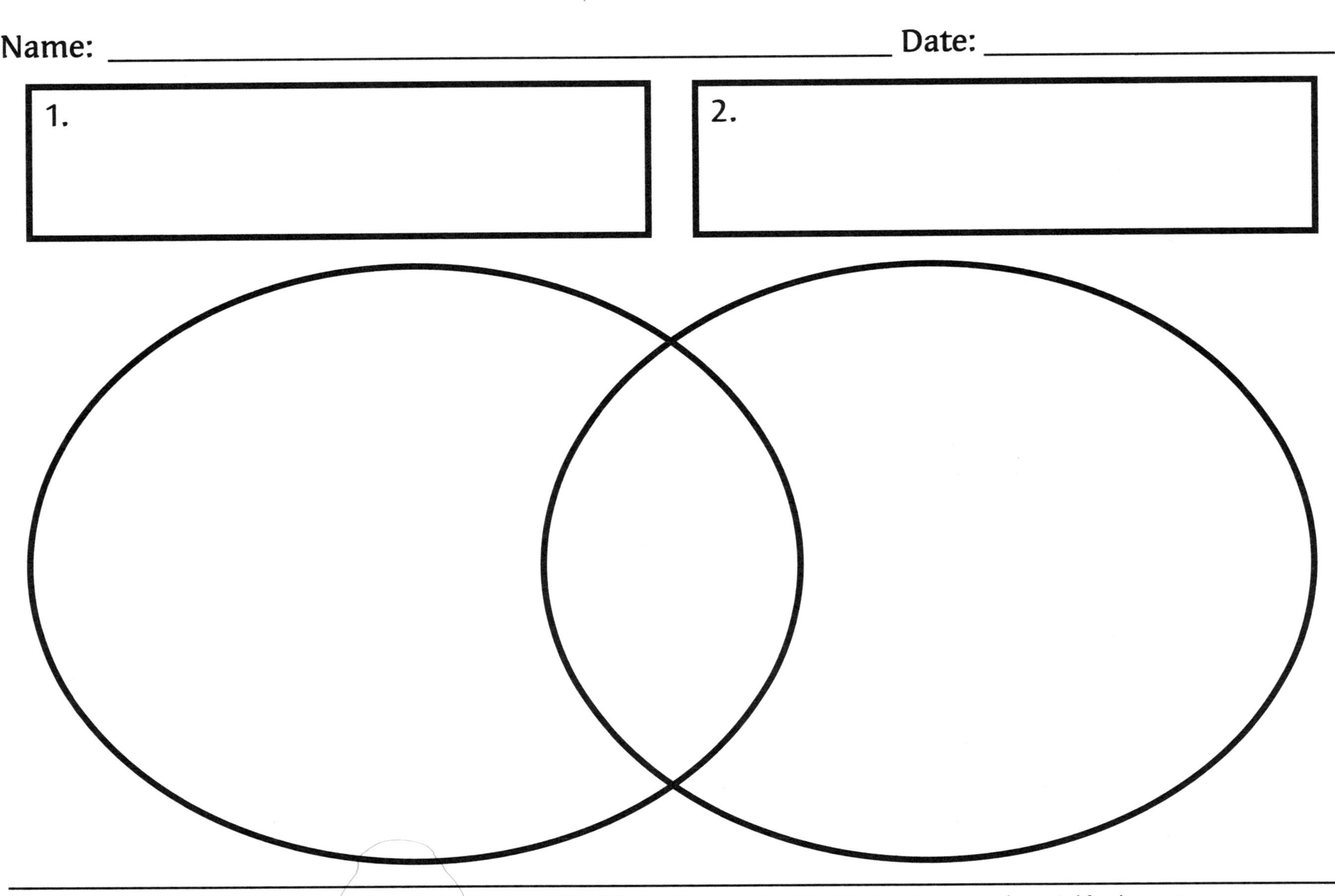

APPENDIX B

Resources for Organizing and Managing Comprehension Centers and Routines

ABC CENTER SEQUENTIAL ROUNDTABLE ALPHABET

Name: ______________________________ Date: ______________

A	B	C
D	E	F
G	H	I
J	K	L
M	N	O
P	Q	R
S	T	U
V	W	X
Y	Z	

ALPHABET BOOKS

Ada, A.F. (1997). *Gathering the sun: An alphabet in Spanish and English.* New York: HarperCollins.
Azarian, M. (2000). *A gardener's alphabet.* Boston: Houghton Mifflin.
Bronson, L. (2001). *The circus alphabet.* New York: Henry Holt.
Browne, P.A. (1995). *African animals ABC.* San Francisco: Sierra Club.
Carle, E. (2007). *Eric Carle's ABC.* New York: Grosset & Dunlap.
Cheney, L. (2002). *America: A patriotic primer.* New York: Simon & Schuster.
Crane, C. (2000). *S is for sunshine: A Florida alphabet.* Chelsea, MI: Sleeping Bear.
Crane, C. (2001). *L is for Lone Star: A Texas alphabet.* Chelsea, MI: Sleeping Bear.
Crosby, E.T. (2001). *A is for adopted.* Gilbert, AZ: SWAK PAK.
Demarest, C. (1999). *The cowboy ABC.* New York: Dorling Kindersley.
Demarest, C. (2000). *Firefighters A to Z.* New York: Scholastic.
Ehlert, L. (1989). *Eating the alphabet: Fruits and vegetables from A to Z.* New York: Harcourt.
Ernst, L.C. (2004). *The turn-around, upside-down alphabet book.* New York: Simon & Schuster.
Fleming, D. (2002). *Alphabet under construction.* New York: Henry Holt.
Gagliano, E. (2003). *C is for cowboy: A Wyoming alphabet.* Chelsea, MI: Sleeping Bear.
Gowan, B. (2002). *G is for Grand Canyon: An Arizona alphabet.* Chelsea, MI: Sleeping Bear.
Hall, B. (2003). *A is for arches: A Utah alphabet book.* Chelsea, MI: Sleeping Bear.
Harley, A. (2001). *Leap into poetry: More ABC's of poetry.* Honesdale, PA: Boyds Mills.
Harris, J. (1997). *A is for artist: A Getty Museum alphabet.* Los Angeles: Getty.
Inkpen, M. (2001). *Kipper's A to Z.* New York: Harcourt.
Jordan, M., & Jordan, T. (1996). *Amazon alphabet.* New York: Kingfisher.
Kalman, M. (2001). *What Pete ate from A–Z.* New York: Penguin.
Kirk, D. (1998). *Miss Spider's ABC.* New York: Scholastic.
Martin, B. Jr. (2000). *Chicka chicka boom boom.* New York: Aladdin.
Martin, B. Jr., & Archambault, J. (2011). *Chica chica bum bum ABC (Chicka chicka boom boom ABC)* (Spanish edition). New York: Simon & Schuster Libros Para Ninos.
Melmed, L.K. (2009). *Heart of Texas: A Lone Star ABC.* New York: Collins.
Morales, Y. (2011). *Just in case: A trickster tale and Spanish alphabet book.* New York: Roaring Brook.
Murphy, C. (1997). *Alphabet magic.* New York: Simon & Schuster.
Nathan, C. (1995). *Bugs and beasties ABC.* Boca Raton, FL: Cool Kids.
Onyefulu, I. (1993). *A is for Africa.* New York: Puffin.
Pallotta, J. (1989). *The yucky reptile alphabet book.* Watertown, MA: Charlesbridge.
Pallotta, J. (1990). *The dinosaur alphabet book.* Watertown, MA: Charlesbridge.
Pallotta, J. (1990). *The furry animal alphabet book.* Watertown, MA: Charlesbridge.
Pallotta, J. (1990). *The icky bug alphabet book.* Watertown, MA: Charlesbridge.
Pallotta, J. (1991). *The bird alphabet book.* Watertown, MA: Charlesbridge.
Pallotta, J. (1991). *The frog alphabet book.* Watertown, MA: Charlesbridge.
Pallotta, J. (1991). *The ocean alphabet book.* Watertown, MA: Charlesbridge.
Pallotta, J. (1991). *The underwater alphabet book.* Watertown, MA: Charlesbridge.
Pallotta, J. (1992). *The Victory Garden vegetable alphabet book.* Watertown, MA: Charlesbridge.
Pallotta, J. (1993). *The extinct alphabet book.* Watertown, MA: Charlesbridge.
Pallotta, J. (1994). *The desert alphabet book.* Watertown, MA: Charlesbridge.
Pallotta, J. (1995). *The butterfly alphabet book.* Watertown, MA: Charlesbridge.
Pallotta, J. (1996). *The freshwater alphabet book.* Watertown, MA: Charlesbridge.
Pallotta, J. (1997). *The airplane alphabet book.* Minneapolis, MN: Econo-Clad.
Pallotta, J. (1997). *The flower alphabet book.* Watertown, MA: Charlesbridge.
Pallotta, J. (1999). *The jet alphabet book.* Watertown, MA: Charlesbridge.
Pallotta, J. (2003). *The boat alphabet book.* Watertown, MA: Charlesbridge.
Pallotta, J. (2004). *The beetle alphabet book.* Watertown, MA: Charlesbridge.
Pallotta, J. (2006). *The construction alphabet book.* Watertown, MA: Charlesbridge.
Picayo, M. (2007). *Caribbean journey from A to Y—Read and discover what happened to the Z.* New York: Campanita.
Pfister, M. (2002). *Rainbow fish A, B, C.* New York: North-South.
Reynolds, C.F. (2001). *H is for Hoosier: An Indiana alphabet.* Chelsea, MI: Sleeping Bear.
Reynolds, C.F. (2001). *L is for lobster: A Maine alphabet.* Chelsea, MI: Sleeping Bear.
Rose, D.L. (2000). *Into the A, B, sea: An ocean alphabet.* New York: Scholastic.
Schnur, S. (2002). *Winter: An alphabet acrostic.* New York: Houghton Mifflin.
Schonberg, M. (2000). *B is for buckeye: An Ohio alphabet.* Chelsea, MI: Sleeping Bear.
Scillian, D. (2001). *A is for America.* Chelsea, MI: Sleeping Bear.
Sendak, M. (1999). *Alligators all around: An alphabet.* New York: HarperCollins.
Shahan, S. (2002). *The jazzy alphabet.* New York: Penguin Putnam.
Shoulders, M. (2001). *V is for volunteer: A Tennessee alphabet.* Chelsea, MI: Sleeping Bear.
Sierra, J. (1998). *Antarctic antics.* New York: Harcourt Brace.
Slate, J. (1996). *Miss Bindergarten gets ready for kindergarten.* New York: Penguin.
Smith, R.M. (2008). *An A to Z walk in the park.* Alexandria, VA: Clarence-Henry.
Stutson, C. (1999). *Prairie primer.* New York: Puffin.
Ulmer, M. (2001). *M is for maple: A Canadian alphabet.* Chelsea, MI: Sleeping Bear.
Wargin, K. (2000). *L is for Lincoln: An Illinois alphabet.* Chelsea, MI: Sleeping Bear.
Weill, C., & Basseches, K.B. (2007). *ABeCedarios: Mexican folk art ABCs in English and Spanish.* El Paso, TX: Cinco Puntos.
Winter, J. (2004). *Calavera Abecedario: A Day of the Dead alphabet book.* Orlando, FL: Harcourt.
Wood, A. (2001). *Alphabet adventure.* New York: Scholastic.
Yolen, J. (1997). *All in the woodland early: An ABC book.* Honesdale, PA: Boyds Mills.
Young, J. (2001). *S is for show me: A Missouri alphabet.* Chelsea, MI: Sleeping Bear.

BOOKS AVAILABLE IN ENGLISH AND OTHER LANGUAGES WRITTEN BY FAVORITE AUTHORS

Eric Carle

Buckley, R., & Carle, E. (1992). *La culebra glotona* (*The greedy python*). New York: Scholastic.
Carle, E. (1994). *La oruga muy hambrienta*. New York: Philomel.
Carle, E. (1996). *La mariquita malhumorada*. New York: Harper.
Carle, E. (2002). *¿El canguro tiene mamá?* New York: HarperCollins.
Carle, E. (2003). *De la cabeza a los pies*. New York: HarperCollins.
Carle, E. (2004). *La araña muy ocupada*. New York: Philomel.
Carle, E. (2004). *Papá, por favor, consígueme la luna*. Madrid, Spain: Kókinos.
Carle, E. (2007). *10 patitos de goma*. New York: Rayo.
Carle, E. (2008). *Animals/animales: My very first bilingual book* (in English and Spanish). New York: Grosset & Dunlap.
Carle, E. (2008). *Colors/colores: My very first bilingual book* (in English and Spanish). New York: Grosset & Dunlap.
Carle, E. (2008). *El mensaje secreto de cumpleaños*. Madrid, Spain: Kókinos.
Carle, E. (2009). *El camaleón camaleónico*. Madrid, Spain: Kókinos.
Carle, E. (2009). *El grillo silencioso*. Madrid, Spain: Kókinos.
Carle, E. (2011). *El artista que pintó un caballo azul*. New York: Philomel.

Doreen Cronin

Cronin, D. (2002). *Clic clac muu: Vacas escritoras*. New York: Lectorum.
Cronin, D. (2003). *Jajá, jijí, cuac*. New York: Lectorum.
Cronin, D. (2004). *Pato para presidente*. New York: Lectorum.
Cronin, D. (2006). *Clic, clac, plif, plaf: Una aventura de contar*. New York: Lectorum.
Cronin, D. (2007). *¡A tu ritmo!* New York: Lectorum.
Cronin, D. (2007). *Dubi dubi muu*. New York: Lectorum.
Cronin, D. (2009). *Pum, cuac, muu: Une loca aventura*. New York: Lectorum.

Gail Gibbons

Gibbons, G. (1983). *Del sol a sol*. New York: Scholastic.
Gibbons, G. (1993). *Las vacas lecheras*. New York: Scholastic.
Gibbons, G. (1993). *Torres de luz: Los faros*. New York: Scholastic.

Bill Martin

Martin, B. Jr. (2000). *Oso polar, oso polar, ¿qué es ese ruido?* New York: Henry Holt.
Martin, B. Jr. (2008). *Oso pardo, oso pardo, ¿qué ves ahí?* New York: Henry Holt.

Laura Numeroff

Numeroff, L. (1985). *Si le das una galletita a un ratón*. New York: HarperCollins.
Numeroff, L. (1991). *Si le das un panecillo a un alce*. New York: HarperCollins.
Numeroff, L. (1998). *Si le das un panqueque a una cerdita*. New York: HarperCollins.
Numeroff, L. (2001). *Si llevas un ratón al cine*. New York: HarperCollins.
Numeroff, L. (2002). *Lo mejor de mamá/Lo mejor de papá*. New York: Scholastic.
Numeroff, L. (2002). *Si llevas un ratón a la escuela*. New York: Rayo.
Numeroff, L. (2006). *Si le haces una fiesta a una cerdita*. New York: Rayo.
Numeroff, L. (2008). *Si le das un panecillo a un alce*. New York: Scholastic.
Numeroff, L. (2010). *Si le das un pastelito a un gato*. New York: Scholastic.

Gary Paulsen

Paulsen, G. (1993). *Nightjohn*. New York: Delacorte.
Paulsen, G. (1993). *Sisters/Hermanas*. San Diego, CA: Harcourt Brace.
Paulsen, G. (1995). *La tortillería*. San Diego, CA: Harcourt Brace.
Paulsen, G. (1996). *El haca*. Logan, IA: Perfection Learning.
Paulsen, G. (1996). *The treasure of El Patrón*. New York: Yearling.
Paulsen, G. (1997). *Caída Libre!* New York: Albatros.
Paulsen, G. (1997). *¡Cautivos!* Buenos Aires, Argentina: Albatros.
Paulsen, G. (1997). *Proyecto—un mundo*. Buenos Aires, Argentina: Albatros.
Paulsen, G. (2011). *El hacha*. Eastsound, WA: Turtleback.

Dav Pilkey

Pilkey, D. (1999). *Dragón y el gato panzón*. Caracas, Venezuela: Ediciones Ekaré.
Pilkey, D. (2000). *Un amigo para dragón*. Caracas, Venezuela: Ediciones Ekaré.
Pilkey, D. (2001). *Hally Tosis: El horrible problema de un perro*. Barcelona, Spain: Editorial Juventud.
Pilkey, D. (2002). *El Capitán Calzoncillos y el ataque de los inodoros parlantes*. New York: Scholastic.
Pilkey, D. (2002). *El Capitán Calzoncillos y el ataque de los retretes parlantes*. New York: Scholastic en Espanol.
Pilkey, D. (2002). *El Capitán Calzoncillos y el perverso plan del Profesor Pipicaca*. New York: Scholastic.
Pilkey, D. (2002). *El Capitán Calzoncillos y la invasión de las horribles señoras del espacio sideral (y el subsiguiente asalto de las igual de horribles zombis malvados del comedor)*. New York: Scholastic en Espanol.
Pilkey, D. (2002). *El Capitán Calzoncillos y la invasión de los pérfidos tiparracos del espacio*. New York: Scholastic.
Pilkey, D. (2002). *Las aventuras del Capitán Calzoncillos*. New York: Scholastic.
Pilkey, D. (2003). *El Capitán Calzoncillos y la furia de la supermujer macroelástica*. New York: Scholastic.
Pilkey, D. (2003). *El Capitán Calzoncillos y las aventuras de superpañal*. Caracas, Venezuela: Ediciones Ekaré.
Pilkey, D. (2003). *Kat Kong*. London: Sandpiper.
Pilkey, D. (2003). *Las aventuras del superbebé pañal*. New York: Scholastic.
Pilkey, D. (2003). *Ricky Ricotta y el Poderoso Robot*. New York: Scholastic.
Pilkey, D. (2005). *El Capitán Calzoncillos y la feroz batalla contra el niño mocobiónico, 1ª parte: La noche de los mocos vivientes*. New York: Scholastic.
Pilkey, D. (2005). *El Capitán Calzoncillos y la feroz batalla contra el niño mocobiónico, 2ª parte: La venganza de los ridículos mocorobots*. New York: Scholastic.

(continued)

BOOKS AVAILABLE IN ENGLISH AND OTHER LANGUAGES WRITTEN BY FAVORITE AUTHORS (continued)

Pilkey, D. (2005). *Las aventuras del Capitán Calzoncillos y el barco de vapor.* New York: Scholastic.
Pilkey, D. (2005). *Ricky Ricotta y el poderoso robot contra los buitres vudú de Venus.* New York: Scholastic.
Pilkey, D. (2007). *Ricky Ricotta y el poderoso robot contra los meca monos de marte.* New York: Scholastic.
Pilkey, D. (2008). *El Capitán Calzoncillos y la ridícula historia de los seres del inodoro morado.* New York: Scholastic.
Pilkey, D. (2009). *Dragón y el día de Halloween.* New York: Scholastic.
Pilkey, D. (2011). *Las aventuras de Uuk y Gluk: Cavernícolas del futuro y maestros de kung fu.* New York: Scholastic.
Pilkey, D. (2012). *El Superbebé pañal 2: La invasión de los ladrones de inodoros.* New York: Scholastic.

Patricia Polacco

Polacco, P. (1997). *El pollo de los domingos.* New York: Lectorum.
Polacco, P. (1997). *Pink and say.* New York: Lectorum.
Polacco, P. (1999). *La colcha de los recuerdos.* New York: Lectorum.
Polacco, P. (2001). *Gracias, Sr. Falker.* New York: Lectorum.

Jon Scieszka

Scieszka, J. (1996). *¡La verdadera historia de los tres cerditos!* New York: Puffin.
Scieszka, J. (1997). *Verdadera tres cerditos.* Pine Plains, NY: Live Oak Media.
Scieszka, J. (1999). *El pirata barbanegra.* Barcelona, Spain: Grupo Editorial Norma.
Scieszka, J. (2000). *Los caballeros de la mesa de la cocina.* Catano, Puerto Rico: Grupo Editorial Norma.
Scieszka, J. (2001). *Tu mamá era neandertal.* Catano, Puerto Rico: Grupo Editorial Norma.
Scieszka, J. (2002). *Nos vemos, gladiador.* Catano, Puerto Rico: Grupo Editorial Norma.
Scieszka, J. (2004). *Domingo, el día del vikingo.* Catano, Puerto Rico: Grupo Editorial Norma.
Scieszka, J. (2006). *En busca de arte.* Barcelona, Spain: RBA Libros.
Scieszka, J. (2008). *¡Ay, Samuray!* Barcelona, Spain: Grupo Editorial Norma.

David Shannon

Shannon, D. (1998). *¡No, David!* New York: Blue Sky.
Shannon, D. (2002). *Pat ova en bici.* New York: Lectorum.
Shannon, D. (2002). *Un caso grave de rayas.* New York: Scholastic.
Shannon, D. (2004). *Alicia, el hada.* New York: Scholastic.
Shannon, D. (2004). *David se mete en líos.* New York: Scholastic.
Shannon, D. (2005). *¡David Huele! David en pañales.* New York: Scholastic.
Shannon, D. (2005). *¡Huy! David en pañales.* New York: Scholastic.
Shannon, D. (2005). *¡Oh David! David en pañales.* New York: Scholastic.
Shannon, D. (2010). *¡Llegó la navidad, David!* New York: Scholastic.

Shel Silverstein

Silverstein, S. (1998). *Lafcadio: El león que devolvió el disparo.* Anaheim, CA: Lumen.
Silverstein, S. (2000). *Batacazos: Poemas para reírse.* Caracas, Venezuela: Ediciones Ekaré.
Silverstein, S. (2000). *La parte que falta.* Buenos Aires, Argentina: Editorial Sirio.
Silverstein, S. (2000). *La parte que falta conoce ala o grande.* New York: Lectorum.
Silverstein, S. (2002). *El árbol generoso.* New York: Lectorum.
Silverstein, S. (2002). *¿Quién quiere un rinoceronte barato?* Barcelona, Spain: Editorial Lumen.
Silverstein, S. (2005). *Donde el camino se corta: Nuevos poemas para reírse.* Caracas, Venezuela: Ediciones Ekaré.
Silverstein, S. (2006). *Hay luz en el desván.* New York: Lectorum.
Silverstein, S. (2010). *La parte que falta.* New York: Lectorum.

Seymour Simon

Simon, S. (2004). *Tiburones.* San Francisco: Chronicle.
Simon, S. (2006). *Aeronaves asombrosas.* San Francisco: Chronicle.
Simon, S. (2006). *Ballenas asesinas.* San Francisco: Chronicle.
Simon, S. (2006). *Pirámides y momias.* San Francisco: Chronicle.
Simon, S. (2006). *Tiburones fabulosos.* San Francisco: Chronicle.
Simon, S. (2007). *Los planetas alrededor del sol.* San Francisco: Chronicle.
Simon, S. (2007). *Tormentas increíbles.* San Francisco: Chronicle.

Chris Van Allsburg

Van Allsburg, C. (1995). *El expreso polar.* Caracas, Venezuela: Ediciones Ekaré.
Van Allsburg, C. (1995). *Jumanji.* San Diego, CA: Fondo de Cultura Económica.
Van Allsburg, C. (1996). *Los misterios del Señor Burdick.* San Diego, CA: Fondo de Cultura Económica.
Van Allsburg, C. (1997). *El higo más dulce.* San Diego, CA: Fondo de Cultura Económica.
Van Allsburg, C. (1999). *La escoba de la viuda.* San Diego, CA: Fondo de Cultura Económica.
Van Allsburg, C. (2000). *Mal día en Río Seco.* San Diego, CA: Fondo de Cultura Económica.
Van Allsburg, C. (2007). *El naufragio del Zéfiro.* New York: Lectorum.

CENTER CHART FOR STUDENTS

Center: ______________________________ Week: ______________________

Directions: If you used this center, sign your name and place a check mark underneath the day you visited.

Students	Monday	Tuesday	Wednesday	Thursday	Friday

CENTER PLANNER

Theme:____

Center Title: ____________________________________

Format: ____Display Board ____Pizza Box ____Folder

Schedule: ____Wall Chart ____Rotation ____Free Choice

Accountability:

Assessment: ___Review Strategy Applications

___Student Self-Assessments

___Other:____________________________

Recordkeeping: ___Guided Comprehension Profiles

___Center Folders

___Other:____________________________

Materials:

Texts:____________________________________

____

Supplies: __________________________________

____

Sample Activity:________________________________

____

____

____

____

CENTER REFLECTIONS

Name: ______________________________ Date: ______________________

Center: ____

1. While I was working at this center, I was able to

____

____

____

2. I learned

____

____

____

3. The next time I plan to

____

____

____

____

CENTER RUBRIC

Name: ______________________________ Date: ______________________

Center: ____

Directions: Think about what you did at the center today. Then use this rubric to describe your performance.

	Minimal 1	Satisfactory 2	Good 3	Excellent 4
My work is complete.	1	2	3	4
I followed the directions.	1	2	3	4
I understood what I did.	1	2	3	4
My presentation is appealing.	1	2	3	4
I made connections that are supported by the text.	1	2	3	4
I used multiple modes of response.	1	2	3	4

Comments:

____

____

____

____

____

CENTER STUDENT SELF-ASSESSMENT

Name: ______________________________ Date: ______________________

Center: ____

1. My goal was

____

____

____

2. I know I reached my goal because

____

____

____

3. My new goal is

____

____

____

CHOOSE YOUR OWN PROJECT

Name: ______________________ Date: ______________

You may work with a partner to do this. Choose a project and follow the directions in the folder.

1. Write a new ending for the story.
2. Make a story collage.
3. Make a character mobile.
4. Create an advertisement for a book.
5. Write a trifold report.
6. Survey the class about authors/books.
7. Make a character puppet.
8. Make a picture collage.
9. Put the characters in a new story.
10. Create a book jacket.
11. Interview a classmate.
12. Write a Lyric Summary and sing it.

CLASS CENTER CHART FOR TEACHERS

Centers					
Students					

CROSS-AGE READING EXPERIENCE SELF-ASSESSMENT

Name: ______________________________ Date: ____________________

Text: ____

1. What is one thing you did to prepare for the Cross-Age Reading Experience that was helpful?

____

____

____

2. What is something you learned in your Cross-Age Reading Experience?

____

____

____

3. How would you rate your Cross-Age Reading Experience?

   great good poor

4. How helpful was today's Cross-Age Reading Experience?

   very helpful somewhat helpful not helpful

5. What will you do to improve your next Cross-Age Reading Experience time?

____

____

____

____

____

CULTURALLY RELEVANT CHILDREN'S LITERATURE

Altman, L.J. (1995). *Amelia's road.* New York: Lee & Low.
Altman, L.J. (2003). *The legend of Freedom Hill.* New York: Lee & Low.
Barasch, L. (2009). *First come the zebra.* New York: Lee & Low.
Burrowes, A.J. (2008). *Grandma's purple flowers.* New York: Lee & Low.
Chinn, K. (1997). *Sam and the lucky money.* New York: Lee & Low.
Cooper, M. (2000). *Gettin' through Thursday.* New York: Lee & Low.
Demi. (2006). *Su Dongpo: Chinese genius.* New York: Lee & Low.
Derby, S. (2008). *No mush today.* New York: Lee & Low.
Elliott, Z. (2008). *Bird.* New York: Lee & Low.
Fine, E.H. (2002). *Under the lemon moon.* New York: Lee & Low.
Fine, E.H., & Josephson, J.P. (2007). *Armando and the blue tarp school.* New York: Lee & Low.
Greenfield, E. (2009). *Paul Robeson.* New York: Lee & Low.
Hale, C. (2009). *The East-West House: Noguchi's childhood in Japan.* New York: Lee & Low.
Hubbard, C. (2008). *The last Black King of the Kentucky Derby: The story of Jimmy Winkfield.* New York: Lee & Low.
Johnson, J.C. (2010). *Seeds of change.* New York: Lee & Low.
Krishnaswami, U. (2007). *Bringing Asha home.* New York: Lee & Low.
Lewin, T., & Lewin, B. (2009). *Balarama: A royal elephant.* New York: Lee & Low.
Louie, T.O. (2006). *Raymond's perfect present.* New York: Lee & Low.
Malaspina, A. (2010). *Yasmin's hammer.* New York: Lee & Low.
Marx, T. (2008). *Everglades forever: Restoring America's great wetland.* New York: Lee & Low.
Marx, T. (2010). *Sharing our homeland: Palestinian and Jewish children at summer peace camp.* New York: Lee & Low.
Medina, T. (2003). *DeShawn days.* New York: Lee & Low.
Medina, T. (2006). *Love to Langston.* New York: Lee & Low.
Miller, W. (1999). *Richard Wright and the library card.* New York: Lee & Low.
Mochizuki, K. (1995). *Baseball saved us.* New York: Lee & Low.
Mora, P. (2009). *Gracias/thanks* (English and Spanish edition). New York: Lee & Low.
Nikola-Lisa, W. (2009). *How we are smart.* New York: Lee & Low.
Reynolds, J. (2009). *Cycle of rice, cycle of life: A story of unsustainable farming.* New York: Lee & Low.
Reynolds, J. (2010). *Celebrate! Connections among cultures.* New York: Lee & Low.
Russell, C.Y. (2009). *Tofu quilt.* New York: Lee & Low.
Schroeder, A. (2009). *In her hands: The story of sculptor Augusta Savage.* New York: Lee & Low.
Steptoe, J. (2001). *In daddy's arms I am tall: African Americans celebrating fathers.* New York: Lee & Low.
Tarpley, N.A. (2004). *Destiny's gift.* New York: Lee & Low.
Taylor, G. (2006). *George Crum and the Saratoga Chip.* New York: Lee & Low.
Vaughan, M. (2005). *The secret to freedom.* New York: Lee & Low.
Vaughan, M. (2009). *Up the learning tree.* New York: Lee & Low.
Watts, J.H. (2000). *Keepers.* New York: Lee & Low.
Weston, M. (2008). *Honda: The boy who dreamed of cars.* New York: Lee & Low.
Wise, B. (2009). *Louis Sockalexis: Native American baseball pioneer.* New York: Lee & Low.
Wolf, B. (2003). *Coming to America: A Muslim family's story.* New York: Lee & Low.
Yoo, P. (2009). *Shining star: The Anna May Wong story.* New York: Lee & Low.

Source: Compiled by Rhonda M. Sutton, East Stroudsburg University of Pennsylvania.

DIRECTIONS FOR MAKING BOOKS

Slotted Book

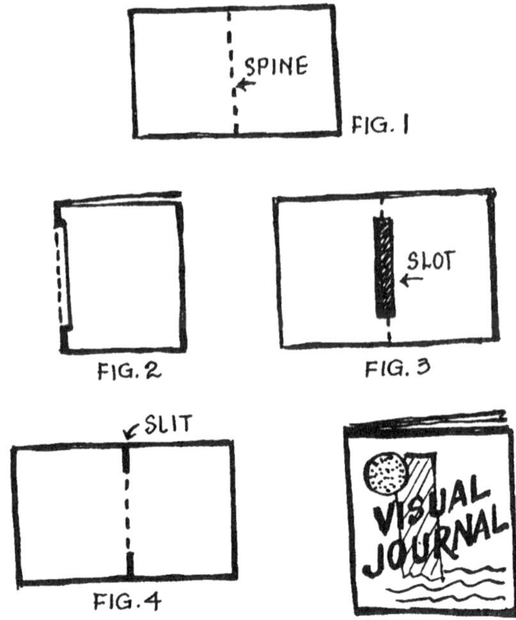

STEP 1: Take at least two pieces of paper and hold them in a landscape (horizontal) position (Fig. 1). You can use more than two pages to create books with more than four pages.

STEP 2—MAKING THE SLOT: Separate one page from the pack of papers. Make sure the fold or SPINE is nice and flat. Measure 1-1/2 inches from the top of the spine and make a mark and do the same at the bottom of the page of the spine.

Cut into the spine and carefully cut away the spine between the marks you have made. Only cut into the spine about 1/16 of an inch (Fig. 2). Open your page and you should see a SLOT (Fig. 3).

STEP 3—MAKING THE SLITS: Take the other page(s) and make sure the spine is nice and flat. Measure the same 1-1/2 inches from the top and bottom of the spine.

This time cut from the bottom of the page up to the mark to create a SLIT. Repeat the process at the top of the page. You should have a SLIT at the top and bottom of the page (Fig. 4).

STEP 4—SLIPPING THE BOOK TOGETHER: Open the slotted page. Take the other page(s) with slits and bend them in half horizontally. SLIP them through the slot until you have reached the center of the book. Carefully slip the slit and slot together and roll the pages open and fold it like a book.

Source: Pinciotti, P. (2001). *Book arts: The creation of beautiful books*. East Stroudsburg: East Stroudsburg University of Pennsylvania.

DIRECTIONS FOR MAKING BOOKS

Dos à Dos Dialogue Journals

Dos à dos is a French expression meaning a couch or a carriage that holds two people sitting back to back. When two people sit back to back, they see different things or they see the same thing from different points of view. This book is really two books in one (or three or more–you decide). There is room for each person's point of view or story. Dos à dos can be a wonderful way to structure a dialogue journal where you and another person write back and forth to each other. Each person has his or her own book and in turn responds to the others' ideas, questions, and feelings. Turn them around and read each other's response!

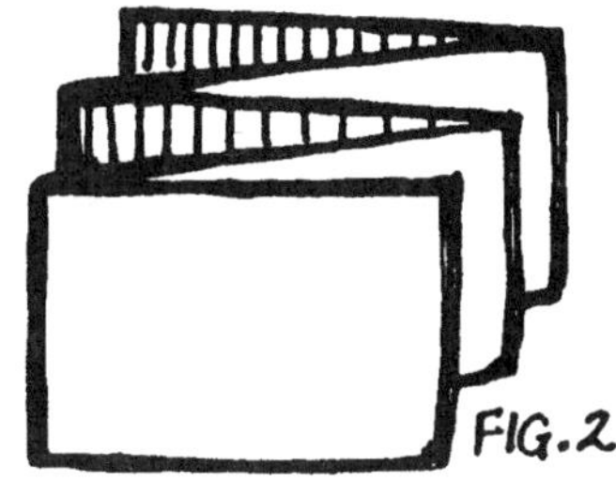

STEP 1: For a two-part dos à dos, take a piece of 11 × 17 paper and cut it lengthwise in half (5-1/2 inches). Take one strip and fold into three equal parts. It should look like a Z (Fig. 1).

STEP 2: Cut all the text pages so they are 8 × 5-1/2 inches. Fold them in half and divide them to create two booklets or signatures with equal pages.

STEP 3: Slip a signature into the first fold. The crease of the signature or booklet should be nested inside the crease of the cover. You can either staple the signature into the cover or sew the signature into the cover. The simplest way is to staple the booklet in by using a book arm stapler that lets you staple deep into the center of the signature.

STEP 4: Repeat step 3 for the other signature, nesting it in the other crease.

STEP 5: Fold the book back and forth so that you can open one signature from the front and one from the back.

STEP 6–DECORATE THE COVERS: Consider these wild variations! As with any book, you can change the shape, size, and materials of this book. Make a dos à dos dialogue journal for three or four people (Fig. 2). Just make an extra long cover or paste together two of them. What an interesting conversation you could have!

Try different types of text pages. If you need some extra long pages, cut some text pages longer than the others, and make fold outs. Cut some pages taller than others and make fold downs. Add some pop-ups.

Source: Pinciotti, P. (2001). *Book arts: The creation of beautiful books*. East Stroudsburg: East Stroudsburg University of Pennsylvania.

DIRECTIONS FOR MAKING BOOKS

Basic Origami Book

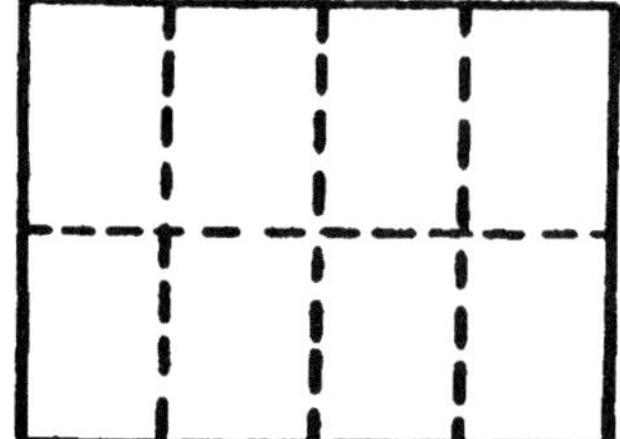

1. Fold an A4 piece of paper into eight equal parts. Lay flat in the landscape position.

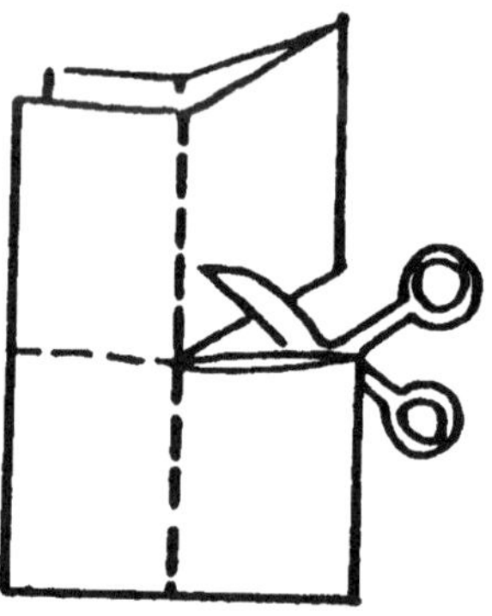

2. Fold in half vertically and cut from the folded edge to the center with scissors.

3. Open out, then fold horizontally. Push left and right ends to center.

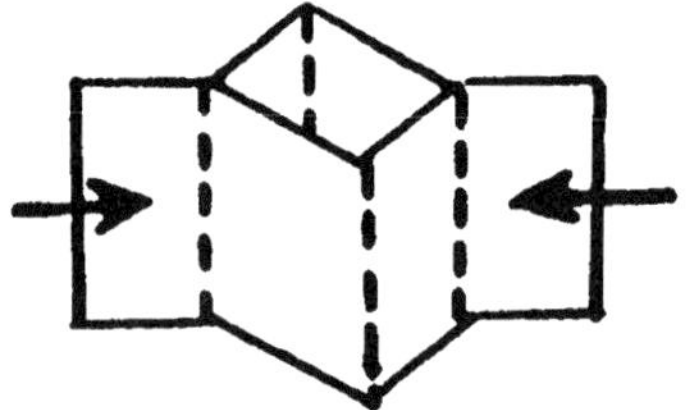

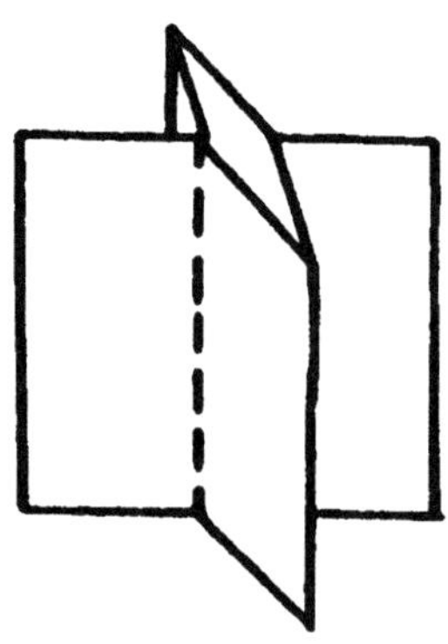

4. Fold around to form a book with six art/writing pages and a front and back cover.

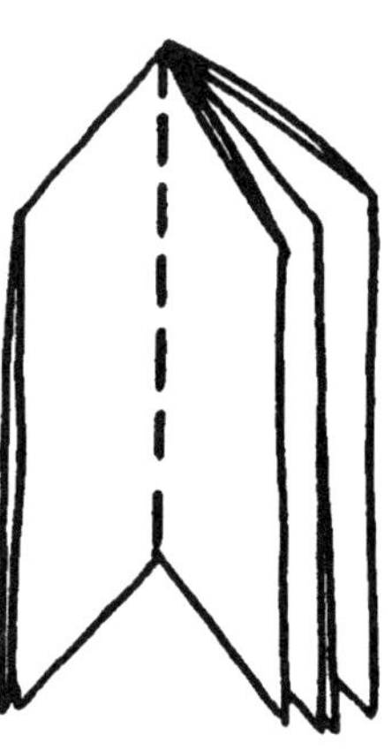

Source: Pinciotti, P. (2001). *Book arts: The creation of beautiful books.* East Stroudsburg: East Stroudsburg University of Pennsylvania.

GROUP REFLECTION SHEET

Name:______________________________ Date:______________________

1. How did your group do today?______________________________________

____

____

2. What did you do to help your group?_______________________________

____

____

3. What did the others do to help the group?__________________________

____

____

4. What will your group do to improve next time?______________________

____

____

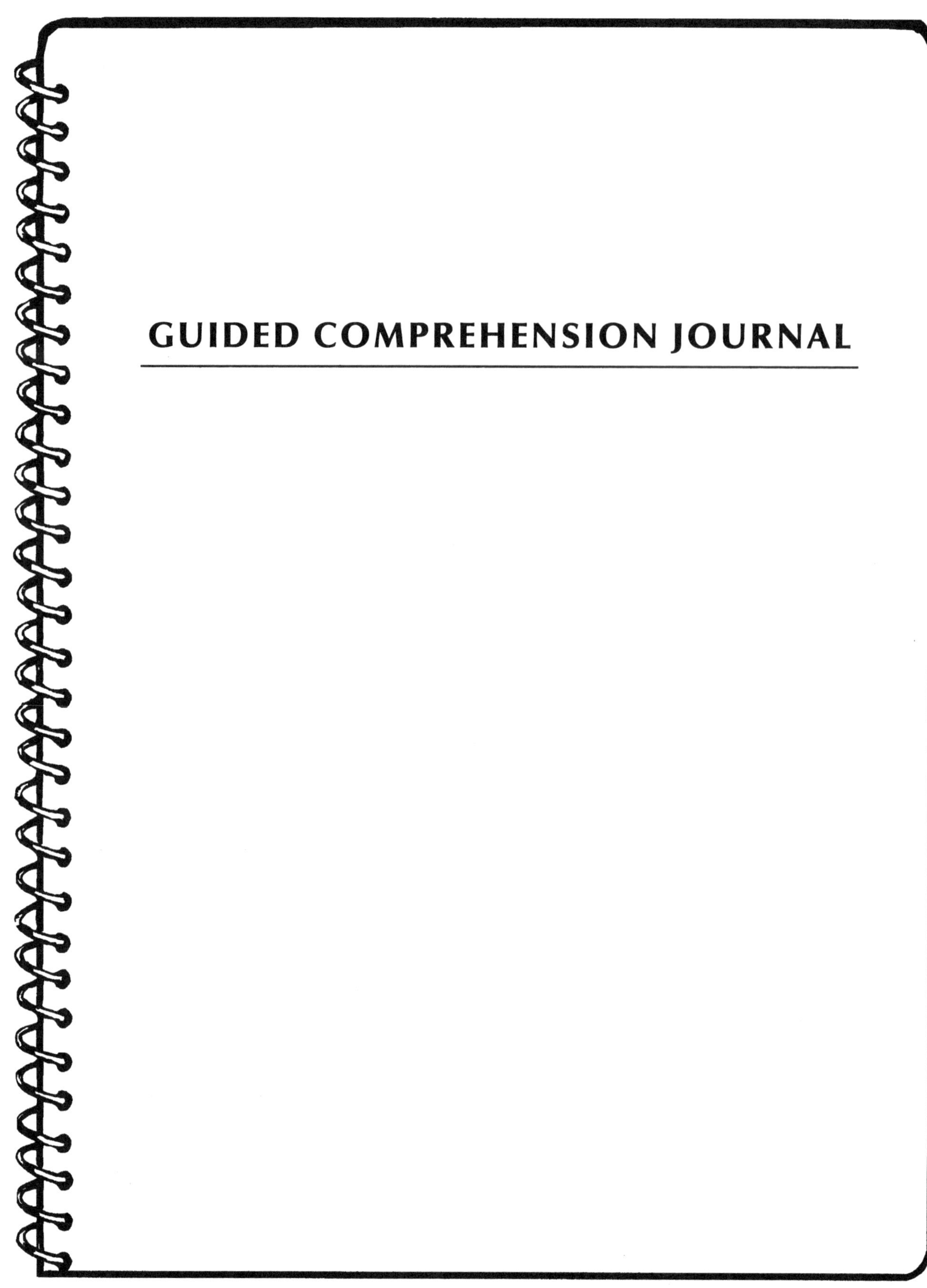
GUIDED COMPREHENSION JOURNAL

"IF I WERE IN CHARGE OF THE WORLD"

If I Were in Charge of____________________________________

by ____

If I were in charge of ____________________________, I'd cancel

____,

____,

____, and also

____.

If I were in charge of __________________________________,
There'd be ____,
____, and
____.

If I were in charge of __________________________________,
You wouldn't have ___________________________________
You wouldn't have ___________________________________
You wouldn't have ___________________________________
Or ____
You wouldn't even have _______________________________

If I were in charge of __________________________________,
____
____
And a person ______________________________________
And ____
Would still be allowed to be in charge of the world.

Source: Adapted from Viorst, J. (1981). *If I were in charge of the world and other worries.* New York: Atheneum.

LITERATURE CIRCLE BOOKMARK

LITERATURE CIRCLE BOOKMARK

Name: ____________________

Date: ____________________

1. I will talk to my group about...

2. I will ask my group about...

3. My favorite part was...

LITERATURE CIRCLE BOOKMARK

Name: ____________________

Date: ____________________

1. I will talk to my group about...

2. I will ask my group about...

3. My favorite part was...

LITERATURE CIRCLE GROUP ASSESSMENT

Group Members

________________________ ________________________

________________________ ________________________

________________________ ________________________

4 = Great 3 = Good 2 = Fair 1 = Poor

1. My group worked well together. ____________
2. My group used its time wisely. ____________
3. I did my best work. ____________
4. I think my group deserves a ____________

Student Comments:

Teacher Comments:

LITERATURE CIRCLE SELF-ASSESSMENT

Name: ______________________________ Date: ____________________

Text: ____

1. What did you do to prepare for the Literature Circle that was helpful?

____

____

____

2. What is something you learned in your Literature Circle?

____

____

____

3. How would you rate your group's Literature Circle?

   great   good   poor

4. How helpful was today's discussion?

   very helpful   somewhat helpful   not helpful

5. What will you do to improve next time?

____

____

____

MAKING AND WRITING WORDS

Name: ______________________________ Date: ____________________

How many words can you make from the word ________________?

Two-letter words:

___ ___ ___ ___ ___ ___ ___ ___ ___ ___

Three-letter words:

______________________________ ______________________________

______________________________ ______________________________

______________________________ ______________________________

Four-letter words:

______________________________ ______________________________

______________________________ ______________________________

______________________________ ______________________________

Longer words:

______________________________ ______________________________

______________________________ ______________________________

______________________________ ______________________________

Source: Adapted from Rasinski, T.V. (1999). Making and writing words using letter patterns. *Reading Online* [Online]. Available: www.readingonline.org/articles/words/rasinski_index.html

MAKING AND WRITING WORDS

Name: ______________________________ Date: __________________

Directions: Use the vowels and consonants provided to make words based on the clues given by the teacher.

Vowels	Consonants

Directions: Listen carefully as your teacher or classmate provides clues to words that you will write in each box.

1.	5.
2.	6.
3.	7.
4.	8.

Source: Adapted from Rasinski, T.V. (1999). Making and writing words using letter patterns. *Reading Online* [Online]. Available: www.readingonline.org/articles/words/rasinski_index.html

MANAGING STAGE THREE

OPTION 1: Participation Chart

Student	Session 1	Session 2

OPTION 2: Center Rotation Chart

Group	Center ____	____	____	____
Blue	1	2	3	4
Green	2	3	4	1
Red	3	4	1	2
Yellow	4	1	2	3

POETRY FORM

Name: ______________________ Date: ______________________

Acrostic Poem

______ ______________________

______ ______________________

______ ______________________

______ ______________________

______ ______________________

______ ______________________

______ ______________________

______ ______________________

______ ______________________

______ ______________________

______ ______________________

POETRY FORM

Name: ______________________________ Date: ______________________

Cinquain

____

one word–noun

__________________ __________________

two adjectives describing line one

__________________ __________________ __________________

three -ing words telling actions of line one

_______________ _______________ _______________ _______________

four-word phrase describing a feeling related to line one

____

one word–synonym or reference to line one

POETRY FORM

Name: ______________________________ Date: ______________________

Diamante

____

subject–one noun

__________________ __________________

two adjectives describing the subject

__________________ __________________ __________________

three participles (-ing) telling about the subject

________________ ________________ ________________ ________________

four nouns–first two relate to the subject,
last two relate to the opposite

__________________ __________________ __________________

three participles (-ing) telling about the opposite

__________________ __________________

two adjectives describing the opposite

____

opposite of subject–one noun

POETRY FORM

Name: ______________________________ Date: ______________________

Bio-Poem

Line 1 – First name ______________________________

Line 2 – Four traits that describe #1 ______________________________

____

Line 3 – Related to/sibling of ______________________________

Line 4 – Cares about/likes ______________________________

Line 5 – Who feels ______________________________

Line 6 – Who needs ______________________________

Line 7 – Who gives ______________________________

Line 8 – Who fears ______________________________

Line 9 – Who would like to see ______________________________

Line 10 – Resident of ______________________________

Line 11 – Last name ______________________________

POETRY FORM

Name: ______________________________ Date: ______________________

Definition Poem

What is ____? (topic)

____
Description of topic

____
Description of topic

____
Description of topic

____
Description of topic

____
Description of topic

____
Description of topic

____
Description of topic

That is ____! (topic)

PRESS CONFERENCE SUMMARY

Name: ______________________________ Date: ________________________

Topic: ____

____

What I read: ____

____

What I learned: ____

____

____

What I will tell the class: ____

____

____

____

____

____

____

QUICK CLOUD

Name: ______________________________ Date: ______________________

This is what I was thinking while I was reading.

RECIPROCAL TEACHING BOOKMARKS

Name: ___________________________

Date: ___________________________

Title: ___________________________

Pages: ___________________________

Make a prediction about what might happen next in the text.

My prediction is...

____

____

____

I think this because...

____

____

____

Prediction Prompts–

I think...	I predict...
I bet...	I anticipate...
I wonder...	I hypothesize...
I imagine...	Based on...I predict...
I suppose...	

Name: ___________________________

Date: ___________________________

Title: ___________________________

Pages: ___________________________

Create questions that help to identify important information and connect prior knowledge with new ideas.

Questions:

1. ___________________________

____

2. ___________________________

____

3. ___________________________

____

Question Prompts–

Who is...?	What if...?
Where...?	I wonder how...?
When...?	Which is better...? Why?
What...?	Why did...?
How...?	What is your opinion...?
Why is...?	Why?

RECIPROCAL TEACHING BOOKMARKS

Name: ______________________

Date: ______________________

Title: ______________________

Pages: ______________________

Identify words or concepts that are difficult to understand. Share how you figured it out.

Word or concept:

____

I figured it out by...

____

____

Word or concept:

____

I figured it out by...

____

____

Clarifying Prompts–

I did not understand...

The confusing part was...

I need to know more about...

A difficult word/phrase is...

Name: ______________________

Date: ______________________

Title: ______________________

Pages: ______________________

Identify the key ideas and summarize them.

Key ideas:

1. ______________________

2. ______________________

3. ______________________

Summary:

____

____

Summary Prompts–

The important ideas so far...

New facts I have learned...

The main character(s) is...

The problem is...

The important story events are...

RECIPROCAL TEACHING SELF-ASSESSMENT

Name: ______________________________ Date: _______________________

Text: ____

1. How would you rate your participation in Reciprocal Teaching?

   just right   too much   too little   not at all

2. What is the main message of the text?

   ____

   ____

   ____

3. How would you rate your group's Reciprocal Teaching?

   great   good   poor

4. How helpful was today's session?

   very helpful   somewhat helpful   not helpful

5. What will you do to improve next time?

   ____

   ____

   ____

   ____

REQUIRED AND OPTIONAL CENTER AND ACTIVITY FORM

Name: ______________________________ Date: __________

	Centers	Monday	Tuesday	Wednesday	Thursday	Friday
D						
D						
W						
W						
W						
W						
W	My Choice: __________					
W	My Choice: __________					

Mark the day with an X when you visit that center.
D = visit center daily; W = visit center weekly

STORY TRIFOLD

Name: ______________________ Date: ______________

Beginning	Middle	End

WRITE YOUR OWN MYSTERY

Name: ______________________ Date: ____________

1. Draw, describe, or explain the crime scene.

2. Write two clues that are in your mystery.

____

____

____

3. Choose the detective, a suspect, or a victim and write two words to describe that character.

Character: ______________________

1. Word: ______________________

2. Word: ______________________

4. Describe how the mystery was or will be solved.

____

____

____

APPENDIX C

Assessment Blackline Masters

ATTITUDE SURVEY 1

Name: ______________________ Date: ________________

1. I think reading is ______________________________

   because ______________________________.

2. I think I am a ______________________ reader

   because ______________________________.

3. I think ______________________ is a good reader because

   ______________________________.

4. I think writing is ______________________________

   because ______________________________.

5. I think I am a ________ writer because ______________

   ______________________________.

6. I think ______________________ is a good writer because

   ______________________________.

ATTITUDE SURVEY 2

Name: ______________________________ Date: ________________________

Directions: Please place a check under the category that best describes your response.

Y = Yes
N = No

	Y	N
1. I read in my free time.	_____	_____
2. I like to receive books as gifts.	_____	_____
3. I like to choose what I read.	_____	_____
4. Reading is a rainy-day activity I enjoy.	_____	_____
5. I would rather read than watch television.	_____	_____
6. I keep a journal.	_____	_____
7. I like to write to my friends.	_____	_____
8. I like to write in school.	_____	_____
9. I use my computer to write.	_____	_____
10. I often revise my writing to make it better.	_____	_____

CLASSROOM READING MISCUE ASSESSMENT

Reader's Name ________________________ Date ________________
Grade Level ________________________ Teacher ________________
Selection Read ______________________________________

I. What percent of the sentences read make sense? — Sentence by sentence tally — Total

____ Number of semantically acceptable sentences

____ Number of semantically unacceptable sentences

____ % Comprehending score:

$$\frac{\text{Number of semantically acceptable sentences}}{\text{Total number of sentences read}} \times 100 \text{ TOTAL } \_\_\_\_$$

	Seldom	Sometimes	Often	Usually	Always
II. In what ways is reader constructing meaning?					
A. Recognizes when miscues have disrupted meaning	1	2	3	4	5
B. Logically substitutes	1	2	3	4	5
C. Self-corrects errors that disrupt meaning	1	2	3	4	5
D. Uses picture and/or other visual clues	1	2	3	4	5
In what ways is reader disrupting meaning?					
A. Substitutes words that don't make sense	1	2	3	4	5
B. Makes omissions that disrupt meaning	1	2	3	4	5
C. Relies too heavily on graphic clues	1	2	3	4	5
III. If narrative text is used:	No		Partial		Yes
A. Character recall	1	2	3	4	5
B. Character development	1	2	3	4	5
C. Setting	1	2	3	4	5
D. Relationship of events	1	2	3	4	5
E. Plot	1	2	3	4	5
F. Theme	1	2	3	4	5
G. Overall retelling	1	2	3	4	5
If expository text is used:	No		Partial		Yes
A. Major concepts	1	2	3	4	5
B. Generalizations	1	2	3	4	5
C. Specific information	1	2	3	4	5
D. Logical structuring	1	2	3	4	5
E. Overall retelling	1	2	3	4	5

Source: Adapted from Rhodes, L.K., Shanklin, N.L., & Valencia, S.W. (1990). Miscue analysis in the classroom. *The Reading Teacher, 44,* 252–254.

GUIDED COMPREHENSION PROFILE SUMMARY SHEET

Student: ______________________ Grade: _______ School Year: ________

Summary of Background Information:

Student's Interests:

Reading Levels:	September	December	March	June
Independent				
Guided				
Strategy Use:				
Previewing				
Self-Questioning				
Making Connections				
Visualizing				
Knowing How Words Work				
Monitoring				
Summarizing				
Evaluating				

Not Observed (NO) – Student does not use the strategy.
Emerging (E) – Student attempts to use the strategy.
Developing (D) – Student is using the strategy on some occasions.
Consistent (C) – Student effectively uses the strategy to make meaning from text.

Comments:

INTEREST INVENTORY 1

Name: ______________________ Date: ______________

1. What is your favorite school subject? Why do you like it? ________

2. What is your favorite book? Why do you like it? ________

3. Do you go to the library? Do you have a library card? ________

4. Who is your favorite author? Why? ________

5. What is a dream or wish you have? ________

6. What do you like to do after school? ________

7. If you had a day off from school, how would you spend the day?

8. What magazine do you like to read? ________

9. If you could meet any famous person, whom would you choose? What would you like to talk about? ________

10. If you could receive any book as a gift, what kind of book would you choose? ________

INTEREST INVENTORY 2

Name: ______________________________ Date: ____________________

1. What is one of your hobbies? What do you like about it? __________

____

2. If you could plan an afternoon to do anything you wanted to do, what would you do? ____

____

3. What kinds of things do you like to draw? ______________________

____

4. What is your favorite food? ___________________________________

____

5. What is your favorite kind of music? Favorite song? Favorite group? What do you like about it (them)? ______________________________

____

6. What is your favorite television show? Why do you like it? _________

____

7. Do you like to read to someone at home? Do you like it when someone reads to you? ____

____

8. If you could choose a book about any topic that someone would read to you, what would it be? ______________________________________

____

LITERACY HISTORY PROMPTS

To learn about your students' literacy experiences, you may wish to have them create their literacy histories. The following prompts will facilitate this process. Having the students illustrate their experiences or provide photos related to their experiences enhances their histories. Be sure to demonstrate this activity by sharing this part of your literacy history as a model for the class.

1. What was your favorite book before you came to school?
2. What was your favorite memory of having someone read to you when you were younger?
3. Can you remember a sign you could read at a young age (McDonald's, Burger King, Toys "R" Us, supermarket, etc.)? What do you remember about that experience?
4. Did you ever read to your stuffed animals, dolls, or younger brothers and sisters? What do you remember about those experiences?
5. What was the first thing you ever wrote (crayon scribbles on a wall, writing in a tablet, note to parents, thank-you note, etc.)? What do you remember about that experience?
6. What was the first book that you read? What do you remember about that experience?
7. What was the first thing you wrote that you were really proud of?
8. What book are you reading outside of school now? Why did you choose to read it?
9. What are some things you are writing outside of school now?
10. Do you and your friends talk about what you read? What is something you would tell them about a book you read recently?
11. Do you think you are a good reader now? Do you plan to continue reading as you get older?
12. Do you think you are a good writer now? Do you plan to continue writing as you get older?

MOTIVATION TO READ PROFILE CONVERSATIONAL INTERVIEW

Student:____________________________Date:________________________

A. Emphasis: Narrative text

Suggested prompt (designed to engage student in a natural conversation): I have been reading a good book...I was talking with...about it last night. I enjoy talking about good stories and books that I've been reading. Today I'd like to hear about what you have been reading.

1. Tell me about the most interesting story or book you have read this week (or even last week). Take a few minutes to think about it. (Wait time.) Now, tell me about the book or story.

Probes: What else can you tell me? Is there anything else? __________________

2. How did you know or find out about this story?________________________

- ☐ assigned
- ☐ chosen
- ☐ in school
- ☐ out of school

3. Why was this story interesting to you? ________________________________

(continued)

Source: Gambrell, L.B., Palmer, B.M., Codling, R.M., & Mazzoni, S.A. (1996). Assessing motivation to read. *The Reading Teacher, 49*, 518–533.

MOTIVATION TO READ PROFILE CONVERSATIONAL INTERVIEW (continued)

B. Emphasis: Informational text

Suggested prompt (designed to engage student in a natural conversation): Often we read to find out about something or to learn about something. We read for information. For example, I remember a student of mine...who read a lot of books about...to find out as much as he/she could about.... Now, I'd like to hear about some of the informational reading you have been doing.

1. Think about something important that you learned recently, not from your teacher and not from television, but from a book or some other reading material. What did you read about? (Wait time.) Tell me about what you learned.

Probes: What else could you tell me? Is there anything else? ________________

____

____

____

2. How did you know or find out about this book/article? ________________

____

____

☐ assigned ☐ in school
☐ chosen ☐ out of school

3. Why was this book (or article) important to you?____________________

____

____

____

____

(continued)

Source: Gambrell, L.B., Palmer, B.M., Codling, R.M., & Mazzoni, S.A. (1996). Assessing motivation to read. *The Reading Teacher, 49,* 518–533.

MOTIVATION TO READ PROFILE CONVERSATIONAL INTERVIEW (continued)

C. Emphasis: General reading

1. Did you read anything at home yesterday? ______What?

____

____

2. Do you have any books at school (in your desk/storage area/locker/book bag) today that you are reading? ______Tell me about them.

____

____

3. Tell me about your favorite author.

____

____

4. What do you think you have to learn to be a better reader?

____

____

5. Do you know about any books right now that you'd like to read? Tell me about them.

____

____

6. How did you find out about these books?

____

____

7. What are some things that get you really excited about reading books?

____

____

8. Tell me about...

____

____

9. Who gets you really interested and excited about reading books?

____

____

10. Tell me more about what they do.

____

____

Source: Gambrell, L.B., Palmer, B.M., Codling, R.M., & Mazzoni, S.A. (1996). Assessing motivation to read. *The Reading Teacher, 49*, 518–533.

CROSS-AGE READING EXPERIENCE OBSERVATION

Student:______________________________Date:________________

Directions: Place a check if the behavior is observed.

Observation:

1. Student was prepared for the Cross-Age Reading Experience. _____
2. Student welcomed his or her cross-age reading buddy. _____
3. Student(s) self-selected an appropriate text from the book basket. _____
4. Student focused on the task. _____
5. Student actively engaged in reading. _____
6. Student successfully engaged in strategy application. _____
7. Student engaged in meaningful discussion. _____
8. Student was competent in his or her role. _____
9. Student's contributions demonstrated depth of understanding. _____
10. Student respected ideas of others involved in the experience. _____

Student's self-evaluation indicated ____________________________

____

____

____

Notes: ____

____

____

____

____

LITERATURE CIRCLE OBSERVATION

Student:______________________________Date:_______________

Directions: Place a check if the behavior is observed.

Observation:

1. Student was prepared for the Literature Circle. _____
2. Student was focused on the group task. _____
3. Student engaged in discussion. _____
   Talk focused on the content of the book. _____
   Talk focused on the reading process. _____
   Talk focused on personal connections. _____
   Talk focused on the group process. _____
4. Student was competent in his or her discussion role. _____
5. Student's contributions demonstrated depth of understanding. _____
6. Student respected ideas of other group members. _____

Student's self-evaluation indicated ____________________________

____

____

____

____

Notes: ____

____

____

____

____

RECIPROCAL TEACHING OBSERVATION

Student:______________________________ Date: ________________

Directions: Place a check if the behavior is observed.

Observation:

1. Student was prepared for Reciprocal Teaching. ____
2. Student was focused on the group task. ____
3. Student was actively engaged in Reciprocal Teaching. ____
4. Student successfully engaged in prediction. ____
5. Student successfully generated meaningful questions. ____
6. Student successfully clarified meaning. ____
7. Student successfully summarized text. ____
8. Student used strategy prompts. ____
9. Student's contributions demonstrated depth of understanding. ____
10. Student respected ideas of other group members. ____

Student's self-evaluation indicated ____________________________

____

____

____

____

Notes: ____

____

____

____

____

PEER INTERVIEW

Family

1. Please tell about your family. Share photos, if possible.

2. When did your family come to the United States? What country did your family come from?

Education

3. What do you like most about school? Why do you like it?

4. If you could change one thing about school, what would it be? Why would you want to change it?

Special Interests

5. How do you use technology in your life (computers, cell phones, digital cameras)?

6. Do you like music? What is your favorite band? What do you like about it?

7. Do you watch television? What is your favorite television program? What do you like about it?

8. What do you like to do when we are not in school?

STUDENT SELF-REFLECTION AND GOAL SETTING

Name: ____________________________ Date: ____________________

Hobby or Special Interest

This activity is designed to help you reflect on one of your hobbies or special interests. Remember that self-reflection involves thinking about what you did, how well you did it, and what you can do to make it better next time. To begin your reflection, focus on your hobby or special interest. Then think about the last time you did it. How well did it go? What is one thing you can do to improve it next time? What is your new goal?

1. My hobby or special interest is ______________________________

____

2. Something I learned to do in my hobby or special interest is __

____

____

3. The last time I did it ___________________________________

____

____

4. One thing I can do to improve it next time is ______________

____

____

5. My new goal for my hobby or special interest is _____________

____

____

STUDENT SELF-REFLECTION AND GOAL SETTING IN GUIDED COMPREHENSION

Name: ______________________________ Date: ______________________

This activity is designed to help you create a self-reflection about your reading. Remember that self-reflection involves thinking about what you did, how well you did it, and what you can do to make it better next time. To begin your reflection, focus on something you have learned during Guided Comprehension. Then think about the last time you did it. How well did it go? What is one thing you can do to improve it next time? What is your new goal?

1. What I read ____

____

2. What I learned ____

____

3. The last time I did it _____________________________________

____

4. One thing I can do to improve it next time is _________________

____

5. My new goal is ____

____

Source: Adapted from McLaughlin, M. (1995). *Performance assessment: A practical guide to implementation*. Boston: Houghton Mifflin.

REFLECTION AND GOAL SETTING

Name: ______________________________ Date: ____________________

1. Today my goal was ____

____

____

2. What I did ____

____

____

3. What I learned ____

____

____

4. Questions I have ____

____

____

5. When I reflect on how well I achieved my goal, I think ________________

____

____

6. Tomorrow my goal will be ______________________________________

____

____

____

TICKETS OUT

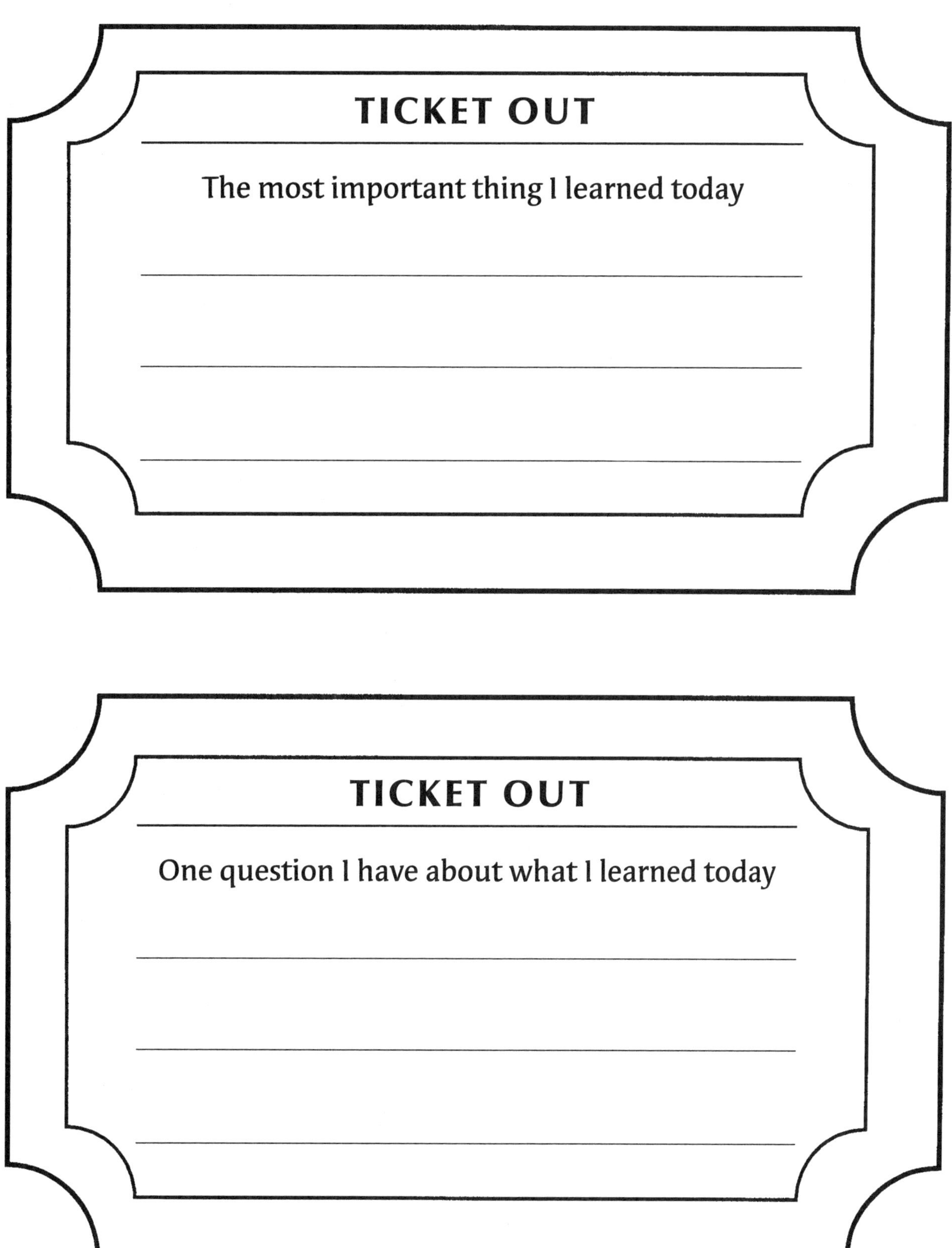
TICKET OUT
The most important thing I learned today
TICKET OUT
One question I have about what I learned today

Sources of Leveled Narrative and Expository Texts

Websites Maintained by Teachers or School Districts

Leveled Book Lists by Nancy Giansante

home.comcast.net/~ngiansante

This site features many book titles easily sorted by title, author, or grade level. The information provided includes title, author, Guided Reading level, and grade level. For example, when you click on grade 3, you get a listing of titles spanning Guided Reading levels L through P. Following are 10 examples from the third-grade list:

Title	Author	Guided Reading Level	Grade Level
Adventures of the Buried Treasure, The	McArthur, Nancy	L	2.50
Airports	Petersen, David	L	2.50
Alexander, Who's Not (Do You Hear Me? I Mean It!) Going to Move	Viorst, Judith	L	2.50
All About Stacy	Giff, Patricia Reilly	L	2.50
Amanda Pig and Her Big Brother Oliver	Van Leeuwen, Jean	L	2.50
Amazing Snakes	Parsons, Alexandra	L	2.50
Amelia Bedelia (other books in series)	Parish, Peggy	L	2.50
Amigo	Baylor, Byrd	L	2.50
Anansi the Spider	McDermott, Gerald	L	2.50

Beaverton School District Leveled Books Database

leveledbooks.beaverton.k12.or.us

This site includes a large collection of titles in English and Spanish that are classified by Guided Reading and Reading Recovery levels. You can search by title, publisher, author, keyword, or level. For example, if you want books that are at an H Guided Reading level, put H in that box, click "Search," click "Sort by Guided Reading Level," and a list of books is displayed. Following are the first 10 titles of that list:

Title	Author
Ben's Tooth	PM Story Books
Just This Once	Sunshine
Letters for Mr. James	Sunshine
Mrs. Spider's Beautiful Web	PM Story Books
Pepper's Adventure	PM Story Books
Bag I'm Taking to Grandma's, The	Neitzel, Shirley
Island Picnic, The	PM Story Books
Water	Wonder World
Clean House for Mole and Mouse, A	Ziefert, Harriet
Animal Tricks	Wildsmith, Brian

If you search for Gary Soto, you will see a list with the 11 titles displayed below. You will also see the Guided Reading levels. For example, the Guided Reading Level for *Baseball in April and Other Stories* is U.

Title	Author	Guided Reading Level
Baseball in April and Other Stories	Soto, Gary	U
Cat's Meow, The	Soto, Gary	O
Jesse	Soto, Gary	Y
Living Up the Street	Soto, Gary	Y
Local News	Soto, Gary	W
Novio Boy	Soto, Gary	X
Off and Running	Soto, Gary	S
Skirt, The	Soto, Gary	N
Summer Life, A	Soto, Gary	Z
Taking Sides	Soto, Gary	S
Too Many Tamales	Soto, Gary	M

Leveled Materials Available From Publishers

National Geographic School Publishing

www.ngsp.com

National Geographic's *Into English ESL Libraries* feature collections of authentic literature for grades K–6. Proficiency levels range from preproduction to advanced fluency. Examples of titles include *One Hot Summer Day* and *Who Eats What?*

InZone Books, which are published for students in grades 6–12, include classic titles written at less challenging levels. Examples of titles include *Frankenstein*, *20,000 Leagues Under the Sea*, and *The War of the Worlds*, as well as biographies of Rosa Parks, Amelia Earhart, and Roberto Clemente.

National Geographic also publishes Theme Sets (differentiated materials related to the same topic) and highly motivational magazines such as *National Geographic Explorer* and *Extreme Explorer.*

Scholastic Teacher Book Wizard

www.scholastic.com/bookwizard

This is a site where you can enter titles and get an approximate level, you can enter levels and get a list of books at that level, or you can enter a title and get other books that are written at that approximate level. For example, if you click on "Find Books" and enter "Seymour Simon" in the search box, the site will display numerous Seymour Simon books. If you click on a title, such as *Wolves*, you can learn the interest level (3–5), grade-level equivalent (5.5), lexile measure (970L), genre/theme (general nonfiction), and related topics (science, animals). For other titles, the search box also provides the DRA levels and Guided Reading levels. For example, if you enter the title *In Enzo's Splendid Garden* by Patricia Polacco, you can learn that the interest level is grades 3–5, the grade-level equivalent is 3.2, the DRA level is 28, the Guided Reading Level is M, and the genre is comedy and humor. You can also click on BookAlike and type in a title to get a list of books that have similar approximate levels. For example, if you enter *The Very Hungry Caterpillar*, 242 books at similar levels will appear. Finally, you can search by putting in a range of grade-equivalent levels and choosing type, topic, and genre. Then a list of books meeting those criteria is displayed.

Scholastic also publishes a variety of leveled books for English learners. These include Scholastic Leveled Readers Spanish and *Guided Reading en Español*, which was created by Gay Su Pinnell and leading bilingual educators.

Lexiles and Readability Graphs

The Lexile Framework for Reading

www.lexile.com

The Lexile Framework levels books according to sentence length and word frequency and assigns each book a lexile based on this information. The site defines *lexile* as "a unit of measurement used when determining the difficulty of text and the reading level of readers." The site has a large book database that is easy to use. Books can be searched by author or by title, and a lexile level is displayed. For example, if you search the title *The Drinking Gourd*, a 370L suggests that this title is in the second-grade level range. (For a chart describing the range of lexiles for each grade, see www.lexile.com/m/uploads/maps/Lexile-Map.pdf.)

Kathy Schrock's Guide for Educators—Fry's Readability Graph: Directions for Use

school.discoveryeducation.com/schrockguide/fry/fry.html

This site offers a clear description of how to analyze a text using Fry's Readability Graph. The Fry Graph uses sentence length and vocabulary complexity for determining levels of reading materials. Although this tool gives an estimate of level, it will give you some ideas about the ease or difficulty of a particular text.

Home–School Connections for English Learners

Creating and maintaining positive relationships with students' families is a valued component of the educational process. A variety of ideas for facilitating such relationships with parents of English learners are presented in this appendix. When participating in these activities, parents and siblings may choose to read in their native language or in English.

Book Pals

English learners practice reading books with classmates or cross-age partners in school. They explore the narrative structure of stories and write retellings of familiar books. The students then read these same books to younger siblings, cousins, and neighborhood children at home.

Environmental Print: Billboards, Street Signs, and Labels

We can invite families to foster the student's knowledge of everyday language by providing multiple exposures to environmental print, including labels, advertisements, store bags, and street names, and using this information to create games in which the students can engage.

Parents or older siblings can also walk with the student throughout the community, pointing out different types of environmental print. Students can notice street signs in their neighborhood and see billboard advertisements. If a stop is made at a local market or if a snack is served after the walk, the students can also make connections between the foods and their labels.

It Happened Just This Way

After reading aloud to an English learner or having the student read to a parent or sibling, invite him or her to retell the story orally, through drawings, through dramatization, or by writing. Books used in this activity should be short, interesting, and culturally relevant.

Library Buddies

Send a list of popular book titles home to parents. Invite a parent or older sibling to become the student's library buddy. The buddies can check out the latest in children's or young adult literature, or listen to an audio book together. When they return home, they can talk about their experience, draw pictures about it, or write about it in a journal.

Parents in the Classroom

Invite English learners' parents to participate in classroom activities. For example, they might read a book in their native language to help students understand how it feels to be second-language learners. They can also demonstrate how important text supports, such as visual aids, are when learning in another language.

Read the Pictures

Families can take photographs during favorite family moments at home, on vacations, or in the community and use them as the basis of storytelling.

Reading Time

Parents should read aloud to their child every day in a special place and at a special time. As the child grows, he or she can read to the parents.

READING = SUCCESS...

...when parents or caregivers

R — Read aloud every day. Read old favorites and new books. Read different kinds of books. Talk when reading with the children. Ask them what pictures they liked or to tell what they think might happen next.

E — Ensure that the environment is literacy-rich, filled with books, magazines, and newspapers for reading as well as papers, cards, pens, and pencils for writing.

A — Allow children to see reading and writing for different purposes every day. Having positive role models will encourage children to read and write.

D — Develop an excitement and enthusiasm about reading when the teacher sends home the classroom's "reading suitcase." It is filled with books that can be shared with everyone in the family.

I — Invite children to talk, read, and write about their favorite experiences. They may even make a family book to which all members can contribute.

N — Nurture children's love of books by taking them to the library on a regular basis and allowing them to buy books that interest them.

G — Guide children's comprehension of a story through responding. You and the children can sketch or dramatize the events of the story.

S — Share stories with predictable texts that will encourage children to read along.

U — Use the Internet as a resource for ideas and materials. Some websites that are helpful include www.famlit.org, www.rif.org, www.ed.gov/pubs/SimpleThings.

C — Create opportunities that foster literacy development. Have the children act out television commercials or put new words to familiar songs.

C — Collect recipes together and make something special with the children. Cooking and eating is a shared bonding experience as well as a learning one.

E — Encourage the children to take risks when they attempt reading and writing. Praise them for their efforts. Leave notes in their lunchboxes.

S — Support the children's learning by reading the "book in the bag" sent home that day. This gives the children opportunities to practice, build confidence, and gain fluency.

S — Stay in regular contact with the children's teachers.

Source: Romano, S. (2002). *Reading = Success: Literacy activities that promote home–school connections* [Emergent Literacy Course Syllabus]. East Stroudsburg: East Stroudsburg University of Pennsylvania.

APPENDIX F

Guided Comprehension Lesson Planning Forms

SAMPLE THEME-BASED PLAN FOR GUIDED COMPREHENSION

Goals and Common Core College and Career Readiness Anchor Standards for Reading, Writing, Speaking and Listening, and Language

Students will

Assessment

The following measures can be used for a variety of purposes, including diagnostic, formative, and summative assessment:

Comprehension Strategies	Teaching Ideas
1.	1.
2.	2.
3.	3.
4.	4.

Text

Comprehension Centers

Students will apply the comprehension strategies and related teaching ideas in the following comprehension centers:

Technology Resources

Comprehension Routines

Students will apply the comprehension strategies and related teaching ideas in the following comprehension routines:

GUIDED COMPREHENSION PLANNING FORM

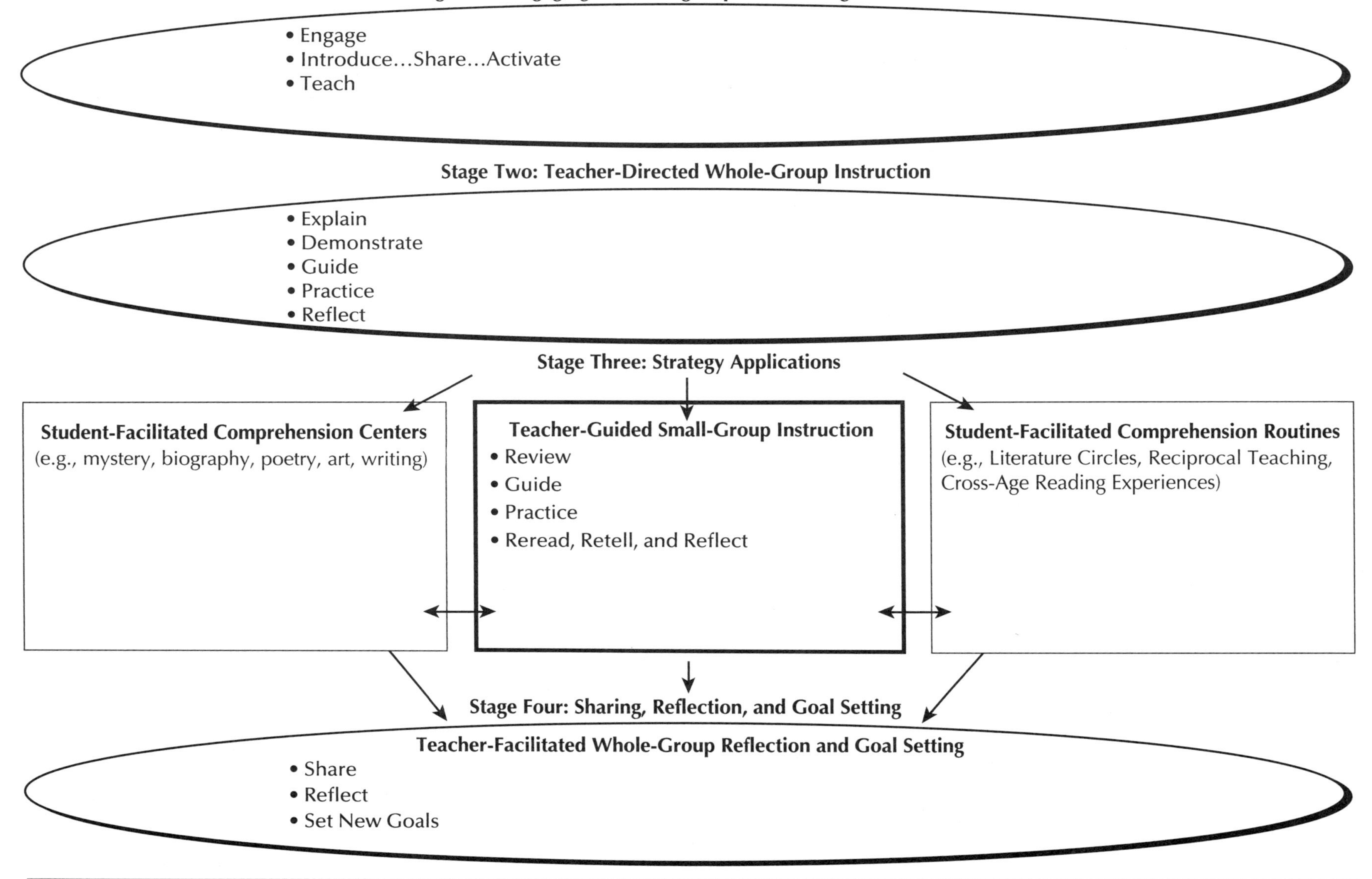

SAMPLE 75- AND 90-MINUTE GUIDED COMPREHENSION SCHEDULES

75-minute	Stage	90-minute
20 minutes	Stage 1 Engaging Prereading Sequence for English Learners	20 minutes
20 minutes	Stage 2 Teacher-Directed Whole-Group Instruction	20 minutes
20 minutes	Stage 3	40 minutes
20 minutes (one group)	Teacher-Guided Small-Group Instruction	40 minutes (two groups)
Students not meeting with the teacher are working on centers and routines.	Comprehension Centers Comprehension Routines	Students not meeting with the teacher are working on centers and routines.
15 minutes	Stage 4 Teacher-Facilitated Whole-Group Reflection and Goal Setting	10 minutes

REFERENCES

Allison, H., & Harklau, L. (2010). Teaching academic literacies in secondary school. In G. Li & P.A. Edwards (Eds.), *Best practices in ELL instruction* (pp. 129–150). New York: Guilford.

Anderson, R.C. (1994). Role of the reader's schema in comprehension, learning, and memory. In R.B. Ruddell, M.R. Ruddell, & H. Singer (Eds.), *Theoretical models and processes of reading* (4th ed., pp. 469–482). Newark, DE: International Reading Association.

Anderson, R.C., & Pearson, P.D. (1984). A schema-theoretic view of basic processes in reading comprehension. In P.D. Pearson, R. Barr, M.L. Kamil, & P. Mosenthal (Eds.), *Handbook of reading research* (pp. 225–253). New York: Longman.

Askew, B.J., & Fountas, I.C. (1998). Building an early reading process: Active from the start! *The Reading Teacher, 52,* 126–134.

Au, K.H. (2009). Culturally responsive instruction: Application to multiethnic, multilingual classrooms. In L.A. Helman (Ed.), *Literacy development with English learners: Research-based instruction in grades K–6* (pp. 18–39). New York: Guilford.

Au, K.H., & Raphael, T.E. (1998). Curriculum and teaching in literature-based programs. In T.E. Raphael & K.H. Au (Eds.), *Literature-based instruction: Reshaping the curriculum* (pp. 123–148). Norwood, MA: Christopher-Gordon.

Au, K.H., & Raphael, T.E. (2010). Using workshop approaches to support the literacy development of ELLs. In G. Li & P.A. Edwards (Eds.), *Best practices in ELL instruction* (pp. 207–221). New York: Guilford.

August, D., Goldenberg, C., Saunders, W.M., & Dressler, C. (2010). Recent research on English language and literacy instruction: What we have learned to guide practice for English language learners in the 21st century. In M. Shatz & L.C. Wilkinson (Eds.), *The education of English language learners: Research to practice* (pp. 272–297). New York: Guilford.

August, D., & Shanahan, T. (Eds.). (2007). *Developing reading and writing in second-language learners: Lessons from the report of the National Literacy Panel on language-minority children and youth.* New York: Routledge; Washington, DC: Center for Applied Linguistics; Newark, DE: International Reading Association.

Avalos, M.A., Plasencia, A., Chavez, C., & Rascón, J. (2007). Modified guided reading: Gateway to English as a second language and literacy learning. *The Reading Teacher, 61,* 318–329.

Baker, L., Afflerbach, P., & Reinking, D. (1996). Developing engaged readers in school and home communities: An overview. In L. Baker, P. Afflerbach, & D. Reinking (Eds.), *Developing engaged readers in school and home communities* (pp. xiii–xxvii). Hillsdale, NJ: Erlbaum.

Baker, L., & Wigfield, A. (1999). Dimensions of children's motivation for reading and their relations to reading activity and reading achievement. *Reading Research Quarterly, 34,* 452–481.

Barone, D.M. (2010). Engaging young ELLs with reading and writing. In G. Li & P.A. Edwards (Eds.), *Best practices in ELL instruction* (pp. 84–102). New York: Guilford.

Baumann, J.F., & Graves, M.F. (2010). What is academic vocabulary? *Journal of Adolescent & Adult Literacy, 54,* 4–12.

Baumann, J.F., & Kame'enui, E.J. (1991). Research on vocabulary instruction: Ode to Voltaire. In J. Flood, J.M. Jensen, D. Lapp, & J.R. Squire (Eds.), *Handbook of research on teaching the English language arts* (pp. 604–632). New York: Macmillan.

Beaver, J., & Carter, M. (2009). *Developmental reading assessment (DRA): Grades K–3* (2nd ed.). Lebanon, IN: Pearson Education.

Beck, I., & McKeown, M. (1991). Conditions of vocabulary acquisition. In R. Barr, M.L. Kamil, P.B. Mosenthal, & P.D. Pearson (Eds.), *Handbook of reading research* (Vol. 2, pp. 789–814). White Plains, NY: Longman.

Bedore, L.M., Peña, E.D., & Boerger, K. (2010). Ways to words: Learning a second-language vocabulary. In M. Shatz & L.C. Wilkinson (Eds.), *The education of English language learners: Research to practice* (pp. 87–107). New York: Guilford.

Blachowicz, C.L.Z., Fisher, P., Ogle, D.M., & Watts-Taffe, S. (2006). Vocabulary: Questions from the classroom. *Reading Research Quarterly, 41,* 524–539.

Blachowicz, C.L.Z., & Lee, J.J. (1991). Vocabulary development in the whole literacy classroom. *The Reading Teacher, 45,* 188–195.

Bogner, K., Raphael, L., & Pressley, M. (2002). How grade 1 teachers motivate literate activity by their students. *Scientific Studies of Reading, 6*(2), 135–165.

Brabham, E.G., & Villaume, S.K. (2000). Continuing conversations about literature circles. *The Reading Teacher, 54,* 278–280.

Brabham, E.G., & Villaume, S.K. (2002). Leveled text: The good news and the bad news. *The Reading Teacher, 55,* 438–441.

Brock, C., Youngs, S., Oikonomidoy, E., & Lapp, D. (2009). The case of Ying: The members of a teacher study group learn about fostering the reading comprehension of English learners. In L. Helman (Ed.), *Literacy development with English learners: Research-based instruction in grades K–6* (pp. 178–195). New York: Guilford.

Brown, L.A. (1993). Story collages: Help for reluctant writers. *Learning, 22*(4), 22–25.

Busching, B.A., & Slesinger, B.A. (1995). Authentic questions: What do they look like? Where do they lead? *Language Arts, 72*(5), 341–351.

Cambourne, B. (2002). Holistic, integrated approaches to reading and language arts instruction: The constructivist framework of an instructional theory. In A.E. Farstrup & S.J. Samuels (Eds.), *What research has to say about reading instruction* (3rd ed., pp. 25–47). Newark, DE: International Reading Association.

Carlo, M.S., August, D., & Snow, C.E. (2005). Sustained vocabulary-learning strategies for English language learners. In E.H. Hiebert & M.L. Kamil (Eds.), *Teaching and learning vocabulary: Bringing research to practice* (pp. 137–153). Mahwah, NJ: Erlbaum.

Carpinelli, T. (2006). Literature circles: A collaborative success story! *Library Media Connection, 25*(3), 32–33.

Casey, H.K. (2008). Engaging the disengaged: Using learning clubs to motivate struggling adolescent readers and writers. *Journal of Adolescent & Adult Literacy, 52,* 284–294.

Ciardiello, A.V. (1998). Did you ask a good question today? Alternative cognitive and metacognitive strategies. *Journal of Adolescent & Adult Literacy, 42,* 210–219.

Ciardiello, A.V. (2007). *Puzzle them first: Motivating adolescent readers with question-finding.* Newark, DE: International Reading Association.

Clarke, L., & Holwadel, J. (2007). Help! What is wrong with these literature circles and how can we fix them? *The Reading Teacher, 61,* 20–29.

Clay, M.M. (1991). Introducing a new storybook to young readers. *The Reading Teacher, 45,* 264–273.

Clay, M.M. (1993). *An observation survey of early literacy achievement.* Portsmouth, NH: Heinemann.

Clemmons, J., Laase, L., Cooper, D., Areglado, N., & Dill, M. (1993). *Portfolios in the classroom.* Jefferson City, MO: Scholastic.

Common Core State Standards Initiative. (2010a). *About the Standards.* Washington, DC: National Governors Association Center for Best Practices & Council of Chief State School Officers. Retrieved September 5, 2011, from www.corestandards.org/about-the-standards

Common Core State Standards Initiative. (2010b). *Application of Common Core State Standards for English language learners.* Washington, DC: National Governors Association Center for Best Practices & Council of Chief State School Officers. Retrieved September 5, 2011, from www.corestandards.org/assets/application-for-english-learners.pdf

Common Core State Standards Initiative. (2010c). *Common Core State Standards for English language arts & literacy in history/social studies, science, and technical subjects.* Washington, DC: National Governors Association Center for Best Practices & Council of Chief State School Officers. Retrieved September 5, 2011, from www.corestandards.org/assets/CCSSI_ELA%20Standards.pdf

Cooper, J.D., & Kiger, N.D. (2001). *Literacy assessment: Helping teachers plan instruction.* Boston: Houghton Mifflin.

Cooter, R.B., Flynt, E.S., & Cooter, K.S. (2006). *Comprehensive Reading Inventory: Measuring reading development in regular and special education classrooms.* Upper Saddle River, NJ: Prentice Hall.

Cunningham, P.M. (2008). *Phonics they use: Words for reading and writing* (5th ed.). New York: HarperCollins.

Cunningham, P., & Allington, R. (1999). *Classrooms that work: They can all read and write* (2nd ed.). New York: Addison-Wesley.

Daniels, H. (2002). *Literature circles: Voice and choice in book clubs and reading groups* (2nd ed.). Portland, ME: Stenhouse.

Daniels, H., & Steineke, N. (2004). *Mini-lessons for literature circles.* Portsmouth, NH: Heinemann.

Darling-Hammond, L.D., Ancess, J., & Falk, B. (1995). *Authentic assessment in action: Studies of schools and students at work.* New York: Teachers College Press.

Davey, B. (1983). Think-aloud—Modeling the cognitive processes of reading comprehension. *Journal of Reading, 27*, 44–47.

Day, D., & Ainley, G. (2008). From skeptic to believer: One teacher's journey implementing literature circles. *Reading Horizons, 48*(3), 157–176.

Day, D., & Kroon, S. (2010). "Online literature circles rock!" Organizing online literature circles in a middle school classroom. *Middle School Journal, 42*(2), 18–28.

de Jong, E.J. (2010). From models to principles: Implementing quality schooling for ELLs. In G. Li & P.A. Edwards (Eds.), *Best practices in ELL instruction* (pp. 189–206). New York: Guilford.

Dewey, J. (1933). *How we think: A restatement of reflective thinking to the educative process.* Lexington, MA: D.C. Heath.

Dixon-Krauss, L. (1996). *Vygotsky in the classroom: Mediated literacy instruction and assessment.* White Plains, NY: Longman.

Duffy, G.G. (2001, December). *The case for direct explanation of strategies.* Paper presented at the 51st annual meeting of the National Reading Conference, San Antonio, TX.

Duke, N.K. (2001, December). *A new generation of researchers looks at comprehension.* Paper presented at the 51st annual meeting of the National Reading Conference, San Antonio, TX.

Duke, N.K., & Pearson, P.D. (2002). Effective practices for developing reading comprehension. In A.E. Farstrup & S.J. Samuels (Eds.), *What research has to say about reading instruction* (3rd ed., pp. 205–242). Newark, DE: International Reading Association.

Durkin, D. (1978). What classroom observations reveal about reading comprehension instruction. *Reading Research Quarterly, 14*, 481–533.

Dzaldov, B.S., & Peterson, S. (2005). Book leveling and readers. *The Reading Teacher, 59*, 222–229.

Edmunds, K.M., & Bauserman, K.L. (2006). What teachers can learn about reading motivation through conversations with children. *The Reading Teacher, 59*, 414–424.

Fashola, O., Slavin, R., Calderón, M., & Durán, R. (1997). *Effective programs for Latino students in elementary and middle schools.* Baltimore: Center for Research on the Education of Students Placed at Risk.

Fielding, L.G., & Pearson, P.D. (1994). Reading comprehension: What works. *Educational Leadership, 51*(5), 62–68.

Fitzgerald, J., & Graves, M. (2004). Reading supports for all. *Educational Leadership, 62*(4), 68–71.

Ford, M.P., & Opitz, M.F. (2002). Using centers to engage children during guided reading time: Intensifying learning experiences away from the teacher. *The Reading Teacher, 55*, 710–717.

Forman, E.A., & Cazden, C.B. (1994). Exploring Vygotskian perspectives in education: The cognitive value of peer interaction. In R.B. Ruddell, M.R. Ruddell, & H. Singer (Eds.), *Theoretical models and processes of reading* (4th ed., pp. 155–178). Newark, DE: International Reading Association.

Fountas, I.C., & Pinnell, G.S. (1996). *Guided reading: Good first teaching for all children.* Portsmouth, NH: Heinemann.

Fountas, I.C., & Pinnell, G.S. (2008a). *Fountas and Pinnell benchmark assessment system: Grades K–2.* Portsmouth, NH: Heinemann.

Fountas, I.C., & Pinnell, G.S. (2008b). *Fountas and Pinnell benchmark assessment system: Grades 3–8.* Portsmouth, NH: Heinemann.

Fountas, I.C., & Pinnell, G.S. (2011). *Fountas and Pinnell sistema de evaluación de la lectura.* Portsmouth, NH: Heinemann.

Fry, E. (1977). Fry's readability graph: Clarifications, validity, and extension to level 17. *Journal of Reading, 21*, 242–252.

Gambrell, L.B. (1996). Creating classroom cultures that foster reading motivation. *The Reading Teacher, 50*, 14–25.

Gambrell, L.B. (2001). *It's not either/or but more: Balancing narrative and informational text to improve reading comprehension.* Paper presented at the 46th annual convention of the International Reading Association, New Orleans, LA.

Gambrell, L.B., Malloy, J.A., & Mazzoni, S.A. (2007). Evidence-based best practices for comprehensive literacy instruction. In L.B. Gambrell & L.M. Morrow (Eds.), *Best practices in literacy instruction* (3rd ed., pp. 11–29). New York: Guilford.

Gambrell, L.B., Palmer, B.M., Codling, R.M., & Mazzoni, S.A. (1996). Assessing motivation to read. *The Reading Teacher, 49*, 518–533.

Gay, G. (2000). *Culturally responsive teaching: Theory, research, & practice.* New York: Teachers College Press.

Gay, G. (2002). Preparing for culturally responsive teaching. *Journal of Teacher Education, 53*, 106–116.

Gibson, V., & Hasbrouck, J. (2008). *Differentiated instruction: Grouping for success.* New York: McGraw-Hill.

Gilles, C. (1998). Collaborative literacy strategies: "We don't need a circle to have a group." In K.G. Short & K.M. Pierce (Eds.), *Talking about books: Literature discussion groups in K–8 classrooms* (pp. 55–68). Portsmouth, NH: Heinemann.
Goldenberg, C. (2010). Improving achievement for English learners. In G. Li & P.A. Edwards (Eds.), *Best practices in ELL instruction* (pp. 15–43). New York: Guilford.
Goldenberg, C. (2011). Reading instruction for English language learners. In M.L. Kamil, P.D. Pearson, E.B. Moje, & P.P. Afflerbach (Eds.), *Handbook of reading research* (Vol. 4, pp. 684–710). New York: Routledge.
Goldman, S.R., & Rakestraw, J.A. (2000). Structural aspects of constructing meaning from text. In M.L. Kamil, P.B. Mosenthal, P.D. Pearson, & R. Barr (Eds.), *Handbook of reading research* (Vol. 3, pp. 311–335). Mahwah, NJ: Erlbaum.
Goodman, Y.M. (1997). Reading diagnosis—Qualitative or quantitative? *The Reading Teacher, 50*, 534–538.
Goodman, Y.M., Watson, D.J., & Burke, C. (1987). *Reading miscue inventory*. Katonah, NY: Richard C. Owen.
Graves, M.F. (2006). *The vocabulary book: Learning & instruction*. Newark, DE: International Reading Association.
Graves, M.F., & Watts-Taffe, S.M. (2002). The place of word consciousness in a research-based vocabulary program. In A.E. Farstrup & S.J. Samuels (Eds.), *What research has to say about reading instruction* (pp. 140–165). Newark, DE: International Reading Association.
Guthrie, J.T., & Alvermann, D. (Eds.). (1999). *Engagement in reading: Processes, practices, and policy implications*. New York: Teachers College Press.
Guthrie, J.T., & Wigfield, A. (1997). *Reading engagement: Motivating readers through integrated instruction*. Newark, DE: International Reading Association.
Guthrie, J., Wigfield, A., Humenick, N., Perencevich, K., Taboada, A., & Barbosa, P. (2006). Influences of stimulating tasks on reading motivation and comprehension. *The Journal of Educational Research, 99*(4), 232–245.
Hadaway, N.L., & Young, T.A. (2006). Changing classrooms: Transforming instruction. In T.A. Young & N.L. Hadaway (Eds.), *Supporting the literacy development of English learners: Increasing success in all classrooms* (pp. 6–21). Newark, DE: International Reading Association.
Hadaway, N.L., & Young, T.A. (2010). *Matching books and readers: Helping English learners in grades K–6*. New York: Guilford.
Hansen, J. (1998). *When learners evaluate*. Portsmouth, NH: Heinemann.
Harris, T.L., & Hodges, R.E. (Eds.). (1995). *The literacy dictionary: The vocabulary of reading and writing*. Newark, DE: International Reading Association.
Harvey, S., & Goudvis, A. (2000). *Strategies that work: Teaching comprehension to enhance understanding*. York, ME: Stenhouse.
Helman, L. (2009). Factors influencing second-language literacy development: A road map for teachers. In L. Helman (Ed.), *Literacy development with English learners: Research-based instruction in grades K–6* (pp. 1–17). New York: Guilford.
Hiebert, E.H. (1994). Becoming literate through authentic tasks: Evidence and adaptations. In R.B. Ruddell, M.R. Ruddell, & H. Singer (Eds.), *Theoretical models and processes of reading* (4th ed., pp. 391–413). Newark, DE: International Reading Association.
Hiebert, E.H. (2006). Becoming fluent: Repeated reading with scaffolded texts. In S.J. Samuels & A.E. Farstrup (Eds.), *What research has to say about fluency instruction* (pp. 204–226). Newark, DE: International Reading Association.
Hiebert, E.H., Pearson, P.D., Taylor, B.M., Richardson, V., & Paris, S.G. (1998). *Every child a reader*. Ann Arbor, MI: Center for the Improvement of Early Reading Achievement.
Hilden, K., & Pressley, M. (2002, December). *Can teachers become comprehension strategies teachers given a small amount of training?* Paper presented at the 52nd annual meeting of the National Reading Conference, Miami, FL.
Hill, B.C., & Ruptic, C.A. (1994). *Practical aspects of authentic assessment: Putting the pieces together*. Norwood, MA: Christopher-Gordon.
Holmes, K., Powell, S., Holmes, S., & Witt, E. (2007). Readers and book characters: Does race matter? *The Journal of Educational Research, 100*(5), 276–282.
Hoyt, L., & Ames, C. (1997). Letting the learner lead the way. *Primary Voices, 5*, 16–29.
Hunt, L.C. (1996). The effect of self-selection, interest, and motivation upon independent, instructional, and frustration levels. *The Reading Teacher, 50*, 278–282.
Iddings, A.C.D., Risko, V.J., & Rampulla, M.P. (2009). When you don't speak their language: Guiding English-language learners through conversations about text. *The Reading Teacher, 63*, 52–61.

International Reading Association. (2000). *Excellent reading teachers: A position statement of the International Reading Association*. Newark, DE: Author.
Johnson, D.D., & Pearson, P.D. (1984). *Teaching reading vocabulary* (2nd ed.). New York: Holt, Rinehart and Winston.
Johnston, P.H. (2000). *Running records: A self-tutoring guide*. Portland, ME: Stenhouse.
Keene, E., & Zimmermann, S. (1997). *Mosaic of thought: Teaching comprehension in a reader's workshop*. Portsmouth, NH: Heinemann.
Ketch, A. (2005). Conversation: The comprehension connection. *The Reading Teacher, 59*, 8–13.
Lasear, D. (1991). *Seven ways of teaching: The artistry of teaching with multiple intelligences*. Palatine, IL: Skylight.
Leslie, L., & Caldwell, J.S. (2010). *Qualitative reading inventory—5* (5th ed.). Boston: Allyn & Bacon.
Lewin, L. (1998). *Great performances: Creating classroom-based assessment tasks*. Alexandria, VA: Association for Supervision and Curriculum Development.
Li, G., & Protacio, M.S. (2010). Best practices in professional development for teachers of ELLs. In G. Li & P.A. Edwards (Eds.), *Best practices in ELL instruction* (pp. 353–380). New York: Guilford.
Lipson, M.Y. (2001). *A fresh look at comprehension*. Paper presented at the Reading/Language Arts Symposium, Chicago, IL.
Lipson, M.Y., & Wixson, K. (2009). *Assessment and instruction of reading and writing difficulties: An interactive approach* (4th ed.). New York: Longman.
Manyak, P.C. (2007). A framework for robust literacy instruction for English learners. *The Reading Teacher, 61*, 197–199.
Manyak, P.C., & Bauer, E.B. (2008). Explicit code and comprehension instruction for English learners. *The Reading Teacher, 61*, 432–434.
McGinley, W., & Denner, P. (1987). Story impressions: A prereading/prewriting activity. *Journal of Reading, 31*, 248–253.
McIntyre, E. (2010). Principles for teaching young ELLs in the mainstream classroom: Adapting best practices for all learners. In G. Li & P.A. Edwards (Eds.), *Best practices in ELL instruction* (pp. 61–83). New York: Guilford.
McLaughlin, E.M. (1987). QuIP: A writing strategy to improve comprehension of expository structure. *The Reading Teacher, 40*, 650–654.
McLaughlin, M. (1995). *Performance assessment: A practical guide to implementation*. Boston: Houghton Mifflin.
McLaughlin, M. (2002). Dynamic assessment. In B. Guzzetti (Ed.), *Literacy in America: An encyclopedia of history, theory, and practice*. Santa Barbara, CA: ABC-CLIO.
McLaughlin, M. (2003a). *Guided Comprehension in the primary grades*. Newark, DE: International Reading Association.
McLaughlin, M. (2003b). *Guided Comprehension in the primary grades: A framework for curricularizing strategy instruction*. Paper presented at the 53rd annual meeting of the National Reading Conference, Scottsdale, AZ.
McLaughlin, M. (2010a). *Content area reading: Teaching and learning in an age of multiple literacies*. Boston: Allyn & Bacon.
McLaughlin, M. (2010b). *Guided Comprehension in the primary grades* (2nd ed.). Newark, DE: International Reading Association.
McLaughlin, M., & Allen, M.B. (2002a). *Guided Comprehension: A teaching model for grades 3–8*. Newark, DE: International Reading Association.
McLaughlin, M., & Allen, M.B. (2002b). *Guided Comprehension in action: Lessons for grades 3–8*. Newark, DE: International Reading Association.
McLaughlin, M., & Allen, M.B. (2009). *Guided Comprehension in grades 3–8* (Combined 2nd ed.). Newark, DE: International Reading Association.
McLaughlin, M., Corbett, R., & Stevenson, C. (2000). Celebrating mathematics: Innovative, student-centered approaches for teaching and learning. In M. McLaughlin & M.E. Vogt (Eds.), *Creativity and innovation in content area teaching* (pp. 157–181). Norwood, MA: Christopher-Gordon.
McLaughlin, M., & Vogt, M.E. (1996). *Portfolios in teacher education*. Newark, DE: International Reading Association.
McTighe, J., & Lyman, F.T. (1988). Cueing thinking in the classroom: The promise of theory-embedded tools. *Educational Leadership, 45*(7), 18–24.
McTighe, J., & O'Connor, J. (2005). Seven keys to effective learning. *Educational Leadership, 63*(3), 10–17.
Minick, N. (1987). Implications of Vygotsky's theory for dynamic assessment. In C.S. Lidz (Ed.), *Dynamic assessment: An interactional approach to evaluating learning potential* (pp. 116–140). New York: Guilford.

Mohr, K.A.J. (2004). English as an accelerated language: A call to action for reading teachers. *The Reading Teacher, 58*, 18–26.

Mohr, K.A.J., & Mohr, E.S. (2007). Extending English-language learners' classroom interactions using the response protocol. *The Reading Teacher, 60*, 440–450.

Morrow, L.M. (1985). Retelling stories: A strategy for improving children's comprehension, concept of story, and oral language complexity. *The Elementary School Journal, 85*(5), 646–661.

Morrow, L.M., & Brittain, R. (2003). The nature of storybook reading in elementary school: Current practices. In A. van Kleek, S.A. Stahl, & E.B. Bauer (Eds.), *On reading books to children: Parents and teachers* (pp. 134–152). Mahwah, NJ: Erlbaum.

Mowery, S. (1995). *Reading and writing comprehension strategies*. Harrisburg, PA: Instructional Support Teams Publications.

National Commission on Teaching and America's Future. (1996). *What matters most: Teaching for America's future*. Retrieved February 3, 2012, from nctaf.org/wp-content/uploads/2012/01/WhatMattersMost.pdf

National Institute of Child Health and Human Development. (2000). *Report of the National Reading Panel. Teaching children to read: An evidence-based assessment of the scientific research literature on reading and its implications for reading instruction* (NIH Publication No. 00-4769). Washington, DC: U.S. Government Printing Office.

Newmann, F.M., & Wehlage, G.G. (1993). Five standards for authentic instruction. *Educational Leadership, 50*, 8–12.

Noe, K.L.S., & Johnson, N.J. (1999). *Getting started with literature circles*. Norwood, MA: Christopher-Gordon.

Ogle, D., & Correa-Kovtun, A. (2010). Supporting English-language learners and struggling readers in content literacy with the "partner reading and content, too" routine. *The Reading Teacher, 63*, 532–542.

Opitz, M.F., & Harding-DeKam, J.L. (2007). Understanding and teaching English-language learners. *The Reading Teacher, 60*, 590–593.

Page, S. (2001). *Tips and strategies for independent routines*. Muncie, IN: Page Consulting.

Palincsar, A.S., & Brown, A.L. (1984). Reciprocal teaching of comprehension-fostering and monitoring activities. *Cognition and Instruction, 1*, 117–175.

Palincsar, A.S., & Brown, A.L. (1986). Interactive teaching to promote independent learning from text. *The Reading Teacher, 39*, 771–777.

Pearson, P.D. (2001). *Comprehension strategy instruction: An idea whose time has come again*. Paper presented at the annual meeting of the Colorado Council of the International Reading Association, Denver, CO.

Peregoy, S.F., & Boyle, O.F. (2005). English learners reading English: What we know, what we need to know. In Z. Fang (Ed.), *Literacy teaching and learning: Current issues and trends* (pp. 18–27). Upper Saddle River, NJ: Pearson/Merrill/Prentice Hall.

Pilgreen, J. (2006). Supporting English learners: Developing academic language in the content area classroom. In T.A. Young & N.L. Hadaway (Eds.), *Supporting the literacy development of English learners* (pp. 41–60). Newark, DE: International Reading Association.

Pinciotti, P. (2001). *Book arts: The creation of beautiful books*. East Stroudsburg: East Stroudsburg University of Pennsylvania.

Pitcher, B., & Fang, Z. (2007). Can we trust leveled texts? An examination of their reliability and quality from a linguistic perspective. *Literacy, 41*(1), 43–51.

Pressley, M. (2000). What should comprehension instruction be the instruction of? In M.L. Kamil, P.B. Mosenthal, P.D. Pearson, & R. Barr (Eds.), *Handbook of reading research* (Vol. 3, pp. 545–561). Mahwah, NJ: Erlbaum.

Pressley, M. (2001, December). *Comprehension strategies instruction: A turn of the century status report*. Paper presented at the 51st annual meeting of the National Reading Conference, San Antonio, TX.

Raphael, T.E. (1986). Teaching Question Answer Relationships, revisited. *The Reading Teacher, 39*, 516–522.

Rasinski, T.V. (1999a). Making and writing words. *Reading Online*. Retrieved February 3, 2012, from www.readingonline.org/articles/words/rasinski_index.html

Rasinski, T.V. (1999b). Making and writing words using letter patterns. *Reading Online*. Retrieved February 3, 2012, from www.readingonline.org/articles/rasinski/MWW_LP.html

Rasinski, T.V. (2010). *The fluent reader: Oral & silent reading strategies for building fluency, word recognition & comprehension* (2nd ed.). New York: Scholastic.

Roehler, L.R., & Duffy, G.G. (1984). Direct explanation of comprehension processes. In G.G. Duffy, L.R. Roehler, & J. Mason (Eds.), *Comprehension instruction: Perspectives and suggestions* (pp. 265–280). New York: Longman.

Rog, L.J., & Burton, W. (2001). Matching texts and readers: Leveling early reading materials for assessment and instruction. *The Reading Teacher, 55*, 348–356.

Romano, S. (2002). *Reading = Success: Literacy activities that promote home-school connections* [Emergent Literacy course syllabus]. East Stroudsburg: East Stroudsburg University of Pennsylvania.

Rosenblatt, L.M. (1978). *The reader, the text, and the poem: The transactional theory of the literary work.* Carbondale: Southern Illinois University Press.

Rosenblatt, L.M. (2002, December). *A pragmatist theoretician looks at research: Implications and questions calling for answers.* Paper presented at the 52nd annual meeting of the National Reading Conference, Miami, FL.

Ruddell, R.B. (1995). Those influential reading teachers: Meaning negotiators and motivation builders. *The Reading Teacher, 48*, 454–463.

Samuels, S.J. (2002). Reading fluency: Its development and assessment. In A.E. Farstrup & S.J. Samuels (Eds.), *What research has to say about reading instruction* (3rd ed., pp. 166–183). Newark, DE: International Reading Association.

Samway, K.D., & Wang, G. (1996). *Literature study circles in a multicultural classroom.* York, ME: Stenhouse.

Schön, D. (1987). *Educating the reflective practitioner.* San Francisco: Jossey-Bass.

Schwartz, R., & Raphael, T. (1985). Concept of definition: A key to improving students' vocabulary. *The Reading Teacher, 39*, 198–205.

Shepard, L.A. (2005). Linking formative assessment to scaffolding. *Educational Leadership, 63*(3), 66–70.

Short, D., & Echevarria, J. (2004). Teacher skills to support English language learners. *Educational Leadership, 62*(4), 8–13.

Short, K.G., & Burke, C. (1996). Examining our beliefs and practices through inquiry. *Language Arts, 73*, 97–103.

Short, K.G., Harste, J.C., & Burke, C. (1996). *Creating classrooms for authors and inquirers.* Portsmouth, NH: Heinemann.

Snow, C.E., Burns, M.S., & Griffin, P.G. (Eds.). (1998). *Preventing reading difficulties in young children.* Washington, DC: National Academy Press.

Stauffer, R. (1975). *Directing the reading-thinking process.* New York: Harper & Row.

Stien, D., & Beed, P.L. (2004). Bridging the gap between fiction and nonfiction in the literature circle setting. *The Reading Teacher, 57*, 512–518.

Szymusiak, K., & Sibberson, F. (2001). *Beyond leveled books: Supporting transitional readers in grades 2–5.* Portland, ME: Stenhouse.

Teachers of English to Speakers of Other Languages (TESOL). (2006). *PreK–12 English language proficiency standards.* Retrieved January 8, 2012, from www.tesol.org/s_tesol/seccss.asp?CID=95&DID=1565

Teachers of English to Speakers of Other Languages (TESOL). (2010, April 2). *Letter to the Council of Chief State School Officers and the National Governors Association.* Retrieved January 8, 2012, from www.tesol.org/s_tesol/bin.asp?CID=86&DID=13225&DOC=FILE.PDF

Tierney, R.J. (1990). Redefining reading comprehension. *Educational Leadership, 47*(6), 37–42.

Tierney, R.J. (1998). Literacy assessment reform: Shifting beliefs, principled possibilities and emerging practices. *The Reading Teacher, 51*, 374–390.

Tierney, R.J., & Pearson, P.D. (1994). A revisionist perspective on "Learning to learn from text: A framework for improving classroom practice." In R.B. Ruddell, M.R. Ruddell, & H. Singer (Eds.), *Theoretical models and processes of reading* (4th ed., pp. 514–519). Newark, DE: International Reading Association.

Tomlinson, C.A. (1999). *The differentiated classroom: Responding to the needs of all learners.* Alexandria, VA: Association for Supervision and Curriculum Development.

Tompkins, G.E. (2006). *Literacy for the 21st century: A balanced approach* (4th ed.). Upper Saddle River, NJ: Prentice Hall.

Townsend, D. (2009). Building academic vocabulary in after-school settings: Games for growth with middle school English-language learners. *Journal of Adolescent & Adult Literacy, 53*, 242–251.

Tyner, B., & Green, S.E. (2005). *Small-group reading instruction: A differentiated teaching model for intermediate readers, grades 3–8.* Newark, DE: International Reading Association.

Vaughn, J., & Estes, T. (1986). *Reading and reasoning beyond the primary grades.* Boston: Allyn & Bacon.

Villegas, A.M., & Lucas, T. (2002). Preparing culturally responsive teachers: Rethinking the curriculum. *Journal of Teacher Education, 53*(1), 20–32.

Villegas, A.M., & Lucas, T. (2007). The culturally responsive teacher. *Educational Leadership, 64*(6), 28–33.

Vygotsky, L.S. (1978). In M. Cole, V. John-Steiner, S. Scribner, & E. Souberman (Trans. & Eds.), *Mind in society: The development of higher psychological processes.* Cambridge, MA: Harvard University Press.

Watts-Taffe, S., & Truscott, D.M. (2000). Using what we know about language and literacy development for ESL students in the mainstream classroom. *Language Arts, 77*(3), 258–265.
Weaver, B.M. (2000). *Leveling books K–6: Matching readers to text.* Newark, DE: International Reading Association.
Weber, E. (1999). *Student assessment that works: A practical approach.* Boston: Allyn & Bacon.
Wigfield, A., & Guthrie, J.T. (1997). Relations of children's motivation for reading to the amount and breadth of their reading. *Journal of Educational Psychology, 89*(3), 420–432.
Wiggins, G., & McTighe, J. (2008). Put understanding first. *Educational Leadership, 65*(8), 36–41.
World-Class Instructional Design and Assessment (WIDA). (2007). *English language proficiency (ELP) standards, 2007 edition.* Retrieved February 3, 2012, from www.wida.us/standards/elp.aspx#2007
World-Class Instructional Design and Assessment (WIDA). (2011). *Alignment study between the Common Core State Standards in English Language Arts and Mathematics and the WIDA English Language Proficiency Standards, 2007 edition, prekindergarten through grade 12.* Retrieved February 3, 2012, from www.wida.us/get.aspx?id=371
World-Class Instructional Design and Assessment (WIDA). (2012). *English language proficiency (ELP) standards, 2012 edition.* Retrieved February 3, 2012, from www.wida.us/standards/elp.aspx#2012
Yoon, B. (2007). Offering or limiting opportunities: Teachers' roles and approaches to English language learners' participation in literacy activities. *The Reading Teacher, 61*, 216–225.
Young, T.A., & Hadaway, N.L. (Eds.). (2006). *Supporting the literacy development of English learners: Increasing success in all classrooms.* Newark, DE: International Reading Association.

Literature Cited

Adler, D.A. (1997). *A picture book of Jackie Robinson.* New York: Holiday House.
Angelou, M. (1986). *All God's children need traveling shoes.* New York: Random House.
Bader, B., & Harrison, N. (2008). *Who was Martin Luther King, Jr.?* New York: Grosset & Dunlap.
Barner, B. (2001). *Dinosaur bones.* San Francisco: Chronicle.
Battle-Lavert, G. (2003). *Papa's mark.* New York: Holiday House.
Benton, M.J. (2000). *The encyclopedia of awesome dinosaurs.* Brookfield, CT: Copper Beech.
Berger, M., & Berger, G. (2000). *Do penguins get frostbite? Questions and answers about polar animals.* New York: Scholastic.
Berger, M., & Berger, G. (2003). *Whales.* New York: Scholastic.
Berne, E.C. (2009). *Helen Keller: Courage in darkness.* New York: Sterling.
Bolden, T. (2007). *M.L.K.: Journey of a king.* New York: Abrams.
Boyden, L. (2002). *The blue roses.* New York: Lee & Low.
Bunting, E. (1989). *The Wednesday surprise.* New York: Clarion.
Bunting, E. (1991). *Fly away home.* New York: Clarion.
Bunting, E. (2006). *One green apple.* New York: Clarion.
Burns, L.G. (2007). *Tracking trash: Flotsam, jetsam, and the science of ocean motion.* Boston: Sandpiper.
Cline-Ransome, L. (2000). *Satchel Paige.* New York: Simon & Schuster.
Cronin, D. (2000). *Click, clack, moo: Cows that type.* New York: Simon & Schuster.
Cronin, D. (2001). *Clic clac muu: Vacas escritoras.* Lyndhurst, NJ: Lectorum. (Spanish version)
Cronin, D. (2003). *Diary of a worm.* New York: HarperCollins.
Cronin, D. (2005). *Diary of a spider.* New York: HarperCollins.
Day, A. (1992). *Carl's masquerade.* New York: Farrar, Straus & Giroux.
Day, A. (1993). *Carl goes to daycare.* New York: Farrar, Straus & Giroux.
Day, A. (2005). *Carl's sleepy afternoon.* New York: Farrar, Straus & Giroux.
Day, A. (2007). *You're a good dog, Carl.* New York: Square Fish.
Day, A. (2008). *Carl's summer vacation.* New York: Farrar, Straus & Giroux.
Deedy, C.A. (2009). *14 cows for America.* Atlanta, GA: Peachtree.
Demi. (2001). *Gandhi.* New York: Simon & Schuster.
Dowswell, P., Malam, J., Mason, P., & Parker, S. (2002). *The ultimate book of dinosaurs: Everything you always wanted to know about dinosaurs—but were too terrified to ask.* London: Parragon.
Elliott, Z. (2008). *Bird.* New York: Lee & Low.
Fine, E.H., & Josephson, J.P. (2007). *Armando and the blue tarp school.* New York: Lee & Low.
Gibbons, G. (2000). *Bats.* New York: Holiday House.

Gibbons, G. (2005). *Sea turtles.* Pine Plains, NY: Live Oak Media.
Gill, S. (2007). *Alaska.* Watertown, MA: Charlesbridge.
Giovanni, N. (2007). *Rosa.* New York: Square Fish.
Holtz, T.R., & Rey, L.V. (2007). *Dinosaurs: The most complete, up-to-date encyclopedia for dinosaur lovers of all ages.* New York: Random House.
Johnson, D. (2002). *Substitute teacher plans.* New York: Henry Holt.
Lambert, D., & Hutt, S. (2000). *Dorling Kindersley guide to dinosaurs: A thrilling journey through prehistoric times.* New York: Dorling Kindersley.
Lessem, D. (2010). *The ultimate dino-pedia: The most complete dinosaur reference ever.* Washington, DC: National Geographic.
Lewin, T., & Lewin, B. (2009). *Balarama: A royal elephant.* New York: Lee & Low.
Lisandrelli, E.S. (1996). *Maya Angelou: More than a poet.* Springfield, NJ: Enslow.
Lowell, S. (1994). *The three little javelinas.* New York: Scholastic.
Malaspina, A. (2010). *Yasmin's hammer.* New York: Lee & Low.
Medina, T. (2001). *DeShawn days.* New York: Lee & Low.
Milton, J. (1989). *Whales: The gentle giants.* New York: Random House.
Mora, P. (2009). *Gracias/thanks* (English and Spanish edition). New York: Lee & Low.
Numeroff, L. (1985). *If you give a mouse a cookie.* New York: HarperCollins.
Numeroff, L. (1998). *If you give a pig a pancake.* New York: HarperCollins.
Numeroff, L. (2008). *Si le das un panqueque a una cerdita.* New York: Scholastic. (Spanish version)
Paulsen, G. (1991). *The monument.* New York: Dell.
Paulsen, G. (1994). *Winterdance: The fine madness of running the Iditarod.* Toronto: Harcourt Brace Jovanovich.
Polacco, P. (1987). *Meteor!* New York: Dodd, Mead.
Reynolds, J. (2009). *Cycle of rice, cycle of life: A story of unsustainable farming.* New York: Lee & Low.
Reynolds, J. (2010). *Celebrate! Connections among cultures.* New York: Lee & Low.
Russell, C.Y. (2009). *Tofu quilt.* New York: Lee & Low.
Silverstein, S. (1974). Sarah Cynthia Sylvia Stout. In *Where the sidewalk ends.* New York: HarperCollins.
Simon, S. (1998). *The universe.* New York: Scholastic.
Simon, S. (2006). *The heart: Our circulatory system.* New York: Collins.
Simon, S. (2007). *Spiders.* New York: HarperCollins.
Simon, S. (2008). *Gorillas.* New York: HarperCollins.
Simon, S. (2009). *Dogs.* New York: Collins.
Simon, S. (2009). *Dolphins.* New York: Collins.
Simon, S. (2009). *Wolves.* New York: Collins.
Slonim, D. (2003). *Oh, Ducky! A chocolate calamity.* San Francisco: Chronicle.
Soto, G. (2003). *Taking sides.* Boston: Sandpiper.
Soto, G. (2006). *Buried onions.* Boston: Graphia.
Soto, G. (2007). *Mercy on these teenage chimps.* New York: Harcourt.
Spinelli, J. (1998). *Knots in my yo-yo string.* New York: Knopf.
Towle, W. (1993). *The real McCoy: The life of an African-American inventor.* New York: Scholastic.
Vail, R. (2001). *Mama Rex & T: Homework trouble.* New York: Scholastic.
Van Allsburg, C. (2011). *Just a dream.* Boston: Sandpiper.
Vogt, G. (2001). *Solar system.* New York: Scholastic.
Weston, M. (2008). *Honda: The boy who dreamed of cars.* New York: Lee & Low.
Wolf, B. (2003). *Coming to America: A Muslim family's story.* New York: Lee & Low.
Wiesner, D. (1991). *Tuesday.* New York: Clarion.
Wiesner, D. (1995). *June 29, 1999.* New York: Clarion.
Wiesner, D. (1999). *Sector 7.* New York: Clarion.
Wiesner, D. (2001). *The three pigs.* New York: Clarion.
Wiesner, D. (2006). *Flotsam.* New York: Clarion.
Wild, M., & Argent, K. (2000). *Nighty night!* Atlanta, GA: Peachtree.
Wise, B. (2009). *Louis Sockalexis: Native American baseball pioneer.* New York: Lee & Low.
Wolf, B. (2003). *Coming to America: A Muslim family's story.* New York: Lee & Low.
Ziefert, H. (2001). *Murphy meets the treadmill.* Boston: Houghton Mifflin.

INDEX

Note. Page numbers followed by *f* and *r* indicate figures and reproducible blacklines, respectively.

C

D

E

F

G

M

N

O

S

T

V

W

Y

Z